Cultural Transfer Reconsidered

Approaches to Translation Studies

Founded by

James S. Holmes

Edited by

Karen Bennett (*Universidade Nova de Lisboa, Portugal*)
Leo Tak-hung Chan (*Lingnan University, Hong Kong*)
Şehnaz Tahir Gürçağlar (*Boğaziçi Üniversitesi*)
Hephzibah Israel (*University of Edinburgh, UK*)
Gabriela Saldanha (*University of Birmingham, UK*)
Tom Toremans (*KU Leuven, Belgium*)
Michaela Wolf (*Universität Graz, Austria*)

VOLUME 47

The titles published in this series are listed at *brill.com/atts*

Cultural Transfer Reconsidered

Transnational Perspectives, Translation Processes, Scandinavian and Postcolonial Challenges

Edited by

Steen Bille Jørgensen
Hans-Jürgen Lüsebrink

BRILL
RODOPI

LEIDEN | BOSTON

Cover illustration: Spiral staircase in Library, Trinity College. Photography by Armelion, pixabay.com.

Library of Congress Cataloging-in-Publication Data

Names: Jørgensen, Steen Bille, editor. | Lüsebrink, Hans-Jürgen, editor.
Title: Cultural transfer reconsidered : transnational perspectives, translation processes, Scandinavian and postcolonial challenges / edited by Steen Bille Jørgensen, Hans-Jürgen Lüsebrink.
Description: Leiden; Boston: Brill Rodopi, 2021. | Series: Approaches to translation studies, 0169–0523 ; vol. 47 | Includes bibliographical references and index.
Identifiers: LCCN 2020047504 (print) | LCCN 2020047505 (ebook) | ISBN 9789004443679 (hardback) | ISBN 9789004443693 (ebook)
Subjects: LCSH: Culture diffusion—Scandinavia. | Language and culture—Scandinavia. | Translating and interpreting—Scandinavia—Social aspects.
Classification: LCC GN365 .C85 2021 (print) | LCC GN365 (ebook) | DDC 303.48/2—dc23
LC record available at https://lccn.loc.gov/2020047504
LC ebook record available at https://lccn.loc.gov/2020047505

Typeface for the Latin, Greek, and Cyrillic scripts: "Brill". See and download: brill.com/brill-typeface

ISSN 0169-0523
ISBN 978-90-04-44367-9 (hardback)
ISBN 978-90-04-44369-3 (e-book)

Copyright 2021 by Koninklijke Brill NV, Leiden, The Netherlands.
Koninklijke Brill NV incorporates the imprints Brill, Brill Hes & De Graaf, Brill Nijhoff, Brill Rodopi, Brill Sense, Hotei Publishing, mentis Verlag, Verlag Ferdinand Schöningh and Wilhelm Fink Verlag.
All rights reserved. No part of this publication may be reproduced, translated, stored in a retrieval system, or transmitted in any form or by any means, electronic, mechanical, photocopying, recording or otherwise, without prior written permission from the publisher. Requests for re-use and/or translations must be addressed to Koninklijke Brill NV via brill.com or copyright.com.

This book is printed on acid-free paper and produced in a sustainable manner.

Contents

Notes on Contributors   VII

Introduction: Reframing the Cultural Transfer Approach   1
Steen Bille Jørgensen and Hans-Jürgen Lüsebrink

PART 1
Transnational Processes of Cultural Mediation – Dynamic Relations

1   What Are Cultural Transfers? The Russian and Scandinavian Cases   23
    Michel Espagne

2   Cultural Transfers in the Shadow of Methodological Nationalism   44
    Magnus Qvistgaard

3   The Meta-Literary History of Cultural Transmitters and Forgotten Scholars in the Midst of Transnational Literary History   64
    Petra Broomans

4   Representations of Brittany in Norwegian and Finnish Women's Paintings: How French Realism and Naturalism Took Over Nordic Art and Contributed to Renew Finnish and Norwegian Painting at the End of the 19th Century   88
    Anne-Estelle Leguy

PART 2
Aspects of Textual Transfers – Comparison, Intertextuality and Translation

5   Cultural Transfer and Intertextuality: Yambo Ouologuem and the Dynamics of Literary and Cultural Rewriting in the (Post)Colonial African Context   105
    Hans-Jürgen Lüsebrink

6 The Cultural Transfer of Genre: The Case of Aphorism in Déwé Gorodé (New Caledonia), *Par les temps qui courent* 124
   Miriam Lay Brander

7 Textual Transfers and the Poetics of Translation: Literature in Translation, Translation in Literature 141
   Steen Bille Jørgensen

PART 3
Perspectives – Types of Distance and Proximity

8 Cultural Transfer and Its Complexities: A Study on Transnational and Transhistorical Mobilities of the Baroque 167
   Walter Moser

9 From *Transferts culturels* to *Transferências culturais*: Interdisciplinary and Methodical Dynamics and Translations of the Concept in the Brazilian Context 198
   Wiebke Röben de Alencar Xavier

10 Relations in a Cultural Triangle: Aspects of Cultural Mediation between Germany, France, and Scandinavia 229
   Karin Hoff, Anna Sandberg and Udo Schöning

Index of Names 251

Notes on Contributors

Petra Broomans
is Associate Professor with *ius promovendi* of European Languages and Cultures (University of Groningen) and a visiting professor at Ghent University. As of 2020 she is appointed honorary doctor at Uppsala University. She is the coordinator of the U4Society network in Cultural Transfer Research and Editor-in-Chief of the book series, Studies on Cultural Transfer and Transmission (CTaT), and has published extensively on cultural transfer, the reception of Scandinavian literature and women writers in literary history. Her research interests include cultural transfer, world literature, meta-literary history, minority literature. She is coordinator of the Dutch translators' dictionary (https://www.vertalers lexicon.nl/). See for publications www.petrabroomans.net.

Michel Espagne
Education: 1971 Ecole normale supérieure de la rue d'Ulm, 1972–1974 studies in German Literature, philology and philosophy at the universities Tübingen and Köln – 1975 agrégation in German Studies, 1976–1978 studies at the University Saarbrücken; 1977 PhD on Robert Musil and Hermann Broch (Saarland University). Work: 1978-French National Center for Scientific Research (CNRS), 1985 second dissertation on the concept of pantheism in Heinrich Heine's manuscripts (Paris Sorbonne); 2011–2019 head of the laboratory of excellence Labex TransferS; since 1993 director of the *Revue germanique internationale*; 2011 Humboldt-Gay Lussac research award. Publications (selected): *Les transferts culturels franco-allemands*, Paris, 1999; Michel Espagne et Li Hongtu (ed.), *Chine France-Europe Asie. Itinéraires de concepts*, Paris, 2018.

Karin Hoff
is Professor of Scandinavian Studies at the University of Göttingen. Her main research interests include 18th century Scandinavian literature, modernism and contemporary literature, drama and theatre (particularly August Strindberg) and European cultural transfer (*Internationale Netzwerke. Literarische und ästhetische Transfers im Dreieck Deutschland, Frankreich und Skandinavien zwischen 1870 und 1945*. Edited with Udo Schöning und Frédéric Weinmann, 2016). She gained her Habilitation on *Die Entdeckung der Zwischenräume. Projekte der Spätaufklärung zwischen Skandinavien und Deutschland*, 2003, and is one of the chief advisors of the 2009 addition of *Kindlers Literatur Lexikon* on the field of Scandinavian literature.

Steen Bille Jørgensen

is Professor at Aarhus University. His main research areas are modern and contemporary French and Francophone Literatures, literary theory, Intercultural Studies and Theory of Translation. Publications on Oulipo, Moroccan Literature and Realism. Co-editor of *Landscapes of Realism*, vol. 2 (published by John Benjamins, forthcoming) and with Lisbeth Verstraete-Hansen (ed.) *Dialogues – Histoire, littérature et Transferts culturels*, Editor-in-Chief of *Revue Romane* (Literature); correspondent at *Société d'Histoire Littéraire de la France*; founder of the *Société danoise de Littérature Contemporaine en langue française* – SLC and translator of literature.

Miriam Lay Brander

is Professor of Romance Literatures and Director of the Centre for Latin American Studies (ZILAS) at Katholische Universität Eichstätt-Ingolstadt. Her research interests include: genre theory, space/time theory, Latin American and Francophone literature, literature and culture of Spanish Siglo de Oro and digital memory studies. She has published *Genre and Globalization. Transformación de géneros en contextos (post-)coloniales / Transformation des genres dans des contextes (post-)coloniaux* (ed., Hildesheim, Zürich, New York, 2017) and *Espacio-Tiempo en transformación. Las estructuras de narrar y mostrar en Sevilla a comienzos de la Edad Moderna* (trans. C.A. Lemke Duque, Kassel, 2017).

Anne-Estelle Leguy

wrote a PhD on the Finnish painter Helene Schjerfbeck (1862–1946) (Université Paris IV – Sorbonne, 2014). Her research interests include History of Art, Literary, Cultural and Political History of the 1800–1950 Nordic countries, Sociology of Art, Gender Studies and Cultural Transfers.

Hans-Jürgen Lüsebrink

is Senior Professor of Romance Cultural Studies and Intercultural Communication at Saarland University. He holds a PhD in Romance Philology (Bayreuth, Germany) and in History (EHESS, France) and is a member of the International Research Training Group "Diversity: Mediating Difference in Transcultural Spaces." His research fields concern cultural transfers between France and Germany and between Europe and non-European societies, conceptual history, francophone literatures and medias (Québec, Sub-Saharan Africa), and the theory of intercultural communication. Recent books: *Transferts de savoirs sur l'Afrique* (co-ed. with Michel Espagne Paris, 2015); *Interkulturelle Kommunikation* (Stuttgart/Weimar 2005, 4th revised edition

2016); *Dialogues interculturels à l'époque coloniale et postcoloniale*, Paris, 2019 (co-ed. with Sarga Moussa); *L'intertextualité dans les littératures sénégalaises. Réseaux, réécritures, palimpsestes*, Paris, 2019 (co-ed. with Ibrahima Diagne).

Walter Moser

earned his PhD in 1968 at the University of Zurich in Romance Languages. He was a professor at Yale University (1969–1971) and at the University of Montreal (1974–2002) before he held the Canada Research Chair on "Literary and Cultural Transfers" at the University of Ottawa (2002–2008). His research interests and activities migrated from text analysis to discourse analysis and to cultural analysis. In his most recent research project, he examined the return of the Baroque in contemporary culture. In 2016, he edited, together with P. Krieger and A. Ndalianis, *Neo-Baroques. From Latin America to the Hollywood Blockbuster* (Leiden/Boston, Brill/Rodopi) and in 2018 he published *La mise à l'essai du roman chez Robert Musil. Une lecture interdiscursive* (Montreal).

Magnus Qvistgaard

is an independent scholar. He holds a PhD in "History and Civilization" from the European University Institute in Florence. He works on processes of cultural exchange and on how cultural value is created and maintained through institutionalisation and public negotiations of aesthetic concepts. He has previously published on the dissemination of Scandinavian drama and on the interplay between theatre and literature in the cultural economy of the late nineteenth century.

Anna Sandberg

is Associate Professor, PhD at the University of Copenhagen. Visiting Professor: CAU Kiel 2018 and UC Berkeley 2016. Research fields: Cosmopolitan and transnational literatures 1800-present, the Scandinavian-German cultural relations. Selected books: *En grænsegænger mellem oplysning og romantik. Jens Baggesens tyske forfatterskab*, 2015; with Karin Hoff & Udo Schöning (ed.) *Literarische Transnationalität. Die kulturellen Dreiecksbeziehungen zwischen Skandinavien, Frankreich und Deutschland im 19. Jahrhundert*, Würzburg, 2015; with Adam Paulsen (ed.) *Natur und Moderne um 1900. Räume, Repräsentation, Medien*, 2013.

Udo Schöning

studied Romance Philology, History furthermore Social and Political Science at Göttingen and Hamburg. He received his Dr. phil. degree and a Dr. phil. habil. degree from the Georg-August-University Göttingen, where he was appointed apl. Prof. (adjunct professor) and taught Romance Philology until 2015. His research interests and publications focus on French and Italian literature, specifically from the Middle Ages and the nineteenth century, as well as intercultural literary relations. Major publications: *Literatur als Spiegel. Zur Geschichte eines kunsttheoretischen Topos in Frankreich von 1800–1860* (Heidelberg, 1984); *Thebenroman – Eneasroman – Trojaroman. Studien zur Rezeption der Antike in der französischen Literatur des 12. Jahrhunderts* (Tübingen, 1991).

Wiebke Röben de Alencar Xavier
is Associate Professor in the Department of Foreign Languages and Literatures at the Federal University of Rio Grande do Norte, Natal/Brazil. Her main areas of research are German Studies and Studies of cultural transfers and translations between Germany, France and Brazil in the 18th and 19th centuries. Among her publications in this area are *Salomon Gessner im Umkreis der Encyclopédie*, (2006); "The Brazilian Novels of José de Alencar translated into German" (book-chapter, 2017) and several other chapters, articles and organized numbers of revues and books. For more information about publications see Researcher ID https://orcid.org/0000-0003-3291-5451.

Introduction: Reframing the Cultural Transfer Approach

Steen Bille Jørgensen and Hans-Jürgen Lüsebrink

0.1 A New Paradigm in (Inter)Cultural Studies

The theoretical approach of cultural transfers was created in the 1980s in a specific academic and intellectual context and on the basis of a set of specific questions and objectives. It aimed at rethinking and renewing, on a conceptual, methodological and theoretical level, the investigation of cultural "relations" and "exchanges", ideas that were attracting increased interest across a range of disciplines (political science, literary studies, cultural studies, history), which nevertheless lacked sufficient theoretical and methodological foundations and a developed heuristic apparatus. Cultural transfers as an approach emerged out of the initiative of historians and specialists in literary studies, mainly from France and Germany, and under the leadership of Michel Espagne and Michael Werner, both initially specialists in German literatures and cultures. The concept of "cultural transfer" and the methodological and theoretical framework which it implied intended, on the one hand, to replace more traditional and unprecise concepts like "cultural relations", "cultural exchanges", "literary influences" and "cultural circulations"; and, on the other hand, to connect with the advances made in the 1970s and '80s in linguistics, anthropology, literary theory and translation studies. This included the theory of linguistic contacts, the theory of intertextuality and the theory of literary reception established in the beginning of the 1970s by Hans-Robert Jauß and Wolfgang Iser[1] and developed closer methodological and theoretical relations with translation studies through the notion of 'cultural translation' created and applied in numerous case studies these past 20 years.

The Cultural Transfer Approach was based on a critique of traditional and established concepts concerning the field of "cultural relations", "cultural exchanges", "cultural mobility" and orthodox conceptions of "influence". For Michel Espagne, one of the major initiators of the Cultural Transfer approach in the 1980s, the concept of "influence", which had for a long time

---

1 Hans-Jürgen Lüsebrink, 'De l'analyse de la réception littéraire à l'étude des transferts culturels', in *Discours social/Social discourse. Analyse du discours et sociocritique des textes*, 7/3–4 (1995), pp. 39–46.

dominated the researches on transnational relations in literature, was vague and problematic.[2] This new approach also intended to put into question attempts to evaluate an 'authentic original work' versus its 'reappropriations', that means its "creative translations" and "reinterpretations". As Matthias Middell, a historian from Leipzig University, has pointed out, Espagne and Werner also argued in their 'first conceptualization of cultural transfers' against 'old-fashioned ideas of diffusion and a historiography in which the weaker culture is thought to be influenced by the somehow stronger one in a process of contact and mutual constituency. Instead, they prioritized the context of perception, that is, the cultural surrounding in which the appropriation of foreign cultural elements takes place'. (Middell 2014, 18–19).

In spite of its broad field of inquiry, the Cultural Transfer Approach does not represent a general theory of relations and contacts between different cultures and societies, nor a theory of interculturality. Rather, it intends as a "theory of intermediate scope" to conceptualize certain forms of intercultural processes: precisely the circulation and reception of texts, discourses, cultural practices and forms of knowledge between different cultural areas. Here, a "cultural area" is defined as a geographical space having in common one or several languages of communication, a specific communication system and specific values and rituals.[3] Fundamentally, the Cultural Transfer Approach is based on the hypothesis that any cultural artifact transferred between different cultures (or cultural systems) undergoes a process of transformation, of re-semanticization, re-interpretation and – in the case of books, paintings and films for example – of re-reading. On a theoretical level, this process resembles the concept of "dynamic functionalism" introduced by Even-Zohar[4] who also underlined the close relationship between translation and cultural transfer connecting different linguistic and cultural systems: "Our accumulated knowledge about translation indicates more and more that translational procedures between two systems (languages/literatures) are in principle analogous, even homologous, with transfers within the borders of the system." (Even-Zohar 1990, 73). This position, which the editors and contributors to this volume defend by

---

2   Michel Espagne, 'La notion de transfert culturel', in *Revue Sciences/Lettres* [online], 1 (2013), pp. 1–9. https://rsl.revues.org/219.
3   Hans-Jürgen Lüsebrink, *Interkulturelle Kommunikation. Interaktion – Kulturtransfer – Fremdwahrnehmung* (Stuttgart, Weimar: Metzler, 2016 [2005]).
4   Itamar Even-Zohar, 'Introduction', in *Polysystem Studies, Poetics today*, 11/1 (1990) (special issue). https://www.tau.ac.il/~itamarez/works/books/Even-Zohar_1990--Polysystem%20studies.pdf.

means of a different terminology and through the conceptual framework of the Cultural Transfer Approach, is based on the fundamental conviction that translation always means shifting not only between two languages, but also between two cultures.[5] The British cultural historian Peter Burke regards the "study of translation" as 'central to the practice of cultural history', pointing out that translators follow a 'strategy of domestication or that of foreignizing, whether they understand or misunderstand the text they are turning into another language, the activity of translation necessarily involves both decontextualizing and recontextualizing.' (Burke 2007, 38). In the case of transferred texts, media, and discourses, processes of recontextualization and consequently re-semanticization entail not only a language change, but also a change in the cultural framework. Following more recent research in this field, Gasimov and Lemke Duque assert that "re-semanticization processes perform a general "semantic shift", caused by the effect of de-contextualization and re-contextualization of the transferred material and structures that accompany the linguistic border crossing". (Lemke Duque/Gasimov 2015, 9). These forms of re-semanticization concern a large variety of types, including forms of adaptation, imitation and productive reception, which always imply processes of transformation of transferred artifacts. Cultural transfer processes are characterized, as Walter Moser underlines in his contribution to this volume, by "transitivity" and "vectoriality", implying the operations of "extraction", "displacement" and "insertion" (into the receiver system) marked by more or less significant forms of transformation of the artifacts themselves, of their social, political and cultural use and of their meanings. As various studies have underlined since the late 1990s[6] and as Petra Broomans also points out in her contribution to this volume, the Cultural Transfer Approach focuses on mediation and cultural transmitters, paying particular attention to the materiality of the transferred artifacts and to the geographical, social and cultural spaces in which cultural transfer takes place.

The Cultural Transfer Approach represents an "agent-centered approach" of cultural relations and circulations which takes into account different types

---

5   Umberto Eco, quoted by Peter Burke, 'Cultures of translation in early modern Europe', in *Cultural Translation in Early Modern Europe*, ed. by Peter Burke/R. Po-Chia Hsia (Cambridge: Cambrige University Press, 2007), pp. 7–38 (p. 7).

6   For instance Michel Espagne, 'Die Rolle der Mittler im Kulturtransfer', in *Kulturtransfer im Epochenumbruch. Frankreich-Deutschland 1770 bis 1815*, ed. by Hans-Jürgen Lüsebrink/Rolf Reichardt, with Annette Keilhauer/René Nohr (Leipzig: Leipziger Universitätsvelag, 1997), (Deutsch-Französische Kulturbibliothek, vol. 9.1), pp. 309–330.

of actors considered and conceptualized as cultural 'brokers and mediators',[7] sometimes also defined as 'passeurs culturels',[8] as 'intermédiaires culturels'[9] or as cultural transmitters (see Broomans in this volume). Actors can represent individual persons acting as intercultural mediators (like translators, teachers of foreign languages and cultures, tourist guides), but also forms of media (like correspondents or reporters working for media in other countries) and cultural institutions being part of the cultural diplomacy system, like the German Goethe-Institutes, the Chinese Confucius Institutes and the French Alliance Française and French Cultural Institutes. In the recent evolution of the mediascape and the growing influence of the internet as a "meta-media", we can observe that human and machine agents are increasingly intervowen. The agency of cultural transfers 'would then be shared between men and machine in proportions determined in each case' (see Moser in this volume). As an actor-centered approach, the Cultural Transfer Theory focuses also the underlying motivations (or "generators") of cultural transfers which can be very diverse, from political and economic motivations to cultural ("learning more about the Other") and emotional factors (like desire and fascination with regard to other cultures).

The Cultural Transfer Approach does not conceptualize cultural relations and exchanges as unilateral and symmetric, but as fundamentally dynamic and multilateral, as well as asymmetric and – in numerous cases – as reciprocal. That means first that, in general, several cultures are implicated in the cultural transfer of a specific cultural artifact, for example in the case of a blockbuster like *Titanic* and a TV-series like *Dallas*[10] which is shown in other media-cultures. And it means secondly that transferred cultural artifacts produce not only effects, reactions and re-interpretations in the "target cultures", but also, in return, in the producing cultures. For example, the translation and critical reinterpretation of a philosophical text in other cultures often generates new perspectives and new interpretations, which are often discussed in the culture where it has been produced. The re-interpretation of the work of

---

7   Antje Dietze, 'Cultural Brokers and Mediators', in *The Routledge Handbook of Transregional Studies*, ed. by Matthias Middell (London: Routledge, 2018), pp. 494–502.
8   Diana Cooper-Richet/Jean-Yves Mollier/Ahmed Silem (eds.), *Passeurs culturels dans le monde des médias et de l'édition en Europe (XIXᵉ et XXᵉ siècles)* (Villeurbanne: Presses de l'ENSSIB, 2005).
9   Michel Vovelle (ed.), *Les Intermédiaires culturels dans l'Histoire. Actes du Colloque d'Aix-en-Provence (16–18 juin 1978)* (Paris: Librairie Champion; Aix-en-Provence: Publications de l'Université de Provence, 1981).
10 Elihu Katz/Tamar Liebes, *The Export of Meaning, Cross-Cultural Readings of Dallas* (New York: Oxford University Press, 1990).

Friedrich Nietzsche through translations and commentaries in French, notably by Gilles Deleuze and Michel Foucault, represents a striking example for this productive "reciprocity" of cultural transfer processes. The asymmetric dimension of cultural transfers is due to assymetric power relations between the two cultural systems, which are particularly important in the contexts of colonialism and military occupation, but can be observed in almost all constellations related to cultural transfers.

0.2 New Questionings and Changing Perspectives

The Cultural Transfer Approach has since its inception been the target of critics. These are partly based on misunderstandings und insufficient knowledge of the numerous, often empirical, research projects and publications it has produced over the past thirty-five years. With regard to the publications over these decades which have employed this approach, we can observe three main trends. First the internationalization of the research stemming from the Franco-German academic community and cultural transfers in Europe to North America, especially Canada,[11] but also China, Vietnam and other Asian countries,[12] and Africa.[13] Second, the scale of the disciplines embracing the Cultural Transfer Approach has widened from the original core disciplines of literary studies and history to art history, musicology, the history of sciences, book history, media studies, gender studies,[14] ethnology/anthropology, cultural studies[15] and translation studies where the concept of 'cultural transfer'

---

11   Laurier Turgeon/Denis Delâge/Réal Ouellet (eds.), *Transferts culturels et métissages Amérique/Europe, XVIe–XXe siècle* (Sainte-Foy: Presses de l'Université Laval, 1996); Sioui, Georges E., 'Point de vue Wendat sur les transferts culturels Europe-Amérique 992–1992', in *Histoires de Kanatha, seen and told. Essays and Discourses, 1991–2008*, ed. by Georges E. Sioui (Ottawa: Presses de l'Université d'Ottawa, 2009), pp. 39–50; Lacroix, Michel, *L'invention du retour d'Europe. Réseaux transatlantiques et transferts culturels au début du XXe siècle* (Québec: Presses de l'Université Laval, 2014).

12   Hoai Huong Aubert-Nguyen/Michel Espagne (eds.), *Le Vietnam. Une histoire de transferts culturels* (Paris: Demopolis, 2015); Espagne, Michel/Hongtu, Li, avec la coll. de Julie Gray et Romain Lefebvre (eds.), *Chine France – Europe Asie. Itinéraire de concepts* (Paris: Éditions Rue d'Ulm, 2018).

13   Michel Espagne/Hans-Jürgen Lüsebrink (eds.), *Transferts de savoirs sur l'Afrique* (Paris: Karthala, 2015).

14   Annette Keilhauer/Andrea Pagni (eds.), *Refracciones/Réfractions. Traducción y género en las literaturas románicas. Traduction et genre dans les littératures romanes* (Wien: LIT Verlag, 2017) (Coll. Representation – Transformation vol. 11).

15   Christine Lombez/Rotraud von Kulessa (eds.), *De la traduction et des transferts culturels* (Paris: L'Harmattan, 2007); Stockhorst, Stefanie (ed.), *Cultural Transfer Through*

is not always defined and conceived in the same sense as by Espagne and Werner.[16] Without referring explicitly to the Cultural Transfer Approach, and using the less theorized concepts of "transposition", "intersection" and "localization", Birgit Trautz embraces fundamentally the same objectives when she underlines, in the foreword of her inspiring book *Translating the World. Toward a New History of German Literature Around 1800*: 'Often, such acts of cultural transposition intersect with actual, linguistic translation. They require acts of localization – the linguistic and cultural rendering to fit the purpose and the idiom of a place [...].' (Trautz 2018, 6).

And third, the concepts and methodological tools stemming from the Cultural Transfer Approach have undergone considerable evolution and developed in different directions and into new fields:

- The category of "cultural mediators" has been reconceptualized successfully through the concepts of "cultural brokers" and "cultural mediators" but also through the concept of network, as articulated in network theory.[17] As Antje Dietze underlines, '[T]he figure of the cultural broker or mediator has gained remarkable prominence in transregional studies as well as in transnational and global history over the last decades. It has been used to study all kinds of cultural entanglements, ranging from early modern cultural encounters and expoloration to the formation of colonial empires as well as of postcolonial nation-states.' (Dietze 2018, 495).

Translation. The Circulation of Enlightened Thought in Europe by Means of Translation (Amsterdam: Rodopi, 2010); Bachmann-Medick, Doris, 'Menschenrechte als Übersetzungsproblem', in *Geschichte und Gesellschaft*, 38 (2012), pp. 331–35; Burke, art. cit.

16 Nikolai Salnikow (ed.), *Sprachtransfer – Kulturtransfer. Text, Kontext und Translation* (Frankfurt/Main, Berlin etc.: Peter Lang, 1995); Gerzymisch-Arbogast, Heidrun/Thome, Gisela/Giehl, Claudia (eds.), *Kultur und Übersetzung. Methodologische Probleme des Kulturtransfers* (Tübingen: Gunter Narr, 2001) (Jahrbuch Übersetzen und Dolmetschen vol. 2); Weissbrod, Rachel, 'From Translation to Transfer', in *Across Languages and Cultures*, 5/1 (2004), pp. 23–41; Fickert, Jan, 'Zum Begriff des Transfers in der Kultur- und Übersetzungswissenschaft am Beispiel eines frankophonen Almanachs', in *Translation als Sinngebung*, ed. by Heidrun Gerzymisch (Berlin: LIT, 2013) (mitSprache. Translatorische Forschungsbeiträge vol. 1), pp. 129–170; Gil, Alberto/Kirstein, Robert (eds.), *Wissenstransfer und Translation. Zur Breite und Tiefe des Übersetzungsbegriffs* (St. Ingbert: Röhrig Universitätsverlag, 2015); Agnetta, Marco, *Ästhetische Polysemiotizität und Translation. Glucks Orfeo ed Euridice (1762) im interkulturellen Transfer* (Hildesheim: Zürich, New York, Olms, 2019) (Crossing Semiotic Borders vol. 2).

17 Michel Lacroix, *L'invention du retour d'Europe. Réseaux transatlantiques et transferts culturels au début du XXe siècle* (Québec: Presses de l'Université Laval, 2014).

- The analysis of reception processes has integrated (and reframed), in a critical manner, the conceptual framework of "hybridity" and "transculturality" developed in the 1990s by researchers like Homi Bhabha and Wolfgang Welsch. In contrast to the analysis of hybrid texts or cultural practices, the analysis of cultural transfers does not focus solely on textual (or mediatic) structures, but on the whole set of processes that lead, in many cases, to Cultural Transfer Approach hybrid phenomena. As Moser points out in his contribution to this volume, he is aiming at the analysis of cultural artifacts characterized by transcultural transitivity and vectoriality, which means that the research process implies to 'cut a window of observation into infinite processes of cultural mobility'.
- Over the last three decades, notions of "culture", "nation" and "cultural area" on which the Cultural Transfer Approach is based, have been fundamentally problematized and put into question.[18] As Carl Antonius Lemke Duque and Zaur Gasimov, and other researchers working on this subject underline, 'cultural areas – similar to nations, regions or other historical subcategories – cannot be modelled as autonomous or hermetic entities, but as dynamic interrelated systems.' (Lemke Duque/Gasimov 2015, 8). The term "culture" can in no way be limited to "national cultures" and must be rethought as dynamic, open, multiscaled and fluid, with changing and permeable borders. In a programmatic article on methods in transregional studies, Antje Dietze and Matthias Middell have pointed out, in a very concise way, the new approaches to the relations between "space" and "culture": 'They reveal that intercultural transfers are complex interplays between the various scalar levels of territory and that they also encapsulate other, non-territorial forms of space. Intercultural transfers could occur between territories, places, and networks. The term of culture does not necessarily suggest a close relationship with one scale of territory that is the nation.' (Dietze 2018, 63).
- The inauguration of the concept of "Histoire croisée"/"Entangled history" by Michael Werner, Bénédicte Zimmermann and other historians has introduced a new perspective on the inquiry into cultural relations and contacts, which was also formulated as a critique of the Cultural Transfer Approach. Still, the focus and the methodological implications of the two approaches are very different, even if there is some conceptual overlap. Focusing on cultural intercrossings which are seen as 'relational, interactive,

---

18   See for example Federico Celestini/Helga Mitterbauer (eds.), *Ver-rückte Kulturen. Zur Dynamik kultureller Transfers* (Tübingen: Stauffenburg, 2003).

and process-oriented',[19] the "histoire croisée" approach associates social, cultural, and political formations, generally at the national level, that are assumed to bear relationships to one another. It furthermore inquires into "the very process of intercrossing in practical as well as intellectual terms." (Werner/Zimmermann 2006, 31). In historical studies, the concept of "Entangled History" has especially been used to analyze cross-cultural historical memories (like the Algerian War, 1954–62), events (like the Battle of Verdun in 1916–17) and encounters (like the violent confrontation between James Cook and the Hawaians leading to his death on February 14, 1779). Cultural transfers may concern either the preconditions or consequences of shared-history-constellations like these, but they focus significantly different questions.

– Finally, research on cultural transfers has paid an increasing attention to "failures", "misunderstandings" and "paradoxes". They can, on closer inspection, often be explained by political, mental or cultural forms of resistance, for example against "foreign influences" or forms of cultural hegemony, as the Iranian Revolution and its pointed refusal of "Americanization" illustrates. Periods and situations of military occupation, like the French occupation of parts of Germany during the Napoleonic era in the early 19th-century or the German occupation of Belgium and parts of France during World War II, are striking examples of paradoxical cultural transfers driven simultaneously by resistance and refusal, but also by underlying forms of interest, even sometimes fascination, and the will to know better the occupant in order to be able to outsmart or even to defeat him in the long run.[20] In numerous cases these constellations have lead also to a radical change of the sense and the use of the transferred artifacts, as the transfer of the French national symbolic to Germany around 1800 shows, a

---

19 Michael Werner/Bénédicte Zimmermann, 'Beyond comparison. *Histoire croisée* and the challenge of reflexivity', in *History and Theory*, 45 (2006), pp. 30–50 (p. 39).

20 Johannes Paulmann, 'Feindschaft und Verflechtung. Anmerkungen zu einem scheinbaren Paradox', in *Vom Gegner lernen. Feindschaften und Kulturtransfers im Europa des 19. und 20. Jahrhunderts*, ed. by Martin Aust (Frankfurt/Main: Campus, 2007), pp. 340–355; Lüsebrink, Hans-Jürgen, 'Interculturalités en temps de guerre. Approches d'une problématique paradoxale', in *Europa zwischen Text und Ort. Interkulturalität in Kriegszeiten (1914–1954)/L'Europe entre Texte et Lieu. Interculturalités en temps de guerre (1914–1954)*, ed. by Hans-Jürgen Lüsebrink/Valérie Deshoulières/Christoph Vatter (Bielefeld: transcript, 2013), pp. 99–110; see also the inspiring reflections of Richard Cobb, *French and Germans, Germans and French. A Personal Interpretation of France under Two Occupations, 1914–1918/1940–1944* (Hanover NH, London: University Press of New England, 1983).

phenomenon which Bruendel proposes to define as 'Negative cultural transfer'.[21]

According to its specific research questions and investigations, the Cultural Transfer Approach can be connected with different methodological tools, which have been enlarged during these last decades, focusing particularly on discourse and network analysis, intersectionality and intermediality. As Celestini and Mitterbauer (2003) as well as Dietze (2018) and Middell (2018) have pointed out, the

> intercultural transfer approach has not developed into a general theory applicable everywhere. On the contrary, it is rather a key for the discovery of new research constellations, open for investigation and appropriation. This makes the approach so compelling for the growing interest in global history, which is in need of an appropriate methodology to conceptualize interactions across borders of regions and continents as a result of global processes. (Middell/Dietze 2018, 64).

0.3 Scandinavian Challenges within Cultural Transfer Studies

In recent years, Scandinavian cinema and television has created a vogue for the "New Nordic", and opened up many countries to disovering new gastronomies and new travel destinations, associated with a certain cultural cachet and fashionable melancholy found in particular in the popular television series *The Killing* (2007). Though trends like this do not last eternally, it is important to consider how an interest in other cultures emerges and can encourage new ways of thinking about other language areas and cultural spheres as "cultural resources" depending on translation in the broadest sense of the word.[22]

In the perspective of Cultural Transfer, the volume *Le prisme du Nord*, published in 2006 by Michel Espagne, contributed to a "rethinking of the North" through the culture of the other.[23] From early thinking in terms of "germanity" over ideas of temperament implied in climate theory, to French political thinker Montesquieu's idea of the 'rational North', representations move from rather negative stereotypes to a more positive image of the other. However, in spite

---

21 Steffen Bruendel, 'Negativer Kulturtransfer. Die "Ideen von 1914" als Aufhebung der "Ideen von 1789"', in *Kulturtransfer im 19. Jahrhundert* ed. by Marc Schalenberg (Berlin: Centre Marc Bloch, 1998), pp. 153–171.
22 François Jullien, *Il n'y a pas d'identité culturelle* (Paris: L'Herne, 2016).
23 Espagne, Michel, *Le prisme du Nord. Pays du Nord, France, Allemagne (1750–1820)* (Tusson: Du Lérot, 2006).

of the cultural unity based on a common Nordic language and reformed idea of religion, Scandinavia did develop national specificities in the 19th century, a period of nation-building. On the political level, Denmark's important territorial position changed when Norway gained independence in 1814 and even more so in 1864, when Denmark lost its southern territories, the dukedoms of Schleswig, Holstein and Lauenburg. Whereas Sweden had developed its own political culture following French Enlightenment ideas, Denmark became so to speak the victim of its geographical, continental position.

Somewhat paradoxically, this 'exposed position' also meant that during the nineteenth century Denmark and Copenhagen were in many ways the catalysts of translations and transfers between Central Europe and the Northern countries as such. Although the circulation and translation of foreign creative texts and works, in terms of Even-Zohar, strengthened the 'national system', Scandinavian writers and artists in general developed their own works and contributed to the specificity of each nation. One example is the importance of the Danish popular movement in the second half of the 19th century, initiated by N.F.S. Grundtvig. As a romanticist, this priest and religious thinker was inspired by Herder's national ideas of *Blut-und-Boden*. However, to fully apprehend the importance of his impact on Danish culture, we must take into account the specificity of his role not only as a thinker but also as a poet (writer of psalms), politician and founder of the pedagogical project related to Denmark's popular *Højskoler*. These became the concrete and lasting result of his idealist view of social coherence and democracy based in a Christian understanding of the national tongue and the bodily presence of the voice.[24] We should also mention that one of Grundtvig's early intellectual achievements was the translation of Saxo Grammaticus's *Gesta Danorum* from Latin into Danish. In the late 19th century, Scandinavian literature even inspired new trends in European theater and literature. One example of this tendency was Ibsen, whose individual work changed the view of aesthetic modernity in Europe.[25]

This suggests that in spite of the conflict amongst the Scandinavian countries, various processes of cultural interaction determine a nation's cultural resources. According to this perspective, Cultural Transfers should not be regarded purely as a simple act of transmission or communication from a transmitting to a receiving culture, but rather as multi-faceted processes transcending frontiers, sometimes thanks to individual agents and their linguistic-cultural

---

24 Paul Ricœur used the Latin expression *vox viva* when he gave a lecture at the University of Copenhagen on the occasion of Grundtvig's 200th birthday in 1983.
25 See Qvistgaard's contribution in this volume.

specialization and commitment. Research in the area of Cultural Transfers was launched by German and French historians and literary scholars, so it is hardly surprising that this research has mainly been published in German and French ... and even in bilingual volumes.[26] Whereas the postcolonial paradigm (and Francophone studies) have been developed quite consistently, mainly at Swedish universities, the concept of Cultural Transfer has been studied more and more widely in the Danish context, first and foremost by literary scholars of Comparative Literature or Language Studies. It is probably no coincidence that in the Scandinavian context, Transfer Studies emerged within Germanic and Romance Languages Departments – both on the level of individual publications, and on the level of larger groups and international collaboration.

To further justify the largely Scandinavian focus of the contributions in this volume, it may be useful to present a brief outline of this paradigm within the Scandinavian context. Significantly, the earliest research in the area of Cultural Transfer was an initiative undertaken by German researchers working in Denmark. Thus, the Network for 'Danish-German Cultural Transfers' was founded at Aalborg University in 2000 by Ernst-Ullrich Pinkert and Klaus Bohnen. In this network, research activities were organized roughly according to socio-historical and linguistic literary approaches. Reception studies played an important role in this project until quite recently. A few years later, Danish universities underwent structural changes due to legislative reform (2002); and with a view to adapting to an increasingly globalized context, researchers were given the opportunity to launch projects that focus on both linguistic and cultural implications of transfer processes. As we shall see in the third section of this book, the University of Copenhagen has hosted an international research project on triangular Scandinavian-German-French relations. The core of this network was personal relations between Danish and German literary scholars, as attested by Anna Sandberg, Karin Hoff and Udo Schöning in their contribution to this volume.

At Aarhus University a process was initiated almost ten years ago to create larger structures and encourage inter-disciplinary research. The development of collaboration between comparatists and researchers from the language departments was facilitated, and the research programme in "Modernity and Cultural Transfers" organized a conference on the topic of "Cultural Transfer Reconsidered" in 2014. This initiative contributed to paving the way for an international Master in Intercultural Studies at the Departement of German and Romance Languages, launched in 2016. This means that in the long term, it

---

26   Christiane Solte-Gresser/Hans-Jürgen Lüsebrink/Manfred Schmeling (eds.), *Zwischen Transfer und Vergleich* (Stuttgart: Franz Steiner Verlag, 2013).

will be a priority to develop research in intercultural dialogue and transfer processes in a cross-disciplinary perspective ranging from cultural history/history of ideas to literature/aesthetics and the current development of media studies.

This book is the result of a project initiated within the department at Aarhus University in association with Hans-Jürgen Lüsebrink (Saarland University, Germany). Reconsidering this notion the question comes up how this paradigm can contribute to a better understanding of intercultural processes of exchange and mirroring. As a theory of "intermediate scope" ("mittlerer Reichweite"), the aim of Cultural Transfer-research is not to substitute any other theory like comparative approaches translational analysis or theory of reception, but rather to reconsider the complexity of relatively abstract research questions and paradigms seeking nonetheless to provide new insights through new framings and analyses. With the extension to phenomena of 'cultural translation' and the growing attention for translations in other disciplines, translation studies in a broad sense of the term have become an important disciplinary field connected with the Cultural Transfer Approach. As we shall see one of the main contributions of this book, beyond its multi-disciplinarity is probably the questioning of range and scope of research questions from large-scale global settings to micro-readings or -analyses.

0.4 Structure of the Book – Epistemology, Textuality and Premises of Transfer

0.4.1 *Dynamic Relations. Transnational Processes of Cultural Mediation*
Given the achievements and developments of Cultural Transfer-research, we intend to point to a number of its heuristic advantages in our times of Globalization. Taking into account the multi-disciplinary foundations of the paradigm, we also retain its definition within the area of historical French-German Studies and the importance a multi-faceted approach to cultural phenomena in various areas and its developments have, in many ways, fulfilled Michael Werner's prophecy of an 'adaptable concept'. In our first section, epistemological complexity is at the very center of interrogations that emphasize the need for new forms of historiography. Examining conceptions of culture within a national framework, the contributions advocate for a transnational view of cultural and literary history, providing examples from a European context with a particular attention to Scandinavian cases. This approach not only subverts the usual center-periphery dichotomy, but points also to more concrete forms of analysis, allowing for a renewed apprehension of transfer processes and the role played by individual agents. Although texts

and translations very often constitute the core objects of these studies, as we shall see, painting (Impressionism, in particular) is also an important case study of an aesthetic style adopted throughout Europe in the last half of the 19th century.

In his epistemological approach to cultural transfers, *Michel Espagne* demonstrates the need for a move away from the paradigm of comparativism established in the 19th century. Taking on insights from *Begriffsgeschichte* (Koselleck), Espagne advocates for a diachronic approach to transnational history and emphasises how cultural transfer modifies the receiving culture. Moving beyond postcolonial contexts, we also need to consider the circulation of notions and objects between conceptual systems. Proposing a study of the Scandinavian and Russian cases, Espagne highlights historical moments of intense mediation. If Scandinavia acts as a mirror of French Culture and Russians read texts in both German and French, these processes of reception and re-semanticization should not be limited to a question of language. Highlighting concrete examples and individuals playing a role in the transfer processes, Espagne insists on the "heterogenous structure of cultural meaning". In this perspective, what is supposed to be the core of Cultural Transfer Studies is the transformation of the receiving culture. Thus, moving beyond the study of bilateral relations, Espagne subverts the idea of center and periphery to insist on the importance of the dynamics of transfer processes as such.

Examining a number of epistemological turns and discussing the crisis of literary historiography, *Petra Broomans* seeks to advocate for a transnational understanding of literary history. Pointing to the missing link in the history of transfer processes, she insists on the importance of individual transmitters detected in early instances of comparative literature versus other transfer and translation theories, and underlines the neglect of both scholars and "cultural transmitters". Considering in particular the reception of the Dutch female writer (Henriette) Roland Holst-Van der Schalk, Broomans draws our attention to a literary translator who has been forgotten in the process of transfer. Arguing for the need to pay attention to translators and other agents, Broomans prefers the term "cultural transmitter" to "literary transmitters". Drawing on Philippe van Tieghem's early reflections, she insists on a broad understanding of the role of individuals. As a part of methodological proposals, Broomans presents concrete "phases of transmission" and seeks to offer concrete tools for apprehending the transfer process. She concludes that a more nuanced understanding of cultural transmitters is essential to a transnational version of literary history.

In his approach, which combines perspectives of world literatures and national literary categories, *Magnus Qvistgaard* uses Casanova's notion of a

"World Republic of Letters" as the starting point for his concrete analysis of the European Ibsen reception. Criticizing the national paradigm underpinning Casanova's model, and the idea of the aesthetic meridian, he develops the idea of the transfer process as a process of metamorphosis. He argues that Naturalist Theater should not be regarded as a common category throughout Europe but rather should be reconsidered in the light of its specific national, cultural context and market. Qvistgaard demonstrates that very often individual critics became responsible for change, as was the case in Germany and Great Britain. In understanding the complexity of cultural transfers, we should consequently pay more attention to specific (creative) appropriations and the complexity of aesthetic negotiation. Thus, the challenge of the foreign implies a national logic of literary norms.

Introducing the perspective of painting in the second half of the 19th century, *Anne-Estelle Leguy* analyses aspects of Impressionist painting as practised by Norwegian and Finnish women and draws our attention to a particular kind of agent. She brings to the fore the role played by Adolf von Becker and his teaching at a private academy in Finland, through which he succeeded in facilitating the transfer process of the French impressionist techniques and style in a Scandinavian context. Accordingly, Leguy demonstrates how Scandinavian painters, female as well as male, travelled to Brittany to paint rural subjects and practice new techniques. In this way, aesthetic modernity was developed in women's paintings and new painters were educated along the lines of women's views of their art and its forms. One of the results of this process can be seen in the Scandinavian style of painting that verges on abstraction.

0.4.2   Aspects of Textual Transfers – Intertextuality, Rewriting and Translation

One of the recent developments of Cultural Transfer Studies is a specifically literary approach related to various forms of mobility. From the perspective of literary studies, cultural transfers are closely related to the mobility of literary texts and works. Where analyses within the frame of traditional comparativism have often been based on the national paradigm and bi-lateral relations, the preoccupation in Cultural Transfer Studies with various levels of observation and analyses point to a variety of potential research questions and objects. In this section on textual transfers, examining critical notions and concepts like intertextuality, rewriting is a core concern. Since these terms have become a part of formalist textual analyses, emerging from the neo-avantgardes of the sixties, various discursive and critical stances have appeared. This means that we will revisit and revise these notions in relation with genre conventions, textual analyses and textual traces of cultural mobility and transformation. The analytically based theoretical proposals we find in the contributions of this section point to individual writers' historical and critical consciousness, but also to their questioning of cultural identity and the "identity of the literary work". The readings presented also make clear that, in spite of the transnational dimension of these theoretical questions, we constantly need to test our various general hypotheses in relation to concrete cultural and historical contexts and situations.

Taking as a starting point the notion of intertextuality, *Hans-Jürgen Lüsebrink* reflects on concepts of inter-discursivity and inter-subjectivity. In distinguishing between the discursive macro-level and the micro-level of the individual's subjectivity, Lüsebrink suggests a further perspective regarding scales of observation and analysis. Through his distinction of different kinds or forms of intertextuality, Lüsebrink brings to the fore the case of Ouologuem and his novel *Devoir de violence* (1968), in which the author rewrites the works of European authors but also African forms of narration. This case of intertextuality and rewriting is highlighted because of its poetics of violence. Intertextuality is seen as a violent counter-discourse and thus as a way of criticizing both the written francophone culture and cultural neo-imperialism but also to criticize African culture and the key figure of the griot, traditional storyteller and wise man, who incarnates oral forms of narration.

We find a parallel reflection on discursivity in general and the concrete case of transfer in New Caledonian transformations of the form of the aphorism. In her article on Déwé Gorodé, *Miriam Lay Brander* emphasises the brevity and the pointedness of the genre. Retracing the use of the aphorism from La Rochefoucauld to its critical adaptation in the context of May 1968, Miriam Lay Brander demonstrates how its recontextualisation produces new critical effects. Through her reading of a poetical practice and its singularity, Lay Brander demonstrates how the literary strategies deployed subvert the European uses of the genre. Her presentation of the graphical dimension of these brief sentences with their critical statement-like style and rhetoric, confronts the reader with a well-known form of which the freshness and effect springs from its rewriting or reconfiguration.

In his contribution on transfer processes and processes of translation, *Steen Bille Jørgensen* investigates the ways in which (cultural) translation is mediated through literary works. He seeks to clarify what happens, when writers and artists make translation a part of their specific and individual literary creativity. On the one hand, we find metafictional strategies, which point to the void or the loss of the loved one or the origins with its tragic dimensions. On the other hand, more concrete avant-garde strategies, if they also point to death, and loss, imply more activist ways of acting in society. In this way, Jørgensen's contribution points to both existential and ethical implications of textual creativity and intertextuality, which focusses on to the otherness maintained, in the dialogue between writer and reader.

0.4.3 *Perspectives – Types of Distance and Proximity*
In this final section we want to raise the question of "Distance and proximity" both in a geographical and a more metaphorical or conceptual sense. Regarding geographical proximity, the approach related to "triangular processes" seems particularly fruitful but, the productive or creative appropriation depends, to a very large degree, on the historical development of cultural and intellectual norms in the receiving culture, as it is the case of transfers between Europe and Latin America. Transfer processes do not only depend on more or less immediate cultural exchange between neighbors, or even of an intracultural kind, but also on intellectual and ideological norms. This becomes particularly clear when we look at transfers between geographically remote continents, countries or regions, where historical and ideological framings and the position of intellectuals become essential to the successful transfer of foreign cultural forms, but also their counter-transfer. In this perspective, we intend to consider institutional initiatives in favor of cultural transfers in Northern Europe and Central Europe but also the case of Brazil as a Latin American country with strong cultural relations to Europe. This dimension is essentially related to institutions like universities.

Discussing the notion of transfer, *Walter Moser* suggests the importance of the Freudian dimension and the dislocation of the subject. He mentions how through the 'wide-ranging zone of intraculturality to cultural analysis, we discover cultural transfers between the most diverse cultural sub-systems'. In this way, Moser draws attention to sub-cultures and cultural differences within a national culture and the importance of micro-analyses. His study of the transhistorical dimension of the Baroque points to the fact that national ideology may imply acceptance or refusal of the 'baroque' as a notion and a style. In Latin America the baroque is to be analyzed in the long duration from the early European conquest to the formation of the nation in the 20th century. The baroque is not just adopted but redefined in relation to Latin American identity in texts by Carpentier and Lima in an intellectual act of counter-conquest. The unsuccessful transfer into the French Culture may help us understand the ideological resistance as opposed to the (national) identity forming process in South America.

In her contribution, *Wiebke Röben de Alencar Xavier* underlines the importance of circulation between the continents. Pondering the fact that Brazil has adopted the cultural transfer paradigm rather late, she analyses its concrete institutional features in the light of the Brazilian notion of *Transferências culturais*. This analysis highlights the notion of resemantization, the translation of the notion as such mirroring aspects of its Brazilian reception. The recent development of the paradigm in Brazil has proven to be particularly adaptable and is used in research contexts such as Translation and Literary Studies, but also Media Studies. Giving priority to transatlantic academic exchanges, the contribution also points to important dynamics between the South and the North.

One of the important perspectives of Cultural Transfer Studies presented in *Anna Sandberg, Karin Hoff* and *Udo Schöning*'s presentation of their research project is related to the triangular structure of transfer processes between Scandinavia, Germany and France in the xixth century. Presenting aspects of the imaginary and material structure of objects transferred, they focus on the ways in which cultural transformations have been carried by translations, and literary-historical scholarship. Although their approach does not dismiss altogether the analyses of bilateral transfer, new insights and nuances are brought about when we rather choose to consider trilateral structures bringing to the fore the French interest in the Germanic, Nordic cultures but also the literary impressionism of the Danish writer Herman Bang.

0.5 Editors' Notice

We wish to thank very much the University of Aarhus for its financial support, Niall Sreenan (PhD) for the linguistic revision of the contributions to this volume. We wish also to thank Carla Dalbeck and Viktoria Lühr, research assistants at Saarland University, for their editorial work on the manuscript.

Bibliography

Agnetta, Marco, *Ästhetische Polysemiotizität und Translation. Glucks* Orfeo ed Euridice (1762) *im interkulturellen Transfer* (Hildesheim: Zürich, New York, Olms, 2019) (Crossing Semiotic Borders, vol. 2).

Aubert-Nguyen, Hoai Huong/Espagne, Michel (eds.), *Le Vietnam. Une histoire de transferts culturels* (Paris: Demopolis, 2015).

Bachmann-Medick, Doris, 'Menschenrechte als Übersetzungsproblem', in *Geschichte und Gesellschaft*, 38 (2012), pp. 331–359.

Bruendel, Steffen, 'Negativer Kulturtransfer. Die "Ideen von 1914" als Aufhebung der "Ideen von 1789"', in *Kulturtransfer im 19. Jahrhundert*, ed. by Marc Schalenberg (Berlin: Centre Marc Bloch, 1998), pp. 153–171.

Burke, Peter, 'Cultures of translation in early modern Europe', in *Cultural Translation in Early Modern Europe*, ed. by Peter Burke/R. Po-Chia Hsia (Cambridge: Cambrige University Press, 2007), pp. 7–38.

Cecovic, Svetlana/Roland, Hubert/Béghin, Laurent (eds.), *Réception, transferts, images. Phénomènes de circulation littéraire entre la Belgique, la France et la Russie (1870–1940)* (Louvain: Presses Universitaires de Louvain, 2018).

Celestini, Federico/Mitterbauer, Helga (eds.), *Ver-rückte Kulturen. Zur Dynamik kultureller Transfers* (Tübingen: Stauffenburg, 2003).

Cobb, Richard, *French and Germans, Germans and French. A Personal Interpretation of France under Two Occupations, 1914–1918/1940–1944* (Hanover NH, London: University Press of New England, 1983).

Cooper-Richet, Diana/Mollier, Jean-Yves/Silem, Ahmed (eds.), *Passeurs culturels dans le monde des médias et de l'édition en Europe (XIXe et XXe siècles)* (Villeurbanne: Presses de l'ENSSIB, 2005).

Dietze, Antje, 'Cultural Brokers and Mediators', in *The Routledge Handbook of Transregional Studies*, ed. by Matthias Middell (London: Routledge, 2018), pp. 494–502.

Espagne, Michel, 'La notion de transfert culturel', in *Revue Sciences/Lettres* [online], 1, (2013), pp. 1–9. https://rsl.revues.org/219.

Espagne, Michel, *Le prisme du Nord. Pays du Nord, France, Allemagne (1750–1820)* (Tusson: Du Lérot, 2006).

Espagne, Michel, 'Die Rolle der Mittler im Kulturtransfer', in *Kulturtransfer im Epochenumbruch. Frankreich-Deutschland 1770 bis 1815*, ed. by Hans-Jürgen Lüsebrink/ Rolf Reichardt, with Annette Keilhauer/René Nohr (Leipzig: Leipziger Universitätsverlag, 1997) (Deutsch-Französische Kulturbibliothek, vol. 9.1), pp. 309–330.

Espagne, Michel/Hongtu, Li, avec la coll. de Julie Gray et Romain Lefebvre (eds.), *Chine France – Europe Asie. Itinéraire de concepts* (Paris: Éditions Rue d'Ulm, 2018).

Espagne, Michel/Lüsebrink, Hans-Jürgen (eds.), *Transferts de savoirs sur l'Afrique* (Paris: Karthala, 2015).

Even-Zohar, Itamar, *Polysystem Studies, Poetics Today*, 11/1 (1990) (a special issue). https://www.tau.ac.il/~itamarez/works/books/Even-Zohar_1990--Polysystem%20studies.pdf.

Fickert, Jan, 'Zum Begriff des Transfers in Kultur- und Übersetzungswissenschaft am Beispiel eines frankophonen Almanachs', in *Translation als Sinngebung*, ed. by Heidrun Gerzymisch (Berlin: LIT, 2013) (mitSprache. Translatorische Forschungsbeiträge, vol. 1), pp. 129–170.

Gasimov, Zaur/Lemke Duque/Carl Antonius (eds.), 'Transfer and Translation', in *Comparativ. Zeitschrift für Globalgeschichte und Vergleichende Gesellschaftsforschung*, 2 (2015), pp. 7–58.

Gerzymisch-Arbogast, Heidrun/Thome, Gisela/Giehl, Claudia (eds.), *Kultur und Übersetzung. Methodologische Probleme des Kulturtransfers* (Tübingen: Gunter Narr, 2001) (Jahrbuch Übersetzen und Dolmetschen, vol. 2).

Gil, Alberto/Kirstein, Robert (eds.), *Wissenstransfer und Translation. Zur Breite und Tiefe des Übersetzungsbegriffs* (St. Ingbert: Röhrig Universitätsverlag, 2015).

Jullien, François, *Il n'y a pas d'identité culturelle* (Paris: L'Herne, 2016).

Katz, Elihu/Liebes, Tamar, *The Export of Meaning. Cross-Cultural Readings of Dallas* (New York: Oxford University Press, 1990).

Keilhauer, Annette/Pagni, Andrea (eds.), *Refracciones/Réfractions. Traducción y género en las literaturas románicas. Traduction et genre dans les littératures romanes* (Wien: LIT Verlag, 2017) (Coll. Representation – Transformation, vol. 11).

Lacroix, Michel, *L'invention du retour d'Europe. Réseaux transatlantiques et transferts culturels au début du XXe siècle* (Québec: Presses de l'Université Laval, 2014).

Lombez, Christine/Kulessa, Rotraud von (eds.), *De la traduction et des transferts culturels* (Paris: L'Harmattan, 2007).

Lüsebrink, Hans-Jürgen, *Interkulturelle Kommunikation. Interaktion – Kulturtransfer – Fremdwahrnehmung* (Stuttgart, Weimar: Metzler, 2016 [2005]).

Lüsebrink, Hans-Jürgen, 'Interculturalités en temps de guerre. Approches d'une problématique paradoxale' in *Europa zwischen Text und Ort. Interkulturalität in Kriegszeiten (1914–1954)/L'Europe entre Texte et Lieu. Interculturalités en temps de guerre (1914–1954)*, ed. by Valérie Deshoulières/Hans-Jürgen Lüsebrink/Christoph Vatter (Bielefeld: transcript, 2013), pp. 99–110.

Lüsebrink, Hans-Jürgen, 'De l'analyse de la réception littéraire à l'étude des transferts culturels', in *Discours social/Social discourse. Analyse du discours et sociocritique des textes*, 7/3–4 (1995), pp. 39–46.

Lüsebrink, Hans-Jürgen, 'De la théorie de la réception littéraire à l'étude des transferts culturels. Ruptures et continuités', in: *Konzepte der Rezeption*, vol 3. *Rezeption und Kulturtransfer: Zur Interaktion literarischer Vermittlungsprozesse*, ed. by Carolin Fischer/Beatrice Nickel/Brunhilde Wehinger (Tübingen: Stauffenberg, 2021), pp. 17–29.

Mein, Georg (ed.), *Transmission. Übersetzung/Traduction, Übertragung/Transfert/ Vermittlung/Médiation* (Wien, Berlin: Verlag Turia+Kant, 2010).

Middell, Mathias/Dietze, Antje, 'Methods in Transregional Studies. Intercultural Transfers', in *The Routledge Handbook of Transregional Studies*, ed. by Matthias Middell (London: Routledge, 2018), pp. 58–66.

Middell, Matthias, 'The Search for a New Place for the 19th Century in Global History Narratives', in *Cultural Transfers. Encounters and Conections in the Global 18th Century*, ed. by Matthias Middell (Leipzig: Leipziger Universitätsverlag, 2014) (Global History and International Studies, 8), pp. 7–40.

Paulmann, Johannes, 'Feindschaft und Verflechtung. Anmerkungen zu einem scheinbaren Paradox', in *Vom Gegner lernen. Feindschaften und Kulturtransfers im Europa des 19. und 20. Jahrhunderts*, ed. by Martin Aust (Frankfurt/Main: Campus, 2007), pp. 340–355.

Salnikow, Nikolai (ed.), *Sprachtransfer – Kulturtransfer. Text, Kontext und Translation* (Frankfurt/Main, Berlin etc.: Peter Lang, 1995).

Sioui, Georges E., 'Point de vue Wendat sur les transferts culturels Europe-Amérique 992–1992', in *Histoires de Kanatha, seen and told. Essays and Discourses, 1991–2008*, ed. by Georges E. Sioui (Ottawa: Presses de l'Université d'Ottawa, 2009), pp. 39–50.

Solte-Gresser, Christiane/Lüsebrink, Hans-Jürgen/Schmeling, Manfred (eds.), *Zwischen Transfer und Vergleich. Theorien und Methoden der Literatur- und Kulturbeziehungen aus deutsch-französischer Perspektive* (Wiesbaden: Franz-Steiner-Verlag, 2013) (Vice Versa. Deutsch-französische Kulturstudien, vol. 5).

Stockhorst, Stefanie (ed.), *Cultural Transfer Through Translation. The Circulation of Enlightened Thought in Europe by Means of Translation* (Amsterdam: Rodopi, 2010).

Trautz, Birgit, *Translating the World. Toward A New History of German Literature Around 1800* (University Park, PA: The Pennsylvania State University Press, 2018).

Turgeon, Laurier/Delâge, Denis/Ouellet, Réal (eds.), *Transferts culturels et métissages Amérique/Europe, XVIe–XXe siècle* (Sainte-Foy: Presses de l'Université Laval, 1996).

Vovelle, Michel (ed.), *Les Intermédiaires culturels dans l'Histoire. Actes du Colloque d'Aix-en-Provence (16–18 juin 1978)* (Paris, Librairie Champion; Aix-en-Provence: Publications de l'Université de Provence, 1981).

Weissbrod, Rachel, 'From Translation to Transfer', in *Across Languages and Cultures*, 5 (1), 2004, pp. 23–41.

Werner, Michael/Zimmermann, Bénédicte, 'Beyond comparison. *Histoire croisée* and the challenge of reflexivity', in *History and Theory*, 45 (2006), pp. 30–50.

PART 1

Transnational Processes of Cultural Mediation – Dynamic Relations

CHAPTER 1

What Are Cultural Transfers? The Russian and Scandinavian Cases

Michel Espagne

Abstract

In contemporary historiography, the representation of the identity of history is undermined by a range of approaches, ranging from comparativism to types of histories highlighting the phenomena of imbrication. It is on this latter dimension that research on cultural transfers focuses. To better understand the differences and complementarities of the two approaches we should, on the one hand, subject comparativism to a historical analysis of its premises and its developments and, on the other hand, consider the contribution of the research on cultural transfers in relation to a particular object of study. In particular, I will be considering here transfers between German, Scandinavian and Russian spheres. We will also highlight the contributions of cultural transfers to postcolonial studies and its distance from and points of convergence with historical comparativism.

Few historians today are satisfied with a national framework.[1] Attempts to enlarge it take different forms and follow diverse theoretical perspectives. The idea of making connections between distinct histories, or more precisely of expanding the history of Europe to include other cultural zones, is very old. It seems to have a theological root that is expressed particularly in the 17th century with the theologian Jacques-Bénigne Bossuet's *Discourse on Universal History*. The idea was to demonstrate the designs of Providence in the development of well-known empires. But beyond this, the growing effort

---

1   See Michel Espagne, *Les transferts culturels franco-allemands* (Paris: PUF, 1999); Hans-Jürgen Lüsebrink, *Interkulturelle Kommunikation. Interaktion – Kulturtransfer – Fremdwahrnehmung* (Stuttgart, Weimar: Metzler, 2005); Michel Espagne, 'La notion de transfert culturel', in *Revue Sciences/Lettres*, 1 (2013), pp. 1–9. https://rsl.revues.org/219; Michel Espagne, 'Comparison and Transfer. A Question of Method', in *Transnational Challenges to National History Writing*, ed. by Matthias Middell/Lluis Roura i Aulinas (Basingstoke: Palgrave MacMillan, 2013), pp. 38–51; Matthias Middell, 'Kulturtransfer, Transferts culturels', in *Docupedia-Zeitgeschichte*. (2016). www.http://docupedia.de/zg/middell_kulturtransfer_v1_de_2016.

to attach the "unknown" to the "known" is evident in the supposition that recently discovered peoples might be the lost tribes of Israel. The history of pre-Columbian America in particular faced from the beginning the question of inclusion in the biblical framework. It was in order to connect the "unknown" to the "known" that China became the descendent of an Egyptian colony, a theory defended well into the 18th century by Joseph de Guignes, one of the first French Sinologists. Integration of still little studied peoples into the historical field was inseparable from the determination of their exact place in the human family as set out in the Bible. History became a science with Scottish empiricism. One cannot overemphasize the importance of the works of David Hume, and of those that William Guthrie devoted to world history. Guthrie's text on world history became a work of reference in Europe, which the scholars of Göttingen, Christian Gottlob Heyne first among them, sought to bring into Germany by means of a translation.[2] At the same time that the Göttingen historians translated Guthrie, they adapted and completed him, encouraging a local school of universal history beginning in the 1760s. This transposition corresponds to a translation often observed of Scottish empiricism in the context of the German Enlightenment.

Comparativism in the narrowest sense of the term, which is based on the placing of objects side by side, is an epistemological attitude characteristic of the nineteenth century, and one that is not to be found first in the domain of historiography. Plants were compared first, in order to establish typologies (Carl Linnaeus) and then organisms, in order to identify descent as much as genesis. Comparative anatomy, as French naturalist, Georges Cuvier, practiced it, disclosed lines of descent in the animal world and allowed the workings of animal's bodies to be understood. The comparative grammar of Indo-European languages was favored both by the romantic search for origins and by the empirical discovery of a potential mother-language, Sanskrit. But even nineteenth-century authors fostered theories of entanglement and Alexander von Humboldt aimed to connect the history of the new continent with migrations from Asia.

Comparison became a yet more radical attitude when philology developed into anthropology. Works like James George Frazer's *The Golden Bough*, or Lewis Morgan's Ancient Society, presuppose that texts or traditions are markers of social realities that must be posed in relation to one another in order to progressively construct a sort of grammar of human comportment, and to discover the primitive building blocks of any social edifice. Comparison undertaken to this end brings together contemporary realities distant in space, as

---

2 Wilhelm Guthrie, *Allgemeine Weltgeschichte von der Schöpfung bis auf gegenwärtige Zeit*, I–XVII (Leipzig: M.G. Weidmanns Erben und Reich, 1765–1788).

well as cultural strata from distinct times. Considered an extension of experimental psychology, *Völkerpsychologie* (folk psychology) favored comparison, and served as a point of departure for ethno-anthropology, or a new kind of universal history. Wilhelm Wundt provided the methodological background for the universal history of Karl Lamprecht.

The function of comparison cannot be underestimated in this situation, because it constitutes a kind of pragmatic precondition for any extension of the field of perception. But for a long time the parallelisms established by comparative social history, or the enumeration of national treatments of such and such an archetypal motif in cultural history, have been reproached for assuming a neutral observer who cannot exist, and for separating the elements being compared from the dynamic of their own genesis and analyzing them as though they were invariant data. There is one case in particular in which historical comparativism shows its limits; this is the question of non-European history. One does not compare England and Burma, or France and Vietnam. Comparativism can hardly begin to treat the historiography of formerly colonized territories, which requires other methodologies. The shaping of modern India or modern Vietnam under the French or English rule can be much easier observed from the viewpoint of cultural transfers working in both directions.

Research on cultural transfers is connected to research on translations if the latter turns away from simple linguistic transpositions to tackle the question of contexts in the broadest sense of the term. The history of the translation of Panchatantra makes it possible to follow the intellectual relations between the Indian Middle Ages and the Western Middle Ages. The question of translations from a first translation, which allows us to observe how the English novel of the 18th century arrived in Germany through French versions, highlights the overlaps between several cultures. This question of second translations can be observed between Europe and China, where many works by European historians or philosophers of the 19th century arrived via Japanese versions which changed the semantic content. We know that the translation of Sanskrit texts from the Buddhist canon into Chinese was one of the largest cultural transfers in Asian history, also involving intermediate languages such as Tokharian or Paleo-Uighur. The attempt to understand the presence of a foreign culture implies taking an interest in the tradition of translations. During the Second World War, the German troops in France immediately started to research the archives to see which parts illustrated German history, but they also produced an exhaustive inventory of what had been translated from German into French since the origins of these archives.[3] This gigantic assessment, which was kept

---

3   Liselotte Bihl/Karl Epting, *Bibliographie des traductions d'auteurs de langue allemande (1487–1944)* (Tübingen: Max Niemeyer Verlag, 1987).

confidential for several decades, was not published until the 1980s. Translation is not only the passage from one language to another, it is also above all the passage from one cultural context to another where translators as cultural mediators play an central role.[4]

The ambition of global history is not limited to see to that every region of the world enters into the historical space, since in order to achieve this it must come to encompass every phenomenon of social life. It is for this reason that it is also a cultural history. But any movement of a cultural object from one context to another results in a transformation of its meaning, a dynamic of re-semanticisation that we can fully recognize only by taking account of the historical vectors of the transfer. Therefore, we can say from the outset that research dealing with cultural transfers concerns most of the human sciences even though its development involved a certain number of precise points of anchorage. Insofar as the perspective on the cultural focuses on real transmission, globality has to be analyzed in a micrological framework.

The notion of cultural transfer was developed in a context of the study of nineteenth-century Germany in its connections to France. The reference to Germany was then a structural element in the development of the French human sciences.

In order to approach this reference it was necessary, on the one hand, to take into account the fact that objective knowledge concerning the German cultural domain was less important than the reorganization of the scientific field it made possible, and on the other hand, it was important to explore the transnational vectors. From this point of view, we find ourselves placed before research of a hermeneutic nature, centered around the determination of new meanings, and faced with a historico-sociological type of inquiry concerning the vectors of transfer between the two countries.

Research concerning transfers ought to admit that the appropriation of a cultural object liberates itself from its origin or model, which is to say that a transposition, however far removed from the original it may be, has just as much legitimacy as the model. The translator is not a traitor, but creates new dimensions of sense. As a result, the notion of comparison as an additional principle of openness to different spaces in the human and social sciences loses its relevance and has to be replaced by the observation of forms of cultural mixing and hybridization. The study of cultural transfers obliges us to diminish the relative importance of comparison. Indeed, this latter tends to confront entities in order to tally their resemblances and dissimilarities, but

---

4 See also in this point Michel Espagne, 'La fonction de la traduction dans les transferts culturels franco-allemands aux XVIIIe et XIXe siècles. Le problème des traducteurs germanophones', in *Revue d'histoire littéraire de la France*, mai–juin 1997, pp. 413–427.

barely takes into account the observer who is making the comparison, who is opposing in order to reassemble, projecting his own system of categories, creating reductive oppositions, and who himself generally belongs to one of the two terms of the comparison.

In the Franco-German context of the 1980s, research rapidly enlarged its terrain of investigation to include other imbrications of national spaces, and even made complex analyses of the interfaces between three or four cultural spaces like Greece, France, and Germany or Italy, France, Germany, and Russia. These investigations brought the role of diverse instances of mediation to the forefront. There are innumerable studies on travellers, work on merchants has been developing rapidly, while investigation has just begun on the military, artists, and translators. On the other hand, the history of the book has already ably explored the role of bookstores and publishers, and collectors have been treated through the history of museums. Above all, one must also emphasize the unavoidable semantic transformation associated with importation to a new context. Particular attention should be paid to the transformation that a cultural import brings about in the context of its reception, and inversely the positive effect of this reception context on the new meaning of the object.

By the same token, the problem of determining if an import is adequate or authentic loses all its pertinence. One notable consequence of this is the new evaluation of the role played by the series of foreign references characteristic of each national space. Each culture makes a foreign pantheon for itself that in no sense corresponds to the pantheon in the country of origin. The questions of semantic transformations connected to the transfer persist in the case of terms which sound similar in many languages, and which may be considered equivalents, but which have a different significance in different contexts. Reinhart Koselleck's *Begriffsgeschichte*, or conceptual history, is potentially very useful, therefore, with the reservation only that this history must be transnational. Concepts do not have a genealogy exclusively connected to a single linguistic zone. Rather, their meaning is also the result of displacements that demand adaptation and linguistic enrichment that must be taken into account.

Archaic transfers in the societies upon which modern Europe's self-perception is founded have already served to legitimate putting its domination into question. Cheikh Anta Diop's book on black Egypt, *Nations nègres et cultures* (1954), reinforced by the hypotheses of Martin Bernal's *Black Athena*, essentially aimed, at the beginning of decolonisation, to designate an archaic African heritage at the heart of European civilization.[5] A Russian

---

5   Michel Espagne, 'Frobenius, Anta Diop et Martin Bernal. Les projections sur l'Europe de connaissances acquises sur l'Afrique', in *Transferts de savoirs sur l'Afrique*, ed. by Michel Espagne/Hans-Jürgen Lüsebrink (Paris: Karthala, 2015), pp. 159–173.

history of German literature is deeply different from a genuine German history of German literature. The question of cultural transfers can, therefore, include elements of postcolonial approaches. However, the term "postcolonial" might seem inadequate. When a Medievalist demonstrates the fact that the German mysticism embodied by Meister Eckhart borrowed its theory of the intellect from Averroes, and when Greek philosophy's detour through Islamic thought has become a classic object of Greek studies, it is not a matter of postcolonialism but rather of the circulation of conceptual systems that, in function of their host context, modifies their meaning. The Platonic keys used by Garcilaso de la Vega to describe his original Inca culture in the late 16th century lead to a double projection: that of Platonic categories onto the Inca, and that of Incan examples to reinforce the Platonic model.

Binary configurations are also transcended by numerous countries considered as peripheral within the European space but which, precisely because of this peripheral situation, can more easily guarantee mediations. Scandinavian countries provide a particularly telling example. The study of multiple-component, complex cultural transfers, particularly those involving a Scandinavian country, often highlight a strange relationship between the alleged periphery, and the places that claim to be at the centre of a European literary and cultural space.

Perhaps because of the low numbers of actors, the bilateral intellectual relationships between Scandinavia and France[6] do not lend themselves easily to a quantitative history of exchanges, mediations, and travels. It is possible, on the other hand, to trace the history of a curiosity that involves whole swathes of French intellectual life. Even when it concerns landscape and travel accounts, this curiosity is focussed on written materials. However, the access to texts from Northern literature demands a linguistic skill that is most often acquired by an extension, often empirical, of linguistic and literary skills in the German domain. The question of Scandinavian studies in France is an interesting case of triangular cultural transfer.

Within the French curiosity about Scandinavia, there is an ancient stratum, marked by a long-standing interest in the European royal courts, particularly in the case of Sweden. To take but one example, memoirs concerning Christine of Sweden have resulted in voluminous publications. But in Voltaire's study of the reign of Charles XII (1731), that is, the tumults of the generalized European conflict termed the 'Great Northern War', Sweden is directly linked with the history

---

6 Michel Espagne, *Le prisme du Nord. Pays du Nord-France-Allemagne (1750–1920)* (Tusson: Du Lérot, 2005).

of Germany. How could Sweden not be associated with the Germanic space, when it appears as the bastion of faith most characteristic of North Germany?

Hans Christian Andersen spoke German and knew Germany well. During a trip that he took to Dresden and Leipzig, notably, he was among the visitors to the old Romantic poet Ludwig Tieck. But his knowledge of France was no less intimate. An initial three-month stay took place in 1833. And later, in 1843, Andersen spent two months in Paris, during which time Xavier Marmier, who discovered Northern literature, introduced him to contributing writers for the *Revue de deux mondes*. It was also here that he met Victor Hugo and Alexandre Dumas.

Another example of mixed culture and of the similarities between French and German literature is supplied by the well-known scholar Georg Brandes, who was the incarnation of a comparativism where the aim is not to draw parallels between literary schools, but rather to adopt the global point of view of a *Weltliteratur* (world literature) where transversal relationships are most important. He quickly encountered a positive response to his work in Germany, where it was published with the title *Die Hauptströmungen der Literatur des 19. Jahrhunderts* (*The Main Currents in 19th-century Literature*) in 1872. A partial French version only appeared in 1902. Yet despite these delays, Georg Brandes still remains no less than one of the Franco-Germanic mediators of the late-nineteenth century, capable of passing on (in both directions) information on literary figures, or methodological reflections concerning the way to approach a global European literature.

It is from the middle of the eighteenth century that the relationships between Germanic and Scandinavian peoples became a subject of reflection in France, and even led to ideological constructions. The key milestone was the voluminous *Histoire de Dannemarc* (*History of Denmark*[7]) by Paul Henri Mallet, which first appeared in 1755.[8] The essential feature of this work is that far from providing an exhaustive chronology of sovereigns and dynasties, it begins with a long introduction where 'monuments of Celtic mythology and poetry and particularly ancient Scandinavians' are presented. Denmark embodies the Scandinavian North, and is, from the outset, endowed with a mythological, intellectual and poetic identity. Mallet's description of Germanic mythology, in French, would be one of Herder's paradoxical sources on the subject.

---

7 Title translation M.E.
8 Michel Espagne, 'Herder-Mallet-Arngrimur. Rückläufige Geschichtsschreibung und Kulturtransfer', in *Kulturelle Dreieckbeziehungen. Aspekte der Kulturvermittung zwischen Frankreich, Deutschland und Dänemark in der ersten Hälfte des 19. Jahrhunderts*, ed. by Karin Hoff/Udo Schöning/Per Øhrgaard (Würzburg: Königshausen & Neumann, 2013), pp. 199–211.

Leaving Berlin in 1827 to visit Sweden, Denmark, and Norway, the philologist and traveller Jean-Jacques Ampère defined his objective thus: 'I was curious to see this great and melancholic environment of the North, to contemplate it, in the heart of their wilderness, these still-pure Germans that Tacitus would almost have recognized.'[9] Denmark is still only the doorway to Scandinavia, 'its link with Germany'. But as Iceland is part of it, it is there that ancient Scandinavian texts have been remembered, and it is in Scandinavia that Ampère was able to meet the philologists versed in the exploration of this traditional heritage. Sweden, whose literary life is encapsulated in the journal *Phosphoros*, appears to him to be, in its philosophy, unlike German idealism.

Another philologist-traveller was Xavier Marmier who was Chair of Foreign Literatures at Rennes. Xavier Marmier travelled extensively in Germany, learnt the language in Leipzig, translated from German, and met Romantic poets. Furthermore, he embodied a Romantic-philological dream of the Germano-Scandinavian North. *Lettres sur l'Islande* (*Letters About Iceland*), published by Marmier in 1837, is one of the great introductions to Scandinavian literature.

Marmier's work, and his calls for further research, did not go unheeded. But the most notable positive result was clearly the collection by the Parnassian poet Leconte de Lisle, entitled *Poèmes barbares* (*Barbaric Poems*) (1862). The Scandinavian part of the collection is but an adaptation of Xavier Marmier, and in passing, Ampère, or the translation by Mallet of the Voluspa.

Several cross-cultural imports should be noted. Adam Gottlob Oehlenschläger (1778–1850), who wrote as much in Danish as in German, was introduced to the French public by Xavier Marmier in a volume of selected theatre plays. Two of his plays, *Hakon Jarl* and *Axel og Valborg*, addressed Nordic subjects: the early Christianization of Norway, and the resistance mounted by Odin's religion when faced with the expansion of Christianity. Mythical Germany, the image of the original Germania, was thus introduced to France via a Danish author. Up to a certain point, Xavier Marmier seems to have wanted, in his introduction to Scandinavian theatre, to establish a counterbalance to Scandinavian Germanism. This provides an interpretation for the fact that his publication of Oehlenschläger's plays was followed by an introduction to the works of the Norwegian author Ludvig Holberg (who translated Molière's plays as early as 1722), which he alternated with his own poetic creations. Moreover, Holberg's book *Nicolas Klimine dans le monde souterrain* (*Nicolas Klimine in the Underground World*) had been translated from Latin to French by the propagandist of the French language, Éléazar de Mauvillon, in 1741.

---

9 Jean-Jacques Ampère, *Littérature, voyage et poésies* (Paris: Didier, 1850), T. 1, p. 1.

If the image of Scandinavia is closely intertwined with the image of Germany, it is also a result of cross-cultural imports. Let us take, for example, the case of Jens Baggesen (1764–1826), a Danish author writing in German and Danish, who became known in France following the translation of his account of his travels from Denmark to Switzerland, via Germany and France, *Le Labyrinthe* (*The Labyrinth*). Baggesen played a role in Franco-Germanic relationships in at least in two other areas. He attended lectures by the philosopher Fichte at Jena, which represented the most sophisticated intellectual contributions about the French Revolution. He then went to Paris, where, as can be read in his correspondence, he attended the meetings of the *Convention Nationale*, and met leading politicians.

To an even greater extent than Baggesen, the Scandinavian connection or convergence with France and Germany seems to be embodied by the Heiberg family, Peter Andreas (1758–1841) and his son Johan Ludvig (1791–1860). The first was a Danish playwright, deeply affected by the French Revolution, who settled in Paris around 1800 where he worked as a translator and publicist. His son, Johan Ludvig, lived in Paris from 1819 to 1822, moving in Parisian literary circles. But Paris was, above all, the opportunity for him to discover a very particular artistic practice: Vaudeville. Heiberg then visited Germany from 1822 to 1825 and discovered another hero of cultural history with whom he forged personal links, Hegel, whose aesthetic system was of particular interest to him. Heiberg, therefore, became both a renovator of Danish theatre in the spirit of the Parisian Vaudeville, as well as one of the people who introduced Hegel to Scandinavia.

The connection in cultural perception between Scandinavia and Germany is almost a rule in the case of a little-studied group in its global context, that of the Norwegian community of late-nineteenth-century Paris. This triangular connection is perhaps even more noticeable in the case of the novelist Knut Hamsun, who settled in Paris from 1893 to 1895. It was in Paris where he wrote, for the *Revue des Revues*, an article on trends in modern Norwegian literature. But more importantly, it was in Paris where Knut Hamsun met the German publisher Albert Langen who would establish his renown in Europe.

The first systematic attempt to introduce teachings on what would be called the "Antiquités du Nord" (or "Northern Antiquities") in French universities was in Strasbourg. When the university created a Chair of Foreign Literature, it was given to Frédéric Guillaume Bermann, who would teach at Strasbourg for 31 years. Bergmann had studied for several semesters at Göttingen and described himself as a disciple of the Brothers Grimm. To highlight the value of his research subject, Bergmann claimed it had a historical depth comparable to that of Pharaonic Egypt and placed dangerous emphasis on a sort of original purity and its decline in the contemporary Christian Scandinavia.

It is clearly necessary to understand Bergmann's Indo-Europeanist excesses to understand the use of Scandinavian philology embodied by the turn-of-the-century Scandinavianist, Maurice Cahen. He was the author of a thesis entitled *Etudes sur le vocabulaire religieux du Vieux-Scandinave: la libation* (*Studies of the Religious Vocabulary of Old Scandinavia: the Libation*), through which Cahen attracted significant attention, when it first appeared in 1921. Cahen, whose premature death prevented him from fully developing his research program, embodied a sort of radical metamorphosis of philology into social science.

From the end of the nineteenth century, further modern Scandinavian studies supplemented research into the "Northern Antiquities". Nevertheless, the umbilical cord with Germany was never fully severed. One of the representatives of early research on Ibsen was the first Professor of German Literature at the University of Lyon, Auguste Ehrhard, from Alsace, who in 1892 published a book on his research entitled *Henrik Ibsen et le théâtre contemporain* (*Henrik Ibsen and Contemporary Theatre*). Ehrhard remained in his position at Lyon until 1931.

In terms of Scandinavian Studies, the Sorbonne was clearly lagging behind Strasbourg, Rennes and Lyon. The first lecturer of Scandinavian literature at the Sorbonne was Alfred Jolivet, a Germanist who undertook a thesis on German eighteenth-century literature. He discovered and remained engaged with the subject of Scandinavia during a visit as Reader at the University of Christiana, and his interest never waned. From the point of view of Scandinavian Studies, he is particularly notable as the author of a book about Strindberg's theatre (1931).

Successor to Alfred Jolivet, Maurice Gravier was also a Germanist who studied in Munich and Berlin during the 1930s and seems to have discovered Scandinavian literature later, while working at the *Institut français de Stockholm* between 1937 and 1940. He also dedicated himself to the mandatory task of studying Ibsen's theatre, as well as that of Strindberg, publishing, in 1949, like his teacher, a book on the former. He actively campaigned for the diffusion of Scandinavian theatre, for translation, and more generally, for a popularization of knowledge about Scandinavia. In the form of both Jolivet and Gravier, it seems that in the French context, the emancipation of the German paradigm in Scandinavian studies was on the point of taking place.

German philosophy has not always been directly introduced into France but has often been subject to intermediary relays. In particular, around 1900, it is possible to speak of a key intermediary role played by Scandinavia. This is notably confused with the philosophy of the Dane Harald Høffding, whose numerous works have been translated into French. As early as 1900, his work

Esquisse d'une psychologie fondée sur l'expérience (*Outline of a Psychology Founded on Experience*), described the state of research in German psychology. *L'Histoire de la philosophie moderne* (The History of Modern Philosophy), probably Høffding's main contribution to the presentation of German philosophy, appeared in French in 1906. Høffding accorded great importance to Lessing's contribution to German philosophy and was interested in the relationship between criticism and positivism. But above all, he introduced a series of important German philosophers who were little-known at the time, such as Hermann Lotze, Eduard von Hartmann, Johann Friedrich Herbart and Hermann von Helmholtz. This work was published by the *Librarie Félix Alcan* and was, without any doubt, one of the best introductions of the time to the history of German philosophy, notably for an approach that was free from the crushing weight of canonical figures. This work was supplemented by a book on contemporary philosophy, published in 1907. Without a doubt, part of the success that Harald Høffding encountered in France in 1900 was due to his ability to understand the points of view of others, the philosophy of a northern country, and the continuities or discontinuities between German and French philosophy. In all his works, he brought together French and German philosophy in order to attempt to reveal hidden points of resonance. Additionally, Høffding was active in French debates around Kierkegaard.

Scandinavia acts as a mirror, reflecting moments of French cultural history. There is the theory of Germanic freedom, gradually becoming accompanied with a Romantic infatuation for the landscapes of the north. There is, on the one hand, the worrying quest for the original, pure race. There is a time when written texts are, on the other hand, used as so many archives of social configurations. There is the formal aesthetical approach of the Parnassians, the infatuation for depth psychology, in the style of Ibsen. If it is not surprising to observe that the history of Scandinavian philology in France is the history of thought, it must be added that the issue is one of a triangular cultural transfer.

Recent research in cultural transfers has focused on the presence of references to Germany or France in nineteenth and early-twentieth century Russian culture. For the last twenty years, work has been undertaken in this area in collaboration with the Institute of World Literature and in particular with Ekaterina Dmitrieva and Russian colleagues which addresses Russian literary history, as well as, increasingly, artistic, philosophical, and even political currents.[10]

---

10   Ekaterina Dmitrieva/Michel Espagne (eds.), *Philologiques IV. Transferts culturels triangulaires France-Allemagne-Russie* (Paris: Éditions de la Maison des Sciences de l'Homme,

Since the Middle Ages, a German Russia has existed. It is as old as the Foreigners' neighbourhood in Moscow (*Nemetskaia Sloboda*). This German population has only grown bigger over the centuries starting with the colonies of the Volga, which were established at the time of Catherine II, to the Baltic aristocrats serving the Tsar and the German scientists working at the Academy of Sciences in St. Petersburg. This Germany exists outside its national boundaries and has been adapted to its Russian context, in which it both leaves its mark and remains attached to the country of origin. However, it is also complemented by a less profound and more elitist French presence, limited to the circles of the upper class and nobility. This interface has resulted in the production of very extensive literature. Just as the German playwright August von Kotzebue contributed to the German theatre of St. Petersburg, the publisher Weitbrecht is a significant part of the history of a city that in 1900 numbered no less than 55,000 German-speaking people. Conversely, the Russian writers of St. Petersburg from Biely to Mandelstam, include in their novels an image of Germany. From Friedrich Maximilian Klinger to Afanassi Fet, there are numerous examples of German and Russian writers whose works are analyzed in terms of cultural transfers. Russian students in Germany or, more precisely, the Russian followers of neo-Kantianism of Marburg, led to studies, which examine their acquisition of a kind of knowledge which provides the origin of their career in Russia. The role played by the University of Göttingen in the training of German teachers who in the nineteenth century populated the first great Russian universities is well known. Since the eighteenth century, the great explorations of Siberia were carried out by German travellers in the service of the Russian Empire. If nineteenth century France was largely formed on the behalf of German imports, this phenomenon is even more striking in the Russian context, in the nineteenth as well as the twentieth century.

The German colonies within the Russian Empire are an obvious point of entry for cultural imports. Along the Volga, colonies of farmers settled from Swabia, whose allegiance to German culture has persisted since the eighteenth century. Baltic territories dominated by Germany are part of the Russian Empire and in Riga Johann Gottfried Herder himself was conscious of having been a subject of the Czar. This population was a pool of resources from which were drawn civil service or Imperial Army administrators, while the case of Maximilian Klinger, the *Sturm und Drang* poet, reminds us that one could at the same time be officer of the Court of St. Petersburg and a German writer.

1996); Michel Espagne, *L'Ambre et le fossile. Transferts germano-russes dans les sciences humaines* (Paris: Armand Colin, 2014).

Another phenomenon is that of exile. This does not date only from the Soviet period, even if, from Bunin to Nabokov, an important part of Russian language literature or literature by writers for whom Russian was their initial language, were originally written abroad. The nineteenth century was also a period of exile. In the 1830s and 1840s, Prince Mestcherski wrote his collections of poems in French. We may also think of Turgenev sharing his time between France and Germany. Of course, exile occurs at different levels. Sometimes the exile of Russian aristocrats in the eighteenth or nineteenth century was an opportunity to develop the literature of the host country at the same time as weaving a closer link with the Russian context. The circle of Münster, founded by Princess Amalie von Gallitzin, where the spiritualist philosopher philosopher and writer Friedrich Heinrich Jacobi, the poet Friedrich Leopold, Count of Stolberg-Stolberg, and the writer Matthias Claudius spent a lot of time, is one of the major sites of German literary sociability in the late eighteenth century. Similarly, the Parisian salon of the Baltic Princess Juliane von Krüdener is a meeting place for representatives of the first forms of French romanticism. But if this Livonian is a French writer, she also retains links with Russia. The Salon of Maria Pavlovna, wife of the Duke of Weimar at the time of Goethe, is obviously one of the important scenes of Russian classical German culture. Russian exile is found to be involved in the creation of European intellectual networks during the twentieth century when Alexandre Kojève, Georges Gurvitch, Alexandre Koyré pass on to the French public knowledge about German philosophy, reconsidered from the perspective of the Russian Orthodox thought.

The representations we have of Russia's eighteenth century derive from official paintings, portraits that have fixed forever the features of the aristocracy, as well as the salons, genre scenes, and families. In 1747, Jakob Stehlin became director of the Department of Fine Arts at the Academy of St. Petersburg. A colony of foreign artists had settled on the island of Wassilievski. Hamburg's portraitist Johann Balthasar Francart, for example, painted the features of the Baroness Count Stroganov or those of Count Sheremetievs. Liudmila A. Markina has highlighted this phenomenon of German painters in post-Petrine St. Petersburg, in which they record for posterity the memories of this time, in her book on the painter Georg Groot.[11] Originally from a family of painters from Württemberg, Groot lived in Russia since at least 1739 and worked as court painter, which did not prevent him from selling paintings and engravings. But especially the official portraits of the Empress and her entourage made

---

11   Liudmila Alekseevna Markina, *Portretist Georg Khristof Groot i nemetskie jivopistsy v Rossii serediny XVIII veka* (Moscow: Pamjatniki Istoričeskoj Mysli, 1999). See as well *Bildende Kunst der Rußlanddeutschen im 18.–20. Jahrhundert* (Moskau: Варяг, 1997).

his glory. There is a clear continuity between the portraits of the Württemberg aristocrats drawn before his departure for Russia and the portraits of the imperial court. One could speak of a projection but in fact it is mostly a compromise between German painting and Russian culture that highlights elements within bourgeois society, moments of family romance, and the splendour of the court of St. Petersburg. It is a German construction of the Russian memory. Incidentally, this continues to be so: in the early-nineteenth century, Gerhard von Kügelgen, Professor at the Dresden Academy, and for long-time court painter in St. Petersburg, also painted portraits of the imperial family, especially of Alexander I, as well as portraits of the pantheon of German literature, including those of Goethe and Schiller.

These examples suffice to show the existence of an entangled history that goes against national narratives, which closely associated Germany with Russia and relegated the French-speaking space to the background as a third party. Certainly, one can always consider that there are distinct entities with multiple bridges between them, which it is useful to identify. But it is also conceivable to show osmotic relations between cultural entities with multiple gradations; where the product of a cultural area also belongs to the other one. Therefore, we will not only highlight bridges, or extend the number of examples observed, but emphasize the shifts that occur, observe the forms of reinterpretation and adaptation that occur in a receiving context. In this case, we observe how Russian culture is built with imported materials, as well as how German or French intellectual productions are inexplicable without a Russian background. Certainly, these are translations, since the most fundamental re-semanticization consists in moving words from one language to those of another. But in the case of the German-Russian network, translation is almost secondary. Russian scientists or writers of the nineteenth century had a direct relationship with German literature and philosophy and had no need of translation to claim it as a possession. Moreover, throughout the nineteenth century, the journals of the Academy of Sciences of Russia gladly welcomed texts in German or French. It is probably in the study of imbrications, those which anchor the claims of identity, that we can best observe the phenomena of cultural osmosis and the dynamics of cultural transfers.

Without the need for translation, the most prominent representatives of the Humanities in Russia, from literary history to art history, philology to anthropology, have always been readers of what Germany produced in the same field. They were also sometimes German or German-speaking or partly trained in German universities. In fact, what Russia retains from the impetus borrowed from German science is not always what German memory itself has preserved from the earlier stages of its own history. There are philosophers, theorists, and historians whose importance has been lost in their original German context, but who have found a new one in the Russian context, the function of which may be, from the perspective of a cultural history of Germany, to preserve traces of German culture. We thus find in the geological strata of the Russian cultural space the fossil strata of a forgotten Germany.

If it is particularly necessary to concentrate on the history of knowledge, it is because we find located within this history forms of identity construction. It takes a literary history and a historiography to constitute a nation. The tools used to build identity have a tendency to suppress and conceal imported materials by reinterpreting them, as they move from one context to another. The choice of subjects made for this demonstration is partly arbitrary. We cannot follow all of the Humanities, but maybe some of them are more likely than others to illustrate areas of transition. German philosophy was a central reference in the philosophical history of Russia, from the period when disputes between Westernizers and Slavophiles took place against the background of the appropriation of Hegel and Schelling, through attempts to stem Kantianism through Bergson, until the discovery of Husserl's phenomenology by Gustave Chpet. While psychology was a dominant human science in Germany in the last third of the nineteenth century, and Russia did not escape this influence. But we can also observe a strong presence, in the Russian sphere of references to German philology, or to a history of art that expanded more than elsewhere in German-speaking countries. The transition from one cultural sphere to another can moreover lead to another transition from one discipline to another.

Mediations, which allow the passage of elements from one scientific culture to another, are diverse in nature. Minorities living on one side or another of the border are, with travellers, the most obvious sociological mediators. And then there are of course the Universities. In this regard, we must especially take a look at Dorpat, a German-language university town, under the direct authority of German officers of the court of St. Petersburg. To be more precise the founder of Dorpat, Friedrich-Georg Parrot, was a Germanized Frenchman from the enclave of Württemberg in France, Montbéliard. Dorpat was a Russian university of German language until the 1880s when it was renamed Iuriew. More generally, we can say that the Baltic territories, home for German subjects of the Russian Empire, represented a bridge between the two cultures while at the same time acting as a resource pool of administrative officers dedicated to the Empire. But there are also areas of German-Russian mediation in Germany. We primarily think of the University of Göttingen. This institution acted as a reservoir from which Sergey Uvarov, the long-time head of higher education in Russia, was sourcing new teachers. August Ludwig von Schlözer also came from Göttingen, who through his work in the *Chronique de Nestor* was one of the first historians of the Russian Middle Ages. And it was also to Göttingen that he returned after a long stay in Russia. The first Russian students came to Leipzig in the nineteenth century, including Aleksander Nikolajevich Radishchev, famous author of the *Journey from St Petersburg to Moscow*. One could also consider the University of Marburg to the extent that this high place of German neo-Kantianism was also a training venue for several generations of Russian philosophers.[12] Mikhail Vasilyevich Lomonosov was trained as a student like later Alexander von Humboldt at the Freiberg University of Mining and Technology. Observing transfers between Germany and Russia such as these helps us to update the geography of the meeting points of culture and knowledge. The Germano-Russian sphere seems to shrink to focused points of extreme imbrication where these transfers mainly occur.

The exploration of German-Russian cultural transfers in the field of the history of knowledge should also incorporate the issue of language. In the Russian sphere, even Russian scientific language was in competition with German or French until the mid-nineteenth century. It is common to find in the scientific journals such as the ones of the Annals of the Academy of Sciences in St. Petersburg, articles in French or German, whose authors are often teachers from Western Europe, and who continue to conduct their scientific life in their native language.

Let us look now at a passionate historian of the German and Russian National Antiquities, Friedrich (Feodor Aleksanderovic) Braun. Born in 1862 in St. Petersburg, he studied Germanic philology there from 1880 to 1885, before becoming a high school teacher, then Privatdozent in 1888, and Professor from 1900 on. He had to leave Russia at the time of the First World War and settled in Leipzig. Later in 1920, the Soviet Commissariat for Education commissioned him to put together a large bibliography of all German scientific work published since 1914. Becoming professor of German in Leipzig in 1922, he remained a Russian language assistant; in 1926 he was co-director of the Leipzig Institute for Research on Eastern Europe. He is credited, in the 1920s, with the German translation of Russian historical works like the story of Vasily Klyuchevsky of whom he had been a pupil.[13] He co-edited with Maxim Gorky a journal of the first emigration, which was published from 1922 to 1923 under the name of *Beseda*. Although he was appointed in 1926 as a corresponding

---

12 Nina Dmitrieva, *Russkoe neokantianstvo. « Marburg » v Rossii* (Moscow: Rosspén, 2007).
13 W. Kliuschewskij [Vasily Klyuchevsky], *Geschichte Rußlands*, ed. by Friedrich Braun/ Reinhold von Walter (Stuttgart, Leipzig, Berlin: Deutsche Verlagsanstalt, 1925). In the introduction to this book, in which the main translator seems to have been Reinhold von Walter, Friedrich Braun emphasizes the need to know the long history of Russia to successfully understand its present, that is the year 1925.

member of the Academy of Sciences, he did not return to Russia, and this title caused him some difficulty during the Nazi era. He died in 1942.

As Dean of the Petersburg Faculty of Arts and President of the philologists' circle, this little-known figure of German Studies, working at the heart of the Russian Humanities after the Veselovski generation, deserves particular attention to the extent that he too was a medievalist. His area of personal investigation was the question of relations between the Goths and Slavs. He investigated the amazing traces of what constituted, until the seventeenth, century the Goths of the Crimea, following the footsteps of their migration, their language, and their absorption by the Tatar ethnic background. More broadly, he was interested in Germanic influences on the legends of ancient Russia, as well as in the history of German Romanticism.[14] Braun is certainly one of those responsible for a shift in the Russian academic curiosity around 1900 in the question of German medieval culture.

A field of Russian history that deserves to be addressed especially in terms of cultural transfers is that of Russian Orientalism. On the one hand, the extension to Central Asia subsequent to the capture of Kazan is one of the fundamental elements of Russian history. It is precisely in Kazan where was developed, since the early-nineteenth century, a Russian science of the east, which involved learning Tatar and other Asian languages.[15] Russian Orientalism was then developed in St. Petersburg, with the conviction of understanding the Eastern cultures that had been integrated into the Empire, but also with the idea of developing a new form of humanism, in which knowledge of Greek antiquity would marry with the knowledge of the East, where one would look for traces of lost Greek works in texts in other languages, such as Persian. But what is striking in this long history of Russian Orientalism, which includes references to Central Asia in Russian Humanities, a trend which was reinforced when some Russian intellectuals were moved to Tashkent in the 1940s, is that it is largely due to the immigration of French or German scholars. Taking, for example, Christian Martin Frähn, from Rostock, who taught Oriental languages at Kazan before moving to St. Petersburg, through to Alexander von Staël-Holstein, who began his career as a Sinologist in St. Petersburg before finishing it in Beijing, Russian Orientalism is largely a matter of foreign scholars, especially Germans.

---

14   Friedrich Braun, *Die letzten Schicksale der Krimgoten in Jahresbericht der reformierten Kirchenschule für 1889–90* (St. Petersburg: R. Golicke, 1890).
15   Michel Espagne/Svetlana Gorshenina/Frantz Grenet/Shahin Mustafayev/Claude Rapin (eds.), *Asie centrale. Transferts culturels le long de la Route de la soie* (Paris: Éditions Vendémiaire, 2016).

After an overview of the examples provided by Scandinavian and German-Russian history, one may wonder what new perspectives and contributions can be derived from the methodology of cultural transfers. The first point relates to the detection of a very heterogeneous structure of cultural memory, which does not reflect any archival order assimilable to nationalism. One assumes more or less that any country develops itself on the basis of internal dynamics. Saxony, as the core of a future German identity, appropriates such foreign cultural objects whose link with a foreign country is gradually repressed in German history. Who will remember that, in the eighteenth century, Polish and Ukrainian Jewish merchants made their fortune in the main fair in Germany? In the dynamics of ownership of something foreign, isolated social groups can play a prominent role disproportionate to their demographic weight. For comparativism, which confronts these historical phenomena, these groups, who fully deserve a historical analysis, play no role. Research on cultural transfers is further able to analyse the transformations that the receiving context owes to foreign exportation. For example, the Leipzig fair has no actual existence independently from Polish, Jewish, and Greek traders' seasonal immigration. The reception of Russian music in France in the late nineteenth century profoundly modified the Parisian musical context by offering an alternative to the dominance of German music. The German merchants who ran the export of Bordeaux wines in the eighteenth and nineteenth centuries changed the face of that province's titular city, despite being mainly interested in their own business. The difference between the original context and the host, which does not have much sense in a historical comparativist context, is crucial to highlight cultural transfers, by showing the imbrication of two cultural systems. From this point of view, Saxony is a piece of Poland or France and the import of any foreign cultural property corresponds to a transformation of the characteristics of the receiving culture.

A second contribution of the research on cultural transfers seems to rest on the fact that the distribution of European space is transformed because of them. The links this mode of study makes between regions creates new perspective by detaching localities from various national frameworks, to the point of making possible a form of historiography that no longer rests on ethnocentrism. A new form of transnational historiography could be based on refusing to consider the territories as comparable units, but as interweaving parts of a puzzle. Besides artificially constructed national or territorial identities, we could in fact introduce a seminal foreignness into historical consciousness. Specifically, as regards the case of historical perceptions of sparsely-populated regions, this approach avoids creating further peripheral positions. Generally, the opposition between a centre and a periphery is irrelevant in the work on cultural transfers. This is because many Scandinavians were crucial enough to the mediation of transfers between France and Germany that their stories deserve as much attention as the European centre. In the same way, Russia is just as central in Europe as France or Germany, because one could not conceive, for example, the French intellectual history of the last hundred years without a structural link with Russia, from Russian novels, to the history of science, and through the aesthetics of the early-twentieth century. Also characteristic here is the history of relationships with Greece, of philhellenism in European countries, from the nineteenth to the twentieth century. On one side, we deal with a common denominator where the political position of the countries crystallizes. Despite the diversity of viewpoints, it is a common aspiration towards asserting cosmopolitanism.

Even though the reference to Ancient Greece in the construction of Berlin as a German Capital during the nineteenth century was central (we think for example of the *Museumsinsel* in the heart of Berlin), we should also remember the case of Munich among the most striking manifestations of German Hellenism in the nineteenth century. Munich is often referred to as the Athens on the Isar, which combined with its prominent role in the political philhellenism of the time, asserts more than other regions the German presence in Greece – as well as helping to show the ambiguity of the Greek reference. We should remember that it was King Ludwig I, initially a liberal ruler who became increasingly despotic, who triggered the Bavarian philhellenic movement, while it was in Munich that Greek decor reached a stage of inauthenticity that contributed to the emergence of the concept of "kitsch". The Greek periphery is at the centre of Germany.

It is clear that an applied method that examines these phenomena of imbrication and the forms of reinterpretation they produce is likely to exceed the national history framework of the Humanities and open a wide field of investigation, which could constitute the form to come of the cultural history of Europe. If there is no need to stress here that Russia is part of Europe, still less that it is part also of German and French cultural history, and conversely that Europe is part of Russia, the systematic history of these imbrications still largely needs to be written. Russia is only one case among many others and it is this *ensemble* of cultural areas, which forms the European space, which can now be examined in this way. It is certainly not a question of denying strong identities, or well-defined differences – Spain is not Germany – but instead showing how these relations are built.

Comparativism has to be replaced by a diachronical oriented study of transnational historiography, including research on cultural transfers. The first attempts to broaden the history of Western Europe to eastern territories or peripheries already involved integrating annals or written records of these outer regions, within a framework that hitherto had not considered their own perspective and were, thereby, reinterpreted. Tracing cultural transfers can supercede comparative perspectives in surveys of transnational historiography, by identifying procedures of re-semanticization of historical objects and mapping the vectors of these transformations. The question of German-Russian or French-German-Scandinavian cultural transfers during the whole of the nineteenth century is a rich field to approach for precisely this method. In particular, it allows us to overcome the problems derived from a binary understanding of centre and periphery that comparativism, in the narrowest sense, has difficulty solving. It is true that the very term comparativism covers various types of historiography and as soon as it incorporates a history of relations (*Beziehungsgeschichte*), it highlights the phenomena of semantic displacement, confronts itself with shared or entangled history, and could be finally better defined as research on cultural transfers.

Bibliography

Braun, Friedrich, *Die letzten Schicksale der Krimgoten in Jahresbericht der reformierten Kirchenschule für 1889–90* (St. Petersburg: R. Golicke, 1890).

Dmitrieva, Ekaterina/Espagne, Michel (eds.), *Philologiques IV. Transferts culturels triangulaires France-Allemagne-Russie* (Paris: Éditions de la Maison des Sciences de l'Homme, 1996).

Dmitrieva, Nina, *Russkoe neokantianstvo. 'Marburg' v Rossii: istoriko-filosofskie očerki*, Humanitas (Moskva: Rosspen, 2007).

Espagne, Michel, 'Frobenius, Anta Diop et Martin Bernal. Les projections sur l'Europe de connaissances acquises sur l'Afrique', in *Transferts de savoirs sur l'Afrique*, ed. by Michel Espagne/Hans-Jürgen Lüsebrink (Paris: Karthala, 2015), pp. 159–173.

Espagne, Michel, *L'Ambre et le fossile. Transferts germano-russes dans les sciences humaines* (Paris: Armand Colin, 2014).

Espagne, Michel, 'Herder-Mallet-Arngrimur. Rückläufige Geschichtsschreibung und Kulturtransfer', in *Kulturelle Dreieckbeziehungen. Aspekte der Kulturvermittlung zwischen Frankreich, Deutschland und Dänemark in der ersten Hälfte des 19. Jahrhunderts*, ed. by Karin Hoff/Udo Schöning/Per Øhrgaard (Würzburg: Königshausen & Neumann, 2013) pp. 199–211.

Espagne, Michel, 'Comparison and Transfer: A Question of Method', in *Transnational Challenges to National History Writing*, ed. by Matthias Middell/Lluís Roura I Aulinas (Basingstoke, New York: Palgrave MacMillan, 2013), pp. 38–51.

Espagne, Michel, 'La notion de transfert culturel', in *Revue Sciences/Lettres*, 1 (2013). http://journals.openedition.org/rsl/219, DOI: https://doi.org/10.4000/rsl.219.

Espagne, Michel, *Le prisme du Nord. Pays du Nord-France-Allemagne, 1750–1920* (Tusson: Du Lérot, 2005).

Espagne, Michel, *Les transferts culturels franco-allemands* (Paris: Presses Universitaires de France, 1999).

Espagne, Michel/Svetlana Gorshenina/Frantz Grenet/Sahin Mustafayev/Claude Rapin (eds.), *Asie Centrale. Transferts Culturels Le Long de La Route de La Soie* (Paris: Vendémiaire, 2016).

Guthrie, William, *Allgemeine Weltgeschichte. Von der Schöpfung bis auf gegenwärtige Zeit*, I–XVII (Leipzig: M.G. Weidmanns Erben und Reich, 1765–1788).

Heeren, Arnold, *Ideen über die Politik, den Verkehr und den Handel der vornehmsten Völker der alten Welt* (Göttingen: Vandenhoeck & Ruprecht, 1805).

Kliuschewskij, W. [Klyuchevsky, Vasily], *Geschichte Rußlands*, ed. by Friedrich Braun/ Reinhold von Walter (Stuttgart, Leipzig, Berlin: Deutsche Verlagsanstalt, 1925).

Lüsebrink, Hans-Jürgen, *Interkulturelle Kommunikation: Interaktion-Kulturtransfer-Fremdwahrnehmung* (Stuttgart, Weimar: Metzler, 2005).

Markina, Liudmila Alekseevna, *Portretist Georg Khristof Groot i nemetskie jivopistsy v Rossii serediny XVIII veka* (Moscow: Pamjatniki Istoričeskoj Mysli, 1999).

Markina, Liudmila Alekseevna, *Bildende Kunst der Rußlanddeutschen im 18-20. Jahrhundert* (Moscow: Варяг, 1997).

Middell, Matthias, 'Kulturtransfer, Transferts culturels', in *Docupedia-Zeitgeschichte. Begriffe, Methoden und Debatten der zeithistorischen Forschung* (2016). www.http:// docupedia.de/zg/middell_kulturtransfer_v1_de_2016.

Trautmann-Waller, Céline, *Aux origines d'une science allemande de la culture* (Paris: Éditions du CNRS, 2006).

CHAPTER 2

Cultural Transfers in the Shadow of Methodological Nationalism

Magnus Qvistgaard

Abstract

The article investigates the problem of methodological nationalism in relation to cultural transfers. Focusing on the field of literature, it takes its outset in a critical reading of Pascale Casanova's seminal work *The World Republic of Letters*, which sets out a model for analyzing the dynamics of the world literary space. The reading shows how Casanova's model reinforces the notion of a priori national categories. Drawing on research on the Norwegian dramatist Henrik Ibsen's path to international success in the late nineteenth century, the article demonstrates how national categories must be historicized. It shows how the agents who facilitated the initial spread of Ibsen's drama, engaged actively with conflicting notions of national literature thereby challenging, subverting, and ultimately, mutating the national categories. The article thereby stresses the importance of an agent-driven approach to cultural transfers that situates the transfer in its historical context and relies on a plurality of perspectives.

This Article is about Cultural Transfers and methodological nationalism. Methodological nationalism is the approach of taking the nation as the *a priori* starting point for any given enquiry, either by confining the investigation exclusively within the country's border, thus cutting off all "foreign" influences, or by comparing countries without reflection upon their suitability as analytical units. In comparative studies, the nation is viewed in isolation as existing alongside other independent nations. In either case, nations are perceived as independent containers that exist independently of one another. To people working on cultural transfers, criticism of methodological nationalism is nothing new. From the outset, research on cultural transfers has acted as a critique of methodological nationalism.[1] Yet, the use of nation as an analytical unit is

---

1 See for instance: Michel Espagne, 'Transferanalyse statt Vergleich. Interkulturalität in der sächsischen Regionalgeschichte', in *Vergleich und Transfer. Komparatistik in den Geschichts- und Kulturwissenschaften*, ed. by Hartmut Kaelble/Jürgen Schriewer (Frankfurt/Main:

deeply wired into the core thinking of many disciplines and the concept of the nation has been the default category for analysis for so long that it often slips back in again, also in the case of international or transnational analyses of cultural transfers. Even in the study of literature, where there has always been a general awareness of the mobility of texts, authors and literary trends, the nation is proving a resilient concept. Thus, the prevalent way of categorising authors has long been according to their presumed place in relation to national traditions. Presently, the question is not so much why this is, as the emergence of vernacular literature has been thoroughly studied and duly historicized, but rather: what should be done about methodological nationalism in the study of literature?

In the following, I approach this question from two directions. First, I investigate the national category: how does it frame perceptions of literature and how might it even thrive in transnational approaches? This is based on a close analysis of Pascale Casanova's influential and very ambitious attempt to construct a model of the world literary space.[2] Analysing Casanova's model is highly relevant as the model partly addresses and partly reproduces the challenges that the use of national categories poses to studies of cultural transfers. Secondly, I provide an example of how notions of national categories may be historicized and analysed by deploying multiple perspectives on cultural transfers. The example draws on my research on the dissemination of the Norwegian playwright Henrik Ibsen's plays in Europe during the latter part of the nineteenth century. Ibsen makes for an excellent case for studying the complex untangling that methodological nationalism requires. As one of the first Scandinavian authors, Ibsen experienced pan-European success in his own lifetime, yet he was from a country hitherto un-associated with the export of literature. In the world of culture, as in that of politics, the late-nineteenth century was a time of high nationalism and, consequently, the reception was predominantly framed in national terms. This complicates matters, as one cannot merely opt to ignore the national framing to which the consumption of literature was subject at the time. Yet, markets for cultural products such as literature and especially theatre were not confined to the nation but were transnational. In the example of Ibsen, I show how national categories were both

---

Campus Verlag, 2003), pp. 419–438 or Silke Neunsinger, 'Cross-over! Om Komparationer, Transferanalyser, Histoire Croisée Och Den Metodologiska Nationalismens Problem', in *Historisk Tidskrift*, 130/1 (2010), pp. 3–24.

2 Pascale Casanova, *The World Republic of Letters* (Cambridge: Harvard University Press, 2004).

constantly challenged and circumvented and intrinsic to the understanding of literature at the end of the nineteenth century.

2.1 The World Republic of Letters: A World of Nations

In her book, *The World Republic of Letters* (2004), Pascale Casanova constructs a model of a world literary space. Casanova has been considered a forerunner in analysing transnational literary relations and the framework that she provides has inspired both insightful and valuable research. I think it is worthwhile to scrutinise her model, however, because she, in effect, merges many stock ideas about nation and literature into a comprehensive model of interaction in the world of literature. This makes it possible to study some of the rather vague but popular notions about authors and literary production, which are otherwise difficult to address. In the analysis below, I show how many such ideas about literature are imported into Casanova's theoretical framework. This is not always wholly unproblematic, some of the ideas that are given new life become hypostatized as part of the methodology with some problematic side-effects. In order to understand both the theory's appeal and its problems, I unravel the specific way in which the model of the world of letters is constructed. Criticism has been levelled at Casanova's concept of the literary world before and especially controversial has been her naming Paris as the capital of the 'world republic of letters'.[3] My analysis, however, focuses closely on national categories and the specific challenge of methodological nationalism.

Casanova's ambitious goal is to provide an account of the dynamics of the world literary space. Special attention is given to the inequality that dominates the space and the difficulty that writers from what she terms small, 'impoverished', or 'peripheral' literatures experience in achieving international recognition.[4] One of the truly laudable things about Casanova's book is that she is concerned with the injustice of this system, which advances the authors from cultural centres and hinders authors from impoverished literary spaces. The true heroes of her narrative are the authors from the periphery, who against all odds manage to break through at the centre. Not surprisingly, one of the writers Casanova highlights who, against the odds, achieved international success is Henrik Ibsen.

---

[3] See for instance: Mads Rosendahl Thomsen, *Mapping World Literature* (New York: Continuum, 2008), p. 36; Prendergast, Christopher, 'The World Republic of Letters', in *Debating World Literature*, ed. by Christopher Prendergast (London: Verso, 2004), pp. 1–26 (p. 8).

[4] Pascale Casanova, *The World Republic of Letter, op. cit.*, pp. 17–18.

This focus on marginalised writers does help shed some light on important dynamics that govern the international literary world and the unevenness that they create. Yet, in spite of the fact that Casanova uses many of the concepts that are also used in connection with cultural transfers, such as centre and periphery, and is concerned with translation and, to some extent, mediation, her book ultimately cements notions about the nation and the national literature as the *a priori* starting point for authors. An unfortunate and definitely unintentional side effect is that Casanova slips back into methodological nationalism and legitimising the very system of suppression and inequality she set out to help in the first place.

The way that methodological nationalism manifests itself is of general interest as it is so common: Casanova simply takes national affiliation as the *a priori* relevant context for authors and builds her theory from there. She writes:

> National literary and linguistic patrimony supplies a sort of a priori definition of the writer, one that he will transform (if need be, by rejecting it or, as in the case of Beckett, by conceiving himself in opposition to it) throughout his career. In other words, the writer stands in a particular relation to world literary space by virtue of the place occupied in it by the national space into which he has been born.
> CASANOVA 2004, p. 41

As already indicated by the reference to Beckett, Casanova's account offers a way in which a few exceptional writers manage to escape the national space and become what she terms 'international writers'. Yet, this does very little, as we shall see, to challenge the fact that national origin is retained as the primary way of understanding authors. That the authors themselves, as Casanova points out, may reject national affiliation does nothing to alter the matter.

Having cemented the importance of national origin of the author, Casanova proceeds to situate the national writer in an international literary world, where competition and rivalry between literatures is the driving force. In this game, the main contenders are nations, and the individual author is viewed as an extension of national tradition. The individual author then adds to the store of national literature and thus bolsters it in the competition with that of other nations. In this international sphere of competition, Casanova's main point is that literary resources, like political and economic resources, are distributed unevenly amongst nations:

> Literary resources, which are always stamped with the seal of the nation, are therefore unequal as well, and unequally distributed among nations. Because the effects of this structure weigh on all national literatures and on all writers, the practises and traditions, the forms and aesthetics that have currency in a given national space can be properly understood only if they are related to the precise position of this space in the world system.
>
> CASANOVA 2004, p. 39

This leads to a hierarchy of literatures. It is given a theoretical underpinning to the extent that it hinges on the notion that each author contributes to the literary prestige of his or her own (national) tradition in the form of literary capital. For the purpose of Casanova's theory, this line of thought is expanded by extending the economic metaphor to encompass the notion that nations are capable of hoarding literary assets. This is achieved through recourse to language, which itself becomes the carrier of literary value. Thus, the languages themselves, which are clearly marked as national languages, in this way become 'literary' to a larger or smaller degree seemingly without the need for human agency to perpetuate this status.

In spite of the objections one may have, Casanova ends up with an outwardly serviceable model of the world of literature. It describes the way in which national literatures may be seen in competition with one another. This system evidently favours Western literatures; the big national traditions are those of the European world powers of the nineteenth century that dominate the smaller literatures in both the West and elsewhere. At the centre, we are told, are the oldest literatures with the richest literary traditions, which is to say the largest store of recognised authors and great works written in its language. At the periphery, the newer literatures that boast fewer 'great works' and which struggle to catch up. It should be remarked that, to scholars working on Ibsen and other authors from other marginalised literatures of the late-nineteenth century, this has been a fruitful approach insofar as it has provided a framework for addressing the question of centre and periphery in the field of literature.

To Casanova, the national level is mirrored by an international level. The idea here is that at some point in history, more specifically during the second half of the nineteenth century, some of the oldest cultural centres managed to become autonomous, which is to say move beyond national political control. The first place to do this was Paris, which then became the 'world capital of literature' (Casanova 2004, p. 87). As Paris was the most richly endowed of the cultural centres, it had the greatest power to consecrate literature, and as it was now autonomous, it had the power not only to consecrate national authors but authors from across the world. This meant that authors from deprived nations now had a chance to escape the confinement of national space by having their works consecrated by 'literary authorities' in Paris. We do not learn much about the process of consecration itself. Casanova vaguely mentions literary authorities, which seems predominantly (or maybe exclusively) to mean autonomous critics, and at some point, she points out, that their judgements take the form of critical studies and commentaries. Rather, she focuses on translation as the chief means for authors from deprived literatures to achieve recognition.

Translation is what ties the world republic of letters together. Yet, the specific function of translation depends on whether one considers translation from a richly endowed language into an impoverished language or the other way around. To impoverished languages, 'translation is a way of gathering literary resources, of acquiring universal texts and thereby enriching an underfunded literature ...' (Casanova 2004, p. 137). Yet, from Casanova's account of translation from a deprived language to a rich language, it is clear that whether or not a country is to be considered deprived does not depend on the actual resources, which were available at a given time, but whether or not the language itself is recognised as a literary language at the centre. Translation from peripheral languages to major languages, on the other hand, is a process with far greater consequences for the author, claims Casanova. For those authors, the translation is equivalent with what she terms *"littérisation"*, which is what provides literary visibility and existence.

> To define the translation of dominated authors as *littérisation*, which is to say as an actual metamorphosis, a change of literary being, makes it possible to resolve a whole series of problems generated by the belief in the equality – or, better, the symmetry – of different types of translations, uniformly conceived as simple transfers of meaning from one language into another. Literary transmutation is achieved by crossing a magic frontier that allows a text composed in an un-prestigious language – or even a non-literary language, which is to say one that either does not exist or is unrecognised in the verbal marketplace – to pass into a literary language.
> CASANOVA 2004, p. 134

Here we are faced with the problem of reducing the complex processes of cultural transfers to functions of language, in this case of substituting one language for another. Being aware of the fact that translated texts frequently fail to be noticed in the literary field of the target language (as Ibsen's did in a number of instances) it is evident that translation alone is not enough to account for the successful transition from one cultural context into another. The process of consecration not only takes place through translation but also through the intermediary of critics, publishers, booksellers, and others active in the field. Translation and consecration do not necessarily walk hand in hand, though translation may be seen as a prerequisite for wider international dissemination. All of these practises cannot be properly understood through the concept of translation alone. Even to the extent that "translation" may be argued to be intended as a metaphor, the description has the unfortunate side effect that it hides a range of complex processes.

The basic outline of the world of letters at the end of the nineteenth century, as Casanova sees it, features a level of national rivalry and an international level where authors, despite their national origin, may have their works consecrated in the autonomous centres of literature. What then follows in Casanova's account is, I think, of chief importance to her conception of 'centre and periphery' and the mobility of literature, because she then introduces what she calls 'aesthetic time'. This is done by coining the term 'the Greenwich meridian of literature', which serves as a way of establishing an absolute time reference for measuring time in the world of letters.

> The continually redefined present of literary life constitutes a universal artistic clock by which writers must regulate their work if they wish to attain legitimacy. If modernity is the sole present moment of literature, which is to say what makes it possible to institute a measure of time, the Greenwich meridian makes it possible to evaluate and recognize the quality of a work or, to the contrary, to dismiss a work as an anachronism or label it "provincial".
> CASANOVA 2004, p. 90

In the quotation, Casanova makes explicit the notion so often implied in the thinking about centre and periphery, namely that the periphery is lagging behind the centre in terms of development. The centre is seen as the source of progress and the periphery is struggling to catch up. To my mind, this description is problematic as it rests on a teleological conception of time. We are presented with a notion of literary history where all literatures eventually travel the path already trodden by the authors consecrated at the centre. In relation to the dynamic of centre and periphery, it draws on a notion of influence, in which the 'modernity' of the centre is gradually disseminated to the periphery.

The problems that provincial writers face when being taken up at the centre is one that concerns Casanova, which is also evident from her work on Ibsen. In her account, 'misinterpretation' is the price that authors from small literatures pay in order to be taken up at the centre; works are stripped of their 'original context' and their reception reduced to fit the categories of perception currently in vogue (Casanova 2004, p. 154ff). The example that she uses to illustrate this point is, in fact, the reception of Ibsen's plays in London and Paris. In Britain, Casanova claims, Ibsen was received as a 'realist' and in France as a 'symbolist'; each nation interpreting Ibsen according to its local fashion. In the process of imposing its own norms, the centre, Casanova points out, understands its own ethnocentrism as 'universalism'. Although Casanova here points to a crucial point about cultural centres' appropriation of literature, it seems to me that there are other modes to receive and interpret foreign material than through reverting to a notion of universalism. As I show below, Ibsen's dramas were appropriated differently in different places and recourse to universalism was one out of a number of approaches.

To sum up, Casanova very efficiently manages to establish the notion of hierarchies in the world of literature and provides an overall model for addressing inequality and the special challenge authors from small literatures face on their path to international recognition. This has provided us with a much-needed framework for addressing such issues and accounts for much of the success with which the book has been met. However, the framework that it provides is problematic as far as national categories are taken as the fundamental building blocks and national literatures are given an existence seemingly independent of mediation and human agency.

2.2 Approaching Notions about Nation: The Transfer of Ibsen's Dramas

In the following, I will give some examples from my research on the transfer of Henrik Ibsen's plays to serve as a case for analysing how notions of nation and national origin played an important role in shaping the transfer when the plays were first exported abroad during the last decades of the nineteenth century. What makes the dissemination of Ibsen's plays an intriguing case is that the notion about the primacy of the national origin of literature not only dominates the historiography, it also pervaded discourses on literature during the time when Ibsen's plays first broke through internationally. After all, at the close of the nineteenth century in Europe, nationalism and essentialist assumptions about national origin were hegemonic across the continent. In challenging methodological nationalism, this landscape causes us significant problems as our as sources seem to vindicate the national categories used in the research.

Looking at the historiography on Ibsen, it quickly becomes clear that there are as good as no comparative or transnational studies, something, which has also been pointed out by Giuliano D'Amico.[5] What one finds almost exclusively in the vast body of research on the reception of Ibsen's dramas are studies that work within a clearly-marked national framework.[6] On the surface, the theoretical approach seems to be well suited to the cultural world at this time as the concept of the national culture was central to all thinking about literature during this period. Yet, as scholars of cultural transfers will agree, confinement to national approaches is not wholly unproblematic. Notwithstanding the many insights into Ibsen's dramas, their origin, and their national reception that more than a century of research has produced, it is nevertheless evident that national frameworks tend to support a specific set of narratives. In these narratives, the importance attached to explanations relating to all things national are emphasised. This happens because the studies of reception are framed based on a notion of a sending and a receiving national context. As Ibsen was Norwegian, Norway is seen as his plays' native context and, more importantly, means that the plays were not native to the receiving country. In historiographic literature, the various national variations on this narrative always have the plays' conflict-filled introduction into the country's literary field as their centrepiece, which is then explained by highlighting differences in the national contexts between the sending and the receiving nation. Frequently, however, the play's original context is merely assumed and framed as Ibsen's "foreignness".

At the same time, these studies quite often revolve around the notion of advanced or backwards literary cultures, the logic of which Casanova's work explains very well. In these cases, the import of Ibsen's plays is universally interpreted as the import of a superior dramatic form compared to those already present in the relevant national space. This is often the case with the studies of exports to non-Western countries, where Ibsen's drama has been contrasted with traditional dramatic forms, as has been demonstrated by Kwok-Kan

---

5 Giuliano D'Amico, 'Six point for a comparative Ibsen reception history', in *Ibsen Studies*, 14/1 (2014), pp. 4–37. For the few transnational exceptions, all comparing the Anglo-French receptions, see Kirsten Shepherd-Barr, *Ibsen and Early Modernist Theatre, 1890–1900* (Westport: Greenwood Press, 1997); Pascale Casanova, *The World Republic of Letters, op. cit.,*; Pascale Casanova, 'The Ibsen Battle. A Comparative Analysis of the Introduction of Henrik Ibsen in France, England and Ireland', in *Anglo-French Attitudes*, ed. by Julien Vincent/Jay Winter (Manchester: Manchester University Press, 2007), pp. 214–235.

6 See for instance Wolfgang Pasche, *Skandinavische Dramatik in Deutschland. Björnstjerne Björnson, Henrik Ibsen, August Strindberg auf der deutschen Bühne, 1867–1932* (Basel: Helbing & Lichtenhahn, 1979) on Germany; Michael Egan, *Henrik Ibsen. The Critical Heritage*, (London, New York: Routledge, 1997) on Britain; Giuliano D'Amico, *Domesticating Ibsen for Italy* (Oslo: University of Oslo, 2011) on Italy; and Liyang Xia, 'Heart Higher than the Sky. Reinventing Chinese Feminism Through Ibsen's *Hedda Gabler*', in *Ibsen Between Cultures*, ed. by Frode Helland/Julie Holledge (Oslo: Novus Forlag, 2016), pp. 113–142 on China.

Tam. However, the trope of the "superior Ibsen" is also evident in the studies of countries with strong, Western literary traditions such as Germany, Italy and Britain.[7] Here, one finds narratives in which the import of the foreign plays gave rise to a division in the receiving nation's cultural field between what are considered progressive and conservative forces.[8] However, what is generally overlooked is to what extent that reception in Norway or in other countries was divided along the same lines. This context helps disprove the idea that the defining features of Ibsen's reception and that of other peripheral authors necessarily hinged on national differences.

In the following examples, I seek to approach the question of national categorisation by stressing that there is nothing self-evident about national literatures. Rather, they are categories that undergo perpetual change as they are being negotiated. One way to approach the constructed nature of national literatures is to historicize it. However, I would argue, it is not enough merely to recognise the historicity of the concept and point to the fact that the paradigm emerged at a certain point and subsequently gained dominance. Because the concept of nation was (and continues to be) highly contested, it is necessary to analyse how the concept of national and literature was negotiated in a specific setting at a specific point in time. This approach has been inspired by Michael Werner and Bénédicte Zimmermann, and the method they term *histoire croisée*, who call for an approach to history which operates with a plurality of perspectives. These negotiations may be analysed as taking place on various levels and across a variety of public arenas.

In my research, I investigate negotiations over the right to define national literature through the concept of field and by mapping the various position that existed in local spaces at given times. In my analyses, I stress that in a given place there will always be stakeholders with conflicting interests who seek to make their influence known. Very often, different aspects are tied together through the people involved and investigating the agents helps situate the analysis of abstract negotiations of concepts in concrete situations and give useful insights as to what was at stake at specific moments. From this point of view, even a hypothetical world capital of literature is an arena where different literary ideals vie for dominance and where no single artistic school or theory may be said to have universal currency. Consequently, artistic time is not a universal time as claimed by Casanova, but something that is constructed

---

7 Kwok-kan Tam, 'Introduction', in *Ibsen and the Modern Self. Acta Ibseniana*, ed. by Frode Helland/Kwok-kan Tam/Terry Siu-han Yip (Hong Kong: Open University of Hong Kong Press, 2010), pp. XII–XXIV.
8 See for instance Thomas Postlewait, *Prophet of the New Drama. William Archer and the Ibsen Campaign* (Westport, Connecticut: Greenwood Press, 1984).

retrospectively and which always represent a specific perspective that may be traced back to specific agents.

In connection with cultural transfers, what is at stake is never merely the fate of the objects of transfer themselves but always the concepts used in framing them. Analysing the transfer of Ibsen's plays, I have reconstructed the positions that the various agents occupied in the receiving field in relation to the import. The question that I pose is how the works were merged into the already existing cultural field – that is to say, how it was perceived in relation to what already existed. In mapping out the various positions, there are always multiple parameters: aesthetic, economic, political and institutional, and at it is on these levels that various notions of nation and national literature can and must be investigated. Furthermore, it is evident that the concept of national literature takes it significance from other associated notions. In the late-nineteenth century, for instance, a popular notion was that literature expressed the properties of its people, which in turn was seen as being shaped by the land it inhabited and its history. Another concern at the time was the idea found in Casanova's concept of 'aesthetic time': the notion of the relative position of national literatures in relation to one another in terms of development. This was an important ingredient in debates over literature and, especially, the perceived risk of falling behind was frequently used to call for artistic renewal and the import of new artistic practices.

In the following, I give a number of examples of how national and national literary categories were negotiated in relation to the initial transfer of Ibsen's plays. Ibsen's path to international recognition may be traced in a number of steps as his dramas were gradually translated, published, and staged in an increasing number of countries. First, I give an overview of Ibsen's first step abroad from Norway to Denmark. This is followed by a short examination of the Berlin naturalists' appropriation of Ibsen's play *Ghosts*, which caused a scandal due to its treatment of the controversial topics of heredity and venereal decease. Finally, I touch on the patterns in the appropriation of the dramas in Paris and London where the path to success was somewhat different from the one in the Scandinavian countries and German-speaking Europe.

2.3 Dissemination to Scandinavia

This step took Ibsen's plays outside Norway and brought them to Norway's neighbouring Scandinavian countries, Denmark and Sweden. Yet, even this first step demonstrates the problems of relying on national categories, when it comes to describing the complex processes of cultural transfer. On the one hand, it testifies to the fact that cultural markets were often entangled across borders; on the other hand, it demonstrates the centrality of national thinking to concepts of literature at the time. In both instances, processes of cultural exchange and categorisation were complex and, therefore, require careful analysis to understand.

Publishing his first work in 1850, Ibsen belonged to a generation of Norwegian writers that sought to create a new national literature. Having been the minor party in a personal union with Denmark until 1814, Norway's cultural field had to a large extent been dominated by Danish cultural products. Import from Denmark to Norway was made easy due to the closeness of their languages, but also because Norwegian elites had strong ties with Denmark. Key to understanding Ibsen and his generation of authors is that the dominion of Danish culture continued even after the dual monarchy ended and Norway, following the Napoleonic wars, was ceded to Sweden. In effect, this meant that Danish publishing continued to dominate the Norwegian book market and that theatre in Norway too continued to be dominated by Danish plays performed in Danish.[9] In Denmark, the reverse was the case. Here Norwegian authors found it very difficult to find an audience: Norwegian publications were almost wholly ignored while Danish publishers were reluctant to publish Norwegians.

This dynamic between Norway and Denmark, which lasted throughout the nineteenth century, may be described as a dynamic between centre and periphery. With reference to Casanova, Mads Rosendal Thomsen has already pointed out that Copenhagen during this period constituted something of a 'semi-centre' because it was susceptible to influences from both France and Germany while taking a leading position in Scandinavia.[10] As I am concerned with the dynamics of transfer, the dichotomy centre and periphery may be used as a framework for describing the uneven relationship. To Ibsen and his generation, being published in Denmark was the logical first step outside Norway. Furthermore, any recognition won in Denmark had the added benefit of also contributing to their standing at home due to the perceived status of Danish culture. Besides, being published in Denmark was not merely a question of winning recognition; it was also a matter of securing a livelihood, as the Norwegian market was still too small to sustain professional authors. Even with supplementary work in theatres, Ibsen and the few others who aimed to pursue a professional career found it difficult to sustain themselves financially.

---

9   Harald Tveterås, *Den Norske Bokhandels Historie* (Oslo: Norsk bokhandler-medhjelperforening, 1964), vol. 2, p. 13 ff.
10 Mads Rosendahl Thomsen, *Mapping World Literature, op. cit.*, pp. 36–37.

To young Norwegians, creating a new national literature inevitably involved a certain opposition to Danish cultural products and choosing Danish publishers may, therefore, seem a paradoxical move. Yet, one of the factors that helped to mitigate the young generation's opposition and which in turn help their eventual transition to Danish publishers, was the ideology of Scandinavianism. This ideology and its related movement insisted on the historical and cultural affinity between Norway, Denmark, and Sweden, and sought to promote cultural exchange between what were seen as kindred nations. To Norwegian authors, Scandinavianism proved a way of insisting on the development of a singular Norwegian literature while still embracing the cultural connectedness to Denmark. Politically, Scandinavianism may be seen to contribute to nation-building efforts; by promoting the idea of the equality of the three countries, it also acted an indirect way of advocating Norwegian emancipation from Sweden. In relation to the contemporary conceptualisation of literature, it is important to note that although nationalism was strong, paradigms or imagined communities existed, which rivalled or modified that of the nation.

What eventually led to the success of Norwegian authors in Denmark must be explained, at least partly, by internal developments in the Danish cultural elite, which resulted in something of a paradigmatic shift in the perception of its national literature. Voices emerged that claimed that Danish literature had stagnated and this claim was followed by a call for aesthetic reorientation. This created an openness in the cultural market that gave the up-and-coming Norwegian writers a chance to break through. It is, however, important to stress that the claim of stagnation must be seen part of a wider development. If one looks at the people who took part in the debates about Danish national literature at the time, it becomes clear that there was a significant overlap in people who led the assault on the ailing Danish literature and those who promoted the young Norwegians.[11] A perspective from publishing history reveals, furthermore, that a reconfiguration of the market for literature occurred simultaneously with the devaluation of the immediate Danish literary past. Scandinavianism, ruptures in the perception of national culture, and developments in the field of publishing were in fact tied together by the people who positioned themselves in the local cultural field with regard to these factors and which, therefore, caused mutual influence. The result of the publications of Ibsen's dramas by a Danish publisher was that the leading Norwegian literature for the next generation was published in Denmark rather than in Norway.

---

11   Magnus Qvistgaard, 'Pioneering Ibsen's Dramas. Agents, Markets and Reception 1856–1893' (unpublished doctoral thesis, Fiesole: European University Institute, Institute of History and Civilization, 2015), pp. 54 ff.

Even though it was at times regretted in Norway that the nation's preeminent writers were published abroad, it was generally pardoned in the light of the international recognition it had brought the emerging national literature.

2.4 Ibsen and the German Naturalists

Just like the idea of the cultural affinity that existed between Scandinavian countries, there also existed a notion of strong cultural ties to Scandinavia in the recently unified Germany. Unlike Scandinavianism, which sought to promote cultural integration in the present, the German emphasis was predominantly on the perceived shared origin of the German and Scandinavian peoples. More than historical, the origin was located in a quasi-mythological past and the North played an important role in the creation a German mythology of origin. The term generally applied to the relationship between Germans and Scandinavians was "*Stammenverwandt*", which conveyed the sense of kindred tribes, a notion that was transplanted to a more general cultural level. In relation to Scandinavia, and Denmark in particular, the insistence on the shared origin also smoothed over the strain that contemporary political conflicts placed on the relationship.

The notion of Scandinavian peoples as kindred tribes played a relatively peripheral role in relation to the increasing success that Norwegian authors and Ibsen in particular, experienced in Germany during the 1870s and 1880s. Given the popularity that Richard Wagner experienced simultaneously with his mythological themed operas that relied heavily on a shared Germanic-Scandinavian mythology, this may seem surprising. In the early part of his career, Ibsen had himself experienced considerable success across Scandinavia with his mythological and historical dramas, but it was not these that drew readers and audiences across Germany. Rather it was Ibsen's so-called problem plays, in which he took aim at contemporary social and moral issue such as the ruthlessness of the capitalist classes, the institution of marriage, and the taboo of venereal decease that soon found an ever-growing audience.

During the 1880s, Ibsen's plays, alongside those of Zola and Tolstoy, served as a major source of inspiration to the German naturalists.[12] Naturalism in Germany started out as a number of different groups all calling for aesthetic

---

12 Vera Moe, *Deutscher Naturalismus und Ausländische Literatur. Zur Rezeption der Werke von Zola, Ibsen und Dostojewski durch die deutsche naturalistische Bewegung (1880–1895)* (Frankfurt am Main, New York: Peter Lang, 1983), pp. 117 ff.

change and a new literature, which was to be the literature of the future. Here it is important to note that more than anything the call that went up was the call for a new national literature. Two of the prominent members of the early movement were the brothers Heinrich and Julius Hart who together published the magazine *Kritische Waffengänge*. In the magazine, the brothers not only violent attacked the current state of German literature, but also adopted a very strong national rhetoric. One of the Harts' chief concerns was that the drama and literature of the preceding generation had been corrupted because it too freely had embraced foreign influence, which primarily meant French literature. At the root of the Harts' dissatisfaction was the belief that the political unification of Germany only a decade before had not fostered a corresponding national cultural renaissance, which they felt was due to the newly-unified nation. Rather, they found that though Germany had emerged victorious from the war with France, it was only to be culturally conquered by the very people they had defeated.[13]

What may seem remarkable is that the object of Harts' attacks was not so much French literature, or the French plays which were continuously adapted for German theatres, but the plays of the German playwrights who wrote in what was perceived to be the French tradition. One particular object of the Harts' attacks was the writer, Paul Lindau, who besides being one of the most successful playwrights at the time was one of the most influential of the Berlin critics. In the Harts' criticism, however, Lindau's aesthetic became emblematic for the preceding decade, the so-called "*Gründerzeit*". For the Harts, this was a way of setting themselves apart as well as announcing that Lindau's aesthetic values were outdated. I find the fact that the Harts targeted Lindau and other German authors like him significant. What was at stake was perhaps not so much a concern with French plays (or the international level) but with local affairs and the Harts' criticism, one may strongly suspect, seems to be aimed squarely at carving out a position in the local cultural field for themselves. The Harts and other naturalists with them were not alone in adopting a national stance when it came to fighting for the literature that they supported, however. Similar positions were taken up by a string of what we (for want of a better term) may call the conservatively-minded critics, such as Karl Frenzel, who throughout the 1880s remained deeply opposed to the new naturalist literature. He also used national borders as demarcation lines to reject the plays he disliked. In his reviews of the Berlin Ibsen productions, for instance, Frenzel

---

13   Lothar L. Schneider, *Realistische Literaturpolitik und naturalistische Kritik. Über die Situierung der Literatur in der zweiten Hälfte des 19. Jahrhunderts und die Vorgeschichte der Moderne* (Tübingen: M. Niemeyer, 2005), pp. 193 ff.

unfailingly deplored the fact that a foreign play had been chosen rather than a German work. In the light of Ibsen's social criticism, he claimed that the audience would not have stomached the 'immorality' of the plays had they been written by one of their own fellow citizens.[14]

Leo Berg was one of the young naturalists who took a very active part in the discussion that arose around Ibsen's relationship with German literature. In his pamphlet on the subject, *Henrik Ibsen und das Germanenthum in der modernen Litteratur*, Berg asserted that although Ibsen was not German he was not foreign either, as he by his Norwegian origin he was 'Germanic'. More important to Berg, however, was that Ibsen had a thoroughly German worldview. With his love for truth and his determinate character, Berg was quick to proclaim him even more German than those of his own country who emulated the French.[15]

Appropriation of foreign literature was, in other words, a practice common to both sides of the aesthetic divide that appeared during the 1880s. However, it did not prevent either side from applying national arguments in their attempt to dismiss foreign aesthetic products of which they disapproved. When Ibsen's plays came to hold a key position within early German naturalism, in spite of the strong national focus of the naturalists, it was due to the fact that no new German plays were found ready to provide a convincing alternative to those that dominated theatrical repertoires. By promoting Ibsen's plays and the works of a few other foreign authors, such as Zola and Tolstoy, the objective was, partly at least, that they were to serve as role models for a future German theatre. Berg's argument in particular shows clearly how national categories were redefined in connection with the transfer of cultural products. Quite often, this was an overt attempt to further specific aesthetic ends such as the promotion of a naturalist aesthetic agenda. Highly contested transfers, such as the import of Ibsen's dramas, were areas where the concept of nation and national literature were debated alongside aesthetic ideals and contemporary social and moral issues.

2.5 Ibsen in London and Paris

Outside Scandinavia and German-speaking Europe, attempts to promote Ibsen's plays could not rely on widely-held notions of cultural affiliation. One

---

14 Karl Frenzel, 'Gespenster (Residenz-Theater)', in *National-Zeitung*, 11 January 1887.
15 Leo Berg, *Henrik Ibsen und das Germanenthum in der modernen Litteratur* (Berlin: R. Eckstein Nachfolger, 1887), pp. 4–5.

of the questions that dominated the early English and French reception of Ibsen was why the inhabitants, of what they themselves perceived to be culturally more advanced nations, should ever concern themselves with literature from as remote a place as Norway? In particular, the well-established critics of large mainstream newspapers looked down upon the hitherto unknown Norwegian dramatist. Yet, Ibsen did have his supporters in the metropolitan cities of Paris and London, and his dramas did find their audiences. Ibsen's reception in in these urban cultural centres is perhaps the epitome of the trope of 'the periphery at the centre' and Casanova has herself used Ibsen in Paris and London as an example of precisely this. However, where Casanova focuses on what she terms misinterpretation, I think a more illuminating approach uses cultural transfers to investigate the fractures within the cultural field of the cultural centres.

What set apart the appropriation of Ibsen's dramas by the theatres of Paris and London from those of the Scandinavia and Germany was the fact that for the most part they remained works for niche-venues. Only in a few instances before the turn of the century did one of Ibsen's dramas make it to the big boulevard theatres. In Paris, the Théâtre de Vaudeville was the only major boulevard theatre to attempt Ibsen but, out of a number of productions, only *A Doll's House* proved a success.[16] In London, the famous actor-manager Herbert Beerbohm-Tree's production of *Pillars of Society* remained the only attempt by a major theatre before the twentieth century, which saw a renewed interest in Ibsen. However, rather than achieving success in the mainstream, Ibsen's dramas were an item for the experimental troupes and the scenes that existed on the fringe of theatrical life. Figures who later gained popular renown such as André Antoine and Aurélien Lugné-Poe with the Théâtre Libre and the Théâtre de l'Œuvre, respectively, produced interpretations of Ibsen's work in small inconspicuous theatres out of view of the mainstream theatregoer. Only in time and then not least due to their success in print did Ibsen's dramas assume the position that they hold today.

The appropriation of Ibsen's plays in Paris and London was a complex process, in which notions of national literature played a role, but where the concept of the nation was only part of the equation. Part of the reason for this was that the vast majority that encountered Ibsen's dramas had any but the haziest notion of what Norway was like or what to expect from the northern country. From the public reception in the media, we see that Norway swiftly became a

---

16   Kirsten Shepherd-Barr, *Ibsen and Early Modernist Theatre*, op. cit., p. 80.

caricature of the country portrayed in Ibsen's plays: a land of mist and gloom inhabited by stern and sombre characters.[17] For Ibsen's local supporters, however, the import of the foreign plays served as a platform from which to attack the current state of local theatre. To Ibsen's English translator, William Archer, Ibsen's plays provided him with an opportunity to chastise the English drama, which he claimed had stagnated as a result of becoming increasingly introverted. Yet even Archer, who arguably was one of the best-informed critics when it came to European drama, and was an internationalist *par excellence*, was ultimately concerned with the renewal of English drama.[18] The international imports were put to work for a national cause.

2.6 Summing Up

Methodological nationalism evidently poses a problem to the study of literature. Yet the study of how cultural transfers are conditioned by notions of "nation" ought to be central to investigating the processes of transfers. In spite of the fact that nationalism and a national perspective on cultural matters seem all-pervasive both in the nineteenth century and later, it is important to insist that national categories do not represent intrinsic features of literature. Meaning-making requires agency and it is people such as critics and scholars of literature who, apart from the authors themselves, invoke the nation and construct as well as reconstruct national traditions. In my example of Ibsen's reception in Europe, I have aimed to show that when investigating specific cases of cultural transfer, one discovers that national categories are stretched, challenged and manipulated by the people involved in the transferral. This is exactly the reason why national categories cannot be treated as existing *a priori*. As I have stressed in my examples with Ibsen, transfers require negotiation and reconfiguration of categories to be accommodated and for investigating these intricate transactions, hypostatizing national categories or perspectives offers insufficient complexity for rigorous analysis. Even less than national categories, national traditions are a given. As shown in my examples, the import of the foreign and the rejection of what is supposedly one's own (in national terms at least) walked hand in hand.

---

[17] See for instance Michael Egan/Tore Rem, "'The Provincial of Provincials'. Ibsen's Strangeness and the Process of Canonisation', in *Ibsen Studies*, 4/2 (2004), pp. 205–225.
[18] William Archer, *English Dramatists of To-Day* (London: T. Fischer-Unwin, 1882).

In my view, the perspectivism such as the one called for by Michael Werner and Bénédicte Zimmermann in their outline of *histoire croisée* is one way to proceed. Although the inclusion of more perspectives complicates matters considerably, it seems that only through this added complexity can one begin to map out the various conflicting positions, which are concealed by the concept of "national perspectives". Thus, one of the problems inherent to Pascale Casanova's account is that conflicting perspectives are lost when they are not considered on the sub-national level. Abandoning methodological nationalism and moving towards a network-based concept of literary history, where the focus is on mobility and exchange has the potential to provide a more accurate picture of how literature actually moves.

Bibliography

Archer, William, *English Dramatists of To-Day* (London: T. Fischer-Unwin, 1882).

Berg, Leo, *Henrik Ibsen und das Germanenthum in der modernen Litteratur* (Berlin: R. Eckstein Nachfolger, 1887).

Casanova, Pascale, 'The Ibsen Battle. A Comparative Analysis of the Introduction of Henrik Ibsen in France, England and Ireland', in *Anglo-French Attitudes*, ed. by Julien Vincent/Jay Winter (Manchester: Manchester University Press, 2007), pp. 214–235.

Casanova, Pascale, *The World Republic of Letters* (Cambridge: Harvard University Press, 2004).

D'Amico, Giuliano, 'Six point for a comparative Ibsen reception history', in *Ibsen Studies*, 14/1 (2014), pp. 4–37.

D'Amico, Giuliano, *Domesticating Ibsen for Italy* (Oslo: University of Oslo, 2011).

Egan, Michael, *Henrik Ibsen. The Critical Heritage* (London, New York: Routledge, 1997).

Espagne, Michel, 'Transferanalyse statt Vergleich. Interkulturalität in der sächsischen Regionalgeschichte', in *Vergleich und Transfer. Komparatistik in den Sozial-, Geschichts- und Kulturwissenschaffen*, ed. by Hartmut Kaelble/Jürgen Schriewer (Frankfurt/Main: Campus Verlag, 2003), pp. 419–438.

Frenzel, Karl, 'Gespenster (Residenz-Theater)', in *National-Zeitung*, 11 January 1887.

Moe, Vera, *Deutscher Nationalismus und ausländische Literatur. Zur Rezeption der Werke von Zola, Ibsen und Dostojewski durch die deutsche naturalistische Bewegung (1880–1895)* (Frankfurt/Main, New York: Peter Lang, 1983).

Neunsinger, Silke, 'Cross-over! Om Komparationer, Transferanalyser, Histoire Croisée Och Den Metodologiska Nationalismens Problem', in *Historisk Tidskrift*, 130/1 (2010), pp. 3–24.

Pasche, Wolfgang, *Skandinavische Dramatik in Deutschland. Björnstjerne Björnson, Henrik Ibsen, August Strindberg auf der deutschen Bühne, 1867–1932* (Basel: Helbing & Lichtenhahn, 1979).

Postlewait, Thomas, *Prophet of the New Drama. William Archer and the Ibsen Campaign* (Westport: Greenwood Press, 1984).

Prendergast, Christopher, 'The World Republic of Letters', in *Debating World Literature*, ed. by Christopher Prendergast (London: Verso, 2004), pp. 1–26.

Qvistgaard, Magnus, 'Pioneering Ibsen's Dramas. Agents, Markets and Reception 1856–1893' (unpublished doctoral thesis, Fiesole: European University Institute, Institute of History and Civilization, 2015).

Rem, Tore, '"The Provincial of Provincials". Ibsen's Strangeness and the Process of Canonisation', in *Ibsen Studies*, 4/2 (2004), pp. 205–225.

Schneider, Lothar L., *Realistische Literaturpolitik und naturalistische Kritik. Über die Situierung der Literatur in der zweiten Hälfte des 19. Jahrhunderts und die Vorgeschichte der Moderne* (Tübingen: M. Niemeyer, 2005).

Shepherd-Barr, Kirsten, *Ibsen and Early Modernist Theatre, 1890–1900* (Westport: Greenwood Press, 1997).

Tam, Kwok-kan, 'Introduction', in *Ibsen and the Modern Self. Acta Ibseniana*, ed. by Frode Helland/Kwok-kan Tam/Terry Siu-han Yip (Hong Kong: Open University of Hong Kong Press, 2010), pp. xii–xxiv.

Thomsen, Mads Rosendahl, *Mapping World Literature* (New York: Continuum, 2008).

Tveterås, Harald, *Den Norske Bokhandels Historie* (Oslo: Norsk bokhandler-medhjelperforening, 1964), vol. 2.

Xia, Liyang, 'Heart Higher than the Sky. Reinventing Chinese Feminism Through Ibsen's *Hedda Gabler*', in *Ibsen Between Cultures*, ed. by Frode Helland/Julie Holledge (Oslo: Novus Forlag, 2016), pp. 113–142.

Zimmermann, Bénédicte/Michael Werner, 'Beyond Comparison. Histoire Croisée and the Challenge of Reflexivity', in *History and Theory*, 45/1 (2006), pp. 30–50.

CHAPTER 3

The Meta-Literary History of Cultural Transmitters and Forgotten Scholars in the Midst of Transnational Literary History

Petra Broomans

Abstract

The field of Cultural Transfer Studies is a relatively young discipline which developed against the backdrop of important events and theoretical and methodological "turns", such as the crisis in literary historiography and the "cultural" turn in translation studies at the end of the twentieth century. It will be argued here that it also has forgotten roots in early comparative literary studies, one object of which was the possibility of writing a world literary history. The early comparatists also argued for more focus on cultural transmitters. This chapter starts from the assumption that a more complete history of Cultural Transfer Studies is required, one that includes the cultural transmitters and leads to a rethinking and finetuning of concepts. It will take the initial steps in this direction. It will become clear that unsuccessful cultural transfer processes and the lack of material complicate the writing of transnational/national literary history. In addition to this complexity, the histories of cultural transfer thus far have commonly relied on metaphors of trade and conquest when describing the literary field in which translators and translations take a visible or invisible position. In this regard, the historiographer will have to decide on the plot regarding the cultural transmitter: will it be one in which the protagonist is a leader and discoverer, or the silent worker and clerk? Throughout the chapter some cultural transmitters from Finland and Sweden will act as illustrative examples.

In his description of cultural translation in his widely read article, "Lost (and Found) in Translation: A cultural history of translators and translating in Early Modern Europe" (2005), Peter Burke uses expressions such as 'negotiation' (4), 'balance of trade' (9) and 'a form of domestication of the alien' (p. 4).[1] These metaphors of trade and conquest are commonly used when describing the

---

[1] Peter Burke, *Lost (and Found) in Translation. A Cultural History of Translators and Translating in Early Modern Europe* (Wassenaar: NIAS, 2005). cf. https://nias.knaw.nl/books/lost-and-found-in-translation/

literary field in which translations take a visible or invisible position, depending on the symbolic power of the foreign author and literary text or the translator herself/himself. These expressions reflect the plot chosen by the author to narrate the story. In this regard, the scholar Hayden White elaborated a theory of discourse within the field of history in his seminal study, *Metahistory. The Historical Imagination in Nineteenth-century Europe* (1973), in which he demonstrated that historians use narrative discourses in their history-telling and that these historical accounts, therefore, do not reflect objective reality or offer analytical representations. As in fictional texts, the historical narrative uses metaphors, a plot, and other features that hold the story together. According to White, this story assists the historiographer to explain the meaning of events. White points out three explanatory strategies: the 'mode of emplotment', the 'mode of formal argument' and the 'mode of ideological implication'. Before setting up a story, the historian gains an overview of the historical field in a process of prefiguring. According to White, this often occurs in an unconscious way: 'the historian both creates his object of analysis and predetermines the modality of the conceptual strategies he will use to explain it'.[2]

In my analysis of texts in literary histories of Swedish women writers, it became apparent that the most often used mode of emplotment was the romantic one (2001), in which, after much trial and error, the author finds her own style, triumphs, and is canonized. Other plots include the tragic (offering an explanation of the failure of the author), the comic (reconciliation), and the satirical (an insight into the inadequacy of human being).[3] I also observed that the argument and the plot are supported by 'strings' which form an associative chain that holds the narrative together. These 'strings' consist of adjectives and metaphors that appear throughout the text (Broomans 2001, p. 59).

In addition to Hayden White, who represents the linguistic turn in the field of history, the French sociologist Pierre Bourdieu could be regarded as the initiator of what we might call a turn to a "conflictual" paradigm within sociology. In his field theory, various actors (whether individuals or institutions) play out their conflicts in different fields in society, based on their "symbolic capital" and "habitus". The trade and conquest metaphors used by Burke and others might well have been inspired by Bourdieu, as his terminology has become widespread in many disciplines. Scholars within the field of the sociology of literature, such as Pascale Casanova, have in fact used and adapted field

---

2 Hayden White, *Metahistory. The Historical Imagination in Nineteenth-century Europe* (Baltimore: The Johns Hopkins University Press, 1973), p. 31.
3 Petra Broomans, *Detta Är Jag. Stina Aronsons Litteraturhistoriska Öde* (Stockholm: Carlsson, 2001), pp. 61–65.

theory to the literary field and the spaces in which different national literary fields meet.

3.1 Development of Cultural Transfer Studies

The meeting of national literatures has been an object of study since the beginning of the nineteenth century and the rise of comparative literature studies. One of the aims of the comparatists was to compile a world literary history or international literary history. In the later decades of the twentieth century, "transnational literary history" also became a common phrase. The aim of this transnational literary history, closely connected to transnational history or *"histoire croisée"* (entangled history), was to move beyond traditional national frames and reveal a broader literary history that crossed borders. The concepts of transnational history and *histoire croisée* were coined by scholars who were critical of the fixation on and confinement within state borders in nationalism studies. Moreover, the creation of these new perspectives was accompanied by the development of Cultural Transfer Studies

As Michael Espagne has pointed out, the field of Cultural Transfer Studies aims to advance a transnational history and should be regarded as an opportunity to unlock new ways of writing transnational history itself.[4] Espagne and Michael Werner first coined the term 'cultural transfer' ("Kulturtransfer") in their article, "Deutsch-Französischer Kulturtransfer im 18. und 19. Jahrhundert. Zu einem neuen Interdisziplinären Forschungsprogramm des C.N.R.S." (1985).[5] In this article they argued, as many before them did and many after have done, including Peter Burke, that more attention should be paid to the individual 'cultural transmitter':

> Selbstverständlich wird ein interkultureller Transfer nicht nur von abstrakten Konjunkturen und geistigen Konstellationen bestimmt: er ist zuallererst das Werk realer Vermitterpersönlichkeiten.

---

[4] Michel Espagne, 'Jenseits der Komparatistik. Zur Methode der Erforschung von Kulturtransfer', *Europäische Kulturzeitschriften um 1900 als Medien transnationaler und transdisziplinärer Wahrnehmung*, ed. by Ulrich Mölk (Göttingen: Vandenhoeck & Ruprecht, 2006), pp. 13–32 (p. 13).

[5] Michel Espagne/Michael Werner, 'Deutsch-Französischer Kulturtransfer im 18. und 19. Jahrhundert. Zu einem neuen interdiszplinären Forschungsprogramm des C.N.R.S.', in *Francia. Forschungen zur westeuropäischen Geschichte*, 13/1 (1985), pp. 502–510.

> (Of course, intercultural transfer is determined not only by abstract conjunctures and spiritual constellations: it is first and foremost the work of real cultural transmitters.)
>
> ESPAGNE and WERNER 1985, p. 506[6]

Espagne and Werner also emphasized the importance of network analysis; what they called the 'Art Matrix' (ibid.). In another article, 'La construction d'une référence culturelle allemande en France: genèse et histoire (1750–1914)', they complemented their framework with research into the sociology of the cultural transmitter as well as the systems in which they are active (1987, p. 905).[7]

Later on, Werner and Bénédicte Zimmermann (2002) pleaded for *histoire croisée* in response to the rise of Cultural Transfer Studies arguing for a transnational discourse rather than a national one, as they were of the opinion that Cultural Transfer Studies had taken the nation as its frame of reference.[8] In 'Jenseits der Komparatistik. Zur Methode der Erforschung von Kulturtransfer' (2006), Espagne formulated an appropriate reply:

> Was transferiert wird, ist im ursprünglichen Zusammenhang national definiert. Es ist der Transferforschung sehr zu Unrecht vorgeworfen worden, sie bleibe selbst in der nationalen Argumentation verankert, die sie aus der Welt schaffen möchte. Man muss zunächst betonen, dass der Ausgangskontext zwar mit nationalen, aber ebenso sehr mit religiösen, dynastischen, ethnischen, sprachlichen oder gar beruflichen Kategorien definiert werden kann.
>
> ESPAGNE 2006, p. 17

(What is transferred is, in the original context, nationally defined. Cultural Transfer Studies has been very unjustly accused of remaining enshrined in the national argument, although it has wanted to get rid of it. Above all, it has to be stressed that the starting point may indeed be defined in terms of the national, but also in terms of religious, dynastic, ethnic, linguistic or even professional categories.)

---

6 All translations from German as well as from French to English by the author.
7 Michel Espagne/Michael Werner, 'La construction d'une référence culturelle allemande en France. Genèse et histoire (1750–1914)', in *Annales. Histoire, Sciences Sociales*, 42/4 (Jul.–Aug. 1987), pp. 969–992. http://www.jstor.org/stable/27583612.
8 Michael Werner/Bénédicte Zimmermann, 'Vergleich, Transfer, Verflechtung. Der Ansatz der Histoire croisée und die Herausforderung des Transnationalen', in *Geschichte und Gesellschaft*, 28/4 (Oct.–Dec. 2002), pp. 607–636.

Espagne, who can be regarded as the most prominent Cultural Transfer Studies scholar, defines the task of such studies as "die Translation eines Kulturgegenstandes von einen Ausgangskontext in einen Aufnahmekontext in ihrem prozessualen Ablauf under die Lupe zu nehmen" (p. 15) ("to take a closer look at the process of translation of a cultural object from a source context into a receiving context").

In his 2006 paper, Espagne pointed out some developments within cultural studies that were important for the study of cultural transfer, particularly in relation to anthropology, philology, and the history of science (pp. 18–22). Speaking more broadly, the development of Cultural Transfer Studies can also be set against the backdrop of other significant events at the end of the twentieth century. In the following, I will demonstrate how these fields enabled the development of Cultural Transfer Studies and, in turn, how this field is related to its predecessors.

As I described in a previous article in Dutch (2012), one of the events in the field of literary theory that made the further development of Cultural Transfer Studies possible was the crisis in literary historiography in the 1980s and 1990s.[9] This arose as the problem of whether or not it was possible to write a complete and true literary history, which was discussed in the forewords and introductions of several literary histories. In his study, *Is Literary History Possible?* (1992), David Perkins argued that it was no longer possible to compile a national literary history.[10] A pessimistic and anti-national attitude to literary history was trending in Western literary historiography. The positive side of this was that cultural studies started to play a complementary role.

At the same time, however, a normative perspective was taken by Harold Bloom in *The Western Canon. The School and the Books of Ages* (1994).[11] Here, Bloom attacked programmatic literary histories such as the Marxist and feminist interpretations, arguing that these politically correct canons neglected the aesthetic standards that, in his opinion, were valid and valuable to the canon. He used tropes such as 'aesthetic authority', 'creative power' and 'originality'; for Bloom, canonical writers ought to be strong and they are mostly male (Bloom 1994, pp. 10–11; p. 37).

Another counter movement to the pessimistic view of national literary history and alternative canons was the return to the national canon debates in

---

9 Petra Broomans, 'Zichtbaar in de canon. Spelregels voor cultuurbemiddelaars', in *Tijdschrift voor Nederlandse Taal- en Letterkunde*, 128/3-4 (2012), pp. 256–275.
10 David Perkins, *Is Literary History Possible?* (Baltimore, London: Johns Hopkins University Press, 1992).
11 Harold Bloom, *The Western Canon. The School and the Books of Ages* (New York, San Diego, London: Harcourt Brace & Company, 1994).

Europe after 2000. In the Netherlands and Denmark, this led to the compilation of lists of events, historical figures and books to be included in the national canon (Broomans 2012, pp. 256–257).

The development of the sociology of literature after the Second World War should be regarded as another event that enabled the rise of Cultural Transfer Studies. It resulted in studies of not only local contributions to the national literary field, but also the role of foreign literature and its reception. This research included the position of publishing houses and the role of networks and institutions. Itamar Even-Zohar's studies, in which he developed the polysystem theory starting in the 1970s, have also been of importance. The polysystem theory led to new insights in the description of national literatures and the description of relations between national literary systems. The basic mechanisms of literary contacts are also extensively studied in this theory. Even-Zohar was criticized by Edwin Gentzler and others for not including "agents and institutions".[12] Agents such as cultural transmitters play an important role in this process, although the focus in reception studies was often only on the author and text translated – not on the translator.

Like the study of history, translation studies also underwent a cultural turn, also called a "social turn" by Wolf. This is meticulously described by Michaela Wolf in her introduction to the volume entitled *Constructing a Sociology of Translation* (2007), in which she focuses on contextualizing the translated text. Wolf discusses a large group of translation studies scholars, including Even-Zohar, Venuti, and Pym, as well as the approaches of Bourdieu, Heilbron, and Sapiro, and, in addition, Latour and Luhmann, who argued for the importance of networks and institutions. After this cultural turn, the background and motives of the transmitter became more important and an awareness that translation is a form of social agency took root. One year before, Mary Snell-Hornby published a study on turns in translation studies (2006) in which she discussed the different turns, starting with the cultural turn.

The last field I consider to have enabled Cultural Transfer Studies is Cultural Studies itself, with cultural historians such as Peter Burke providing the impetus. Burke, for example, wrote the short but influential essay mentioned above, "Lost (and Found) in Translation: A Cultural History of Translators and Translating in Early Modern Europe" (2005), in which he investigated the sixteenth and seventeenth centuries, mapping what was translated and by whom. Other cultural studies scholars regarded cultural transfer as an interesting

---

12   Michaela Wolf, 'Introduction. The emergence of a sociology of translation', in *Constructing a Sociology of Translation*, ed. by Michaela Wolf/Alexandra Fukari (Amsterdam, Philadelphia: John Benjamins Publishing Company, 2007), pp. 1–36 (p. 7).

domain, not least because cultural studies is such a broad discipline and Cultural Transfer Studies is more defined and focused.

In summary, we may say that there were two apparently contrasting and overlapping discourses in the 1980s and 1990s: the transnational perspective and a renewed national discourse. Espagne attempted to combine the two (2006).

A Cultural Transfer Studies perspective is crucial to the study and compilation of a transnational history, as it requires a different approach to traditional "world literary history", demanding greater focus on mediation and the cultural transmitters, more attention to material and, as Espagne points out, more focus on the space(s) in which cultural transfer takes place (Espagne, 2006, pp. 28–32).

3.2   Transnational Literary History

Before further discussing the theory, history and practice of cultural transfer studies we need to define transnational literary history. Or should we call it post-national literary history? And is it international or transcultural? I propose to define the act of writing transnational literary history as follows: Mapping and following flows of literary texts (translated or not) across national, linguistic, ethnic, and temporal borders and placing authors/texts/genres in global, national, and local contexts, while using this form of history as a tool to describe the influence of changing contexts on literary capital.

I use the term "mapping" as it is employed by Franco Moretti in his study *Graphs, Maps, Trees; abstract models for a literary history* (2005). According to Moretti, it is important to visualize the literary field with 'graphs', 'maps' and 'trees'.[13] In our context, what this means is that mapping includes the use of all the quantitative and digital instruments available to visualize the flows of cultural and literary mediation from, to and across borders. Moretti calls this 'distant reading', in opposition to close reading (2000, pp. 56–57).

Following the flows of literary texts does not always mean following translated texts. During some periods, a *lingua franca* might be used, such as Latin, with scientific and religious texts not always translated into the vernacular. Moreover, in societies with upper and middle classes that had reading skills in foreign languages, literary texts were read in the original. As Espagne

---

13   Franco Moretti, *Graphs, Maps, Trees. Abstract Models for a Literary History* (London, New York: Verso, 2005); Franco Moretti, 'Conjectures on World Literature', in *New Left Review*, 1 (January–February 2000), pp. 54–68.

demonstrated, German was used as the *lingua franca* by scholars in the field of Slavic studies (2006: 21). Nevertheless, in general, cultural transfer entails the transferring of a literary text across national and linguistic borders. This transfer may also occur within state borders, with translations from a minority culture into the major culture, such as Sámi literature into Swedish or Norwegian for example.

Thus, there are still many borders to cross in transnational literary history, although not necessarily state borders. The issue of borders seems to be the political (and a powerful) point of departure for all thinking about and describing fields, whether economic, cultural, and/or literary.

In addition to national, state, or political borders, as suggested above, there are also linguistic borders within countries where various groups speak different languages, such as in Belgium and Finland. There are also ethnic borders in states with different ethnic groups, such as Denmark, with Inuit people who migrated from Greenland (part of the Kingdom of Denmark) to Denmark; or Canada with its First Nations population, its migrants from the Caribbean, as well as French-speaking Quebec and the Acadians.

The temporal border can be stretched across many ages or over a shorter period. Texts might be forgotten and translated much later, or they might not have been published immediately after the translation was done and be forgotten for many years. According to the discipline of literary historiography, authors, genres and texts are placed within periods and classified within global, national, and local contexts and compared with each other. When texts are transferred to a new context do they still have the same symbolic capital? A good example is the novel *Stoner* (1965) by John Williams (1922–1994). In the US, the author is known to a small inner circle, but in Europe the novel was read by many and was highly regarded. Thus, cultural transfer does not always entail general transmission; it may be limited to specific cultural and linguistic regions and not always be a worldwide event, such as the success of Dan Brown's *Da Vinci Code* (2003).

Another reason that the term "transnational" is preferred, is because it is about opening up national borders to allow inspiration from outside, and crossing national borders to seek inspiration. To use the term "international" still implicitly suggests the maintenance of national borders. I endorse Édouard Glissant's argument, referring to Gilles Deleuze and Félix Guattari[14], that when we use the term "international" the singular roots are still implied rather than

---

14   Gilles Deleuze/Guattari, Félix, 'What is a Minor Literature?', in *Kafka. Towards a Minor Literature*, by Gilles Deleuze/Félix Guattari (Minneapolis, London: University of Minnesota Press, 1986), pp. 16–27.

the rhizome that is 'an enmeshed root system', a multiple, non-hierarchical rootedness that challenges the 'totalitarian root'.[15] The act of mapping that aims to detect the transmission of literary texts can be combined with the act of tracing how the transmission took place and whether or not it has been successful, as well as the factors playing a role in an interrupted, unsuccessful, or successful transfer.

At the same time, it might be argued that the "national" is still found in the term "transnational". Another possible term could thus be "transcultural". Wolfgang Welsch developed the concept of "transculturality", arguing against Herder's 'traditional concept of single cultures' and the modern concepts of 'interculturality' and 'multiculturality'. According to Welsch, whether from an intercultural or multicultural perspective, culture is still regarded as folk-bound. One might correlate such a notion of a single and folk-bound culture with the notion of the nation as a singular entity: 'It still proceeds from a conception of cultures as islands or spheres' (3). Interculturality, however, reflects another understanding of cultures and how they interact with each other. For Welsch, cultures are never isolated or in simple conflict with each other but are in fact entangled. This perspective could be compared with a *histoire croisée* approach or as Jani Marjanen describes it, referring to Werner and Zimmermann, an 'interconnectedness in history'.[16]

Glissant and Welsch are not alone in their critique of the notion of the nation. How should we define it? The field of nationalism studies is immense, with several important studies in the field published in the 1980s, including Ernest Gellner's *Nations and Nationalism* (1983) and Benedict Anderson's *Imagined Communities: Reflections on the Origin and Spread of Nationalism* (1983). In his famous comparative study on small nations in Europe, *Social Preconditions of National Revival in Europe: A Comparative Analysis of Patriotic Groups among Smaller European Nations* (1968, 1985), Miroslav Hroch formulated some essential characteristics of nation-building. These included, firstly, a memory of a common past; secondly, linguistic and cultural ties; and, thirdly,

---

15   Édouard Glissant, *Poetics of Relation* (Ann Arbor: University of Michigan Press, 1997), p. 11.
16   Jani Marjanen, 'Undermining Methodological Nationalism. *Histoire croisée* of Concepts as Transnational History', in *Transnational Political Spaces. Agents – Structures – Encounters*, ed. by Mathias Albert/Gesa Bluhm/Jan Helmig/Andreas Leutzsch/Jochen Walter (Frankfurt/Main, New York: Campus, 2009) (Historische Politikforschung 18), pp. 239–263 (p. 239).

a feeling of equality of all members.[17] Hroch also emphasized the importance of literature and language for nations.

It is difficult to ignore the significance of nation, place, ethnicity, language, and identity to oral literature and storytelling, as well as to written and published/digitalized/performed literature. The meaning of mobility, migration and flight are also indispensable, with cultural transfer taking place in relation to all these markers of position.

3.3 World Literature

In a literary transnational space, shared memory of a common past, as well as linguistic and cultural ties, and the feeling of equality of all members of a nation exist in a mobile, transitional zone and might be transferred to other spaces. Is there a continuity of thinking in a transnational literary space and does world literature exist? According to Casanova, '[i]nternational literary space was formed in the sixteenth century at the very moment when literature began to figure as a source of contention in Europe, and it has not ceased to enlarge and extend itself since'.[18] It goes without saying that the point of departure here is the European region and its geopolitical ties. Chinese literature, for example, has a tradition that began more than three thousand years ago, with poetry the dominant genre and many poets still remembered. For example, in a park in the city of Chengdu, a certain area is dedicated to the poetess Xue Tao (AD 768–831). Although Casanova describes China as a 'completely neglected area' (151), at least until the year 2000 when the Nobel Prize in Literature was awarded to Gao Xingjian, she does not give more extensive attention to Chinese literature in her work. A reflection on the types of literature, whether philosophical Confucian literature, religious texts or historical texts, as well as a long era of imitation, could have added another dimension to the debate about what constitutes literature. The notion of world literature is thus indeed a highly Western-oriented concept.

---

17 Miroslav Hroch, *Social Preconditions of National Revival in Europe. A Comparative Analysis of the Social Composition of Patriotic Groups Among the Smaller European Nations* (Cambridge: Cambridge University Press, 1985), p. 79.
18 Pascale Casanova, *The World Republic of Letters* (Cambridge: Harvard University Press, 2004), p. 11.

Other scholars have criticized the notion of world literature, arguing that there is a great deal of literature that has not been translated. In her challenging book, *Against World Literature: On the Politics of Untranslatability* (2013), Emily Apter discusses several world literature perspectives, approaches and practices, and presents the hypothesis "that translation and untranslatability are constitutive of world forms of literature".[19] Apter endorses 'World Literature's deprovincialization of the canon and the way in which, at its best, it draws on translation to deliver surprising cognitive landscapes hailing from inaccessible linguistic folds' (2). Apter thus takes translation as a point of departure; as a prerequisite for the concept of world literature.

The term "world literature" has its origins in the nineteenth century. Most famously, it was used by Goethe in 1827 in his diary and in an essay written while reading a translation of Chinese poetry.[20] It appears that Goethe's notion of world literature was inspired by the increasing number of non-European works available in translation and was thus, according to Said, a "German" version of Orientalism (1978). As Yi Chen demonstrates in "Who is the Other? Goethe's encounter with 'China' in his concept of *Weltliteratur*" (2015), Goethe's perspective is complicated and ambivalent; nevertheless, on the basis of a comparative analysis, Yi Chen comes to the conclusion that Goethe still situates intellectual authority in the Western canon, 'despite his insightful and intuitive understanding of Chinese aesthetic qualities' (251). Thus, at the core of Goethe's concept of world literature is 'the realization of the West's own classic exemplariness' (ibid.).

In the twentieth century, early French comparatists such as Paul Van Tieghem took a step further, not only reflecting on the concept of world literature but also defining a new approach to world literatures as the study of comparative literature.

> Elle ne prétendra nullement remplacer les diverses histoires littéraires nationales : elle les complétera et les unira ; et en même temps elle tissera, entre elles et au-dessus d'elles, les mailles d'une histoire littéraire plus génerale. Cette discipline existe ; elle fait l'object de ce livre; elle s'appelle la *Littérature comparée*.
> VAN TIEGHEM 1931, p. 17

---

19   Emily Apter, *Against World Literature. On the Politics of Untranslatability* (New York, London: Verso Books, 2013), p. 16.

20   Yi Chen, 'Who is the Other? Goethe's Encounter with "China" in his Concept of Weltliteratur' in *Major Versus Minor? Languages and Literatures in a Globalized World*, ed. by Theo D'haen/Iannis Goerlandt/Roger D. Sell (Amsterdam, Philadelphia: John Benjamins, 2015), pp. 241–252 (p. 242).

(It does not pretend to replace the various national literary histories: it will complement and unite them; and at the same time, it will weave between them and above them, the mesh of a general literary history. This discipline exists; it is the object of this book; it is called Comparative Literature.)

Van Tieghem calls for a general literary history. The term 'tissera' (literally 'will weave') reminds us of 'croisée', used in the notion 'histoire croisée' that was introduced in 2002 by Werner and Zimmermann in a similar context. In the chapter "Vers l'histoire littéraire internationale" (Towards an international literary history), Van Tieghem discusses similar literary histories that had already been published in the nineteenth and early-twentieth centuries, such as Georg Brandes' *Main Currents in the Literature of the Nineteenth Century* (published in four volumes in Danish between 1872 and 1875 and in in English from 1901–1905) and *Europas litteraturhistoria från medeltiden till våra dagar I–II*, by Otto Sylvan and Just Bing in 1910 (202–203). He also presents an outline of what he regards as a true international literary history:

> La combinaison des influences et les traditions avec les diversités irréductibles des esprits et des races fait jaillir des qualités d'âme demeurées jusqu'alors latentes. Et ce n'est pas un des moindres privilèges de l'histoire littéraire ainsi conçue, que de nous faire mieux connaître à nous-mêmes, d'agrandir et d'enrichir notre idée de l'âme humaine.
> VAN TIEGHEM 1931, p. 17

(The combination of influences and traditions with the irreducible diversity of minds and races allows qualities of the soul to emerge that hitherto remained latent. And it is not one of the lesser privileges of literary history thus conceived that it allows us to better know ourselves, to expand and enrich our idea of the human soul.)

Thus, Van Tieghem sees the writing of a world literary history as a romantic, moralistic, and psychological undertaking. Another, later example of a comparatist working in another linguistic area is the Slovak Dionýz Ďurišin. In his study from 1972, he offers an overview of comparative literature studies, referring to Paul Van Tieghem as one of the scholars who attempted to understand 'den eigentlichen interliterarischen Prozeß' (the actual interliterary process).[21] Ďurišin discusses the term "world literature" and presents three

---

21   Dionýz Ďurišin, *Vergleichende Literaturforschung* (Berlin: Akademie-Verlag, 1972), p. 41.

basic interpretations: 1) world literature as a summary of the literature of the entire world and thus all the national literatures side by side; 2) world literature as the canon of the best literature produced by the separate national literatures; and 3) world literature as "irgendwie voneinander abhängige oder ähnliche Schöpfungen aus allen Nationalliteraturen" (somehow interdependent or similar creations that come from all national literatures) (1972, p. 39).

According to Ďurišin, the first interpretation is merely static in nature and does not include the idea of an interweaving of literatures. In this regard, it might be argued that Ďurišin expresses an early form of the *histoire croisée* idea. In the second interpretation, terms such as 'übernational' and 'universal' are used, and Ďurišin points out that from this point of view, the essential national characteristics of the literary works are not sufficiently considered. Thus, he argues that the third notion is the most appropriate for comparative literature studies because it includes all literary expressions that exhibit mutual relationships and connections, as well as being genetically and typologically related (p. 40).

Paul Van Tieghem and Ďurišin, as well as others, all argue for more focus on cultural transmitters. While Apter and Casanova present inspiring studies in this respect, they do not offer any deep insight into the cultural transfer process. What phases do literary texts pass through as they travel from the source area to the target area? What characteristics and skills does the cultural transmitter need? A micro-analysis of the cultural transfer process and the skills of the figures involved may give us valuable insight and serve as a supplement to the distant reading of the flows. Moreover, if the material is stored in databases, a more profound picture of the why and by whom might also be discerned.

In this respect, Espagne proposes the study of cultural transfer between places on the level of Mikroräume (micro places), arguing that this could create the foundations of a European cultural history (p. 31). I prefer to use the terms 'phases' or 'steps', which can be situated in certain places but might also include people and the temporal dimension. According to scholars like Matthias Middell (2014), Cultural Transfer Studies focuses on three moments: contact with another culture, research on the mediators (translators, institutions and media), and the new context of the text.[22] This approach has been applied by Christine Mayer (2019) and others.[23]

---

22   Matthias Middell, 'The Search for a New Place for the 18th Century in Global History Narratives', in *Cultural Transfers, Encounters and Connections in the Global 18th Century*, ed. by Matthias Middell (Leipzig: Leipziger Universitätsverlag, 2014), pp. 7–43.
23   Christine Mayer, 'The Transnational and Transcultural. Approaches to Studying the Circulation and Transfer of Educational Knowledge', in *The Transnational in the History*

Espagne's 'prozessualen Ablauf' can in fact be divided into six phases, some of which may be skipped or combined depending on the actual steps taken:

1. The phase of introduction: After the "discovery", the cultural transmitter reviews a literary work, publishes interviews with the author or publishes other introductory texts. Proof translations might be made and the material may or may not be published. One example in this respect: the Finnish-Swedish literary critic, writer and translator, Hagar Olsson (1893–1978) stated that in the 1920s she read one poem by the Dutch writer and politician, Henriette Roland Holst-Van der Schalk (1869–1952) in Finnish translation. We still do not know which poem this was, who translated it, or the medium it took; this material is lost.[24]

2. In the second phase, the selected author is "in quarantine". A cultural transmitter attempts to find an interested publisher or another way to publish the work and proof translations may circulate. The writer and lecturer in Dutch literature in Sweden, Martha A. Muusses (1894–1981), tried to introduce Henriette Roland Holst-Van der Schalk to the Swedish public but the poems she translated were only published in her own publications. A large publishing house such as Bonniers never published a collection of poems. (ibid.)

3. In the third phase, the author's work is translated. The translation is an important event in the process. However, it can also imply a new phase of "quarantine": will the translation be published? A fine example is the Swedish writer, Kerstin Ekman, whose international breakthrough came with the novel *Blackwater* (published in Swedish in 1993, in Dutch in 1994, and in English in 1996). Prior to this, in 1984 and 1985, two of her novels were published in Dutch and a third was translated, but because of a lack of commercial success the Dutch publisher decided not to publish the latter. After the bestselling success of *Blackwater* in the Netherlands, this novel from the 1980s was finally published in Dutch – translated anew by another translator – fourteen years later in 1998.[25]

---

of Education. Global Histories of Education, ed. by Eckhardt Fuchs/Vera E. Roldán (Cham: Palgrave Macmillan, 2019), pp. 49–68.

24 Petra Broomans, 'A Cultural Transfer History. Possibilities and Prerequisities. The Case of Henriette Roland Holst, Martha Muusses and Hagar Olsson', in *The Dynamics and Contexts of Cultural Transfers. An Anthology*, ed. by Margaretha Fahlgren/Anna Williams (Uppsala: Uppsala University, 2017) pp. 79–99 (p. 91).

25 Petra Broomans/Ester Jiresch, 'The Invasion of Books' in *The Invasion of Books in Peripheral Literary Fields. Transmitting Preferences and Images in Media, Networks and Translation. Studies on Cultural Transfer and Transmission (CTaT)*, ed. by Petra Broomans/Ester Jiresch (Groningen: Barkhuis Publishing, 2011), vol. 3, pp. 9–21 (pp. 12–13).

4. The translation is published. Is the translator mentioned and visible?
5. The translation might be bought and read, but not reviewed. Cultural transmitters might actively inform journalists and reviewers. The material used might be letters, meetings, and conversations on social media.
6. In the final phase, the literary work undergoes a second phase of reception in the form of reviews, articles, lectures, and so forth. It is due to this follow up that we can speak of a successful cultural transfer. The transmitter might become visible and receive awards and/or translation prizes.

Henriette Roland Holst-Van der Schalk never came to be known in Sweden or Finland, although her cultural transmitters, Martha A. Muusses and Hagar Olsson, both had cultural capital. Hagar Olsson was as a central figure in the literary debate in Finland, while Muusses lectured in Dutch literature in Stockholm in the 1930s, in Gothenburg the 1940s, and, from 1947, in Uppsala. She acted as literary critic and historian, translator, and cultural transmitter (in both directions, Dutch-Swedish/Swedish-Dutch). Furthermore, she was regarded as an authority in the field of Dutch literature and was an advisor to the Swedish Academy. Muusses also wrote articles and essays on Dutch literature and compiled a Dutch literary history in Swedish and, in addition, she was also a poet. While cultural transmitters have not always been visible and active in the various phases of cultural transfer, it is clear that both Olsson and Muusses held various positions and were visible cultural transmitters. (Broomans, 2017: 91).

3.4 Forgotten Scholars

As mentioned above, both Paul Van Tieghem and Ďurišin discuss the concept of the cultural transmitter and the process of cultural transfer, emphasizing that literary mediators should be studied. So the development of Cultural Transfer Studies in recent decades has had some forefathers who have been forgotten. Naturally, we could also mention Madame de Staël, who wrote *De l'Allemagne* (1810) and introduced the ideas of German Romanticism to the French and European public. To a certain extent, she also paved the way for comparative literature studies. The example of Madame de Staël demonstrates that cultural transmitters are important to literary history, not only because they mediate and translate an important part of the literature that readers consume (sometimes not even aware that they are reading a translation), but also because they have profound knowledge about the society and culture in which the source text was produced.

Peter Burke has defined two different categories of cultural transmitters: groups and individuals. In the period he investigated – the sixteenth and seventeenth centuries – translations were produced within professional groups: scholars translated scholars, lawyers translated lawyers, and so on. Other professional groups included diplomats and emigrants. Michel Espagne studied the eighteenth and nineteenth centuries and observed that members of the merchant class, the Jewish community and language teachers also acted as cultural transmitters. In 2006 Espagne remarked once again that foreign cultural imports cannot be realized without mediators and that it seems to be 'eine Konstante der Kulturgeschichte' (an unchangeable feature of cultural studies) that this mediation is always neglected (Espagne 2006, p. 24).

On the basis of my investigations of cultural transmitters in the nineteenth and twentieth centuries, I have formulated a working definition. I prefer the term "cultural transmitter" and not "literary transmitter" because, through literature, there is also a mediation of culture: translations are instruments that mediate ideas/ideologies/images from one cultural/linguistic area to another. Moreover, cultural transmitters are actors in a transnational space, and ideas and images travel through time and across borders. Thus, I propose the following definition:

> A cultural transmitter or mediator basically works within a particular language and cultural area. She/he often takes on various roles in the field of cultural transfer: translator, reviewer, critic, journalist, (literary) historian, scholar, teacher, librarian, bookseller, collector, literary agent, scout, publisher, editor of a journal, writer, travel writer, counsellor, or even businessman. Transmitting another national literature and culture, and its cultural context to one's own national literature and cultural context is the central issue in the work of a cultural transmitter. Transmission often reflects a bilateral situation. Even the transmission of one's own literature and culture takes place. The motivation can be aesthetically, ideologically, politically and/or economically based.[26]

All these different roles, functions and positions in different periods demonstrate that the concept of the cultural transmitter is dynamic. This is also apparent in Anthony Pym's description of translators: they do more than

---

26 I have elaborated on this working definition on the basis of previous articles (e.g. 2006, 2009).

translate, they have personal interests and preferences, they can move, and they have their own names that we should respect.[27]

As mentioned above, Espagne argues for an interdisciplinary approach and that the material evidence, the space of transfer, and a focus on transmitters should be included in studies of cultural transmission. Regarding the material, cultural transmitters use it, produce it and leave it behind during the cultural transfer process. A study of such material might tell us more about the people who used it and about their position in networks; however, this material often disappears or is lost in archives. This can be regarded as a reflection of the neglected and underestimated position of the cultural transmitter. This concerns especially women cultural transmitters. Luise von Flotow (1997),[28] Susanne Stark (1999)[29] and Michaela Wolf (2005) among others, wrote about forgotten women translators in the past. To locate these 'lost' translators requires historical research and finding material.

There are also different categories of material: concrete and virtual. Concrete material consists of physical and visible objects, such as manuscripts, awards (medals), images. In this respect, for example, we still have no clear picture of Muusses on the basis of such material. Virtual material can refer to lost objects, whether hidden away in archives or destroyed, but also invisible elements, such as characteristics of transmitters, their language skills, knowledge of the culture, and so on. (Broomans 2017, p. 82). Thus, it is not only people, knowledge, and culture that are involved in transfer, but the material as well, and the rediscovery of unknown or not yet located material in archives is essential for Cultural Transfer Studies.

One example of figures lost to the discipline are the forefathers of Cultural Transfer Studies discourse itself. I have observed that in the works of Espagne, Werner, Sapiro, Pym and many others, including my own work to date, no references are made to early comparatists such as Paul Van Tieghem. Therefore, let us ask explicitly what they have written about cultural transfer, cultural transmitters, and world literature.

Paul Van Tieghem (1871–1948) writes about cultural transmitters in a chapter entitled, "Les intermédiaires", in his study *La Littérature comparée* (1931). Here he defines the following categories of cultural transmitters:

---

27   Anthony Pym, 'Translators', in *Method in Translation History* (Manchester: St Jerome, 1998), pp. 160–176 (p. 176).
28   Luise von Flotow, *Translating and Gender. Translating in the 'Era of Feminism'* (Ottawa: University of Ottawa Press, 1997).
29   Susanne Stark, *'Behind inverted commas'. Translation and Anglo-German Cultural Relations in the Nineteenth Century* (Clevedon, Philadelphia, Toronto, Sydney: Multilingual Matters Ltd., 1999) (Topics in Translation 15).

1. "Les individus" (individuals): he mentions the traveller Xavier Marmier and Carl Chr. Gjörwell, who started the journal of literary criticism, *Den Svenska Mercurius* (*The Swedish Mercury*), in the eighteenth century.
2. "Les milieux sociaux" (literary groups, associations, salons): he mentions the Swedish authors Hedvig Charlotta Nordenflycht and Anna Maria Lenngren, and Madame de Staël among others.
3. "Critiques: journaux et revues" (literary criticism: newspapers and journals).
4. "Traductions et traducteurs" (translations and translators) (152–167).

The wide range of names Van Tieghem mentions shows that he was familiar with both central and peripheral cultures (such as the Scandinavian). Van Tieghem states that we should learn more about the cultural transmitters, "il est souvent besoin de connaître les *traducteurs*" (it is often necessary to know the translators), we need to learn about their biographies, literary careers and social positions (166). This is what Espagne, Meylaerts, and Sapiro argued for much later. Reine Meylaerts argued for the need to study the 'socio-biography' of the cultural transmitter: their life, the linguistic and cultural environment and their networks.[30] Sapiro even suggests this is a new domain. However, it should be added that Meylaerts and Sapiro do not refer to early comparatists such as Paul Van Tieghem, or scholars such as Burke and Espagne. We might say that there was no "prefiguring" of the field of Cultural Transfer Studies to use White's term. We pursued, perhaps unconsciously, the plot of neglect, as I would formulate it. Why Paul Van Tieghem was forgotten in the field of Cultural Transfer could be an interesting topic to examine in more detail. He published many works regarding international literary history which were often translated, yet he was not a professor at university, but a secondary school teacher. In the French context, this may explain why he found less recognition among scholars than he deserves.

If one was to present an overview of scholars who have dealt with cultural transfer, we would observe three groups. Interestingly, the first two groups do not refer to each other, nor does either refer to the third group.

1. Translation studies scholars such as Venuti and Pym, and sociologists oriented towards translation studies such as Heilbron and Sapiro.
2. Scholars related to cultural studies who are also concerned with transfer, such as Burke and Espagne.
3. The early comparatists: the forgotten cultural transfer scholars such as Van Tieghem.

---

30   Reine Meylaerts, 'Habitus and self-image of native literary author-translators in diglossic societies', in *Translation and Interpreting Studies*, 5/1 (2010), pp. 1–19.

The method Paul Van Tieghem proposes is "mésologie" (mesology), the study of how a culture receives literary works, ideas and forms that belong to another culture. As a son of the well-known botanist Philippe Édouard Leon Van Tieghem (1839–1914), Paul Van Tieghem derived the term from the discipline of biology, in particular its study of the interrelationships between creatures and their surroundings.[31] His son, Philippe Von Tieghem, added "flair" as another skill that the cultural transmitter should have: the ability to discover new authors, to trace what should be transmitted, and what might provide a new impulse to the culture from elsewhere. The transmitter should thus have an open mind towards other cultures (1961, p. 4).

As his father pointed out, this sensitivity to something new also requires profound knowledge about one's own culture. The above-mentioned Ďurišin also argued for a more profound study of the role of the cultural transmitter (1972, 61) and divided cultural transfer into two categories: 1. "Einfach", that is, not complex, such as academic studies and reviews; and 2. complex cultural transfer, that is, translations. Ďurišin regards a translation as an important expression of an 'interliterary symbiosis' (65) and focuses in his study on translations. His approach can be compared with Even-Zohar. Worth noting here is that both published their theories in 1972. Of interest are Ďurišin's remarks on national myths, quoting the Czech scholar, K. Krejčí:

> Die Völker schaffen sich über sich, wie auch über andere Völker fiktiv komplexe Vorstellungen, die zwar aus der Wirklichkeit stammen und sie fragmentarisch erfassen, sie jedoch unter dem Einfluss verschiedener Umstände stilisieren, mehr oder weniger definieren.
> ĎURIŠIN 1972, p. 55

> (The people create fictionally complex ideas about themselves, as well as about other peoples, which, although derived from reality and presented in a fragmented way, are stylized under the influence of circumstances and are more or less defined.)

The myths and stereotypes of other cultures and nations are now studied within the field of imagology, developed by Joep Leerssen and Manfred Beller among others.[32] Thus, we could also add the field of imagology to the disciplines that are relevant to Cultural Transfer Studies.

---

31 Margareta Dubois, *Algot Ruhe. Kulturförmedlare och europeisk visionär* (Lund: Lund University Press, 1989), p. 6.
32 Manfred Beller/Joep Leerssen (eds.), *Imagology. The Cultural Construction and Literary Representation of National Characters; a Critical Survey* (Amsterdam: Rodopi, 2007) (Studia Imagologica, 13).

Although the early comparatists such as Paul Van Tieghem argued that more attention should be paid to cultural transmitters, they did not develop a deeper instrument to analyse and investigate the positions and backgrounds of the actors and the process. As I have demonstrated, the field of Cultural Transfer Studies is interwoven with various disciplines: literary history, *histoire croisée*, the sociology of literature, translation studies, and cultural studies. We might, through Ďurišin to Leerssen, now complete the list with imagology. Concerning methodology, the discipline will also benefit to a large extent from the instruments and opportunities offered by the digital humanities. In the light of this, where, then, do we position cultural transmitters in relation to transnational literary history?

3.5 Plots

It goes without saying that transnational literary historians will have to make a decision. Will they consider cultural transmitters as the invisible bridges between different languages or will they present them as a visible "power"? There are also other agendas. The rewriting of literary history with the aim of including women, as well as ethnic and minority groups, requires a critical rereading of the sources (the debates in various media, archives, etc.). This also demands the collection and digitalization of the material, and the design of databases is also of fundamental importance.

Another question is the position of the peripheral language versus dominant central literatures. As Olsson wrote, Roland Holst was unknown in Finland and Sweden; however, 'if RH had written in a central language she would have become "famous" and "one of Europe's leading intellectuals"'.[33] This is a fine example of the problem of cross language borders in a modern world and further evidence that it is always easier for writers of central languages. Digging through archives and scrutinizing journals makes it possible to map more of the connections between different peripheral languages as well as between central and peripheral languages. This would open up a more diverse and layered transnational literary history conducted in a contextualizing mode.

I would like to conclude with a note on the results of a meta-literary analysis of entries in two translators' encyclopaedias, a genre within Cultural Transfer Studies that will generate material for transnational literary history. One of the goals of these translators' encyclopaedias is to make forgotten cultural transmitters visible. The content of the entries in these encyclopaedias usually concerns an overview of facts; for example, a list of translations and the life story

---

33   Hagar Olsson, 'Ljuset från Holland', in *Samtid och Framtid*, (Stockholm: Natur och kultur, 1945), p. 15.

of the cultural transmitter. However, aspects such as "habitus" (Bourdieu), self-image, and "self-fashioning" (Stephen Greenblatt) are also important in the presentation of the motives of the cultural transmitter and their literary preferences. We need to understand why a cultural transmitter selects a certain author and why they translate certain texts and not others. On the basis of an investigation of the entries, I came to the conclusion that plots are used and they are supported by strings: the metaphors of the pioneer, the discoverer, and the explorer (Broomans, 2016). The clerk metaphor is not used. Without doubt, a meta-literary historical understanding is essential when writing transnational literary history.

Bibliography

Apter, Emily, *Against World Literature. On the Politics of Untranslatability* (New York, London: Verso Books, 2013).

Beller, Manfred/Leerssen, Joep (eds.), *Imagology. The Cultural Construction and Literary Representation of National Characters. A Critical Survey* (Amsterdam: Rodopi, 2007) (Studia Imagologica, 13).

Bloom, Harold, *The Western Canon.The School and the Books of Ages* (New York, San Diego, London: Harcourt Brace & Company, 1994).

Broomans, Petra, 'A Cultural Transfer History. Possibilities and Prerequisities. The Case of Henriette Roland Holst, Martha Muusses and Hagar Olsson', in *The Dynamics and Contexts of Cultural Transfers. An Anthology*, ed. by Margaretha Fahlgren/Anna Williams (Uppsala: Uppsala University, 2017), pp. 79–99.

Broomans, Petra, 'Vergessener Held oder dienender Handwerker. Zur Diskursstrategie in Übersetzerbiographien', in *Übersetzerforschung. Neue Beiträge zur Literatur- und Kulturgeschichte des Übersetzens*, ed. by Andreas F. Kelletat/Aleksey Tashinskiy/Julija Boguna (Berlin: Frank & Timmer, 2016), pp. 255–264.

Broomans, Petra, 'Zichtbaar in de canon. Spelregels voor cultuurbemiddelaars', in *Tijdschrift voor Nederlandse Taal- en Letterkunde*, 128/3-4 (2012), pp. 256–275.

Broomans, Petra, 'Introduction. Women as Transmitters of Ideas', in *From Darwin to Weil. Women as Transmitters if Ideas. Studies on Cultural Transfer and Transmission (CTaT)*, ed. by Petra Broomans (Groningen: Barkhuis Publishing, 2009) vol. 1, pp. 1–20.

Broomans, Petra, 'Om vårt sätt att forska i kulturförmedling. Exempel: Marie Herzfeld (1855–1940)', in *Der Norden im Ausland – das Ausland im Norden. Formung und Transformation von Konzepten und Bildern des Anderen vom Mittelalter bis heute*, ed. by Sven H. Rossel (Wien: Praesens Verlag, 2006) (Wiener Studien zur Skandinavistik, 15), pp. 201–210.

Broomans, Petra, *Detta Är Jag. Stina Aronsons Litteraturhistoriska Öde* (Stockholm: Carlsson, 2001).

Broomans, Petra/Ester Jiresch, 'The Invasion of Books', in *The Invasion of Books in Peripheral Literary Fields. Transmitting Preferences and Images in Media, Networks and Translation. Studies on Cultural Transfer and Transmission (CTaT)*, ed. by Petra Broomans/Ester Jiresch (Groningen: Barkhuis Publishing, 2011), vol. 3, pp. 9–21.

Burke, Peter, *Lost (and Found) in Translation: A Cultural History of Translators and Translating in Early Modern Europe* (Wassenaar: NIAS, 2005). https://nias.knaw.nl/wp-content/uploads/2018/01/KB_01_Peter-Burke.pdf

Casanova, Pascale, *The World Republic of Letters* (Cambridge: Harvard University Press, 2004).

Chen, Yi, 'Who is the Other? Goethe's Encounter with "China" in his Concept of *Weltliteratur*', in *Major Versus Minor? Languages and Literatures in a Globalized World*, ed. by Theo D'haen/Iannis Goerlandt/Roger D. Sell (Amsterdam, Philadelphia: John Benjamins, 2015), pp. 241–252.

Deleuze, Gilles/Guattari, Félix, 'What is a Minor Literature?', in *Kafka. Towards a Minor Literature*, by Gilles Deleuze/Félix Guattari (Minneapolis, London: University of Minnesota Press, 1986), pp. 16–27.

Dubois, Margareta, *Algot Ruhe. Kulturförmedlare och europeisk visionär* (Lund: Lund University Press, 1989).

Ďurišin, Dionýz, *Vergleichende Literaturforschung* (Berlin: Akademie-Verlag, 1972).

Espagne, Michel, 'Jenseits der Komparatistik. Zur Methode der Erforschung von Kulturtransfer', in *Europäische Kulturzeitschriften um 1900 als Medien transnationaler und transdisziplinärer Wahrnehmung*, ed. by Ulrich Mölk (Göttingen: Vandenhoeck & Ruprecht, 2006), pp. 13–32.

Espagne, Michel/Werner, Michael, 'La construction d'une référence culturelle allemande en France. Genèse et histoire (1750–1914)', in *Annales. Histoire, Sciences Sociales*, 42/4 (1987), pp. 969–992. http://www.jstor.org/stable/27583612.

Espagne, Michel/Werner, Michael, 'Deutsch-Französischer Kulturtransfer im 18. und 19. Jahrhundert. Zu einem neuen Interdiszplinären Forschungsprogramm des C.N.R.S.', in *Francia. Forschungen zur westeuropäischen Geschichte*, 13/1 (1985), pp. 502–510.

Flotow, Luise von, *Translating and gender. Translating in the 'Era of Feminism'* (Manchester, Ottawa: Routledge, 1997).

Glissant, Édouard, *Poetics of Relation* (Ann Arbor University of Michigan Press, 1997).

Hroch, Miroslav, *Social Preconditions of National Revival in Europe. A Comparative Analysis of the Social Composition of Patriotic Groups Among the Smaller European Nations* (Cambridge: Cambridge University Press, 1985).

Marjanen, Jani, 'Undermining methodological nationalism. *Histoire croisée* of Concepts as Transnational History', in *Transnational Political Spaces. Agents – Structures – Encounters*, ed. by Mathias Albert/Gesa Bluhm/Jan Helmig/Andreas Leutzsch/Jochen Walter (Frankfurt/Main, New York: Campus 2009) (Historische Politikforschung 18), pp. 239–263.

Mayer, Christine, 'The Transnational and Transcultural. Approaches to Studying the Circulation and Transfer of Educational Knowledge', in *The Transnational in the History of Education. Global Histories of Education*, ed. by Eckhardt Fuchs/Eugenia Roldán Vera (Cham: Palgrave Macmillan, 2019), pp. 49–68.

Meylaerts, Reine, 'Habitus and Self-image of Native Literary Author-translators in Diglossic Societies', in *Translation and Interpreting Studies*, 5/1 (2010), pp. 1–19.

Middell, Matthias, 'The Search for a New Place for the 18th Century in Global History Narratives', in *Cultural Transfers, Encounters and Connections in the Global 18th. Century*, ed. by Matthias Middell (Leipzig: Leipziger Universitätsverlag, 2014), pp. 7–43.

Moretti, Franco, *Graphs, Maps, Trees. Abstract Models for a Literary History* (London, New York: Verso, 2005).

Moretti, Franco, 'Conjectures on world literature', in *New Left Review*, 1 (2000), pp. 54–68.

Olsson, Hagar, 'Ljuset från Holland', in *Samtid och Framtid* (Stockholm: Natur och kultur, 1945), pp. 15–19.

Perkins, David, *Is Literary History Possible?* (Baltimore, London: Johns Hopkins University Press, 1992).

Pym, Anthony, 'Translators', in *Method in Translation History* (Manchester: St Jerome, 1998), pp. 160–176.

Sapiro, Gisèle, 'The Sociology of Translation. A New Research Domain', in *A Companion to Translation Studies*, ed. by Sandra Bermann/Catherine Porter (New York: John Wily & Sons, 2014), pp. 82–94.

Snell-Hornby, Mary, *Turns of Translation Studies. New Paradigms or Shifting Viewpoints?* (Amsterdam, Philadelphia: John Benjamins Publishing Company, 2006).

Stark, Susanne, *'Behind inverted commas'. Translation and Anglo-German Cultural Relations in the Nineteenth Century* (Clevedon, Philadelphia, Toronto, Sydney: Multilingual Matters Ltd, 1999).

Van Tieghem, Paul, *La Littérature comparée* (Paris: Libraire Armand Colin, 1931).

Van Tieghem, Philippe Édouard Léon, *Les influences étrangères sur la littérature Française 1550–1880* (Paris: Presses Universitaires de France, 1961).

Welsch, Wolfgang, 'Transculturality. The Puzzling Form of Cultures Today', in *Spaces of Culture. City, Nation, World*, ed. by Mike Featherstone/Scott Lash (London: Sage, 1999), pp. 194–213.

Werner, Michael/Bénédicte Zimmermann, 'Vergleich, Transfer, Verflechtung. Der Ansatz der *Histoire croisée* und die Herausforderung des Transnationalen', in *Geschichte und Gesellschaft*, 28/4 (2002), pp. 607–636.

White, Hayden, *Metahistory. The Historical Imagination in Nineteenth-century Europe* (Baltimore: The Johns Hopkins University Press, 1973).

Wolf, Michaela, 'Introduction. The Emergence of a Sociology of Translation', in *Constructing a Sociology of Translation*, ed. by Michaela Wolf/Alexandra Fukari (Amsterdam, Philadelphia: John Benjamins Publishing Company, 2007), pp. 1–36.

Wolf, Michaela, 'The Creation of A "Room of One's Own". Feminist Translators as Mediators Between Cultures and Genders', in *Gender, Sex and Translation. The Manipulations of Identities*, ed. by José Santaemilia (Manchester, Northampton: Routledge, 2005), pp. 15–25.

Wolf, Michaela/Fukari, Alexandra, *Constructing a Sociology of Translation* (Amsterdam, Philadelphia: John Benjamins Publishing Company, 2007).

CHAPTER 4

Representations of Brittany in Norwegian and Finnish Women's Paintings: How French Realism and Naturalism Took Over Nordic Art and Contributed to Renew Finnish and Norwegian Painting at the End of the 19th Century

Anne-Estelle Leguy

Abstract

This article aims to demonstrate the relevance of notion of "cultural transfer" and "hybridity" in the field of art history, and accordingly challenges the "centre" and "periphery" paradigm that is held to account for global trends in art history and its official canons.

At the end of the nineteenth century, most Nordic female and male artists travelled to France to complete their artistic education, many of which were to make significant contributions to their home countries' respective histories of art at the turn of the twentieth century. Most of these artists are not particularly famous outside Nordic countries and specialist circles – despite the fact that, over the past thirty years, many travelling exhibitions featuring "the Light of the North" have been organised in Europe or in North America.[1]

Nordic research has single-handedly undertaken to study the artistic paths of these artists and how they adopted the aesthetic values of Paris to create their own take on the various schools that constitute pictorial modernity and forge their national variations.[2] So far, these artists have been largely disregarded by continental art historians. This is mostly because these historians still

---

1   With the exception of a few names such as Edvard Munch (1863–1944) from Norway, whose production tends to overshadow his Nordic colleagues, or Vilhelm Hammershøi (1864–1916) from Denmark, whose art stands apart from the main aesthetic trends of the time.
2   In the middle of the 19th century, Nordic artists went mostly to Germany or Denmark to complete their artistic education. From the 1860s, partly because of the 1864 war between Germany and Denmark and partly because of the latest French pictorial evolutions, they began to travel to Paris. The 1878 Universal Exhibition in Paris played also a decisive role.

follow the "centre" and "periphery" paradigm, in conjunction with the dominant avant-garde approach, according to which innovation stems from the rejection of the past by a central "avant-garde" that "dominates" lesser, peripheral trends. The avant-garde approach is itself derived from a traditional pictorial modernity narrative, dating back to France, Germany, and Russia at the turn of the twentieth century, in which avant-garde artists promoted a succession of innovative trends. Inevitably, this dismisses the local variations present in geographical peripheries. This paradigm still structures the discourse of art history, even if it is increasingly disputed.

In contrast, Nordic research breaks free from this traditional "centre" and "periphery" approach, by insisting on exchange, mutual influences, interrelation, circulation, transfer, hybridation of ideas, aesthetic standards and values, pictorial experimentations, to name but a few.[3] These new analytic tools enable Nordic art historians to show that the artists they support have the makings of international painters.

This article provides an example of how the notion of "cultural transfer" can be deployed in the field of art history and challenges the "centre and periphery" paradigm. For this purpose, it focuses on women artists from Norway and Finland. According to the "centre and periphery" approach, they are doubly disadvantaged as women, originating from small and distant countries which are isolated from a long pictorial tradition.

For the purpose of this analysis, I have selected the Norwegian women artists Harriet Backer (1845–1932) and Kitty Kielland (1843–1914),[4] the Finnish women artists Amélie Lundahl (1850–1914), Helene Schjerfbeck (1862–1946) and Helena Westermarck (1857–1938), to whom one could add their friends Maria Wiik (1853–1928) and Elin Danielson (1861–1919).[5] For all of these artists, sojourns in Paris and in Brittany (the coastal region in the Northwest of France) had a profound personal and artistic effect and subsequently made an impact on Norwegian and Finnish art history.

At the end of the 19th century, when a new "centre" of modernism grew in Germany, a great number of Nordic painters went also to Berlin to participate to these radical artistic debates.

3   See for example Hubert van Den Berg et al. (eds.), *A Cultural History of the Avant-Garde in the Nordic Countries 1900–1925* (Amsterdam, New York: Rodopi, 2012).

4   For an introduction to these two artists, see Marit Lange, 'Harriet Backer och Kitty Kielland I Paris på 1880-talet', in *De drogo till Paris: nordiska konstnärinnor på 1880 – talet* (Stockholm: Föreningen Norden, 1988), pp. 113–147.

5   For an introduction to these artists, see Riitta Konttinen, 'Finska konstnärinnors 1880-tal. Ljus, luft och färg. Elin Danielson, Amélie Lundahl, Helene Schjerfbeck, Helena Westermarck och Maria Wiik', in *De drogo till Paris, op. cit.*, pp. 221–253.

This piece will first highlight the significant role of teachers as intermediaries and connecting factors between Christiana (Oslo) or Helsingfors and Paris. Secondly, the article will give some examples of how painting in Brittany has exercised significant influence on the artistic evolution of these women painters and on the evolution of their home countries' art. Thirdly, it will give an insight into the reception of their Brittany works on national and international (i.e. Parisian) art scenes.

4.1 The Role of Teachers as Go-Betweens / Intermediary Agents

4.1.1 *Adolf von Becker (1831–1909) in Helsingfors*
As agents of "cultural transfer" in art history, teachers are critical to the circulation of ideas and aesthetic values.

In the case of Finnish women artists and their male colleagues, Adolf von Becker is a case in point. He was one of the first Finnish artists to travel to Paris to complete his artistic education, at a time when his colleagues usually went to Germany. Most Finnish artists born in the 1860s and 1870s went to Becker's private academy in Finland, and very much appreciated his teaching. What they valued most were his teaching methods, which were inspired by his own experiences as a Parisian student of Gustave Courbet (1819–1877), Édouard Frère (1819–1886), Léon Bonnat (1833–1922), and Thomas Couture (1815–1879). Adolf von Becker's methods were to teach his students the principles of French realism, make them familiar with the aesthetic debates of the time, and show them reproductions of French contemporary art. He convinced them of the importance of copying old masterpieces or more contemporary paintings in order to study their composition, interpret their effects, and undertake the challenge of copy from memory. He trained them also to master the "draft" or "sketch" technique, which insisted on composition and moderate use of colours over details, enabling his students to deliver a personal impression. Adolf von Becker also taught how to use a knife and a dynamic brush stroke in oil painting and how to combine the observation of nature with a simple and authentic representation of reality.

Interestingly, the painters whom Adolf von Becker referred to in his teaching did not really belong to the French avant-garde of the time. At the end of the 1870s, in France, Naturalism and Realism were becoming more or less mainstream compared to Impressionism,[6] whose subjects and techniques

---

6 Comparatively, Impressionism was les well received by Nordic artists than Realism and Naturalism or Symbolism and Synthetism later on. See for example *Impressionism and the*

were considered as more radical at that time. However in Finland, this was not yet the case – at the time, Naturalism and Realism were considered the height of modernity in pictorial practice.[7]

Through his teaching, Helene Schjerfbeck, Helena Westermarck, to speak of only women artists, became familiar with these methods and fitted happily in Paris when they travelled there at the beginning of the 1880s – having been encouraged to do so by von Becker.

Likewise, the cases of Harriet Backer and Kitty Kielland in Norway is also interesting. They received a more traditional education in Germany. Harriet Becker trained mostly in Munich (1874–1878) with a German teacher, Lambert Linder (1841–1889), and two Norwegians, Christian Meyer Ross (1843–1904) and Eilif Peterssen (1852–1928). Kitty Kielland trained in Karlsruhe, taught by the Norwegian Hans Fredrik Gude (1825–1903), and subsequently Munich, with Harriet Backer and Eilif Peterssen. Despite being older and more experienced than their Finnish colleagues when they came to Paris, they also succeeded in adapting to the French academies' rules without rejecting what they had learnt in Germany. For example, Harriet Backer repeated throughout her life that drawing was the only thing that truly mattered. This was what she was taught in Germany and what Léon Bonnat also wanted his students to be convinced of. Harriet Backer reckoned that German and French pictorial traditions shared some of the same principles.[8] The two friends headed for Paris in 1878 hoping for recognition by the Salon; they lived there for ten years, returning to Norway mainly in summer.

In contrast, the Dane Peder Severin Krøyer (1851–1909), who hadn't been introduced to such breakthroughs, remembers having been "frightened" (sic)

North. Late 19th Century French Avant-Garde Art and the Art in the Nordic Countries 1870–1920, (Stockholm: Nationalmuseum, 2002). According to the Swedish art historian Torsten Gunnarsson, Realism and Naturalism played in Nordic countries in the 1870s and 1880s the same role as Impressionism in France, giving rise to wide-ranging debates between Realism and Idealism followers, the latters originating from the German cultural legacy. The emergence of Symbolism renewed the Idealism's issues. (Torsten Gunnarsson, 'Impressionism and the North', in *Impressionism and the North, op. cit.*, pp. 8–45, (p. 19)).

7 In the beginning of the 1880s in Finland, Naturalism was perceived as dangerously linked to Darwinism and Socialism and, as such, exceeded the aesthetic challenges at stake, to be part of a more comprehensive social debate. (Riitta Konttinen, 'Finska konstnarinnors 1880-tal', *op. cit.*, p. 246).

8 Marit Lange, 'Les artistes norvégiens en Bretagne et en Normandie', in *Peintres du Nord en voyage dans l'Ouest. Modernité et impressionnisme 1860–1900* (Caen: Musée des Beaux-arts de Caen, 2001), pp. 100–106 (p. 100).

at the 1877 Salon, because of such a collection of "daubs, aberrations" and of "coarse, crude artistic feeling".[9]

4.1.2 Teachers in Paris

As can be expected, first-hand experience of an artists' life in Paris is also a critical factor for cultural transfers.

At the end of the nineteenth century, Paris attracted foreign artists mainly for two reasons: to achieve their artistic education and to attempt to exhibit a work of art at the annual Salon de Paris. The Salon remained at that time a very important event in the French and international artistic calendar, which drew attention from critics, public, collectors, art dealers, and official institutions. To be admitted to the Salon constituted the first step of an official career, especially if the work of art submitted received a prize.[10]

Norwegian and Finnish women artists who stayed in Paris often attended the Académie Julian, the Académie de Mme Trélat de Vigny, and the Académie Colarossi, all of which were open to women. The renowned Parisian École des Beaux-arts did not accept women until 1897, at the very moment of its decline as an influence on French artistic field. In these art schools, female artists could work like their male colleagues, with the same methods of teaching, working with live and partly nude models, which at that time was specific to French teaching. Nordic women artists benefitted greatly from this first-hand approach to anatomical study, which helped them meet their objective of being recognized as professional artists.[11] Interestingly, none of the teachers who came to correct their works such as Tony Robert-Fleury (1837–1911) and William Bouguereau (1825–1905) at the Académie Julian, Léon Bonnat, Jean-Léon Gérôme (1824–1904), and Jules Bastien-Lepage (1848–1884) at the Académie de Mme Trélat de Vigny, or Gustave Courtois (1852–1923), Raphaël Collin (1850–1916), and Jean-Charles Cazin (1841–1901) at the Académie Colarossi – could really be described as avant-garde, and Pierre Bourdieu would have characterised them as "established artists" in the artistic field.[12] Under their supervision, these women artists hoped to deepen their techniques and to have one of their pictures selected for exhibition at the Salon. Some of them

---

9   Peder Severin Krøyer, in a letter dated 9th July 1877. Quoted by Annette Johansen, 'Le périple français de Peder Severin Krøyer, 1877–1880', in *Peintres du Nord en voyage dans l'Ouest, op. cit.*, pp. 70–74.

10   International recognition at the Salon gave foreign artists more opportunities to receive scholarships and sell their paintings in their home countries.

11   For gender studies authors specialized in art history, unequal access to artistic skills reveals the male domination over the artistic field, which prevents women to fulfill a professional career. See texts by Griselda Pollock, Norma Broude or Tamar Garb for example.

12   See Pierre Bourdieu, *Les Règles de l'art. Genèse et structure du champ littéraire* (Paris: Le Seuil, 1992).

did fulfil their ambitions, like Harriet Backer, Kitty Kielland, Amélie Lundahl, Helene Schjerfbeck.

Personal relationships with these French painters were considered very fruitful – a sure sign of cultural transfer. Their correspondences reveal how much mere conversations or even single sentences could have a very strong effect on their artistic paths.

Once home, these women artists passed on the techniques they had learnt abroad to their students, for them to apply. This was done either through their own schools (Harriet Backer had her own private school in Christiana/Oslo) or through the courses they gave at the drawing school of the Finnish Art Society in Helsingfors (Helene Schjerfbeck) or Åbo (Elin Danielson). Another way to spread these new techniques was to exhibit their paintings in their home countries.

In addition to all they learnt in Paris, these women artists also followed their teachers to Brittany, mostly in the summer months when the academies were closed. Kitty Kielland travelled to Douarnenez in 1880, and Harriet Backer to Rocherfort-en-Terre with Léon Germain Pelouse (1838–1891) in 1881. Amélie Lundahl, Helene Schjerfbeck, and Helena Westermarck travelled to Pont-Aven, Douarnenez, and Concarneau respectively, from 1879 to 1885. For Nordic research, these trips to Brittany are critical as it is mostly there that these women applied as autonomous and professional artists the principles of Naturalism, Realism, and *plein-airism* principles they learnt from their French teachers.[13] Abroad, it was easier for Nordic women artists to live a life exclusively dedicated to their art and artistic ambitions, far removed from the social conventions that burdened their existence at home. They discovered a new way of living that liberated their personal, artistic, and professional horizons. The artists' colonies they were part of in Paris, in Brittany or elsewhere, enabled them to confront their art and their aesthetic ideas with the ones of their male peers and were also an extraordinary vector for cultural transfers.

4.2   In Brittany

In the visual arts, the distinction between Naturalism and Realism is not always clear. From the 1850s, Realism depicts as accurately as possible the life and environment of common people. Such folk scenes in the countryside or seaside are idealized because of the fear of their imminent disappearance as a

---

13   As examples, see *De drogo till Paris, op. cit., Peintres du Nord en voyage dans l'Ouest, op. cit.*, and *Taiteilijoiden Bretagne 1800-luvun lopussa / The Brittany of Artists in the Late 19th century / La Bretagne des artistes à la fin du XIXe siècle* (Helsingfors: Musée Gallen-Kallela, 1998).

result of urbanisation. Jules Breton (1827–1906) is one of the best-known representatives of this trend, specifically through his monumental depictions of the people of his region of birth, Douarnenez, painted from 1860 to 1880, which combine apparent realism with dignity and beauty. In contrast, Naturalism in the 1880's, as understood by Jules Bastien-Lepage (1848–1884), exclusively promotes nature, particularly peasantry from his region of birth, la Meuse, in north-eastern France. In an article from 1881, Helena Westermarck noted: "Bastien-Lepage follows the course of a never-ending study of nature [...] He focuses on it down to the smallest details."[14] Under the influence of natural sciences, art sought to represent types which could embody the social and ethnic groups subject to its study. Faces or figures were to be seized in the contemporary surrounding environment. It must be said that both Jules Breton and Jules Bastien-Lepage were idolized by Finnish and Nordic artists.

4.2.1　Harriet Backer, Kitty Kielland and Léon Pelouse

Kitty Kielland had already worked with Léon Pelouse near Paris, in Cernay-la-Ville, in June 1879. She learnt there how to paint outdoors, directly in front of the nature, with a sketch effect brush. In Brittany, during the Summer of 1880, she met Jules Breton, whose depiction of relationships between human characters and nature is perceptible in Kielland's paintings of that time. Likewise, the Norwegian art historian Marit Lange analysed how Harriet Backer's work in Britanny in 1881 shows the influence of the Barbizon school in her local landscapes, which she carried forward to the Norwegian landscapes of Jæren. In the 1880s, these surprised a Norwegian public, more accustomed to the representations of a wild, monumental, and primitive nature, because they depicted a familiar environment that had not heretofore been chosen as a pictorial motif, which was executed with modern techniques.[15] With her landscapes and her paintings of summer nights with reflecting water, Kitty Kielland largely participated in National Romanticism in Norway and even created a new kind of nocturnal landscape of the mind (*Summer night* (1886), Fleskum). By absorbing the techniques of French Naturalists and the Barbizon school, and adapting them to her own artistic requirements and to the Norwegian environment, Kielland plays a decisive role as an intermediary between French and Norwegian art.

14　Quoted by Elina Antilla, 'Brittany in Finnish Art', in *Taiteilijoiden Bretagne 1800-luvun lopussa, op. cit.*, pp. 79–101 (p. 83).

15　Marit Lange, 'Harriet Backer och Kitty Kielland I Paris pa 1880-talet', *op. cit.*, p. 122.

Likewise, in Rochefort-en-Terre, Harriet Backer painted her first "plein-air interior scenes" as she herself called them: contemporary but traditional renderings of detailed Breton interiors, with subtle lighting effects.[16] In these three seminal pictures, Harriet Backer applies the techniques learnt from Léon Bonnat (the study of light effects and strict composition) and Pelouse (*plein-air* painting). It has to be said, however, that this was not the first time Harriet Backer painted interiors. In Germany and in her first months in Paris, she had already produced paintings of interiors, but these featured heavily historical settings and dark colours. She had made her debut at the 1880 Salon with a painting of this kind, *Solitude* (1878/1880), which was even prized with an "Honourable Mention".[17] By contrast, Harriet Backer learnt in Brittany how to work with the natural light of the room she wanted to depict. She borrowed from Pelouse the technique of "*ébauche sur ébauche*", making perceptible on the canvas the layers of sketches as a kind of record of the genesis of the painting. In doing so, she wanted to preserve lightness and a feeling of spontaneity. This is a technique she would in turn teach to her students, echoing a lesson Bonnat taught her, which she would never forget: the importance of construction and composition. Back in Paris and Norway, Harriet Backer pursued her work on interior natural light and vivid colours, through the depiction of modern rooms with or without characters painted in modern clothes. She painted her first Norwegian interior in 1883 in Fåberg, and her first landscape painting in 1884, in Jæren with Kitty Kielland. In 1883, a few months after coming back to Paris, Harriet Backer painted *Blue Interior*, which built on all she had learnt so far in France and especially in Brittany. With a rather strong composition, she worked a considerable amount on light effects and colours, which struck the Norwegian public. She is now considered as one of the most subtle colourists in Norwegian art history.

4.2.2 *The Finnish Women Artists and Brittany*
It is possible to find some common features in the Brittany productions of Finnish women painters. The experimentations of *plein-air* painting affect the subject as much as their technique.

---

16 *Interior from Rochefort-en-Terre* (*Morning light*) (1882) (without any characters); *Interior from Rochefort-en-Terre* (*Afternoon light*) (1882) (with two characters, one mother and her boy) and *Fourre-tout* (1882) (with one woman in the cellar of the Hôtel Lecadre where Harriet Backer was staying).
17 Marit Lange, 'Harriet Backer och Kitty Kielland I Paris pa 1880-talet', *op. cit.*, p. 123.

Under the influences of Jules Breton and Jules Bastien-Lepage, Finnish women artists showed interest in Breton fishermen, their families, and their work, as well as in the peasantry. They tried to demonstrate the connection between ordinary people and their environment. These works often merged two distinct genres, landscape and portraiture, with figures painted outdoors. However, if old folk traditions fascinated the Finns, paradoxically, they didn't play a major role in their paintings. They painted Breton people in everyday life, but this did not extend to show them actually working, or to paint folk costumes or church services.

For example, in Helene Schjerfbeck's *Funerals in Brittany* (1884), the procession in the background is just outlined and barely visible – the main figure is an old man kneeling in the foreground, more carefully painted, without depicting him in folk costume. This opposition between a detailed foreground and a more suggestive background is redolent of Bastien-Lepage's approach. As another example, the woman of Amélie Lundahl's *Girl at the cabbage plot* (1884) has stopped gathering cabbage as in Bastien-Lepage's *Hay Harvest* of 1877. There is no actual intention to achieve a documentary form of realistic painting, even if the composition of the picture strengthens the connection between the figure and surrounding nature.

Interestingly, there is gradual trend towards depicting figures as they are, without embellishment, even in representations of children or women. This is particularly the case for Helena Westermarck and Helene Schjerfbeck, who did not seek in their work to conceal poverty or grime. Finnish critics will criticise this feature of their works, notably Helene Schjerfbeck's *Little boy feeding her little sister* (1881) or Helena Westermarck's *Ironing women* (1883). Folk costumes do not dissimulate the harshness of daily lives. Content and execution reflect the Naturalism crystallized in the works of Bastien-Lepage, where idealisation has been replaced by an unembellished depiction of common people (as in his *Hay Harvest*). This style inaugurated a new trend of idealist depiction of common people. According to the Finnish art historian Elina Antilla, this was because they were considered close to the primeval origins of man.[18] Finnish viewers were shocked by this lack of embellishment that was still unusual in national iconography. Realism implies a lack of embellishment, and seeks to be a true expression of authenticity. This primitivist approach to the depiction of Breton features became popular nonetheless and was later also applied to the portrayal of Finnish people. It changed the aesthetic criteria and the definition of beauty in the Finnish artistic field. Most of all, over the following years, it questioned the primitive state and authenticity of Finnish people by

---

18   Elina Anttila, 'Brittany in Finnish Art', *op. cit.*, p. 88.

the male defenders of a strictly Finnish Finland.[19] These women artists introduced a new way of representing the people in Finnish visual arts.

The technical implications of outdoor painting, discovered in Brittany, are various. As their Norwegian colleagues, Finnish women artists learnt to work like their French teachers with the light and colour in Brittany. By painting outdoors, they freed themselves from the academic conventions of perspective and space. In the 1880s, outdoor painting (*en plein-air*) was a major trend in visual arts, from the French Naturalists mentioned earlier (Bastien-Lepage) to the Impressionists. As a technique, it entailed depicting atmosphere and daylight as they were and portraying figures as spontaneously as possible. This was made possible by the mild climate of Brittany, even if some paintings were finished indoors. This practical advantage has been noticed by many artists in their letters. This technique had an impact on both the content, as we have seen, and on the form of painting. Academic conventions were abandoned in favour of natural light, leading Finnish women to reconsider some of their compositional habits shaped by artificial studio light. Likewise, their palette changed, becoming dominated by blues and greys, in accordance with the Brittany's sights and buildings. Wide brushes were frequently used, and visible brush strokes remind the viewer of the work's spontaneity and create a new feeling of space. This focus on light and brushwork tends to reintroduce two-dimensionality and to soften the rendering of forms, freed from the contrasts between light and shade. From a technical viewpoint, these works are a decisive step in the process that leads to Symbolism and Synthetism in Finland in the 1890s, marked by a shift in content from an actual subject to what lies beyond the signs, and in form towards less detail.

Critically, in Brittany, some Finnish women artists discovered that artistic execution could be the main goal for art. In some of their paintings, the study of light became the central theme, as in Helena Westermarck's *Poor boy* (1884) or Amélie Lundahl's *Young girl on the beach* (1884). The young Helene Schjerfbeck experimented the most with the possibilities of pure painting, like in *Drying linen* (1883), *Street in Brittany* (1884), *Shadow over the wall* (1883), *Alley* (1881), and *The Door* (1884), all of which appear unfinished and are devoid of what usually characterizes Naturalism and mimetic Realism. These pictures bear no narrative, no hidden story, they are on the verge of abstraction. Most of these paintings by Helene Schjerfbeck were not shown until 1917, in Helsingfors, more than thirty years after having been made.

---

19   See for example Timo Huusko, 'Finnish Nationalism and the Avant-Garde', in *A Cultural History of the Avant-Garde in the Nordic Countries 1900–1925, op. cit.*, pp. 557–572.

Of course, these features of Breton painting do not imply at all that these women artists would follow the same artistic path and have an equal claim to fame. Helene Schjerfbeck stands out as one of the most important modern artist in Finnish art history.

4.3 Reception

Some of the works painted in Brittany by these Norwegian and Finnish women artists were exhibited in Paris, at the annual Salon and at the 1889 Paris World Exhibition. A few of them gained positive reviews in France, such as Harriet Backer, Kitty Kielland, Helene Schjerfbeck, and Maria Wiik. I shall not provide a detailed survey of the reception of their exhibited works here, but will give a few general insights that characterise the main responses they and their work encountered.

Arguably, these women artists travelled to Brittany because, in the early 1880's, Breton subjects were fashionable and could enable these women artists to gain recognition in Paris. By doing so, they hoped to sell paintings on the international art market, given, at that time, that Finnish or Norwegian subjects were not yet particularly popular. Nonetheless, it is true that many reviewers criticized foreign artists for painting and exhibiting French subjects in France and would have preferred them to produce paintings that are closer reflections of their own region.[20] If these women artists were to receive little recognition at the cultural centre of the dominant form of European artistic production, they could at least use the know-how they accrued in Brittany back in their home countries and in the international art market. One must not forget that both Norwegian and Finnish artistic fields were still in their early stages in the 1880s. Here, one can see the paradigm of "centre" and "periphery" at work: at that time, for foreign artists, who considered themselves peripheral, Paris remained at the centre of artistic life, playing a guiding role and, to quote Pierre Bourdieu, offering cultural and symbolic capital.

Yet, this strategy was unsuccessful. In Finland, Breton works by Finnish women were met with strong resistance in the 1880s. As a paradigmatic example of their reception, we can discuss a national contemporary art exhibition in 1885, arranged for the visit of the Czar Alexander III.

---

20   The huge number of Breton paintings exhibited ended up irking art critics, such as Philippe Burty, 'Le Salon de 1881 (1)', in *L'Art*, 1881, quoted by Elina Anttila, 'Brittany in Finnish Art', *op. cit.*, p. 96: "Today, when all are in command of their profession as artists, may each paint with enthusiasm the beauties of his own country. Real art will languish under cosmopolitanism just as it was about to languish under academism."

Helene Schjerfbeck and Helena Westermarck were violently criticized, both because of the content and the form of their works of art. These new practices and the vernacular ideology they conveyed generated violent reactions and debates. These paintings challenged society's prevailing definition of the role and the place of women in social and artistic fields. Female artists could not be innovative but only imitative and had to contain themselves to the modest depiction of beauty. Technically, female artists were required to follow the prescriptions of the Düsseldorf school and banned from sketching, wide brush-strokes, or light colours. In fact, at that time, with these paintings, Finnish women artists introduced some French contemporary art trends in Finland, even if what was qualified as "radical" and "extreme" was nothing more than the "juste milieu" (or balanced view) over there, in France.[21] Some press reviews went so far as to mock and condemn these new pictorial trends only because they were French, that is to say, not Finnish, and because they were imported by women. But above all, the gender bias was predominant in the press reviews.[22]

Indeed, in the mid-1880s, there were increasing numbers male artists who claimed to be professional, and who feared that the artistic field could be undermined by the dilettante artistic practice of female artists. As a consequence, they sought to control the national artistic field; that is to say, to define who could be an artist, and what art should be, in the context of rising tensions with Russia (which implied a definition of a great national art). This obviously conflicted with the claims of many women artists to professional status, such as Amélie Lundahl, Helena Westermarck or Helene Schjerfbeck, and the fact that they ended up challenging their male colleagues, particularly with their Breton works, considered for some of them as the most radical Finland had ever produced. This conflict was aggravated by the fact that these women artists had lived very independent lives abroad, travelled alone etc. The French and Breton works threatened not only academic traditions, but also the socio-ideological definition of what a woman artist should be in a male-dominated artistic field. Until recently, these "painting women",[23] as they were depicted in many press reviews, were overshadowed by their male colleagues who had

---

21   Riitta Konttinen indicates that the Naturalism school is perceived as avant-garde by Finnish artistic circles as late as 1889. (Riitta Konttinen/Ulla Savojärvi, *Elin Danielson – Gambogi* (Helsinki: Publications of the Hämeenlinnan Art Museum, no. 3, Otava, 1995), p. 127.)
22   See for example the texts by Axel Berndtson, *Nya Pressen*, 09.09.1885 and by Charybdis and Scylla, *Finsk Tidskrift*, quoted by Riitta Konttinen, in *De drogo till Paris, op. cit.*, p. 222 and p. 246.
23   This is an expression that can be found in most of European press at that time. As gender studies authors underline it, there is no such expression to qualify male artists.

long been considered by traditional historiography as the ones who introduced French Realism and Naturalism in Finland.

In this example, one can see how the "centre" and "periphery" paradigm operates within a national context, between a "centre" dominated by male artists and a "periphery" to which their female colleagues have been assigned for a long period of time. Nordic historiography, as well as in other parts of the world, has attempted over the past forty years to re-evaluate the position of women artists in visual arts, by disputing this prevailing form of "centre" and "periphery" paradigm.

The concept of "cultural transfer" is a useful analytical tool, which enables us to understand how pictorial modernity spread rapidly across Europe at the end of the nineteenth century and how it generated its own local variations. Conversely, the "centre" and "periphery" paradigm is inadequate to analyse the numerous exchanges between artists who made artistic (r)evolution possible. Additional concepts are needed to undertake an accurate history of modern art. This traditional paradigm divides artists along national lines but also, internally, within domestic national boundaries. Accordingly, women were the most peripheral artists both at home and on the international market – not to speak of the history of modern art until recent years. This example of Finnish and Norwegian women artists gives an insight into how these doubly-marginalized painters imported modern pictorial techniques in their home countries according to the definitions and descriptions made possible by the notion of "cultural transfer" and contributed profoundly to the modernisation of their national aesthetic conventions. Regardless of their aesthetic choices and techniques, Nordic women artists did participate with their male peers to the artistic effervescence in Europe at the turn of the twentieth century.

Bibliography

Anon., *Peintres du Nord en voyage dans l'Ouest. Modernité et impressionnisme 1860–1900. Catalogue de l'exposition coproduite par l'Office franco-norvégien d'échanges et de coopération (ofnec), le musée des Beaux-Arts de Caen et l'Ateneum d'Helsinki* (Caen: Presses Universitaires de Caen, 2001).

Anon., *Taiteilijoiden Bretagne 1800-luvun lopussa / The Brittany of Artists in the Late 19th century / La Bretagne des artistes à la fin du XIXe siècle* (Helsingfors, Musee Gallen-Kallela, 1998).

Antilla, Elina, 'Brittany in Finnish Art', in *The Brittany of Artists in the Late 19th century* (Helsingfors: Musee Gallen-Kallela, 1998).

Bourdieu, Pierre, *Les règles de l'art. Genèse et structure du champ littéraire* (Paris: Seuil, 1998).
Broude, Norma/Mary D. Garrard (eds.), *The Expanding Discourse. Feminism and Art History* (Boulder: West View Press, 1992).
Cariou, André, 'Le voyage en Bretagne', in *Peintres du Nord en voyage dans l'Ouest – Modernité et impressionnisme 1860–1900* (Caen: Presses Universitaires de Caen, 2001), pp. 40–48.
Gunnarsson, Torsten, *Impressionism and the North. Late 19th century French Avant-Garde Art and the Art in the Nordic countries 1870–1920* (Stockholm: Nationalmuseum, 2002).
Johansen, Annette, 'Le périple français de Peder Severin Krøyer, 1877–1880', in *Peintres du Nord en voyage dans l'Ouest. Modernité et impressionnisme 1860–1900* (Caen: Presses Universitaires de Caen, 2001), pp. 70–74.
Konttinen, Riitta/Savojärvi, Ulla, *Elin Danielson-Gambogi* (Helsingfors: Tavastehus Konstmuseets publikationer, 1995).
Konttinen, Riitta, 'Finska konstnärinnors 1880-tal. Ljus, luft och färg. Elin Danielson, Amélie Lundahl, Helene Schjerfbeck, Helena Westermarck och Maria Wiik', in *De drogo till Paris. Nordiska konstnärinnor på 1880 – talet* (Stockholm: Foreningen Norden, 1988), pp. 221–253.
Lange, Marit, 'Les artistes norvégiens en Bretagne et en Normandie', in *Peintres du Nord en voyage dans l'Ouest – Modernité et impressionnisme 1860–1900* (Caen: Presses Universitaires de Caen, 2001), pp. 100–106.
Lange, Marit, 'Harriet Backer och Kitty Kielland I Paris på 1880-talet', in *De drogo till Paris. Nordiska konstnärinnor på 1880 – talet* (Stockholm: Foreningen Norden, 1988), pp. 113–147.
Pollock, Griselda, *Differencing the canon. Feminist Desire and the Writing of art's Histories* (London, New York, Routledge, 1999).
Sinisalo, Soili, 'Un pays où les femmes ont du talent', in *Peintres du Nord en voyage dans l'Ouest – Modernité et impressionnisme 1860–1900* (Caen: Presses Universitaires de Caen, 2001), pp. 80–86.
Supinen, Marja, 'Les Finlandais sur les rives de la Manche', in *Peintres du Nord en voyage dans l'Ouest. Modernité et impressionnisme 1860–1900* (Caen: Presses Universitaires de Caen, 2001), pp. 88–98.
Tapié, Alain, 'La nouvelle peinture dans la nébuleuse moderne', in *Peintres du Nord en voyage dans l'Ouest. Modernité et impressionnisme 1860–1900* (Caen:, Presses Universitaires de Caen, 2001), pp. 30–38.
Van Den Berg, Hubert /Hautamäki, Irmeli/Hjartarson, Benedikt/Jelsbak, Torben/ Schönström, Rikard/Stounbjerg, Per/Ørum, Tania/Aagesen, Dorthe (eds.), *A Cultural History of the Avant-Garde in the Nordic Countries 1900–1925* (Amsterdam, New York: Rodopi, 2012).

PART 2

*Aspects of Textual Transfers – Comparison,
Intertextuality and Translation*

∴

CHAPTER 5

Cultural Transfer and Intertextuality: Yambo Ouologuem and the Dynamics of Literary and Cultural Rewriting in the (Post)Colonial African Context

Hans-Jürgen Lüsebrink

Abstract

This contribution deals with the relationship between the concepts and critical practices of cultural transfers and intertextuality, beginning at the theoretical level by offering definitions of these critical ideas and articulating their specifically methodological interrelationship. The three following parts of the article concern their conceptual interweaving and their related methodological issues through the example of postcolonial literature(s), with a specific focus on the paradigmatic case of Malian novelist Yambo Ouologuem's work *Le Devoir de violence* ('Bound to violence', 1968). Taking into consideration a multiplicity of texts stemming from disparate cultural contexts, this contribution points out how intertextuality in sub-Saharan African literatures reveals and illustrates creative practices that can be understood as direct consequences of the processes of cultural transfer.

5.1 Problematics and Concepts

Cultural Transfer and Intertextuality, and their respective theoretical and methodological fields, are both closely related and distinct concepts. The theory of intertextuality, developed during the 1960s, especially by Julia Kristeva, can be considered as one of the major theoretical backgrounds for the cultural transfer approach, together with the reception theory (articulated first in the early 1970s, almost at the same time as the theory of intertextuality) as well as other comparative approaches in literary and cultural studies. Intertextuality can be defined, in a very general manner, as the "relationship between one literary work and other literary works"; Laura Buzzard and Don LePan elaborate further on this definition with the following forms of intertextuality: 'Allusion, imitation, parody and satire'.[1] For Julia Kristeva, who elaborated the concept in different works between 1966 and 1974, intertextuality implies the idea of both "connectedness" (of one text with a multiplicity of others), of "dialogical interaction" (of one text with a multiplicity of other explicitly or implicitly quoted texts) and of "productivity", resulting from the dynamics of dialogue and connectedness. The meaning of intertextuality, explored on the basis of its natural linguistic logic, can thus be defined, following Kristeva, as the "interweaving of texts", "weaving of one text into another", "connectedness and interdependence of at least two related texts", the characteristic of intertextuality being the establishment of "a relation with (an) other text(s) or having another or multiple texts woven in it".[2] As Judith Still and Michael Worton have pointed out, the phenomenon of intertextuality, even if the term dates only from the 1960s, is far older and replaced especially, in a renewed theoretical perspective, the notions of "influence" and "source": 'Unsurprisingly, therefore, we can find theories of intertextuality wherever there has been discourse about texts – both because thinkers were aware of intertextual relations and because our knowledge of the theory makes us, as readers, keen to re-read our source texts in that light.'[3] Finally, Tiphaine Samoyault, considers "intertextuality" as a "practice" ("pratique") which constitutes the "memory of literature", embracing forms like citation, allusion, reference, pastiche, parody, collage and plagiarism and connecting a given text to a multiplicity of textual references it is based on and which it is using, re-appropriating and transforming in a creative way.[4] Kristeva and the theory of intertextuality is thus closely related to Bakhtin's concept of dialogism and his theory of the dialogic text which "culminates in the new term, intertextuality". As Kristeva stated in 1980, in her book *Desire in language:*[5] 'any text is constructed as a mosaic of quotations; any text is the absorption and transformation of another. The notion of 'intertextuality' replaces that of intersubjectivity, and poetic language is read as at least double.'[6]

---

1 Laura Buzzard/Don LePan, *The Broadview Pocket Glossary of Literary Terms* (Toronto: Broadview, 2013), p. 78.
2 Marko Juvan, *History and Poetics of Intertextuality*, transl. from Slovenian by Timothy Pocacar (West Lafayette: Purdue University Press, 2008), p. 13.
3 Judith Still/Michael Worton, 'Introduction', in *Intertextuality. Theories and Practices*, ed. by Michael Worton/Judith Still (Manchester, New York: Manchester University Press, 1990), pp. 1–2.
4 Tiphaine Samoyault, *L'intertextualité. Mémoire de la littérature* (Paris: Armand Colin, 2008), p. 5.
5 Graham Allen, *Intertextuality* (London, New York: Routledge, 2000), p. 39.
6 Julia Kristeva, *Desire in Language. A Semiotic Approach to Literature and Art* (New York: Columbia University Press, 1980), p. 66.

Intertextuality is also closely connected to the notion of "Interdiscursivity", a more recent concept, opening the field of explicit or implicit references, quotations and dialogic reappropriations to a very broad, semiotic scope, including not only written, printed or oral texts, but also visual and audio-visual discourses and non-verbal practices like music, sound, gestures and mimicries. Often establishing relations between different medias – for example when a written novel uses filmic references or is even based, in its very structure, on cinematographic forms of narration, as in the West-African writer Tierno Monénembo's film *Cinéma* (1998)[7] – interdiscursivity includes often, but not always, intermedial relations and is thus linked to the concept of "intermediality".

If the theory of intertextuality represents, together with the reception theory, one of the major theoretical backgrounds for the Cultural Transfer Approach, it constitutes, on a theoretical level, also one of its integral components. If we define cultural transfer as the process of transmission, mediation, and reception of cultural artefacts between cultural areas, we can, in fact, distinguish between the dimension of selection, mediation, and reception, the last dimension being constituted by processes of imitation, adaptation, productive reception, commentary, and intertextual reference. The presence of intertextual references in texts of very different structures (literature, periodicals, essays), are generally based on cultural transfers in all the cases where different cultures and languages play a role. And they represent their long-lasting impact, their 'memory', to quote Samoyault's concept of intertextuality as memory. As in intracultural configurations – configurations within given cultures and their often linguistically based boundaries – intertextuality represents one of the major impulses (or "empowerments") for literary and cultural creation and productivity, which create frames of references with different functions and produce adaptations and forms of creative reception. Related to cultural transfers and to intercultural forms of selection, mediation and reception, and in spite of the structural similarities with 'intracultural' intertextuality, 'intercultural' intertextuality generally embraces very different functions, which I would like to focus on in part 2 and 3 of this contribution. In order to point out the specificities of intertextual relations in an intercultural context, connected to cultural transfers, I will take especially into consideration colonial

---

7 Hans-Jürgen Lüsebrink, 'Afrikanische Ausprägungsformen einer "littérature-monde". Transkulturelle Räume, intertextuelle Netze und intermediale Bezugnahmen im Werk von Tierno Monénembo', in *Transkulturelle Begegnungsräume? Ästhetische Strategien der Überlagerung, Pluralisierung und Simultaneität in den zeitgenössischen romanischen Literaturen*, ed. by Alessandro Bosco/Ursula Moser/Julia Pröll (Würzburg: Königshausen & Neumann, 2020) pp. 71–88.

and post-colonial examples and paradigms referring to very distinct cultures and historical situations.

Taking a systematic approach, I propose to distinguish three main configurations connecting intertextuality and cultural transfers, each of which imply specific forms, functions, and processes:

- First, cultural transfers and intertextual references introduce new literary and cultural forms and generic structures, including "processes of imitation" and "adaptation", but also "transcultural creative dynamics";
- Secondly, cultural transfers and intertextual references often lead to the constitution of "transcultural identity canons" which compete or even replace traditional cultural canons in given societies and cultures;
- Thirdly, cultural transfers and intertextual references produce, often in different cultural contexts and systems, "counter-discourses" sustained by militant positions to rewrite history, to reconsider values, and to put into question hegemonic legitimation of social positions and power-relations.

5.2 The Creative Dynamics of Transcultural Intertextuality and the Constitution of Identity Canons

Innovations and new creative dynamics in literatures and cultures are often consequences of cultural transfers, which frequently in their first stage take the form of imitations. The publication of Goethe's novel *Werther* in 1774, for example, created throughout Europe a phenomenon of literary and cultural imitations which can be considered as one of the major constitutive elements of the Western romanticism. Generic models like the *Almanach Royal*, published in France since the late seventeenth-century, the *Almanach des Dames*, also created in France in the 1760s, or the *Brockhaus Konversationslexikon*, created by the Brockhaus Publishing House in Leipzig in 1796, were imitated in numerous European and even non-European print-cultures, like Canada, the United States of America and Haiti. However, often these were not only adapted to their new cultural and linguistic context, in their formal structures, paratexts, and contents, but also transformed, creating thus new and autonomous generic traditions.

These phenomena of productive reception and rewriting, embracing a dialectic process of transfer, imitation, adaptation, and transformation, which have been described and analyzed for example in Patrick Chamoiseau's and Raphaël Confiant's *Lettres creoles. Tracées antillaises et continentales de la littérature* (1991) play a particularly important role in non-European colonial and post-colonial societies and cultures. European literary texts and cultures were transferred to colonial and post-colonial societies by two major institutions including specific hermeneutic forms and practices of approprations and reading: the school (and university) system, on the one hand; and the media in the public sphere, especially periodicals, on the other hand. For example, the Mexican writer and intellectual Octavio Paz, in his 1990 Nobel Prize speech in Stockholm, *La busquéda del presente*, underlined the impact of European classics like Daniel Defoe, Miguel de Cervantes, and Alexandre Dumas, which were generally transferred and mediated through the school system in Latin America, pointing out their impact on his personal imagination: 'We travelled with Sindbad and Robinson, struggled with d'Artagnan and took Valencia with the Cid.'[8]

5.3 Intertextuality, Cultural Transfers and Counter-Discourses – The Example of Yambo Ouologuem (Mali)

The literary and journalistic works of Yambo Ouologuem, born in 1940 near Bandiagara in the modern West African state of Mali, constitute one of the most fascinating and contested oeuvres of the modern African literature. It may at first seem paradoxical that Ouologuem's literary works – essentially one novel, an essay, several poems published in *Présence Africaine*, and other periodicals, as well as a collection of pornographic short stories edited under the pseudonym of Utto Rudolph, entitled *Les Mille et une Bibles du sexe* – appeared quite suddenly between 1967 and 1969, while the author has since observed an almost complete silence, with the exception of few contributions in literary historical textbooks in the early seventies, written in collaboration with the French scholar, Robert Pageard. This fact is indeed remarkable when one considers that Ouologuem was the first francophone African writer to obtain the very prestigious Prix Renaudot for his novel *Le Devoir de Violence (Bound to Violence)*. After the Prix Goncourt, the most important literary prize in France, these prestigious literary prizes have only been won by few other writers of francophone literature outside Europe, like the Carribean writers René Maran in 1921 and Patrick Chamoiseau in 1992. No other book of the African literature of the 1960s and 1970s has, therefore, been discussed more intensively or more widely reviewed in periodicals and literary supplements in France and in other European countries, as well as in Africa and in the United States. In a study

---

8   Octavio Paz, *La búsqueda del presente. La quête du présent. Discours de Stockholm*, édition bilingue (Paris: Gallimard, 1991), pp. 46–47: "Naufragamos con Simbad y con Robinson, nos batimos con d'Artagnan, tomamos Valencia con el Cid".

published in 1973 in the journal *Présence Africaine*, Anita Kern called the novel 'undoubtedly one of the most talented works ever to come out of Africa, or anywhere in the world' (Kern 1973, p. 230). It became, as Thomas Hale formulated in 1980, 'the most controversial novel ever written by an African writer' (Hale 1980, 137).

Ouologuem's novel, published a few months before his provocative essay, *Lettre à la France nègre*, is a vast, extremely dense narrative epic, a kind of historical fresco, telling the history of the imaginery West African kingdom of Nakem-Ziuko. The history of Nakem-Ziuko condenses in a sense the general history of the great West African empires of Mali, Ghana, and Songhay situated in the Sahel area, between the 13th century and the end of the colonial era in the 1950s, even through, as Thomas Hale has pointed out, numerous precise references to the history of the Songhay empire.

The novel is divided into four main chapters. The first two chapters, entitled "The legend of the Saïf" and "Ectasy and Agony", treat the historical period from the assumption of power of the Islamic dynasty of the Saïf which conquered the Sahel area from the north to the borders of the coast of Guinée. The two following chapters, 'The night of the giants' and 'Dawn' ('L'Aurore'), close the novel, pursuing a double narrative perspective. They tell the story of Colonial West Africa, first, from the viewpoint of the rulers, the 'scene of power', that is the Saïf dynasty, which succeeded in maintaining a position of power even during the colonial period as a result of their extremely skillful, ambivalent relations with the French colonial power and its representatives; and secondly from the viewpoint of the oppressed majority of Africans: the former subjects of the Saïf dynasty, some of whom were slaves, who had become indigenious subjects during the French colonization. In the novel, the African student Raymond Spartacus Kassoumi, as one of the first Africans of his country, frequents the colonial school and then the University in Paris, appears as the main positive figure in the last two chapters of the novel. However, even he must finally recognize that his career has been entirely directed by the Saïf clan, the ancient slaveholders of his own family. This dynamic is even more critical for the tragic fate of Kassoumi's sister, who dies as a prostitute in a Parisian brothel. The very last scene of the novel symbolizes Ouologuem's pessimistic view of African history: a game of chess between a descendant of the Saïf-dynasty and one of the representatives of the colonial power, Bishop Henry. Being the only uncorrupted protagonist of the novel, in terms of his exercise of power, Bishop Henry also represents the values of true Christianity in supporting, as much as he can, the oppressed masses of African peoples. During the chess game he informs Saïf that he is fully aware of his Machiavellian strategies and power secrets. The last gesture of Saïf, throwing an asp, intended to kill the bishop, leaves the reader without closure, providing an enigmatic and mysterious ending.

Telling the history of the last decade of the colonial period, the final sequences of the novel thus illustrate Ouologuem's underlying thesis that both the colonial and the post-colonial power in Africa were closely linked to pre-colonial, Islam-dominated structures of power which – in Ouologuem's eyes – were predominantly characterized by violence, oppression, slave-holding, and slave-trade, based on social hierarchy and military force. This sustains a general vision of African history in which the rupture of the Islamic conquest appears vitally important, while the colonial conquest seems to have left mostly untouched, in Ouologuem's view, the general structures of authoritarian power established in the pre-colonial era. The colonial conquest, far from representing a radical break, causing deep alienation and a complete overthrow of inherited structures and values, only changed, in Ouologuem's eyes, the exterior or visible forms of the public staging of power and the foundations of its legitimacy. 'But projected into the world', says Ouologuem's narrator at the end of the last chapter of the novel entitled 'The Dawn', 'one cannot help recalling that Saïf, mourned three million times, is forever reborn to history beneath the hot ashes of more than thirty African republics'. (Ouologuem 1971, 181–182).

Ouologuem's view of African history constitutes, in this sense, a radical "counter-discourse" to contemporary African visions of precolonial history, like those represented by the works of Cheikh Anta Diop and Léopold Sédar Senghor. In the same manner as Ayi Kwei Armah's novel *Two Thousand Seasons*, published in 1966, *Bound to violence* belongs to a form of historiography – using here the medium of literary fiction – which I propose to call "Critical historiography", as opposed to "Annalistic historiography", "Exemplary historiography" and "Genetic historiography" (Rüsen 1982), the last one being represented by the works of Cheikh Anta Diop, who relates the origins of African Civilizations to Ancient Egypt. Like other types of historical narratives belonging to the form of "critical historiography" in Rüsen's sense, Ouologuem's novel *Bound to violence* brushes against the grain of traditional schemas and certainties in proposing new perceptions of a given historical process. As John D Erickson formulates in his essay on Yambo Ouologuem, in his 1979 book *Nommo: African Fiction in French South of the Sahara*, the novel *Bound to Violence* readjusts through irony and paradox a view of history as 'mis-represented by ethnologists, historians, theoreticians, and writers - European and African.' (Erickson 1979, p. 238). Ouologuem himself pointed out in an interview published in 1971 in the *New York Times Review of Books*, that '[i]t is unfortunate that African writers have written only about folklore and legend. Until now African history has been shown only as a conflict between blacks and whites; all African novels deal with this colonial conflict. However, actions taken only in opposition to whites create an atmosphere of paranoia – one does not deal with reality but with the proclamations of others.' (Watkins 1971, pp. 7–8).

Ouologuem's novel includes, indeed, a threefold form of counter-discourse: first, a counter-discourse (or a form of "Critical historiography" in Rüsen's sense) directed against the idealization of pre-colonial African societies as egalitarian and free societies. Through the history of the part-imaginary, part-historical empire of Nakem-Ziuku (which refers, often in a very precise manner, to numerous elements of the history especially of the Songhay-Empire between 1202 and 1947), Ouologuem underlines, albeit in an hyperbolic, selective, and exaggerated manner, the existence of slavery and the use of tyrannical violence in the exercize of power in the West African empires. The fact that Ouologuem belonged to the ethnic group of the Dogon who successfully resisted the Islamic conquest in keeping their animist religion and retiring into the mountain area of south Mali, explains partly his profoundly critical attitude to Islam and its close relation to temporal power.

Secondly, *Bound to Violence* formulates a radical counter-discourse to the idealizing representation of precolonial rural Africa by European ethnologists in particular. This form of discourse appears in the novel through the personality of Fritz Shrobenius, a name scarcely masking the name of Leo Frobenius, one of the major figures of 20th-century German ethnology, who had a significant influence on the Negritude movement of Léopold Sédar Senghor, Léon-Gontran Damas, and Aimé Césaire. By means of parody and irony, Ouologuem shows the reader, through the eyes of an omniscient narrator, that Frobenius' scientific discourse called "Shrobeniusology", which is based on the myth of the "noble savage", omits critical dimensions of African reality: the sophistic, Machiavellian strategy of the preservation of power embodied by the Saïf dynasty, which mobilises traditional symbols for its own legitimacy; the presence of violence, which Shrobenius willingly seeks to ignore; the existence of complex political organizations and extremely stratified, unequal societies, being in complete contradiction with the idyllic image of a profoundly egalitarian society in a rural environment; and the relation between sexuality and violence, a truly obsessive theme in Ouologuem's works. This last aspect of African reality is clear in many passages of the novel, notably in the seduction of Shrobenius's daughter, Sonia, by Saïf's son Madouba, an act which is intimately connected to the brutal murder of the slave-woman, Awa, by her husband, Sankolo, who has been surprised while voyeuristically observing the love-making of Madouba and Sonia. Ouologuem also points out how the Saïfs manipulate information about African art and cultures in presenting an extremely idealized view of them:

Saïf made up stories and the interpreter translated. Madoubo repeated in French, refining on the subtleties to the delight of Shrobenius, that human crafish afflicted with a groping mania for resuscitating an African universe-cultural autonomy; dressed with the flash elegance of a colonial on holiday, a great laughter, he was determined to find metaphysical meaning in everything, even in the shape of the palaver tree under which the notables met to chat. Gesticulating at every word, he displayed his love of Africa and his tempestuous knowledge with the assurance of a high school student who slipped through the final examinations by the skin of his teeth. African life, he held, was pure art, intense religious symbolism, and a civilization once grandiose – but alas a victim of the white man's vicissitudes.

OUOLOGUEM 1971, p. 87

'I have horror of "folkloric" attitudes to Africa', stated Ouologuem in 1968, in an interview given to the English newspaper *The Guardian*. 'These only help to reassure those philistines, the Negrophiles – generally people who have neither real obligations nor the power of sanctions. We find that among the infantile left related in France.' (Ouologuem 1968, p. 8). This remark is related to a third kind of counter-discourse concerning Western attitudes to Africa which Ouologuem seems to consider both condescending and ambivalent. It is directed against colonial paternalism, but also against militant identification with Africa (as was characteristic for the the anti-parliamentary left during the 1960s). This latter attitude was often linked to socialist projects that Ouologuem denounced, especially in his article *Marx ou l'étrangeté d'un socialisme africain*, which points out certain false historical presuppositions. African socialism is indeed based, in Ouologuem's view, on an idealized perception of precolonial African societies, following the concept of "Ur-Kommunismus" ("Primitive communism") developed by Karl Marx and Friedrich Engels themselves.

'My aim is to do violence to the mis-conceptions of Africans so that we can realize what the real problems are. This is our "duty of violence"', asserted Ouologuem in one of the numerous interviews he gave after the publication of his most important novel (Ouologuem 1968, p. 1). The expression 'duty of violence' used here concerns not only the proper representation of violence as such – as the second obsessional theme of his novel, just beneath sexuality – but also "textual violence", in its various possible registers. In his study on Ouologuem. James Olney characterizes his style as an 'extremely rich, colorful, intense, and sensorily heightened vehicle'. Olney uses also in this context the terms and expressions of 'stylistic vitality' (Olney 1973, p. 235), of 'bizarre, intense, highly colored prose' (p. 233), of 'surrealistic hypertension' (p. 232), of 'stylistic variety' (p. 235), of 'brilliant, exotic sensuousness' (p. 218) and even of 'syntactic insanity' and 'mad brilliance' (p. 229) in order to describe Ouologuem's style. Olney affirms in his book *Tell me Africa: An Approach to African Literature*, published in 1973: 'For a good part of *Bound of Violence* language is hardly a conceptual thing at all, but rather a voluptuously and violently sensuous creature that Ouologuem treats as a living thing: he makes love to it, both tenderly and violently, he caresses and tortures and rapes it, and he often surprises the reader into sharing the same relation of it.' (p. 230).

5.4 The "Operative Gymnastics of Writing"[9] – The Dynamics of Intertextuality and Cultural Transfers

The predominant violence in Ouologuem's style occurrs on the intertextual level, that means the re-writing, re-interpretation, and a radically new use of an extremely wide and complex range of literary sources which are only sometimes, and generally not, explicitly quoted.

Six types of textual references (or 'intertexts') may be distinguished in his novel:

1. References to European fiction, especially *Le Dernier des Justes* by André Schwarz-Bart, *It's a Battlefield* by Graham Greene, the poems of Arthur Rimbaud, and the novel *Salammbô* by Gustave Flaubert;
2. Global references to the European genres of the detective novel (in the third part of the novel), the sentimental novel (especially in the love-scenes between Awa and Sankolo) and the pornographical novel;
3. European ethnology, in particular the works of Leo Frobenius and Maurice Delafosse, quoted explicitly;
4. The sacred texts of the Bible and the Koran, often explicitly quoted, through italicised extracts, mostly in the first two parts of the novel;
5. The major Arab chronicles of West Africa, especially the *Tarikh-el-Fetach* and the *Tarikh-el-Sudan* of the 16th century, quoted explicitly on the very first pages of the novel;
6. The African oral tradition, in particular that of the Malinké and Dogon cultures.

---

9   Yambo Ouologuem, *Lettre à la France Nègre* (Paris: Edmond Nalis, 1968), p. 176. He underlines in this context: "[...] le texte pourra se lire et se combiner en millions de possibilités, dans tous les sens". ('The text can be read and combined with a million of possibilities, in all directions').

Ouologuem applies in this huge intertextual network a technique of distancing, by means of parody, irony and satire. In quoting the two main Arab chronicles of Early Modern times, he is thus referring to the major sources for medieval West African history. If both texts – Ouologuem's novel and the chronicles – represent violence as necessarily connected with war and conquest, their narrative perspectives differ considerably: in contrast to the two *Tarikhs*, which tell the history of the Arab conquest as a gradual triumph of wisdom over irreligion and barbaric violence, Ouologuem's ironic narrator perverts this perspective in underlining the continuity of violence towards the oppressed masses. Exclamations, ritual Muslim formulas, like "Bismillah" ("in the name of Allah"), "Glory to the Almighty God", "Blessed be the Eternal One!" or "So be it!", often put in parenthesis, are interspersed also in the discourse of the two *Tarikhs* and thus appear in his novel in total contradiction with the represented events. Whereas in the Arab chronicles, the representation of cruelties – for example those of the historical figure of the "bad ruler" Askia Mohammed personified in Ouologuems's novel by Isaac El Heit – intends to underline the outstanding qualities of the predominant "good" emperors, it belongs in *Bound to violence* to the very structure of the Islamic exercise of power in West Africa. At the same time, Ouologuem reduces considerably the complexity of the history of the major African empires from the Middle Ages to the colonial period. The threefold story of the great empires of Songhay, Mali, and Ghana, situated in the same geographical area as Ouologuem's novel, meaning the territories situated between the Senegalese region of Futa-Toro in the West to Bornu-Kanem on Lake Tchad in the East, are reduced to the history of a single imaginary empire of Nakem-Ziuku, which leads to the independent Republic of Nakem alias Mali. Instead of inspiring, like the *Tarikh*-chronicles, admiration for good Islamic rulers, Ouologuem's view of history, based on a selective rewriting of traditional texts, calls forth the reader's indignation because cruelty and its official, religious legitimation are explicitly connected to one another by the discourse of the narrator.

The same technique of distancing and parody is applied to the discourse of oral literature, the sixth type of intertext outlined above. As James Olney underlines, "the method by which [he] probes the authenticity of the legend is to rewrite history in the voice, in the tone, and in the very language of the griots and the Arab historians [...]. He adopts the narrative attitude of the *Griot* towards his subject." (p. 237, p. 239). In contrast to oral literature, Ouologuem's *Griot* voice provides some very precise dates in the first part of the novel in predicting, for instance, that a child would overthrow Saïf Moche Gabbai de Honaine, in the year 1420 (pp. 9–11). The enigmatic inexactitude of time in oral texts is thus undermined. Another example of the subversion of the discourse of the Griot is the specific use of genealogy in Ouologuem's novel. In oral epic texts such as the epic of Soundjata, written down by Djibril Tamsir Niane, or in written genealogies truly imitating oral traditions, like the first chapter of Birago Diop's autobiographical memoirs entitled *La plume raboutée* (1978), the genealogical form focuses on the magnanimity of the rulers, their wisdom, justice, and charity, contrasting sharply with the characters of some rare, quite exceptional, negative rulers. Ouologuem turns this tradition literally upside down: in his history of the Saïf-dynasty he presents a true caricature of a traditional genealogy, because nearly all his rulers are negative, duplicitous and extremely violent figures, with only two exceptions: Saïf El Hilal whose government was remarkably short, and Saïf Isaac El Heit, 'le doux et juste empereur' (p. 14) ('the gentle and just emperor of Nakem-Ziuku'). All the other rulers are proper anti-heros, and the narrator takes a kind of perverse pleasure in portraying them extensively and in complaining about their victims. Saïf El Haram, for example, who assassinated his father and his brother who preceeded him on the throne, is described by the Griot, in the same pathetic manner as used in traditional pro-Islamic texts, as knavish and tricky; his successor Abdoul Hassana is shown as 'gentle in his cruelty' ('doux dans sa cruauté'). This emperor is followed by Halongo, with his 'buffulo-brutal gaze' ('avec son regard brutal de buffle'), who ultimately expires in the arms of the prostitute Aiosha; his successor Saïf Ali is presented to the reader as a 'homosexual full of religious devotion' ('un pédéraste aux manières devotes') who died from gluttony, and so on.

These two discursive techniques of oral texts – to which could have been added the subversion of the traditional form of the prediction – illustrate Ouologuem's profoundly iconoclastic attitude also towards the African intertext of *Bound to Violence* and its implicit morality and ideology. His essay *Lettre à la France Nègre* ('Letter to Negro France', 1968), published a few months after his prize-winning novel, pursues, in a kind of polemic orientation, themes and reflections found in *Bound to Violence*. The essay consists of twelve 'open letters' ('lettres ouvertes') written in an autobiographical form and addressed to different individual and collective persons – General De Gaulle, the French people, the Africans as a whole, the African immigrants in France, the African writers, and so forth. Through stylistic registers which may be characterized as both manifesto-like and sarcastic, Ouologuem attacks, for instance, the politics of "Francophonie", meaning the politics of economic, military, and cultural cooperation established by General De Gaulle since the end of the colonial era (1960/1962) to preserve the French influence in most of the former colonies. Ouologuem sees the politics of "Francophonie" as a neo-colonial form of paternalism, characterized by a racist perception of intercultural relations just as its apparent opponent, the "Négritude" ideology, is defined as a new kind of "self-mystification", an 'exhibition of chimera and fantasies' ('foire aux chimères'; Ouologuem 1968, p. 191).

Even if the deconstruction of collective ideologies and myths determining the relations between Africa and the western world – like "Francophonie" and "Négritude" – occupy a similar importance in *Lettre à la France Nègre* and *Bound to Violence*, Ouologuem's essay is nevertheless far more oriented towards the phenomena of everyday life in Europe and towards current social and political events like the Biafra-War, the Vietnam-War, the events of May 1968, and the Civil War in the Republic of Congo after its declaration of independence in the early 1960s. In a series of very subtle, properly philological reflections Ouologuem points out how the hidden racism of French everyday language, which appears obviously in expressions like 'blanchir le criminel' ('whiten' meaning 'to declare innocent a criminal') or 'donner carte blanche' (meaning 'to give someone full power, or authority') (Ouologuem 1968, p. 40). By means of a sarcastic, truly biting anecdote which refers to the narrative structure of the parable, Ouologuem intends to reveal the illusions and ambiguities behind the western aid for Biafra, which is supposed to guarantee good conscience for the western world. He describes how a refugee from Biafra is first received by the French Red Cross and then by a French citizen who charitably takes care of him, but intends also to transform him entirely, both his spirit and his body, into a white man. Even if the physical assimilation turns out to be successful, from the blanching of the skin and the hair, to surgical modifications of the nose and the lips, his mental and cultural resistance proves finally to be insurmountable. The Biafra-refugee whose body seems to be perfectly assimilated to the exterior appearance of a white Frenchman, and who demonstrates overwhelming gratitude towards his "benefactor", seems to be incapable of – or unconsciously resistant to – relinquishing either his africanized French language ("Petit Nègre") or those inherited forms of thought and perception which the narrator of the anecdote qualifies sarcastically as a 'primitive mentality' ('mentalité primitive'; Ouologuem 1968, p. 149).

One of the final chapters of the essay, addressed explicitly to African writers, contains systematic reflections on the necessary "patchwork-structure" of any literary creation, and especially of popular genres. In demonstrating how narrative sequences from different genres of popular mass literature (the erotic novel, pornographic novel, sentimental novel, detective novel) can be recomposed in new stories according to an almost infinite number of combinations, Ouologuem describes creative writing as a process of both imitative and productive receptions of existing literary and cultural forms, schemes and models, a process which he calls the 'operative gymnastics of writing' ('gymnastique opératoire de l'écriture', Ouologuem 1968, p. 176).

These reflections seem to anticipate accusations of plagiarism levelled at Ouologuem in the early seventies which damaged his reputation considerably and problably led to his sudden and surprising retirement from the literary scene. Critics, such as János Riesz (1998), Kaye Whiteman (1972) and Seith Wolitz (1973), have shown, however, that the accusations of plagiarism, especially concerning passages inspired by Graham Greene and André Schwarz-Bart, were unfounded and that Ouologuem's accusers have misunderstood the whole structure of his novel which intended precisely to deconstruct inherited African *and* European discourses by quoting and rewriting them. Comparing in detail the incriminated passages taken from Graham Greene's 1934 novel, *It's a Battlefield*, Wolitz demonstrates in *L'Art du plagiat, ou, une brève défense de Ouologuem* ("The Art of plagiarism, or a brief defence of Ouologuem") that the author of *Bound to Violence* completely rewrites and transforms the passage in question, according to the artistic and ideological strategy of the work: 'Parler d'emprunts, voire de plagiat, ne touche pas à l'essentiel. [...]. Greene nous présente un texte plutôt décousu et presque dépourvu de résonance. Ouologuem resserre tout, intensifie tout, et fait un devoir de nous ouvrir les yeux' ('To speak of borrowings, even of plagiarism, does not touch upon the essential concern of Ouologuem. Greene presents a rather incoherent text without almost any real impact on the reader. Ouologuem contracts all, intensifies all and obligates us to open our eyes'; Wolitz 1973, p. 133).

Ouologuem's theory of African creative writing which is closely linked to the concepts of "Intertextuality", "Patchwork", "Productive Reception" and "Deconstruction", is without any doubt related to the structuralist and post-structuralist paradigms of literary and cultural theory emerging in France in the 1960s and early 1970s, especially in the *Tel Quel*-group. Yambo Ouologuem, as a student of literature and sociology at the Sorbonne in Paris at the time, was certainly familiar with these theoretical and epistemological implications. *Bound to Violence* can be considered a more or less sucessful and convincing, and on the whole fascinating attempt to inscribe African literature in the modernity of deconstructivist thinking (in the manner of Julia Kristeva for instance). In presenting an image of Africa 'as far removed from the romanticism of Negritude as from the anticolonial realism of the novelists' (Mbelolo ya Mpiku 1971, 140), Ouologuem adopted, indeed, a radically negative attitude, close to the role and function of the historiographical narrator in the works of Michel Foucault, for example. In manipulating an extremely complex and rich network of African and European discourses and texts, and in using the stylistic registers of parody, irony, and sarcasm, Ouologuem intended to break up inherited, schematically dichotomous schemes of thought, symbolic representations, and mental perceptions in relation to Africa, such as the oppostions of "black" and "white", of colonialism and precolonial purity, and of violence and innocence.

Bound to Violence strenghtens, often very provocatively, two main structural elements that characterize African literatures in foreign languages since their rise in the 1920s: first their hybrid, composite structure, combining intertextual elements and genres from both oral and written literatures and cultures; and secondly their structure of counter-discourse, or of reply ('Replik-Struktur'[10]), directed against the colonizer and his symbolic and discursive universe. Outstanding representatives of the first generation of African writers, like Bernard Dadié and Abdoulaye Sadji, intended to present an inside view of African reality and African history, close to the oral traditions of their own societies and radically different from that of the colonial discourse. Dadié, accused of 'Anti-French activities' and imprisoned for about a year, declared in a 1949 speech addressed to the tribunal of Grand Bassam, what is today the Ivory Coast, that African writers should consider it their duty to write about their own heros, like the anti-colonialist religious leader Amadou Bamba and the queen Aoura Pokou, their own "Vercingétorix" and "Jeanne D'Arc" (Dadié 1981, p. 207), and reject European perceptions of African History by using and rewriting oral traditions. In his major theoretical work *Éducation Africaine et Civilisation* published in 1964, Abdoulaye Sadji urged African writers and intellectuals to use the foreign media of French-language writing and printing to dig out the African-language subtext of their own culture, beginning with patronyms and topographical denominations, which he proposed to de-colonize in order to re-discover the hidden symbolic and semantic dimensions of names like "N'Dar", the ancient name of the town of Saint-Louis in northern Senegal. Yambo Ouologuem, together with contemporary writers like Amadou Kourouma and Ayi Kwei Armah, goes a step further in this dialectic evolution of African Literature in resolutely leaving behind him what we could call the "identification-pattern". Using the possibilities of literary fiction which include the duty and the right to be hypothetical, provocative, and to take risks – in contrast to non-fictional historiography – Ouologuem produced new insights not only in the structure of African literatures and cultures, but also in the structure of pre-colonial, colonial, and post-colonial power. Despite

---

10   See on this concept, its definition and its historical dimension: Hans-Jürgen Lüsebrink, 'Interkulturelle Dialogizität. Europäisch-außereuropäische Dialoge bei La Hontan und Clavijero', in *Dialog und Dialogizität im Zeichen der Aufklärung*, ed. by Gabriele Vickermann-Ribémont/Dietmar Rieger (Tübingen: Gunter-Narr-Verlag, 2003), pp. 49–67.

a silence of almost 25 years since the publication of his books *Bound to Violence* and *Letter to Negro France*, until the recent rebirth of interest in Ouologuem's biography and work,[11] both provocations have lost nothing of their force and acuteness.

5.5 Conclusions

Intertextuality in sub-Saharan African literatures and the creative processes they provoke, are direct consequences of cultural transfers. This includes, on the one hand, the "intercultural" transfer of texts – both literary and non-literary – from Europe and the non-African world. On the other hand, "intra-cultural" dynamics entails intra-African cultural transfers between oral and written cultures, as well as, in the case of the Arab chronicles written in the Sahel region in the 16th century, between written African cultures and African cultures in European languages, like French. Colonialism in Africa and on other continents represents a significant force of cultural transfers affecting a multiplicity of social and cultural fields: literature, media, photography, art, music, but also technologies (like the printing press), literary and mediatic genres (like the novel or the movie), forms of clothing (like the European or Western suit), pedagogic styles and institutions (like the school and the university in a western sense) and political and social organizations (like political parties or trade unions). The example of Ouologuem's work and that of other African writers who have been mentioned (like Sadji and Dadié) demonstrate that such processes of cultural transfer are closely related to the colonial project of acculturation, political domination and the social transformation of the colonized countries and their societies, which characterize relations between Western societies and African societies between the 17th and the mid 20th century. However, these works also illustrate that, while being embedded

---

[11] See Jean-Loup Amselle, 'Au-delà et en deçà du postcolonialisme. Hommage à Yambo Ouologuem', in *Les Temps modernes*, 699 (2018), pp. 76–84, Sarah Burnautzki, 'Masculinites "noires", renegociées. Yambo Ouologuem au prisme de ses représentations d'ethnicité et de genre', in *HeLix. Dossiers zur romanischen Literaturwissenschaft*, 6 (2013), pp. 12–35, Sarah Burnautzki, *Les frontières racialisées de la littérature française. Contrôle au faciès et stratégies de passage* (Paris: Honore Champion, 2017), Christopher Wise (ed.), S*elections. The Yambo Ouologuem Reader* (Trenton: Africa World Press, 2008), Christopher Wise (ed.), *Yambo Ouloguem. Postcolonial Writer, Islamic Militant* (Boulder: Rienner, 1999) and Hans-Jürgen Lüsebrink, 'De l'incontournabilité de la fiction dans la connaissance historique. Questionnements théoriques, à partir de romans contemporains d'Alejo Carpentier, de Yambo Ouologuem et d'Ousmane Sembène', in *Neohelicon* (Budapest), 16/2 (1989), pp. 107–128.

in a colonial project of domination, processes of cultural transfers produced a dynamic of critical distancing and creative transformation. Often, this occurs first, during the colonial era, in a hidden and fragmentary way. Subsequently, since the beginning of the postcolonial period at the end of the 1950s, this transformation takes place in an open, often radical and violent manner, a process Ouologuem's *Le devoir de violence* (*Bound to violence*), published in 1968, illustrates forcefully.

Bibliography

Allen, Graham, *Intertextuality* (London, New York: Routledge, 2000).

Amselle, Jean-Loup, 'Au-delà et en deçà du postcolonialisme. Hommage à Yambo Ouologuem', in *Les Temps modernes*, 699 (2018), pp. 76–84.

Burnautzki, Sarah, 'Masculinités "noires", renégociées. Yambo Ouologuem au prisme de ses représentations d'ethnicité et de genre', in *HeLix. Dossiers zur romanischen Literaturwissenschaft*, 6 (2013), pp. 12–35.

Burnautzki, Sarah, *Les frontières racialisées de la littérature française. Contrôle au faciès et stratégies de passage* (Paris: Honoré Champion, 2017).

Buzzard, Laura/LePan, Don, *The Broadview Pocket Glossary of Literary Terms* (Toronto: Broadview, 2013).

Chamoiseau, Patrick/Confiant, Raphaël, *Lettres créoles. Tracées antillaises et continentales de la littérature. Haïti, Guadeloupe, Martinique, Guyane, 1655–1975* (Paris: Hatier, 1991).

Dadié, Bernard B., *Carnet de prison* (Abidjan: CEDA, 1981).

Diop, Birago, *La plume raboutée. Mémoires I* (Paris: Présence Africaine, Dakar: Les Nouvelles Éditions Africaines, 1978).

Erickson, John D., 'Yambo Ouologuem', in *Nommo. African Fiction in French South of the Sahara*, ed. by John D. Erickson (York: French Literature Publications Company, 1979), pp. 225–247.

Hale, Thomas A., *Scribe, Griot, & Novelist. Narrative Interpretations of the Songhay Empire, followed by* The Epic of Askia Mohammed *recounted by Nouhou Malio* (Gainesville: University of Florida Press/Center for African Studies, 1990).

Hébert, Louis/Guillemette, Lucie (eds.), *Intertextualité, interdiscursivité et intermédialité* (Québec: Presses de l'Université Laval, 2009).

Holthuis, Susanne, *Intertextualität. Aspekte einer rezeptionsorientierten Konzeption* (Tübingen: Stauffenberg, 1993).

Juvan, Marko, *History and Poetics of Intertextuality*, transl. by Timothy Pogacar (West Lafayette: Purdue University Press, 2008).

Kern, Anita, 'On "Les soleils des indépendances" and "Le Devoir de violence"', in *Présence Africaine*, 85/1 (1973), pp. 209–230.

Kristeva, Julia, *Desire in Language. A Semiotic Approach to Literature and Art* (New York: Columbia University Press, 1980).

Lüsebrink, Hans-Jürgen, 'Afrikanische Ausprägungsformen einer *littérature-monde*. Transkulturelle Räume, intertextuelle Netze und intermediale Bezugnahmen im Werk von Tierno Monénembo', in *Transkulturelle Begegnungsräume. Ästhetische Strategien der Überlagerung, Pluralisierung und Simultaneität in den zeitgenössischen romanischen Literaturen*, ed. by Julia Pröll/Ursula Mathis-Moser (Würzburg: Königshausen & Neumann, 2020) (Saarbrücker Beiträge zur Vergleichenden Literatur- und Kulturwissenschaft), pp. 71–88.

Lüsebrink, Hans-Jürgen, 'Interkulturelle Dialogizität. Europäisch-außereuropäische Dialoge bei La Hontan und Clavijero', in *Dialog und Dialogizität im Zeichen der Aufklärung*, ed. by Gabriele Vickermann-Ribémont/Dietmar Rieger (Tübingen: Gunter-Narr-Verlag, 2003), pp. 49–67.

Lüsebrink, Hans-Jürgen, 'De l'incontournabilité de la fiction dans la connaissance historique. Questionnements théoriques, à partir de romans contemporains d'Alejo Carpentier, de Yambo Ouologuem et d'Ousmane Sembène', in *Neohelicon* (Budapest), 16/2 (1989), pp. 107–128.

Mbelolo Ya Mpiku, Joseph, 'From one Mystification to Another. "Negritude" and "Négraille" in "Le Devoir de Violence"', in *Review of National Literatures*, 2 (1971), pp. 124–147.

Murdoch, H. Adlai/Donadey, Anne (eds.), *Postcolonial Theory and Francophone Literary Studies* (Gainesville: University Press of Florida, 2005).

Olney, James, *Tell me Africa. An Approach to African Literature* (Princeton: Princeton University Press, 1973).

Orr, Mary, *Intertextuality. Debates and Contexts* (Malden: Polity, 2003).

Ouologuem, Yambo, *Le devoir de violence* (Paris: Seuil, 1968). English transl.: *Bound to Violence*, transl. by Ralph Manheim (London: Heinemann, 1971.)

Ouologuem, Yambo, *Lettre à la France nègre* (Paris: Edmond Nalis, 1968).

Ouologuem, Yambo, 'Malien Prizewinner [Interview]', in *West Africa*, 2698 (December 14, 1968), p. 1474.

Ouologuem, Yambo, 'The Rulers Obligations. Interview with the Winner of the Prix Renaudot', in *The Guardian* (November 28, 1968), p. 8.

Paz, Octavio, *La quête du présent. Discours de Stockholm*, Édition bilingue (Paris: Gallimard, 1991).

Riesz, János, 'Abwehrstrategien gegen afrikanische Autoren. Der "Plagiats"-Vorwurf', in *Europäisch-afrikanische Literaturbeziehungen, II: Französisch in Afrika – Herrschaft durch Sprache*, by János Riesz (Frankfurt/Main: IKO-Verlag, 1998), pp. 167–189.

Rüsen, Jörn, 'Formen des historischen Erzählens', in *Formen der Geschichtsschreibung. Beiträge zur Historik*, ed. by Reinhart Koselleck/Heinrich Lutz/Jörn Rüsen, (München: DTV, 1982), vol. 4, pp. 514–606.

Samoyault, Tiphaine, *L'intertextualité. Mémoire de la littérature* (Paris: Nathan, 2001).

Watkins, Mel, 'Talk with Ouologuem', in *New York Times Book Review* (March 3rd, 1971), pp. 7–8.

Whiteman, Kaye, 'In Defence of Yambo Ouologuem', in *West Africa* (July 21st, 1972), pp. 939–941.

Wise, Christopher, 'Qur'anic hermeneutics, Sufism, and "Le Devoir de violence". Ouologuem as Maraout novelist', in *Religion and Literature*, 28 (1966), pp. 85–112.

Wise, Christopher (ed.), *Selections. The Yambo Ouologuem Reader* (Trenton: Africa World Press, 2008).

Wise, Christopher (ed.), *Yambo Ouloguem. Postcolonial Writer, Islamic Militant* (Boulder: Rienner, 1999).

Wolitz, Seith I., 'L'art du plagiat. Ou une brève défense de Yambo Ouologuem', in *Research in African Literatures*, 2 (1973), pp. 130–134.

Wood, Michael, *Literature and the Taste of Knowledge* (New York etc.: Cambridge University Press, 2005).

Worton, Michael/Still, Judith (eds.), *Intertextuality. Theory and Practices* (Manchester, New York: Manchester University Press, 1991).

CHAPTER 6

The Cultural Transfer of Genre: The Case of Aphorism in Déwé Gorodé (New Caledonia), *Par les temps qui courent*

Miriam Lay Brander

Abstract

Genre can be considered one of the configurations of cultural organization most conducive to the study of cultural transfer. Using the example of the aphorisms of New Caledonian writer Déwé Gorodé in *Par les temps qui courent* (1996), I will show that genre is an instrument of intercultural communication that is transformed and subverted in processes of cultural transfer. Gorodé appropriates the European tradition of aphorism by enriching and subverting it through borrowings from political graffito, on the one hand, and concepts from the repertoire of her Kanak ancestors, on the other. This subversive transformation of European practices of genre – moralist aphorism and "mural aphorism" in the context of events in France in May 1968 – is reflected in at least one more procedure of appropriation: Gorodé imitates the rhetorical structures of the discourse of cultural assimilation in a consciously exaggerated way, exposing the neo-colonial strategies of the latter. As an originally European genre in the postcolonial context of New Caledonia, the cultural transfer of aphorism thus constitutes a fruitful example of intercultural communication that can help us perceive political, linguistic, and epistemological implications of cultural transfer between hexagonal France and its peripheries.

6.1 Cultural Transfer of Genre

Cultural transfer of genre has occurred in all phases of accelerated globalization.[1] These processes were largely asymmetrical during the imperialist epoch as receiving, colonized cultures imitated European genre models

---

[1] I follow the model of four phases of accelerated globalisation proposed by Ottmar Ette. See also, with respect to the French speaking countries, Ute Fendler/Hans-Jürgen Lüsebrink, 'Introduction', in *Francophonie et Globalisation Culturelle*, ed. by Ute Fendler/Hans-Jürgen Lüsebrink (Frankfurt/Main, London: IKO, 2008), pp. 3–14.

without transforming them, whereas the influences of colonized cultures on the European centre did not lead to a transformation of the genre system as a whole. For instance, the extensive reception of non-European, orally transmitted texts by European anthropologists in the late nineteenth and early twentieth centuries initially had little influence on European literary trends. Instead, the category of "oral literature" located alien texts as part of the Other, which could consequently be subjected to folkloric curiosity.[2] It was only in the 1920s that the European genre system began to evolve under the influence of non-European literature. For instance, the transfer of the concept of the novel from European culture to the black diaspora produced a confrontation between two different types of genre: the notion of the European bourgeoisie novel, which had completely dissociated itself from oral tradition, and the black genre system, based on orality. When Black author René Maran subtitled his novel *Batouala* with *Véritable roman nègre* (*A True Black Novel*), he created a contradiction between the notion of the novel as a genre belonging to the European bourgeoisie and the application of this genre by a non-European Black author. In this way, the publication of the novel *Batouala* in 1921 and its recognition by the Prix Goncourt gave rise, in the francophone world, to an entire form of literary production that privileged the novel as an expression of postcolonial emancipation.

The transfer of a genre from one culture to another requires contact between two different and possibly incompatible manners of categorizing aesthetic symbolic forms. As Marion Gymnich explains, European models of genre, which originally responded to European social problems, may be inappropriate for representing experiences and traditions crucial to colonial, postcolonial, or intercultural societies. The adaptation of traditional European genres within a new cultural context with different social needs can thus serve as a catalyst for the modification of genres.[3] In the words of Gymnich 'those aspects of genre that reflect European cultural knowledge and European ways of thinking are transformed in the process of "decolonizing genre" thus making possible the articulation of alternative non-European points of view and areas of experience'.[4]

---

2 Erhard Schüttpelz, 'Weltliteratur in der Perspektive einer Longue durée I. Die fünf Zeitschichten der Globalsierung', in *Wider den Kulturenzwang*, ed. by Özkan Ezli/Dorothee Kimmich/Annette Werberger (Bielefeld: transcript, 2009), pp. 339–360 (p. 351).
3 Marion Gymnich, '"Decolonizing Genre"? Das Konzept der literarischen Gattung in englischsprachiger postkolonialer und interkultureller Literatur', in *Was sind Genres? Nichtabendländische Kategorisierungen von Gattungen*, ed. by Stephan Conermann/Amr El Hawary (Berlin: ED-Verlag, 2011), pp. 299–315 (p. 301).
4 Gymnich, *"Decolonizing Genre", op. cit.*, p. 305.

What can be observed is a high number of reciprocal and transversal intersections in cultural transfer processes arising from the context of economic liberalization and growing media-related interconnectivity that has been aided by new technologies since the 1980s. In the domain of genre, this is articulated in manifold forms of hybridization and productive reception. Hans-Jürgen Lüsebrink describes productive reception as 'kinds of creative appropriation (and not imitation) and transformation of cultural discourses, texts, practices and institutions from other linguistic and cultural areas'.[5] In this context, genre can be considered an instrument of intercultural communication that is transformed and subverted in processes of cultural transfer. These processes can be described as follows: They start with the reception of a certain foreign genre within a given culture. The second step consists in the modification of the transferred genre through the insertion of elements taken from the receiving culture. As Pannewick and Szyska state, '[t]he resulting new and modified form is neither a cultural misunderstanding nor a failed reading. Rather, it is a kind of "inventive syncretism", to use James Clifford's term'.[6]

Gymnich identifies two tendencies in the productive reception of genre models in postcolonial or intercultural societies: the critical modification of European genre traditions as an act of intellectual and artistic self-affirmation and the inscription of literary forms that are not rooted in the European genre system and often associated with marginalized, Indigenous, cultural traditions.[7] From my point of view these two aspects cannot be separated. The inscription of archaic oral forms is always an act of critical modification as opposed to mere imitation. The presence of oral elements from non-European languages in written texts challenges, in fact, the Western concept of genre being based on writing by invalidating the transcendence of the written text.[8] This conflict between orality and literacy contains creative potential, resulting, in some cases, in a completely new literary form that can no longer be located within either genre system.

I would like to illustrate these considerations using the example of the transfer of aphorism from hexagonal France to one of its former colonies. Such a transfer can be observed, for example, in the collection of aphorisms *Par les*

---

5   Hans-Jürgen Lüsebrink, *Interkulturelle Kommunikation. Interaktion, Fremdwahrnehmung, Kulturtransfer* (Stuttgart, Weimar: Metzler, 2005), p. 134.
6   Friederike Pannewick/Christian Szyska, 'Crossings and Passages in Genre and Culture. An Introduction', in *Crossings and Passages in Genre and Culture*, ed. by Friederike Pannewick/Christian Szyska (Wiesbaden: Reichert, 2003), pp. 1–9 (p. 3).
7   Gymnich, *"Decolonizing Genre"*, op. cit., p. 300, pp. 301–304.
8   Edouard Glissant, *Traité du Tout-Monde* (Paris: Gallimard, 1997), pp. 108–115.

temps qui courent (1996) by New Caledonian writer Déwé Gorodé.[9] As I will show, Gorodé's aphorisms are the result of a complex, at least twofold cultural transfer: (1) the transfer of key concepts of Kanak[10] culture to French culture and the repercussions of this transfer within the culture of origin and (2) the transfer of the genre of aphorism from French to post-colonial New Caledonian culture.[11] Gorodé not only adopts certain characteristics of European aphorism, whose prototype can be found in 17th century French moralistic literature, but also mixes them with themes from both Kanak tradition and postcolonial thought, as well as introducing visual effects in the presentation of her aphorisms that evoke the agitation posters and graffiti from the events in Paris in May 1968. By imitating the visual techniques of this movement, in conjunction with the expression of political thought, Gorodé modifies French aphorism in an already transformed version. As such, her aphorisms demonstrate a complex and by no means unilinear cultural transfer of genre.

One of the main topics of Gorodé's aphorisms is the perversion of elements and practices of Kanak culture by Western politics of assimilation. To do this she introduces archaic elements of Kanak culture into an originally European genre alongside demonstrating how French politicians have appropriated these elements in order to justify measures of assimilation. By using a European genre to reflect on French appropriation of Kanak cultural practices, Gorodé reverses this process of transfer. Although she cannot directly reclaim the Kanak practices that have been adapted to French political discourse, she regains the sovereignty of its discourse for her culture by unmasking processes of illegitimate appropriation, transforming French language and literary traditions in a creative-subversive way.

---

9   Déwé Gorodé, *Par les temps qui courent* (Nouméa: Grain de sable, 1996).
10 'Kanak' is the adjective derived from 'Kanaky', the denomination for New Caledonia chosen by the members of the separatist movements. It comprises the Indigenous Melanesian inhabitants and elements of New Caledonia.
11 With the expression *post-colonial* (with hyphen) I refer to what chronologically follows the colonial period and to a lesser extent to the contemporary debate on culture and history of the colonial era and its heritage (Ashcroft). New Caledonia is a special collectivity (*collectivité sui generis*) of France, currently governed under the Nouméa Accord of 1998. In accordance with this accord, New Caledonians were allowed up to three referendums on independence; the first in 2018, then two more in 2020 and 2022 if the previous ones had not resulted in independence, but one-third of members of the Congress of New Caledonia voted for another one. The first was held in November 2018, the second in October 2020 with voters rejecting independence in both instances.

6.2 Productive Reception of (Muralist) Aphorism in *Par les temps qui courent*

6.2.1 *The Development of Aphorism*

The Greek term *aphorismos* denoted a scientific principle formulated in a short form. Modelled on a treatise by Hippocrates that presented medical principles using short sentences, this form was widely used by Tacitus (~58–120 AD), who considered himself the "political Hippocrates". The form resurfaced during the Renaissance when commentaries citing and explaining the propositions of Tacitus appeared. Spanish writer Baltasar Gracián imitated this combination of proposition and commentary by commenting on his own sentences. Furthermore, he invested aphorism with literary value by increasing its linguistic concision in his *Oráculo manual y arte de prudencia* (commonly translated as *The Art of Worldly Wisdom*). However, the form as it is known today was mainly developed by the French Moralists of the seventeenth and eighteenth centuries, who continued its linguistic perfection by joining the two parts of aphorism into one single form. Most German critics of aphorism now consider the maxims of these moralists, like La Rochefoucauld, La Bruyère, Vauvenargues, and Chamfort, as the cradle of literary aphorism.[12] Their maxims, which circulated in literary salons of the epoch, contain observations on the human condition and society. For example, the nucleus of the maxims by La Rochefoucauld consists of the affirmation that things are never as they appear: 'Nos vertus ne sont, le plus souvent, que des vices déguisés'[13] ('Our virtues are most frequently but vices disguised.'[14]). In this sense, all human actions, even those that appear altruistic, are products of *amour propre* ("self-love"). It is in this context that the word "aphorism" and the literary genre that today carries this denomination interconnect. While the German language assumes the French term, which is restricted to literary aphorism, the English "aphorism" and the Spanish "aforismo" also include non-literary types of the genre.

As the genre of aphorism in the case of Gorodé is appropriated from French language and culture, I use the French, and accordingly the German, notion of literary aphorism. Gerhard Neumann in his famous definition of the genre describes aphorism as a 'single and unrelated sentence [...] that is thought

---

12 E.g. Harald Fricke, *Aphorismus* (Stuttgart: Metzler, 1984), p. 48.
13 François de La Rochefoucauld, *Maximes et réflexions diverses* (Paris: Garnier-Flammarion, 1977), p. 45.
14 François Duc de La Rochefoucauld, *Reflections; or Sentences and Moral Maxims*, transl. by J.W. Willis Bund, M.A. LL.B/J. Hain Friswell (London: Sampson Low, Son, and Marston, 1871). https://www.gutenberg.org/files/9105/9105-h/9105-h.htm.

against the dominant order of thinking'.[15] In this way, La Rochefoucauld used the genre to foil the idea of man established in his courtly environment (see, for example, Clark). There are divisions among critics over the necessary characteristics of aphorism, but the intersections between most of the definitions by French and German critics consist of co-textual autonomy, brevity and concision, linguistic originality, and pointedness.

The short texts of *Par les temps* tie in with a specific version of aphorism which emerged during the protest movements in France in May 1968, which Werner Helmich has called "mural aphorism" ("Maueraphoristik"). During her studies of literature in Montpellier from 1969 to 1973 Gorodé was involved with the post-68 student movement. Here she came into contact with the Marxist ideals that influenced her first collection of poems *Sous les cendres des conques*[16] (1985), which she began in 1970, and that shaped her entire corpus.[17] In *Par les temps*, traces of the May 1968 events are particularly visible in the graphic design of the short texts. Gorodé's play with different font sizes is reminiscent of the graffiti and agitation posters seen decorating institutions of higher education and administration both in Paris and across France during and after the student occupation (see, for example, the photographic collections of Gasquet and Lewino). By taking up the political art of graffiti, Gorodé implies at least three points. First, she marks her writing as an act of rebellion against political domination. In *Par les temps* she not only expresses resistance against political and cultural dependence from France, but also against the opportunism and parasitism of Kanak chief.[18] Second, Gorodé imitates the collective spirit of the protest movements from which this graffiti emerged. Although the graffiti shows individualistic and anarchistic traits, it displays a shared political will by invoking an individualistic ideology.[19] In this way, Gorodé emphasizes that the political opinions expressed in her aphorisms correspond with collective

---

15 Gerhard Neumann (ed.), *Der Aphorismus. Zur Geschichte, zu den Formen und Möglichkeiten einer literarischen Gattung* (Darmstadt: Wissenschaftliche Buchgesellschaft, 1976), p. 8. Unless otherwise stated, the translations are mine.

16 Déwé Gorodé, *Sous les cendres des conques* (Nouméa: Edipop, 1985).

17 Raylene Ramsay, 'Déwé Gorodé. The Paradoxes of Being a Kanak Woman Writer', in *Kunapipi*, 2 (2005), pp. 23–42 (p. 30); Veronica Ntoumos, 'Déwé Gorodé. Une esthétique militante ou l'art de cultiver des identités plurielles', in *Dialogues Francophones*, 17 (2011), pp. 213–216 (p. 213).

18 Dominique Jouve, 'Les modalités du voyage. Trajets temporels et itinéraires identitaires dans les œuvres de Déwé Gorodé (1985–2009)', in *Nottingham French Studies*, 51/1 (2012), pp. 26–40 (p. 30).

19 Werner Helmich, 'Maueraphoristik. Einige kommunikationstheoretische Überlegungen zu den Graffiti des Mai' '68', in *Cahiers d'histoire des littératures romanes*, 5 (1981), pp. 281–295 (p. 283).

concerns. Moreover, if the production of her aphorisms is thus based upon a shared political attitude, their reception also contains a moment of collectivism, in the sense that Gorodé imitates the reading of graffiti by an urban public. Since the reader of a graffito can be considered 'a single person who is nevertheless, through the reading in public space, connected with a collective with whom he shares similar experiences',[20] the graphic and linguistic designs as well as the content of the aphorisms allow the reader to imagine himself as an observer of political graffiti even if enjoyed in a private space. Third, Gorodé emphasizes the relation between her aphoristic writing and her political activism: affixing a graffito or an agitation poster is not only a political act *per se*; it accompanies and corroborates other political acts like strikes and demonstrations.[21] However, Gorodé's aphorisms support her political activism against French politics of assimilation rather than her involvement with a post-68 student movement as she applies the graphic characteristics of the political graffiti to the content of the New Caledonian separatist movement, for which she had been fighting since 1974. It is this second, much longer phase of her political activism which becomes aesthetically manifest in *Par les temps*.

Apart from the political potential of muralist aphorism, Gorodé might have opted for the genre for two reasons: because its resistance to dominant orders of thinking, in the sense of Neumann, makes aphorism notably applicable in postcolonial contexts and because of its similarity with sententious traditional forms of Kanak culture. In the context of postcolonial literature, the transfer of genre includes processes of transculturation, meaning, following Ángel Rama's use of the term, a confrontation between traditional and modern literatures. In this process, the receiving literature selects elements of the other as well as archaic elements of its own culture. In the case of Gorodé, aphorism is not only adapted to the actual context of the receiving culture but also fuses with traditional genres in the process of creative reception. This combination is probably not random, given the similarity of the two forms that attract each other. Both proverbs and aphorisms can be considered as concise texts which sum up a series of experiences or observations (Jolles). Their distinction resides in the different contexts in which they are used. While proverbs are closely linked to practices of everyday life, aphorism, as a result of the evolution of the genre in Europe, largely remains restricted to literary situations of communication. Of course, there are exceptions – proverbs that appear in literary texts or written collections of oral literature, as well as literary aphorisms that are articulated in every day communication – but, in general, we can say that the proverb

---

20 Helmich, 'Maueraphoristik', *op. cit.*, p. 290.
21 Vasco Gasquet, *Les 500 affiches de mai 68* (Paris: Balland, 1978), p. 8.

belongs to the sphere of orality, while aphorism forms part of literacy. By using aphorism as an aesthetic means of political engagement, Gorodé surpasses mere literary communication and thus values it, like proverbial communication, as an expression of practical knowledge.

6.2.2 Creative Appropriation of Aphorism

After returning to her home country, Gorodé joined the independence movement *Foulards Rouges*, founded in 1969 by young New Caledonians inspired by the Parisian student revolts. As an active member of the separatist-Marxist party PALIKA (*Parti de Libération Kanak*), which she helped found in 1976, Gorodé campaigned for the independence of the Kanak nation during the 1970s. Despite various stays in jail for participating in demonstrations, Gorodé went on to become a member of the New Caledonian government, which she represented as vice president from 2001 to 2009.

While the graphic design of *Par les temps* is affected by the public art of Parisian May revolt, the language and content of the aphorisms stem from Gorodé's engagement with New Caledonian independence. She considers her work the ethical instrument of a collective fight that will open the way to a liberty still to be realized.[22] Part of her political and social engagement reflected in her (aphoristic) work is dedicated to the preservation and strengthening of New Caledonian native languages. Like most authors from ex-French colonies, Gorodé writes in French and subordinates the implications of doing so, in relation to the history of ideas, to her own, Kanak, style of thought. As Hamid Mokaddem writes: 'Ce n'est plus la langue dominante qui impose la pensée, mais la pensée qui expose et qui transpose la langue dans le style kanak'[23] ('It is not any more the dominant language which imposes the thought, but the thought exposes and transposes the language into Kanak style.'). As neither hexagonal French nor the mother tongue of the author are sufficient to express a way of thinking transformed by intercultural processes, an *interlangue* is required.[24] Gorodé achieves this by enriching hexagonal French with structures taken from *paicî*, a New Caledonian language that Gorodé taught at various public schools.

---

22 Ntoumos, 'Dewe Gorode', *op. cit.*, pp. 213–214.
23 Hamid Mokaddem, 'Par les temps qui courent de Déwé Gorodé ou l'Exigence de la pensée dans la parole kanak', in *Notre librairie. Revue du livre. Afrique, Caraïbes, Océan Indien*, 134 (1998), pp. 95–102 (p. 9).
24 Jean-Marc Moura describes *interlangue*, following the term coined by Bill Ashcroft, as a rupture with the linguistic norms of a language to create an individual literary language.

One example of a term used by Gorodé which can neither be attributed to hexagonal French nor the *paicî* language, and thus forms part of an *interlangue*, is *parole*. It refers to one of the key concepts of Kanak culture[25] that has fallen prey to the linguistic inflation of the Matignon Agreements of 1988. Rather than referring to linguistic enunciations, *la parole* represents an intuitive relation with the world. Therefore, it is pitted against the French political discourse present on the radio, television, or newspaper but often lacking content in the sense that it does not mean what it suggests. As we will see later, the term *consensus* exemplifies the distortion of concepts by French politicians according to Gorodé. While words can be deceptive, *la parole* forms part of a direct expression of things and feelings without the detour of language.

La parole est le fruit du silence

FIGURE 6.1
GORODE 1996, p. 6
('The word is the fruit of silence')

Although silence means the absence of acoustic signals, it does not mean the absence of communication.

Le silence ne veut rien dire

FIGURE 6.2
GORODE 1996, p. 7
('Silence means nothing.' Literally:
'Silence does not want to say anything')

The double signification of the last cited aphorism emphasizes the ambiguities of spoken language whilst appropriating it in a creative way: the spoken or written word can be used for selfish purposes instead of serving understanding and agreement.

While those aphorisms related to Kanak cultural practices may seem opaque to the European reader, sentences like the following present themselves more transparently. Nowhere else does Gorodé articulate her ideological attitude more clearly than in this aphorism:

---

25   Mokaddem, 'Par les temps qui courent de Dewe Gorode', *op. cit.*, p. 96.

L'Etat français
veille encore au grain
de son caillou ***stratégique***
du Pacifique

FIGURE 6.3
GORODE 1996, p. 39 ('The French State still keeps an eye on its strategic stone in the Pacific')

In this example, aphorism not only coalesces with political graffito but also with epigram. The political affirmation of France's neo-colonial intentions in New Caledonia is clad in a poetic garment in which an assonant rhyme is followed by a perfect rhyme. By harmonizing the cadences of the verses, Gorodé presents her affirmation in a coherent linguistic formation and thus enhances its persuasive power.

While the previous aphorism is aimed at the colonizer, the following fragment criticizes Gorodé's fellow countrymen who use French assimilation politics to pursue their own interests. She does this using a combination of an elaborate graphic design, Kanak orality, and elaborated literacy:

FIGURE 6.4
GORODE 1996, p. 33

The figure combining text and graphical elements can be read in two ways: If one reads the text literally, one provides us with the proverb-like sentence 'La mort nourrit le charognard' ('Death nourishes the vulture'). Furthermore, the visual arrangement of the single elements as a laughing face suggests the proposition 'La mort nous rit' ('Death laughs at us'). The paronomasia of 'nourrit' ('nourishes') and 'nous rit' ('laughs at us') points to the ambiguity of language, which in turn suggests the hypocrisy of those New Caledonians who avail themselves from French assimilation politics.[26] In this way, they not only bring about the death of Kanak culture but, like vultures, benefit from it. This reproach of self-enrichment aimed at France-oriented groups in New Caledonia also constitutes the thematic frame of the following aphorism:

La paresse
des uns
se nourrit de la coutume
des autres

FIGURE 6.5
GORODE 1996, p. 44
('The laziness of one person nourishes itself from the custom of another')

This aphorism can be read as the reproach that Kanak custom (*la coutume*) has been removed from its original context and has become an instrument of unjust enrichment. The ceremonies of Kanak custom were held within the context of collective events which were frequented by the members of the concerned clans.[27] They included the exchange of gifts and of ceremonial speeches whose content, order, and duration reflected social hierarchies and family relations. While these ceremonies had originally served to strengthen social relationships between ancestral lines, clans, and families, they developed into sources of individual profit under the influence of Western capitalism. By graphically highlighting 'des uns' ('of one person') and 'des autres' ('of another'), Gorodé emphasizes the contrast between the groups of New Caledonian society who subject themselves to the influence of French politics and culture out of sheer accommodativeness and those who adhere to traditional Kanak values.

---

26   In general, the paronomasia often used by Gorodé (for example in "Consensus comme censure ou encore concensus comme sang-sue", p. 17 or "Consensus sans conscience n'est que ruine de soi", p. 18) reinforce the affirmation that the agreements between the French and the New Caledonian governments only appear as consensus at first sight and are not congruent with this concept.
27   Mokaddem, 'Par les temps qui courent de Dewe Gorode', *op. cit.*, p. 98.

Gorodé underlines the fact that the latter are exploited by the first by writing 'des uns' in larger letters than 'des autres'. In this way Gorodé takes up the Western, imperial strategy of marking certain ethnic groups as Other, which must be subjected and civilized. For Gorodé, this imperial logic perseveres in French assimilation politics. From her point of view, the adversarial, New Caledonian political groups play into the hands of the French state by availing themselves of its assets and thus betraying their own culture. For Gorodé and her sympathizers, the heart of political betrayal resides in the *Accords of Matignon*, which included an apparent consensus between the political forces of the archipelago: the separatist movement, to which Gorodé belonged, and the *Rassemblement pour la Calédonie dans la République* (RPCR), which was in favour of French politics. Although the Matignon agreements precipitated a period of relative stability in New Caledonia, the political situation remained tense, as shown by the assassination of one of its proponents by a Kanak extremist on May 4th, 1989.

One key word of the agreements was 'consensus' (*le consensus*), which, as one of the foundations of Kanak culture, ensures the functioning of society.[28] By using this key word more often than any other – in eleven of about eighty aphorisms – Gorodé imitates its increased usage in French political discourse. She unmasks the term of consensus as a neo-colonial dictate that is the result of a misunderstanding and not of an agreement between two equal parties.

Qui est qui dans le **quiproquo** du **consensus** **?**

FIGURE 6.6
GORODE 1996, p. 21
('Who is who in the misunderstanding of consensus?')

By applying different font sizes she marks the equality of the two contractual partners suggested by the symmetry of 'Qui est qui' ('Who is who') as feigned. The disproportionally large question mark imitates a typical structure of political graffito used to indicate the explicit questioning of established opinion and institutions.

Apart from its function as a critical challenge, the question asked in this aphorism is only a rhetorical one, because the answer already has been given in the previous aphorism.

---

28   Mokaddem, 'Par les temps qui courent de Dewe Gorode', *op. cit.*, p. 99.

> Consensus
> est le **maître-mot**
> du seul **maître** à bord

FIGURE 6.7 GORODE 1996, p. 20 ('Consensus is the keyword of the only master aboard')

The expressions 'Consensus' and 'maître' conflict with each other, which Gorodé underlines by highlighting the corresponding keywords and opposing them by using different typographic styles. Gorodé recurs to a typical rhetorical figure of aphorism – the paradox – which she reinforces with the help of graphic instruments borrowed from political graffito in order to denounce the asymmetry of power inherent in an apparent consensus.

The following aphorism makes clear that a key concept of Kanak culture has been converted into an instrument of cultural and political assimilation in the apparent agreement between two parties, where one single voice prevails:

> Consensus
>
> entre
>
> premier   deuxième
> partenaire   partenaire
>   ..   ..
> **pour**   **contre**
>
> arbitre
>   ..
> « l'Etat, c'est moi »
> « Et moi… et moi… et moi »
>
> (air bien connu)

FIGURE 6.8 GORODE 1996, p. 14 ('Consensus between / first partner – for it / second partner – against it / arbitrator / "the State, it is I" / "and I … and I … and I" / (well-known tune)')

This aphorism also begins by visually suggesting a symmetry which is not destroyed graphically but by the colossal 'moi'. Again, Gorodé alludes to the Matignon Agreements, which were presented by the French government as an understanding between equal partners, but which, from her point of view, are a new, hidden version of absolutism. The famous sentence of Louis XIV is echoed in the song *Et moi, et moi, et moi,* released in 1966, in which French rock musician Jacques Dutronc sings about abysmal egoism and Gorodé takes up to again denounce the parasitic attitude of New Caledonian assimilationists.

By dint of the figure of Louis XIV, Gorodé creates a link between her own neo-colonial society and seventeenth century French courtly society. Her references to the themes of the seventeenth-century Moralists implicitly reinforce this link. The material self-enrichment for which Gorodé reproaches the "betrayers" of her culture is, in moralistic terms, the manifestation of delusions of grandeur ('la folie des grandeurs',[29] 'the madness of grandeur') and the pursuit of reputation ('La gloire est une poupée gonflable',[30] 'Reputation is an inflatable doll'). Gorodé turns to the Moralist idea of *amour propre* as a human condition to elucidate a historical context whose particularities foster selfishness.

6.2.3 *The Transformation of French Aphorism*

As we have seen, in addition to some formal aspects of European literary aphorism, like co-textual autonomy, brevity and concision, linguistic originality, and pointedness, Gorodé adopts one of aphorism's major themes and adapts it to the specific problems of New Caledonian society. In this way a diachronic and a synchronic, temporal and spatial, transfer can be observed: thematic features of seventeenth century Moralistic maxims as well as graphical techniques of events from France in May 1968 are transferred to an actual political context. At the same time, a geographical transfer of European aphorism to the peripheral context of New Caledonia takes place. This cultural transfer cannot leave the genre of aphorism untouched. First of all, the appropriation of French aphorism has linguistic consequences. Gorodé uses the French language without letting herself be governed by its epistemological implications; instead, she subordinates it to Kanak style. While French politicians transferred concepts of Kanak culture, like custom, consensus, and *parole* to their political discourse, Gorodé appropriates their arguments by imitating and subverting this discourse from a Kanak point of view. By presenting Kanak cultural practices as having been corrupted by neo-colonialism, she does not merely root the genre of aphorism in an untouched Kanak heritage, but adapts it to the

---

29 Gorodé, *Par les temps, op. cit.,* p. 65.
30 Gorodé, *Par les temps, op. cit.,* p. 69.

current state of her culture. This complex combination of archaic and modern elements also manifests itself in the use of Anglicism and Argot slang, like *fric*[31] and *magot*[32] for money or *came*[33] for drugs. These elements from modern colloquial speech accommodate the fact that processes of urbanization and the resultant sociolects have also affected the islands.[34]

The problem of how to enable social and individual life within a culture whose principles have been perverted, which is constantly present in Gorodé's aphorisms, requires new aesthetic symbolic forms. Due to the fact that neither cultural assimilation nor the instauration of a Kanak culture untouched by European influences is possible, forms of expression capable of representing the complex postcolonial situation need to be found. As an answer to this need Gorodé presents a modified concept of aphorism that combines the thematic constants of European aphorism with both political graffito and New Caledonian social topics, orality with literacy, and written with iconic forms.

As the example of aphorism in Gorodé's work shows, postcolonial literature can be considered neither a mere re-writing of Western canonical genres nor still rooted in so-called "traditional" oral forms (Gehrmann/Veit-Wild). Rather, modified and even new genre forms emerge from the transfer of Western genre conventions and their fusion with non-Western oral forms and postcolonial thought, and such forms cannot be classified within existing categories of genre. Thus, the short texts of *Par les temps qui courent* go beyond existing categories of genre like visual poetry or aphorism. At the same time, taking (mural) aphorism as a basis for reading Gorodé's short texts can help not only illustrate processes of transculturation but also highlight possibly intended paths of reception. The category of genre is highly relevant in intercultural studies because it provides norms that can serve as clues in complex processes of intercultural communication at the same moment as uncovering the way in which established generic categories are transformed in processes of cultural transfer. In this sense, the productive reception of aphorism as an originally European genre in the post-colonial context of New Caledonia can help us

---

[31] Gorodé, *Par les temps, op. cit.*, p. 41.
[32] Gorodé, *Par les temps, op. cit.*, p. 57.
[33] Gorodé, *Par les temps, op. cit.*, p. 68.
[34] Gorodé explains in an interview: "Nous vivons dans une situation *déclanisée, détribalisée*. Même si on essaie de reformer le groupe à Nouméa, on est confronté là-bas aux problèmes urbains …" (Blandine Stefanson, 'Entretien avec Déwé Gorodé', in *Notre Librairie. Revue des Littératures du Sud*, 134 (1998), pp. 75–86 (p. 85)) ('We live in a *declanised, detribalised* situation. Even if we try to reform the group in Nouméa, we are confronted there with urban problems …').

perceive political, linguistic, and epistemological aspects of intercultural communication between hexagonal France and its peripheries.

Bibliography

Ashcroft, Bill, 'On the Hyphen in "Post-Colonial"', in *New Literatures Review*, 32 (1996), pp. 23–31.

Clark, Henry C., *La Rochefoucauld and the Language of Unmasking in Seventeenth-Century France* (Paris: Droz, 1994).

Ette, Ottmar, *TransArea. A Literary History of Globalization* (Berlin, Boston: de Gruyter, 2016).

Fendler, Ute/Lüsebrink, Hans-Jürgen, 'Introduction', in *Francophonie et Globalisation Culturelle*, ed. by Ute Fendler/Hans-Jürgen Lüsebrink (Frankfurt/Main, London: IKO, 2008), pp. 3–14.

Fricke, Harald, *Aphorismus* (Stuttgart: Metzler, 1984).

Gasquet, Vasco, *Les 500 affiches de mai 68* (Paris: Balland, 1978).

Gehrmann, Susanne/Veit-Wild, Flora *Conventions & Conversions. Generic Innovations in African Literatures. Innovations génériques dans les littératures africaines* (Trier: WVT, 2012).

Glissant, Édouard *Traité du Tout-Monde* (Paris: Gallimard, 1997).

Gorodé, Déwé, *Par les temps qui courent* (Nouméa: Grain de sable, 1996).

Gorodé, Déwé, *Sous les cendres des conques* (Nouméa: Edipop, 1985).

Gracián, Baltasar, *Oráculo manual y arte de prudencia* (Zaragoza: Guara, 1983).

Gymnich, Marion, '"Decolonizing Genre"? – Das Konzept der literarischen Gattung in englischsprachiger postkolonialer und interkultureller Literatur', in *Was Sind Genres? Nicht-abendländische Kategorisierungen von Gattungen*, ed. by Stephan Conermann/Amr El Hawary (Berlin: ED-Verlag, 2011), pp. 299–315.

Helmich, Werner, 'Maueraphoristik. Einige kommunikationstheoretische Überlegungen zu den Graffiti des Mai' 68, in *Cahiers d'histoire des littératures romanes*, 5 (1981), pp. 281–95.

Jolles, André, *Simple Forms. Legend, Saga, Myth, Riddle, Saying, Case, Memorabile, Fairytale, Joke*, transl. by Peter Schwartz (New York: Verso, 2017).

Jouve, Dominique, 'Les modalités du voyage. Trajets temporels et itinéraires identitaires dans les oeuvres de Déwé Gorodé (1985–2009)', in *Nottingham French Studies*, 51/1 (2012), pp. 26–40.

La Rochefoucauld, François de, *Maximes et réflexions diverses* (Paris: Garnier-Flammarion, 1977).

Lewino, Walter, *L'Imagination au pouvoir* (Paris: Le Terrain Vague, 1968).

Lüsebrink, Hans-Jürgen, *Interkulturelle Kommunikation. Interaktion, Fremdwahrnehmung, Kulturtransfer* (Stuttgart, Weimar: Metzler, 2005).

Maran, Rene, *Batouala. Véritable Roman Nègre* (Paris: Albin Michel, 1938).

Mokaddem, Hamid, '*Par les temps qui courent* de Déwé Gorodé ou l'Exigence de la pensée dans la parole kanak', in *Notre librairie. Revue du livre. Afrique, Caraïbes, Océan Indien*, 134 (1998), pp. 95–102.

Moura, Jean-Marc, *Littératures francophones et théorie postcoloniale*, (Paris: Presses Universitaires de France, 2005).

Neumann, Gerhard (ed.), *Der Aphorismus. Zur Geschichte, zu den Formen und Möglichkeiten einer literarischen Gattung* (Darmstadt: Wissenschaftliche Buchgesellschaft, 1976).

Ntoumos, Veronica, 'Déwé Gorodé. Une esthétique militante ou l'art de cultiver des identités plurielles', in *Dialogues Francophones*, 17 (2011), pp. 213–216.

Pannewick, Friederike/Szyska, Christian, 'Crossings and Passages in Genre and Culture – an Introduction', in *Crossings and Passages in Genre and Culture*, ed. by Friederike Pannewick/Christian Szyska (Wiesbaden: Reichert, 2003), pp. 1–9.

Rama, Ángel, *Transculturación narrativa en América Latina* (México: Siglo Veintiuno, 1982).

Ramsay, Raylene, 'Déwé Gorodé. The Paradoxes of Being a Kanak Woman Writer', in *Kunapipi*, 2 (2005), pp. 23–42.

Schüttpelz, Erhard, 'Weltliteratur in der Perspektive einer Longue Durée I. Die Fünf Zeitschichten der Globalisierung', in *Wider den Kulturenzwang. Migration, Kulturalisierung und Weltliteratur*, ed. by Özkan Ezli/Dorothee Kimmich/Annette Werberger (Bielefeld: transcript, 2009), pp. 339–360.

Stefanson, Blandine, 'Entretien avec Déwé Gorodé', in *Notre librairie. Revue des Littératures du Sud*, 134 (1998), pp. 75–86.

CHAPTER 7

Textual Transfers and the Poetics of Translation: Literature in Translation, Translation in Literature

Steen Bille Jørgensen

Abstract

Within the field of Cultural Transfer Studies, traditional terms linked to national systems like "reception" and "influence" have been problematized. An increasing focus on process and metamorphosis has pointed to the necessity of considering culture as relational, and quite recently, the status of the literary work and its textual transfers has become a legitimate part of research in cultural transfer. These elements have mainly been studied through the prism of intertextuality, which can be seen as the logical textual and literary equivalent of cinematographic remakes. Taking into account the parallel development of Cultural Transfer Studies and Cultural Translation Studies, I want to argue that creative appropriation and the idea of textual transfers may open perspectives in relation to processes of cultural transfer on the level of individual works and at various other scales as well as culturally and linguistically determined modes of reading. Through concrete readings of experimental literary works, I want to suggest that we must think in terms of a "poetics of translation" to be analysed at the level of individual literary works. This approach may bring to the fore how neo-avant-garde strategies of the sixties imply translation and rewriting but also how metafictional novels integrate concrete examples of (commented) translations on the levels of works. Through readings of Daniel Spoerri's *Topographie anecdotée du hazard* (1962), or rather his and Emmett Williams' collective English version, *An Anecdoted Topography of Chance* (1966), and metafictional novels such as Vladimir Nabokov's *Pale Fire* (1962) and Aragon's *Blanche ou l'oubli* (1967), I want to pinpoint these writers' awareness of the cultural implications of textual transfers. Thus, translation and rewriting imply strong indications of the reader's position as a potential rewriter and literature as a necessary existential remedy for a sense of loss and exile.

As the reader of this volume may realize, recent research in Cultural Transfer has moved beyond the perspectives of bilateral relations. Although it may be tempting to consider the very notion of "transfer" as a simple question of exchange between two national, linguistic and cultural spheres, it is important to consider that notions such as "nation" and "culture" never refer to well-established and stable unities. Since early studies by historians French-German bilateral relations, the research field of Cultural Transfer has expanded, and also been explicitly reconsidered by Michel Espagne (2009, 2013), who was one of the founding fathers of the discipline. In his article 'The Notion of Cultural Transfer' from 2013, he comments on his own research on the German nation and the Germanistic cultural sphere and argues in favor of notions such as "hybridity" and *métissage*. No transfer can be limited to two cultural spaces and Espagne insists on the dynamics of the process of transfer, even using the term "metamorphosis" to characterize the transformation of the cultural elements involved:

> Transférer, ce n'est pas transporter, mais plutôt métamorphoser, et le terme ne se réduit en aucun cas à la question mal circonscrite et très banale des échanges culturels. C'est moins la circulation des biens culturels que leur réinterprétation qui est en jeu
>
> ESPAGNE 2013, p. 1.

The research area of Cultural Transfer, understood as emerging from historical and anthropological thinking, has rapidly evolved. Vague ideas about "reception" and "influence" have made way an effort at comprehending both concrete individual and institutional aspects of the transfer dynamics.[1] M. Espagne even suggests that transfer does not necessarily imply a specific object. This points to the fact that the transfer of literature takes the form of books and translations and highlights the idea that literature and varied poetics is can be a privileged space for experiencing, analyzing, and interpreting what is at stake regarding literary transfers. In the same essay, M. Espagne mentions adaptations of literary models as one such example of a literary space for cultural transfer. Still, how can we study the transfer of literary models and "creative appropriation" (Lüsebrink), which we analyze in cinematographic remakes. To do so, Hans-Jürgen Lüsebrink suggests we look at intertextual adaptations of literary works. We find yet another approach in Ute Heidmann's proposal on "differential textual transfers". Taking as my starting point the common grounds of Cultural Transfer, as articulated by M. Espagne and others, and

---

1 For example in his fascinating account of the development of art history as an academic discipline in central Europe. Michel Espagne, *L'Histoire de l'art comme transfert culturel* (Paris: Belin, 2009).

Translation Studies, I want to emphasize the metamorphosis of the transfer process as it occurs on the level of the individual literary work.[2]

Taking into account the necessity of thinking about the hybridity that is involved in multiculturalism, my question concerning the literary work and the poetics of translation will point to the fact that translation presupposes different languages as well as processes of rewriting. In this perspective, the literary work, more than any other cultural form, has the potential through the process of textual transfer to reflect on the tensions between cultures of cultural resources or meaning potential. It therefore becomes crucial to understand the specifically literary aspects of bilingual or multilingual positioning. I will suggest though that a more specifically literary approach can be deployed by reading concrete examples of translation (and comments on translations) within the novel, which in itself becomes the place for (images of) cultural transfer. In the area of literary translation, the notion of "poetics of translation" has been used to identify the effort of the translator to render the works' "stylistic-literary values". In my perspective, the term will be used as a way of dealing with the way in which translation becomes an integrated part of the literary work. I shall focus on works problematizing the limits of fiction.

Taking as my starting point the avant-garde strategies of 1960s literature, I want to point to (minimalist) concrete poetry/writing's proposition that the idea of potential storytelling simultaneously implies an important idea of "cultural resources". I am thinking mainly of texts by the Nouveau Realist Spoerri but also Fluxus-artists like Emmett Williams and George Brecht. In these artists' works, translation becomes a part of the artistic-literary work, such as when Daniel Spoerri and Emmett Williams collaborate on an extended English version of *La Topographie anecdotée du hasard* (1962). Within the following five years, novelists creating experimental hybrid metafictional novels also structured their books around questions and examples of translation, and we shall see how this works in *Pale Fire* (1962) by the exiled Russian writer Vladimir Nabokov, as well as *Blanche ou l'oubli* (1967) by Louis Aragon. Through readings of these three examples, I will suggest that strategies of translation as rewriting may pave the way for new thinking about the complexity of cultural transfer as process. Neither translation nor literature can be limited to simple questions of selection and mediation. On the contrary, contemporary theories of translation tend to consider the literary work as "always translated" as an intertextual form carrying various cultures and languages.

---

2   In Clive Scott's book *The Work of Literary Translation* (Cambridge: Cambridge University Press, 2018), notions such as *work* and *reader* have become essential in new theoretical orientations seeking to surpass linguistic translation to question among other things our complex experience as readers of translations.

7.1 Translation, Reception and Reading

The myth of Babel is traditionally considered as a parable of chaos and cultural conflict. However, the opposite position could also be defended, as it is in Heinz Wismann's book, *Penser entre les langues* (2012). As a bilingual writer, editor, and translator, working between German and French, Wismann has emphasized the importance of a knowledge of languages, two as a minimum, to any idea of "culture" or, in German *Bildung*. In a similar vein, François Jullien argues that translation is crucial to any kind of intercultural thinking, relativizing any thinking in terms of cultural identity.[3] Reflecting on the French notion of *écart* as opposed to the English "gap", he considers the importance of thinking between and developing a thinking on the relational or what lies between more or less specific, local cultures. Considering the notion of *ressources culturelles* (cultural resources), he has emphasized the importance of 'reinvesting' in the present historical context resources that are or can be adapted in specific local contexts.

In literary terms, the key question relates to the way in which we read literature in translation. In his book *How to Read World Literature* from 2009, David Damrosch includes a chapter on the topic of "Reading in translation", arguing that it is possible to read literary texts in translation without necessarily considering the source text and its context. Proposing to his own reader a quite traditional comparative analysis based on classics like *Candide* and *A Thousand and one nights*, Damrosch claims that we do not necessarily need to know the source text(s) and context(s) to understand the text sufficiently. When one considers that Damrosch argues that *World Literature* is, by definition, translated literature that circulates, one would expect Damrosch to be more concerned with the broader reception of literary works and their impact in society than with philologically based close readings of the works as such. On the one hand, one could argue, that the circulation of texts paves the way for dynamics between cultures, but on the other hand, "reading in translation" should not just be a, more or less ideological, mono-linguistic reading or reading without "awareness of translation".[4] It seems obvious that this position is based on a kind of quantitative or serial fallacy related to the canon. The implicit valorizing of re-translations of the same works as a necessary basis for this kind of fairly traditional comparative reading of works hardly takes into account the transgressive force of contemporary experimental forms which often circulate within smaller circles of writers, translators, and academics.

---

3 François Jullien, *Il n'y a pas d'identité culturelle* (Paris: L'Herne, 2016).
4 In the best of cases, this approach can be considered as an attempt at opening to readings of texts from various cultures and the "reading of translations" as such.

If we turn to the discipline of Translation Studies developed after the early systems theories by Even-Zohar and others, its inherent criticism of more philologically oriented comparative studies has emphasized the importance of the target culture and the weight of "cultural institutions" and ideology as such. Adapting the sociological term of "cultural capital" (Bourdieu), Gisèle Sapiro, among others, has drawn our attention to the quantitative-institutional perspective on translation and linguistic domination which has been developed further by Pascale Casanova.[5] Together they have made it clear that translation implies power and ideology, and that institutional implications determine cultural life considerably.

Given the fact that theories of translation have, since the "Cultural Turn", relativized the approach of the specific work in favor of more ideological perspectives, it is crucial to ask whether quite recent suggestions on "rewriting" from the perspective of post-Translation Studies necessarily imply neglecting the meaning potential (between cultures). As an important thinker of the "cultural turn", André Lefevere has radicalized the way of conceiving literary translation through notions such as "manipulation" and "rewriting".[6] One could say that Lefevere's thinking of translation pinpoints exactly the translation problem of *écart*, mentioned above, drawing attention to the fact that every kind of cultural translation implies adaptation or manipulation. Any literary translation adapts its wording to a specific historical-cultural context with its view of literature/poetics on the one hand and morals/ideology on the other. Specifying the components and cultural agents operating at different levels, Lefevere argues that any textual-literary translation is the result of economic and institutional interest, but also a question of cultural-literary tensions or battles. One observation that becomes increasingly evident is the tendency of big publishing houses with general market strategies publishing mainly bestsellers and smaller idealistic publishers assuring publication of mainly innovative writing, various genres (poetry and drama for instance) and experimental writing.[7] One might think that Lefevere has abandoned or neglected the

---

5   Gisèle Sapiro, 'Translation and the field of publishing', in *Translation Studies*, 1/2 (2008), pp. 154–166 and Pascale Casanova *La langue mondiale. Traduction et domination* (Paris: Seuil, 2015).
6   In their book *Constructing cultures* (Bristol: Multilingual Matters, 1998), Susan Bassnett and André Lefevere present their common view of *Translation Studies* trying to understand the context of historical-cultural processes determining a specific ideological-poetological understanding of literature, any translation being the result of different demands and audiences.
7   It is important to note that small idealistic editors selecting exclusively what they consider to be important literature, very often use para-texts such as the translators Foreword/Postface to legitimize their criteria of selection and to explain difficulties in translating formally self-conscious works.

original. However, more positively, it is crucial to think further about the textual and cultural dynamics implied in the positive notion of "rewriting". The traditional source text/target text-dichotomy is abandoned in favor of the larger notion of "rewriting" (1992: 138).

Following Lefevere's line of reflection, Edwin Gentzler takes into account the new conceptual status of the source text, developing further the notion of rewriting. Reading for instance 'pre-Shakespeare translations of Hamlet', he acutely reminds us of the Nordic and Norse historical-mythological origins of Shakespeare's *Hamlet* and presents important insights into the work of Saxo Grammaticus' *Gesta Danorum*.[8] In his perspective, rewritings should not merely be considered in terms of institutional (poetological or ideological) norms defended by patrons but also, in the larger context of historical dynamics. Rewriting is not merely a question of selection but also a question of contextual, artistic-intellectual as well as individual or personal relevance. Even though Lefevere was right pointing out that a better understanding of foreign literatures and cultures is far from being the most important reason for translating literature, it becomes crucial, developing Gentzler's point of view further, to argue that rewriting is a literary strategy implying individual artistic impulse, both the writer's and the reader's:

> Further, he [Clive Scott] suggests that criticism has tended to avoid dealing with the individual input by the reader because of its idiosyncratic and subjective nature. Yet these impressions, often triggered by personal associations, old memories, and unpredictable intertexts, are precisely those aspects that reveal what the reader finds useful and why
> GENTZLER 2017, pp. 229–230.

Reading Scott, Gentzler reminds us that intertextuality and rewriting is already there before translation as such. This is probably even one of the main reasons why we read literature if we accept that literature constitutes a privileged opening for an understanding of the other, either at an individual or a cultural level.[9] If research in cultural transfer has shown that translation plays a central role when it comes to the circulation of literature, this is also very much the

---

8　As we shall see in the analyses of translation in the metafictional novel, this aspect of the Hamlet myth is also present in the metafiction from the second half of the 20th c.
9　One of the core elements of Michel Espagne's view of cultural transfer is related to the "altérité des langages" (otherness of languages), as underlined by Joseph Jurt, 'Traduction et transfert culturel', in *De la traduction et des transferts culturels*, ed. by Christine Lombez/Rotraud von Kulessa (Paris: L'Harmattan, 2007), pp. 93–111.

case of translation studies of rewriting according to Gentzler's logic. Although editorial and ideological aspects of transfer must be taken into consideration as an essential part of our ways of understanding literature, just as important are new ways of understanding intertextuality through reading writers in other languages, which can bring about new insights into writing as a particular potential or dynamics in transfer processes.[10]

7.2 Differential Reading

As we have seen, the idea of rewriting is crucial to a theory of translation as well as the use of literary models from foreign cultures. This is also one of the important aspects, we find in Ute Heidmann's reading of European tales. In her work, she brings to the fore the way in which stories circulate as models between European countries.[11] Pointing to the written and intertextual quality of these tales, considered by many as an oral legacy, Heidmann has emphasized the importance of a discursive perspective, avoiding in this way to neglect either the textual or the contextual-cultural implications of the different languages. U. Heidmann's analysis of differences between cultures becomes crucial.[12] Considering liminal literary experiences what remains, nevertheless, to be determined, implying exploration of literary potentiality and the limits of the literary work as such, is the fact that many works from the 20th C and onwards adopt rewriting strategies according to more or less explicit models. This involves translation as rewriting but also different sorts of intertextual strategies (Filion 2013)

The opposite example would be bilingual publications urging the reader to consider the accurateness of the translation and appreciate the possible double reading. This kind of publication is very often strictly artistic-academic and thus marginal, obeying either a research logic or another more subjective

---

10   As early as 1984, Michel Espagne insists on the importance of textual genesis, intertextuality and impact, underlining at the same time the importance of historically situated readers: 'lecteurs successifs qui confèrent à l'œuvre son historicité' (Jurt 'Traduction et transfert culturel', *op. cit.*, p. 100).
11   The textualist understanding of literature was as we all know theorized in a consequent manner by Kristeva in the context of sixties. Since then, a broader understanding of intertextual writing has brought attention to the memory of texts and reading.
12   See Ute Heidmann, 'La Différence n'est pas ce qui nous sépare', in *Zwischen Transfer und Vergleich*, ed. by Christiane Solte-Gresser et al. (Stuttgart: Franz Steiner Verlag, 2013), pp. 331–343.

impulse and is often considered elitist.[13] Nevertheless, the double perspective on the work and its way of exposing the *écart* mentioned above, should be studied further both regarding the way it might influence patrons and determine their awareness of the cultural-linguistic dimension of the reading in-between or the formal-textual dimension opening to the impact of the foreign poetics.[14]

Regarding poetics and translation, this coupling is at the core of Marjorie Perloff's thinking about the ontological status of the work implying both a formalist approach and readings of literary works based on contextualization. In her book *Differentials* from 2007, two of her essays deal with literary translation as a way of determining and analyzing literary strategies. In other words, in her view translation becomes a means for detecting which kind of poetry and poetics we are dealing with, and which would be the most apt ways of reading. Examining lyrical classics, namely Rilke, she demonstrates how four translators have found different approaches to the same couple of verses. Lyrical poetry presents a series of challenges to translators, which is of course one major reason why bilingual editions of neighbor languages, mentioned above, become relevant. However, at the same time, we witness new contemporary poetical forms, which can almost be translated literally, and Perloff has argued that this is exactly the way of showing that we are dealing with conceptual poetry. This demonstrates that a translator cannot not simply do what they wish with a literary text; there are limits to manipulation and rewriting, limits that relate to the formal-literary premises presented by the work itself. Every reading is rooted in a context, and every text should be translated by a translator observing and respecting both of a referential, contextual, and a poetological dimension.

Given Perloff's own conceptual framework and references to the philosophy of Wittgenstein, investigations into everyday language is essential, and it is no coincidence that Perloff analyses a text by Oulipo-writer Jacques Roubaud, who is himself inspired by Wittgenstein. Offering a reading of the poem *Ce morceau de ciel* (*This patch of sky*) published in *Quelque chose noir* (1986)/*Some thing black* (translated by Rosmarie Waldrop in 1999), a book of poetry written

---

13   A few examples from the contemporary Danish context could be the bilingual edition of Hölderlin's *Hyperion* and Brecht's *Svendborger Gedichte*: Friedrich Hölderlin, *Hyperion* (Copenhagen: Rævens Sorte bibliotek, 2011). Bertolt Brecht, *Svendborgdigte* (Copenhagen: Multivers Klassiker, 2017).

14   This point draws on the recent insight, which I personally gained as an editor and as a translator contributing to two bilingual Danish editions: Jacques Jouet, *På ... / En ...* (Aarhus: J&J-Aarhus Litteraturcenter and SLC, 2016); *Franske stemmer / Captations littéraires* (Copenhagen: Etcetera Editions and SLC, 2017); *Poetiske rum / Espaces poétiques* (Copenhagen: Bobo Editions and SLC, 2020).

in a language without images or metaphors, Perloff emphasizes the importance of the literal aspect of Roubaud's language and its rewriting of Dante's *Vita nouva*.[15] The English translation of the title as Perloff points out, is in fact literal and renders the French very well. Through her "differential reading", Perloff brings to the fore the necessary awareness of the most concrete aspects of the text in its dynamic relation to its conceptual-intertextual dimension. These strategies point to Roubaud's existential situation or context of being alone after the death of his partner, the photographer and artist Alix Clio.

Regarding the transfer aspect of similar concrete textual strategies, it is particularly interesting to examine the neo-avantgarde strategies of the sixties between the art world and concrete poetry. If groups such as Fluxus and the Nouveaux Réalistes do not exactly adopt the surrealist idea of a world revolution based on nebulous ideas about the Freudian unconscious, they did in fact transcend national borders to travel both throughout Europe and in the USA. In this way, they developed relatively intimate friendships, rooted in practices related to everyday life and commonplace objects and expressions. Such international and multicultural partnerships complicated lifestyles defined along merely linguistic and cultural lines and even demonstrated the dynamics of translation or transfer as the very essence of artistic practices, not without parallel to detective-like investigations seeking traces of the past in the concreteness of the present moment.

In the context of the concrete poetry practiced by Emmett Williams, it is interesting to observe early uses of translation within the written work, and we find one of the most appealing forms in the ironic and *infra-literary* work *An Anecdoted Topography of Chance* (1966) by Rumanian-French Daniel Spoerri, as translated by Williams. This book is dominated by its para-textual dimension, through a series of preliminary texts and concluding appendixes.[16] As an "augmented" English version of Spoerri's *Topographie anecdotée du hasard* (1962), the book can be seen as a prototypical example of translation as rewriting. In its Introduction, the reader even learns that Spoerri himself had wanted to augment his French version, and agreed to participate in the collective project of translating his own work into English, adding notes and new texts[17] in order to move beyond "chance" and paradoxically insist on order through the para-text entitled *An Anecdoted Topography of Order*. Thus, the writers

---

15   Nevertheless its systematized intertextual strategies or patterns clearly make it a text with a poetic impact and an autobiographical meaning. Both Wittgenstein are mentioned explicitly, Wittgenstein's name is even the title of one of the poems.
16   The function of the seven *Appendix*-texts and the *Index*, at the end of the book, is both a ludic and a documentary one. Text is certainly proliferating, but the reader is also informed about various artistic practices and processes of the period.
17   In this way, a new larger volume appears and is signed by the writer but also the translator.

deliberately adopt a ludic-ironic posture, which is signaled from the beginning on the double title page, where we read:

> *An Anecdoted Topgraphy of Chance* / *(Re-anecdoted Version)* / Done with the help of his very dear friend / Robert Filliou and / Translated from the French, / and further anecdoted / at random by their very dear friend / Emmett Williams / With One Hundred / Reflective Illustrations by / Topor. (See Appendix, fig. 7.1)

The para-textual dimension, thus creates a space for play, and the meaning of the quite enigmatic word "re-anecdoted" is suggested by formal and structural means. In this clearly experimental work, the reader soon finds out that the idea or the concept behind the work arises from the way in which the writer and the translator had agreed to expand the work, in particular through the translator's notes on concrete, even insignificant, aspects of everyday life and personal relations, creating also a humoristic mode of writing. The written and the pictorial qualities are both emphasized in this *narrative* or *prose poem* and a more developed commentary of this title page should necessarily deal with both the graphic qualities and the collective dimension of the whole project. All in all the conventional and institutional textual space is transgressed in order to reflect the creative dynamics of a French-Roumanian artist (Daniel Spoerri), a British poet (Emmett Williams), a French Fluxus-artist (Robert Filliou) and the Polish-Jewish writer and painter (Roland Topor).

The narrative strategies developed in the notes present a new kind of literary dimension through altering and metamorphosing the status of the work as such. In other words, it becomes a clearly conceptual (literary) work. In this way, the French text, a simple description by the artist of objects (some with textual inscriptions) in his room, becomes a collective work based on friendship and a common view of art or creative life as ludic intervention regarding both material and linguistic aspects of everyday life. From the point of view of the reader, translation and cultural transfers, clearly, become a central part of the text. Living in Denmark and being a Dane myself, I spontaneously retain the Danish references. In text 6, we find the first of these Danish occurrences on a Jar of Nescafé, which had clearly been a part of an exhibition in a Danish art gallery:

> 6. Jar of Nescafé. With Danish label^y that I brought back from Copenhagen Sept. 30 and which is almost empty now. I was in Denmark to help organize the "Art in Motion" (Bevaegelse I Kunsten) exhibition (Nos. 34d,

42). Since the museum decided it could get along without my assistance I took advantage of the opportunity that ADDI KOEPCKE gave me to have a show in his gallery. Fate willed that I live at ROBERT FILLIOU'S, who since he had been ordered to leave the country, gave up his apartment and let me "snare" everything I could find there: altogether ten pictures. The exhibition opened Sept. 28, 1961, at 6:30 p.m., and ran through Oct. 28.

SPOERRI 1962, pp. 15–16

Reading this passage today, we actually obtain an account of intercultural Art History of the sixties. Since then, we have been able to find Spoerri's snare pictures in museums. However, it is crucial also to think of the way language is "snared" in this passage. Presenting both the English and the Danish wording, the writers themselves play the role as translators: "Art in Motion (Bevaegelse I Kunsten)" (p. 15). A Danish storyline, clearly connected to the collaboration with the Galleri Köpcke, can even be detected. This theme even implies individual relations, and Robert Filliou actually met a Danish girl and lived for a while in Denmark.

Though this kind of avant-garde approach is an ontological interrogation of everyday life in particular Parisian places like the Place Mouffetard and its most banal serially produced objects, the artistic, textual and cultural dimension is essential. The two artists exchange flats moving across the Atlantic but the multilingual dimension itself is the most important aspect of this endeavor. On the one hand, this can be seen as obscuring understanding, but on the other, it also suggests the international dimension of avant-garde activities. The partly ironical cultural references make us wonder about the particular way of ceasing the present, almost like a *nature morte* without representation, through the interventionist, artistic project. In other words, the translational-intercultural dimension, with its meaning potential, became an essential aspect of (a concrete) thinking about artistic activity as a process equivalent to the dynamics of life itself.

Following M. Espagne's point of view, the cultural transfer implies more than the two languages and cultures, and this point of view has even become a part of artistic consciousness reflected on the level of the work and its structure. What was at the beginning a simple notation of the objects of everyday life (close to Spoerri's snare-pictures) became a sophisticated formal reflection on languages and cultures. The ironic-ludic approach of language(s) makes translation and (re)writing appear as essential elements creating meaning potential through description and narration of a non-heroic kind.[18]

7.3 The Metafictional Novel and the Poetics of Translation

Through their post-Duchampian ontological strategies these neo-avantgarde artists interrogated the art world as such through their inter-medial artistic and literary experiments. If we turn to the metafictional novel, we find a similar attention towards concrete words and expressions; however, literary intertextual strategies, which make apparent the "readymade quality" of language, as we shall see, imply a very strong consciousness of literary tradition. Since the nineteenth century and the development of both literacy and the press, writers have constantly pushed the limits of literary genres and modes of expression. An increasing liberty of expression made writers aware of the possibility of nourishing their own (nationally determined) writing through the reading, translating and rewriting of foreign texts which entered into dialogue with to their own literary ideas and contributed to defining their (modernist) poetics.[19]

From a theoretical point of view, it has become increasingly clear, that the notion "poetics of translation"[20] is related not just to writing and reading literature but also to a particular kind of reflection on languages and intercultural understanding. This was probably one of the intuitions of the French modernist writer Marcel Proust when deciding to translate texts by the British critic John Ruskin. Edward Bizub publishing an essay on this particular aspect of Proust's novelistic writing emphasized the psychoanalytic aspect of the work. As such his reading also brings to the fore the formal-literary approach to

---

18   Further perspectives on this kind of avant-garde strategy can be found in the more individual works of contemporary poets like German-Japanese Yōko Tawada and multicultural poet Cia Rinne. Both of these female writers are excellent examples of poets constantly exploring languages and transfers between cultures, investing their bodily presence in an attempt to grasp our contemporary historical and globalized world.

19   This is the case of Baudelaire translating Poe and rewriting Thomas de Quincey's *Confessions of an English Opium-Eater* and *Suspiria de Profundis* in *Les Paradis artificiels*.

20   Meschonnic's notion "poétique du traduire" refers specifically to the formal-stylistic dimension of translation and could be translated by "translational poetics". This is the term which has been suggested in a book on Angela Carter (Martine Hennard Dutheil de la Rochère, *Reading, Translating, Rewriting. Angela Carter's Translational Poetics* (Detroit: Wayne State University Press, 2013)) and which brings us closer to thinking about translation as a part of the literary work and even the way the individual writers conceive of literature.

psychology and interior life. In the case of Proust, it is nonetheless important to remember the particular kind of intertextual or intra-linguistic translating of the *pastiche*. In this perspective, writing is, first and foremost, understood as style or "the manner" of the individual writer.[21]

Considering such strategies of rewriting with their inherent self-conscious meta-fictional dimension, the poetics of the novel presents more and more overt interrogations of language and the limits of representation. Following and developing the aesthetics of fragmentation that could be found in Joyce's *Ulysses*, writers like Nabokov and Aragon would in similar ways explore the "textual and narrative potential" related to translation. As we shall see, their two novels *Pale Fire* (1962) and *Blanche ou l'oubli* (1967) are both fragmented metafictional novels. Both of them have extensive references to both German and English literary classics and it is striking that Shakespeare is at the core of the intertextual play in both as well as the translation of his works, *Timon of Athens* in Nabokov's novel and *The Tempest* in Aragon's. Still, formal differences are also important. Nabokov is a very playful and overtly ironic (and parodic) writer. Aragon stays attached to interrogations of society, politics, and the reality of everyday life.

As an exiled Russian writer in USA and as an academic, Nabokov remolded the novel with respect to exile and multilingualism.[22] This is also the case of Aragon, whose partner was the Russian, Elsa Triolet, with whom he translated Céline's *Voyage au bout de la nuit* into Russian. In his metafictional novels *La Mise à mort* (1965) and *Blanche ou l'oubli*, he examined the difficulties of dialogue and communication between individuals. The narrator, Gaiffier, who investigates the lack of personal pronouns in Javanese, points to the absent dialogue and Aragon indirectly questions his suffering at the level of subjectivity.

Thus, both of these writers have integrated translation at the thematic and structural levels of their extremely fragmented works. In this light, it is important to examine the ways in which novels reflect on dialogue and processes of transfer to make the distinctive poetics of the work itself a question of linguistic-cultural processes. In many ways, we can claim that the metafictional novel points to the limits of notions such as "culture" and "identity" in favor of the dynamics and the potential of the in-between or the metamorphosis of textual transfers.

---

21   Proust rewrote the *fait divers* referred to as "L'Affaire Lemoine" according to the style of a whole series of writers. Marcel Proust, *Pastiches et mélanges* (Paris: NRF, 1919).
22   He considers himself an American writer born in Russia who studied French literature at Cambridge.

7.3.1 Pale Fire

As critics have observed, translation is an essential part of Vladimir Nabokov's artistic and intellectual preoccupations.[23] Translation is one of the core themes of the novel *Pale Fire*, constantly linked to the intertextual dimension of the book, on the one hand, and to the construction of a fictional language on the other. As theories (or perhaps just as much practices) of translation have often proved, we simultaneously find meaning potential and experience loss in the processes of translation. Given the importance of commentary and 'textual anthropophagy', as developed by Brazilian poet Haroldo de Campos, it is critical to understand the way the thematic of translation is intertwined with the structure of the novel.

As a matter of fact, the novel is structured around the fictional poet, John Shade's unfinished poem of 999 verses entitled 'Pale Fire'. The poem is followed by a *Commentary* section, which develops a narrative of the creative process and the 'exegete's' own role in the process as well as biographical elements relating to his former position as the king of Zembla. In this commentary the reader actually finds a suggestion regarding a potential, final verse no. 1000. Finally in the *Index*, Nabokov signals a concrete dimension blending comments on authentic and fictional elements in a structure suggestion that the idea of 'word golf', or an elaborate game of words is what the books is all about. As the *Index* seems to suggest through the following words:

> *Translations, poetical*; English into Zemblan, Conmal's versions of Shakespeare, Milton, Kipling, etc., noticed 962; English into French, from Donne and Marvel, 678; German into English and Zemblan, *Der Erlkönig*, 662; Zemblan into English, *Timon Afinsken*, of Athens, 39 Elder Edda, 79; Arnor's *Miragarl*, 80.
>
> NABOKOV 1987, p. 247

This passage clearly illustrates the blurring of boundaries between the fictional and the real. Poetry and literature are closely connected to the process of translation and its meaning potential, which is emphasized through the many references to literature from various language areas. No essence or authorial identity seem to lie behind the words that are always a part of new situations and contexts. The reader is even warned in the *Foreword* that the unachieved poem is translated through the commentary, and reading as such becomes a question of personal motivation and imagination and even potential writing.

---

23   He translated Pushkin, rewrote his own novels in American because of the poor state of existing translations, and he developed a strong idea of the importance of literal translation.

From the macro-level to the micro-level, the idea of rewriting, variation, and metamorphosis seems essential. In the case of *Pale Fire*, we may speak of a metafictional novel, and still we recognize crime fiction, literature of exile, as well as a campus novel, with conflicts related to Shade's manuscript and responsibility for editing the book to be published. Intertextuality establishes rewriting as the fundamental task of the author, and if we can talk about originality, this seems to stem from the capacity of combining various pre-existing forms. All levels of expression and forms can be redefined and reformulated. Consequently, we must ask if the writer and the novel as such do not appear as functions of rewriting and translation understood as cultural transfer. Thus, the reader understands that the writer invites him to play a word game, which is at the same time a "game of worlds". The combinatory aspect is very close to the practice of the translator of literature and the uncertainty concerning the fictional or real (historical) references implies that knowledge and insight (into languages) is necessary to make decisions regarding the ways to read and understand Nabokov's text.

Although English is the clearly predominant language of *Pale Fire*, it is also in many respects multilingual. As a kind of a campus novel on an American language department, the theme of philology, erudition, and multilingualism is constantly present. The reader is confronted with various linguistic expressions both from historical Latin and various modern languages such as Russian, Spanish (*ombre*) and Danish (p. 107). In this multilingual context, even the Zemblan fictitious examples are all the more easily accepted as possible expressions of a particular culture. One passage is particularly interesting as a pastiche of philological discourse, taking the form of commentaries on translations from German and French. Thus, the highly canonical text of the *Erlkönig* and its (fictitious) translation from German into English is commented at considerable length:

> Line 662: Who rides so late in the night and the wind
> This line, and indeed the whole passage (lines 653–664), allude to the well-known poem by Goethe about the erlking, hoary enchanter of the elf-haunted alderwood, who falls in love with the delicate little boy of a belated traveler. One cannot sufficiently admire the ingenious way in which Shade manages to transfer something of the broken rhythm of the ballad (a trisyllabic meter at heart) into his iambic verse
> 662 Who rides so late in the night and the wind
> 663 ...
> 664 ... It is the father with his child
> Goethe's two lines opening the poem come out most exactly and beautifully, with the bonus of an unexpected rhyme (also in French): *vent-enfant*, in my own language:

> *ret woren ok spoz on natt ut vet?*
> *Eto est votchez ut mid ik dett ...*
> Another fabulous ruler, the last king of Zembla, kept repeating these haunting lines to himself both in Zemblan and German, as a chance accompaniment of drumming fatigue and anxiety, while he climbed through the bracken belt of the dark mountains he had to traverse in his bid for freedom. (188–189; see Appendix, fig. 7.2)

This comment on translation also implies intertextual reference and diverges into obsessional idiosyncratic discourse of the novel's (mad) narrator, Kinbote, imagining that he is the king of Zembla in exile; this can be understood through intertextual allusions to Shakespeare and *Hamlet* but also Nordic history and mythology as a source or uncertain origin of the great literary work. The Danish capital Copenhagen is mentioned several times as a part of the flight itinerary of the enigmatic murderer Jakob Gradus. At the level of formal expression, the philological commentary turns to existential preoccupations and even an obsession with inscribing the absent story/history of Zembla in the poem. The praise of the poet seems ironic considering the fact that commentary as storytelling replaces the actual form of poetic expression.

The following passage of the *Commentary* section is devoted to the translation of poems from English into French published by a Canadian scholarly journal. The narrator's harsh and ironic critic of the Sibyl Shade translator seems to stem from ("*Line 678*: into French" (p. 190)) his homosexuality and the whole passage is clearly very ironic. Both of these passages appear as academic commentaries of translations, which turn to delusional constructed partly historical and partly phantasmagoric and constructed reality. Both are end up in references to the Zemblan (a Zemblan version of Goethe's poem) and the "magic Zemblan (the tongue of the mirror)" (p. 191).

The attentive reader will discover that references to the fictional language Zemblan run through the whole *Commentary* section with it numerous translations of specific expressions or words ... 'A crested bird, called in Zemblan sampel ("silktail") ...' (p. 61); "Wodnaggen" (p. 68); "A mow (in Zemblan *muwan*) is the field next to the barn" (p. 185). Clearly, this kind of "dictionary" or "language manual" aspect, presenting a mythological (lost) language in itself becomes an allegorical expression of exile. At least this could be one possible reading of a more enigmatic passage on translation in the commentary *Line 615*: two tongues (p. 186). Here we find a list of language couples opened by the couple 'English and Zemblan' followed by 'English and Russian' but also 'English and Lettish' 'English and Estonian' 'English and Lithuanian' ... the list is concluded by 'American and European' (p. 186). The coupling in itself underlines the construction of meaning between cultures and languages. However, the numeric privilege of the English-Russian coupling, which is repeated several times, should signal the autobiographical dimension of the novel, with its specific writing of the in-between of the Russian-American. The Zemblan should, in this perspective, be seen as a phantasmagoric, literary construction both of the lost biographical Russian and the literary England (p. 186). We hear that 'Gloomy Russians spied' (p. 192), ant this element can be read as a relativizing view of national cultural identity. In this long passage on cultural translation, questions of origin related to fatherhood in the *Erlkönig* could be retained, and yet, memory appears as a phantasmagoric construction out of fragmented stories and images.

The theme of exile points to an interpretation of the melancholic dimension of the intellectual reverie. At the very least, the way a language is constructed out of more or less historical elements from earlier languages appears to contribute to the blurring of the limits between the real (the philologically documented) and the fictitious. This illuminates the reference to an (imaginary?) translation of the Elder *Edda*, which is mentioned (p. 88); but it is chiefly important to note the way Nabokov connects Shakespearean intertextuality with the (imaginary) translation into Zemblan. We learn about 'Conmal the great translator of Shakespeare' (p. 63) and 'Conmal's translation of *Timon of Athens* into Zemblan' (p. 66 and p. 224).

In our times of writing in exile, it is interesting to note that Nabokov used literature and the literary tradition to construct "a nation" and an "origin" along the lines of Shakespeare's mythological Kingdoms with a touch of culture, writing, and mythology based on Norse language.[24] However, the limits of this kind of melancholic and obsessional phantasmagoric imagination also appears through an abandoned project of translation. In fact, Kinbote fails in translating Shade into Zemblan, and the unachieved status of the central poem is reflected in the very act of translating as commentary or rewriting.

7.3.2   *Blanche ou l'oubli*

With his two books *La Mise à mort* (1965) and *Blanche ou l'oubli* (1967), Louis Aragon makes the autobiographical quest of the other (his Russian companion Elsa Triolet) a central thematic aspect of the novel.[25] At the same time, he constantly interrogates the cultural and linguistic distance between the two of them. Much like in *Pale Fire*, Shakespeare becomes an important intertextual reference, mirroring the novel's tragic existential dimension, while simultaneously problematizing translational aspects of language. An interesting example

---

24   Somehow anticipating the above mentioned theoretical suggestions by E. Gentzler.
25   French translations of Shakespeare and references to Russian literature play an important role.

is the way that he imagines Denmark through the writings of the Danish national chronicle by Saxo Grammaticus. However, the extent to which language itself becomes the theme and the subject of Aragon's writing becomes clear in *Blanche ou l'oubli*. The main character and narrator Geoffroy Gaiffier is also a linguist working on Javanese language, culture, and dialects.[26]

Nevertheless, Gaiffier's expertise in foreign languages with a lack of personal pronouns doesn't help him much in apprehending why his wife Blanche left him. In Aragon's fragmented novel, the construction is less focused on the play with genres and (academic) commentary than we find in Nabokov than on the limitations of perception and narration. Though the narrator is probably close to losing his senses, much in the way it is suggested in *Pale Fire*, this aspect is linked more closely to emotions and the relationship between man and woman and, significantly the structure of the narration shifts perspective (Gaiffier inventing the female narrator Marie-Noire) according to the logic of *mise en abyme* and interchangeable narrators.

Using Flaubert's *L'Éducation sentimentale* as a model for rewriting (Jørgensen 2013), the fictional-phantasmagoric and the autobiographical are constantly intertwined. This is certainly one of the reasons why Hölderlin's *Hyperion* also becomes an important intertextual reference and translation is integrated directly in the first chapter. As an intertextual reference Hölderlin's *Hyperion* runs through the whole book and is quoted in the very last page. If the first occurrence is clearly related to Aragon's youth in the twenties, this reference becomes essential and is far from being merely nostalgic. It implies a whole worldview and, significantly, Hölderlin is also present, next to Flaubert and an autobiography related to Élisa Schlésinger's destiny in Germany, as an image of oncoming madness. The blurring of the limits between the fictional and the real is constantly accompanied by intertextual reflections and translation:

> C'était que sous le prétexte de la philologie, il voulait s'assurer, Maxime, d'une traduction qu'il en avait faite. J'y jetai un coup d'œil sans trop comprendre l'intérêt de ces poires jaunes et de ces églantines ... Le nom de l'auteur ne me disait rien. C'est pourtant ainsi que je fis connaissance avec Hölderlin, et je fus après longtemps poursuivi par l'impossibilité de traduire cette *Hälfte des Lebens* qui semble si simple à première vue. Je

---

26 This choice may have been motivated by the political reality of the times, which is suggested through a couple of articles evoking civil war and repression of communists and 87000 who died in Indonesia (p. 219 and p. 289). Another reason for choosing these cultural areas may find its motivation in the theory of Benveniste who argues that dialogue is based on the pronouns *je* and *tu*.

n'arrivais pas à me resoudre aux mots français du dictionnaire. Et je craignais d'inventer, par exemple, si, à *ins heilignüchterne Wasser*, je donnais pour équivalent dans *l'eau saintement dégrisante*, ce que par la suite des temps je n'ai trouvé ni chez Maxime Alexandre, en 1942 ni chez Geneviève Blanqui en 1943.

ARAGON 1967, p. 21

Evidently, translation is no simple matter either from a linguistic, ideological, or an existential point of view. But although the collective memory of the French-German relationship at the time of World War II is documented just as much as philology and translation, the passage is just as much about individual memory and the historical period of the 1920s. The following two chapters also present developments of a linguistic character, related to Asian languages and personal pronouns, 'Le *je* et le *vous*' (the *me* and the *you*) and English language, integrated directly in the third chapter where we also find a simple comment on the narrator's lack of competences in Danish.

Throughout the book, languages and memory become stepping stones in an effort to comprehend the loss of a loved one. Imagination, invention, and fiction (and fictional narrators of a *mise-en-abyme* structure) become the only means for trying to figure out how Blanche slipped away. Considering the "translational poetics", one important passage can make us understand such implications. Aragon quotes Shakespeare's *The Tempest* as an effort to grasp the specificity of his position as a human between languages. The narrator deplores the limitations of the French when it comes to the sound of the language:[27]

> Et après comment est-ce après? *voices* ... *voices* ... la rime à *noises* arrête ma mémoire. Les rimes au bout des vers lèchent la terre des mots comme l'écume autour de l'île. Il y a toujours une idée de la mort comme l'écume autour d'une île. (243)
>
> *L'île est pleine de bruits, de sons et de doux airs, qui donnent plaisir et ne blessent point ... et parfois mille instruments miauleurs vont me tinter aux oreilles ... et parfois ce sont des voix telles que j'en suis éveillé d'un long sommeil, elles vont me rendormir, – et alors en un rêve, les nuages me semblent s'écarter et montrer des richesses prêtes à me tomber dans le bec, si bien que m'éveillant j'implore de rêver encore ...*
>
> C'est bien mal traduit, cela oscille entre le mot à mot et l'interprétation, parce que l'idée de Java s'y glisse et chasse l'idée Bermudes. [...]

---

27 At the same time the political situation of the 1960, massacres of communist in Indonesia become a part of the tragic perspective and the loss of perspectives loss of faith in the communist social ideal.

> Une langue qui n'est pas l'ANGLAIS, c'est une misère pour tout ce qui touche le bruit, le son, le chant, mélodie ou discordance.
>
> ARAGON 1967, p. 244.

In spite of the academic and intellectual character of the commentary, evidently the problem is that the French is insufficient when it comes to understanding the nature of things in the Orient and that the narrator obtains this insight through mediations via English. French does not render the music in this passage on the sounds of nature and, thus, proves limited regarding the sensuous dimension of a reality that is out of reach. The atmosphere is lost in translation. In many ways, the passage suggests that the technical "expert approach" of languages does not help us a lot when it comes to emotions and comprehending "the other".

As we have seen, the dialogic and almost intimate relation between writer and translator characterized the English version of Spoerri's work. In the case of the exiled writer Nabokov, words and linguistic strategies became a way of negotiating loss and melancholia through literature, and finally in Aragon's case, translation could be seen as an effort to bridge the gap between the narrator and the other. In all cases, the readers find themselves facing textual transfer and metamorphosis. We can even say that the "poetics of translation" is intertwined with the idea of loss and a deficient language, and still literature becomes the necessary means, which allows the author to reach the reader as the potential other and, more so, potential rewriter.[28]

7.4 Textual Transfers and the Real – The Intercultural Dynamics

In contemporary literature, both linguistic and cultural translation as forms of rewriting have become an essential part of the literary work itself. Still, until very recently, the critical impulse has been to consider in a postcolonial mainly ideological and thematic perspective "writings between cultures". In the francophone context, different kinds of textual adaptations and creative rewritings between cultures have emerged.[29] Nevertheless, with the metafictional way of representing language and problems of communication, multilingualism and problems of translation have become increasingly present. Even in the case of *migrant literature*, it seems important to consider the element "literature" just

---

[28] In *Pale Fire*, this idea is expressed quite explicitly in the very last pages "... – a bigger, more respectable, more competent Gradus." (p. 236).

[29] One example is *Les bouts de bois de Dieu* (Paris: Le Livre contemporain, 1960) by the Senegalese writer Ousmane Sembène, which is a rewriting of Zola's *Germinal* (Paris: Charpentier, 1885).

as much as the "migrant" part. In Kim Thúy's work *Ru* (2009), for instance, the narrator constantly mediates reality through specific expressions and words as is the case of the title with its two different meanings in Vietnamese (a lullaby) and French (a stream). When Thúy writes about her trip as a lawyer from her exile in the USA to Vietnam, people tell her that she has become fat. Even the simplest of words thus appear as rooted in different cultural and anthropological contexts. One last example that should be mentioned is *Allah n'est pas obligé* (2000) de Ahmadou Kourouma with its child narrator Birahima and his way of interrogating African reality through linguistic investigations and use of dictionaries. Using brackets to translational purposes, A. Kourouma, stages an ironic narration of the African reality without neglecting any formal mean of the European modernity.[30] All in all the poetics of translation makes it possible for us to detect literary models adapted in different geographical and historical contexts with different literary implications, aesthetic effects and cultural impact.

In relation to textual transfers, the readings I have performed in this essay demonstrate the necessity of reflecting on different aspects of translation theory as well as the poetics of translation, which define the literary work. The notion of "rewriting" seems particularly apt for interrogating the implications of textual dynamics, implying specifically literary ways of "thinking in-between" and revitalizing cultural resources. Both from a practical-artistic and a theoretical point of view, it becomes crucial to reflect further on various analytical levels of textual transfers and various scales of cultural transfer. The individual texts and individual readers should be taken seriously with their linguistic-cultural impulses.[31] We must perhaps even reconsider the term of identification and talk about hybrid or formal identification.[32] In spite of our globalized world and its cultural-linguistic hybridization, multilingual formal-literary practices point to the fact that, as individuals, our sensibilities and intellectual capacities are, to most of us, connected to different languages, and that we must read differentially both when it comes to formal and cultural-linguistic aspects of the literary work.

---

30 Jørgensen, 'Poétique de la traduction. Intertexte mondial et sensibilités francophones', in *Des littératures nationales à la littérature monde en français. Questionnements, positionnements, enjeux et perspectives*, ed. by Sylvère Mbondobari (Saarbrücken: universaar, 2021, forthcoming).

31 An idea, which I have tried to suggest through observation of Danish and Nordic details with their structural implications.

32 The motivation for reading the text of the other has nothing obvious about and it is no coincidence that I have suggested the presence of Danish/Nordic examples in my readings. This is also one of the theoretical perspectives, I find in Clive Scott's book *The Work of Literary Translation, op. cit.*

Appendix

Daniel Spoerri
An Anecdoted Topography of Chance
(Re-Anecdoted Version)

Done with the help of his very dear friend
Robert Filliou
and
Translated from the French,
and further anecdoted
at random by their very dear friend
Emmett Williams
With One Hundred
Reflective Illustrations by
Topor

1966
Something Else Press, Inc.
New York   Cologne   Paris

FIGURE 7.1   Daniel Spoerri, *An Anecdoted Topography of Chance*

662 Who rides so late in the night and the wind
663 ....
664 .... It is the father with his child

Goethe's two lines opening the poem come out most exactly and beautifully, with the bonus of an unexpected rhyme (also in French: *vent-enfant*), in my own language:

Ret woren ok spoz on natt ut vett?
Eto est votchez ut mid ik dett.

Another fabulous ruler, the last king of Zembla, kept repeating these haunting lines to himself both in Zemblan and German, as a chance accompaniment of drumming fatigue and anxiety, while he climbed through the bracken belt of the dark mountains he had to traverse in his bid for freedom.

FIGURE 7.2   Fragment from Vladimir Nabokov, *Pale Fire*

Bibliography

Literary Works
Aragon, Louis, *Blanche ou l'oubli* (Paris: Gallimard, 1967).
Kourouma, Ahmadou, *Allah n'est pas obligé* (Paris: Seuil, 2010 [2000]) (coll. Opus).
Nabokov, Vladimir, *Pale Fire* (Middlesex: Penguin Books, 1987 [1962]).
Spoerri, Daniel, *An Anecdoted Topgraphy of Chance* (New York: Something Else Press, 1966).
Thúy, Kim, *Ru* (Québec: Les Éditions Libre Expression, 2009).

Theory and Critical Studies
Bassnett, Susan/Lefevere, André, *Constructing Cultures* (Bristol: Multilingual Matters, 1998).
Bizub, Edward, *La Venise intérieure* (Neuchâtel: À la Baconnière, 1991).
Casanova, Pascale, *La langue mondiale. Traduction et domination* (Paris: Seuil, 2015).
Damrosch, David, *How to Read World Literature* (New Jersey: Wiley-Blackwell, 2009).
Dutheil de la Rochère, Martine Hennard, *Reading, Translating Rewriting. Angela Carter's Translational Poetics* (Detroit: Wayne State University Press, 2013).
Espagne, Michel, 'La notion de transfert culturel', in *Revue Sciences/Lettres* [online], 1 (2013), pp. 1–9. http://journals.openedition.org/rsl/219.
Espagne, Michel, *L'Histoire de l'art comme transfert culturel* (Paris: Belin, 2009).
Filion, Louise-Hélène, 'Nouvelles perspectives sur l'intertextualité interculturelle', in *Zwischen Transfer und Vergleich*, ed. by Christiane Solte-Gresser/Hans-Jürgen Lüsebrink/Manfred Schmeling (Stuttgart: Franz Steiner Verlag, 2013), pp. 137–149.
Gentzler, Edwin, *Translation and Rewriting in the age of Post-Translation Studies* (London: Routledge, 2017).
Heidmann, Ute, 'La Différence n'est pas ce qui nous sépare', in *Zwischen Transfer und Vergleich*, ed. by Christiane Solte-Gresser/Hans-Jürgen Lüsebrink/Manfred Schmeling (Stuttgart: Franz Steiner Verlag, 2013), pp. 331–343.
Jørgensen, Steen Bille, 'Poétique de la traduction. Intertexte mondial et sensibilités francophones', in *Des littératures nationales à la littérature-monde en français. Questionnements, positionnements, enjeux et perspectives*, ed. by Sylvère Mbondobari (Saarbrücken: universaar, 2021, forthcoming).
Jørgensen, Steen Bille, 'Réécritures de Flaubert. Poétique de la traduction et soucis de la littérature', in *Dialogues. Histoire, Littérature et Transferts Culturels*, ed. by Steen Bille Jørgensen/Lisbeth Verstraete-Hansen (Copenhagen: Museum Tusculanum Press, 2013).
Jullien, François, *Il n'y a pas d'identité culturelle* (Paris: L'Herne, 2016).

Jurt, Joseph, 'Traduction et transfert culturel', in *De la traduction et des transferts culturels*, ed. by Christine Lombez/Rotraud von Kulessa (Paris: L'Harmattan, 2007), pp. 93–111.

Lefevere, André, *Translation, Rewriting and the Manipulation of Literary Fame* (London: Routledge, 1992).

Lüsebrink, Hans-Jürgen, 'Universalisme des Lumières. Résistances (inter)culturelles, traductions, transferts, fictionnalisations', in *Des Apories de l'universalisme aux promesses de l'universel*, ed. by Mourad Ali-Khodja (Laval: Presses universitaires de Laval, 2013), pp. 145–160.

Perloff, Marjorie, *Differentials* (Alabama: Alabama University Press, 2004).

Sapiro, Gisèle, 'Translation and the field of publishing', in *Translation Studies*, 1/2 (2008), pp. 154–166.

Scott, Clive, *The Work of literary Translation* (Cambridge: Cambridge University Press, 2018).

Wismann, Heinz, *Penser entre les langues* (Paris: Albin Michel, 2012).

PART 3

Perspectives – Types of Distance and Proximity

∴

CHAPTER 8

Cultural Transfer and Its Complexities: A Study on Transnational and Transhistorical Mobilities of the Baroque

Walter Moser

Abstract

In this chapter, I present two thoughts in two successive parts. The first part puts forward a general reflection on the concept of cultural transfer (CT) that focuses on its operationality in cultural analysis. The second part follows up with a case study applied to some transnational as well as transhistorical transfers of the Baroque. These studies will be result-oriented, that is, the analysis concentrates on the final stage of the process of transfer, when the cultural material transferred is integrated – or not, as we shall see – into the cultural receiver system.

8.1 General Considerations on Cultural Transfer (CT)

Cultural transfers are as old as culture itself, and as a matter of principle, they cannot be dissociated from the comprehension and analysis of culture. Obviously, such a general statement has to be contextualized. For quite a few decades already, there has been a tendency in social sciences and in the humanities to consider the processual more than the substantial aspect in cultural objects.[1] Culture thus tends to be viewed as a process, and even more as a complex interaction of processes rather than as given objects, artifacts or fixed substances. All this goes along with an implicit axiomatic change, too. Basically, mobility seems to be more valued than stability; therefore, culture in a state of flux attracts more cognitive interest than culture in a state of stasis.

---

[1] This was not always the case, though. If we look back to the 1960s, we find Paul Ricœur, as a historical thinker, in a minority position against the up-and-coming structuralist paradigm represented by Claude Lévi-Strauss. Structuralism was gaining momentum in what might be considered an epistemic turn. Against "structure", which is focused on how cultural objects are made and function, and interested in historical changes, Ricœur upheld the notion of process.

This can be recognized symptomatically in the arsenal of terms and concepts inhabiting and even to a certain degree dominating the research in cultural analysis. "Transculturation", "hybridization", "syncretism", "de- and reterritorializaton", "métissage", and more specifically in the Ibero-romance languages "miscigenação" and "misigenación". All these terms and concepts have a common denominator in that they presuppose a plurality of cultural identities and imply mobility within or between them.

Concomitantly, we observe the trend of putting the word culture in the plural. That is, on a purely theoretical level, we can still strive to determine what culture (in the singular) is or ought to be. However, as soon as we move on to the empirical level, where cultural analysis is located, we have to deal with concrete, empirically given cultural processes which usually imply a plurality of cultural entities. As a dynamic concept, the CT fits well into this general paradigm of cultural analysis.

Indeed, the more recent interest in the concept of CT plus its actual use takes part in this general tendency and confirms it.[2] At the most basic level, working with the concept of CT could be labelled an epistemic strategy to know processes that take place between cultures. Etymologically, the term "transfer" goes back to the Latin combination of "trans" + "feri" that means "to carry over". It has the same semantic structure and lexical program as other terms such as English "translation", French "traduction", even as Greek "meta-phorein", as well as the more general term "transport". All these words have in common the composition of the prefix "trans-" (that means "beyond", "over", "across") with a transitive verb (that can mean "to carry", "to put", "to take").

With this background in mind, let us then venture a tentative definition of a cultural transfer (CT). In a cultural transfer, we deal with the processes arising when an agent carries cultural material from a giver system (S1) over to a receiver system (S2). This minimalist definition should help us to develop the heuristic value of the CT as a paradigm for cultural analysis. If what interests us is a cognitive access to cultural mobility, then the CT constitutes a minimal dynamic unit of cultural mobility that can be treated analytically. This minimal unit is obtained through a heuristic gesture of "contingent closure".[3] That is to

---

[2] This is not to say that the history of the concept of "transfer" does not have deep roots. See, for instance, Daniel Simeoni, 'De Quelques Usages Du Concept de Transfert dans la réflexion sur la traduction', in *Transfert : Exploration d'un Champ Conceptuel*, ed. by Nicolas Goyer/ Walter Moser/Pascal Gin (Ottawa: University of Ottawa Press, 2017) (Transferts Culturels | Cultural Transfers), pp. 103–117.

[3] The term "contingent closure" is freely adapted from Homi Bhabha, *The Location of Culture* (New York: Routledge, 1994).

say, we have to cut a window of observation into infinite processes of cultural mobility. Unable to cognitively capture all these infinite processes at once, we have to proceed analytically by reducing their complexity to a binary vectorial unit. This artificial, yet heuristically necessary, window creates an analytically manageable object of study. On the one hand, it contains the essentials of cultural mobility; i.e. two different cultural systems in contact, an active process through which elements from one of the two systems move (in)to the other. In this sense, a CT operates with three basic ingredients: 1) more than one cultural system, 2) a process, and 3) a vector orienting that process. This reduction of complexity in the set-up of research in cultural analysis makes empirical analysis possible hence it has a heuristic value. On the other hand, we cannot and do not ignore the fact that, beyond the window of our dynamic unit, both up-stream and down-stream, cultural mobility is already active and will continue to be; that binary relations are often integrated into multiple, network-like relations; and that unilaterally oriented processes can gain in complexity as soon as there is feedback.

The paradigm, as phrased above in our tentative definition, adopts the syntactical structure corresponding to the notion of action: subject – transitive verb – object (SVO). In the logics of action, there must be a subject at the origin of action. In principle, the agent in the subject position has the force to act, can make and execute a plan of action, as well as assume responsibility for its results. Normally a transitive activity must be attributed to that subject, and lastly, the action must be oriented toward an object upon which the action has an impact. Now, let us have a closer look at each of these three components of our paradigm.

8.1.1 *The Subject or Agent of a Cultural Transfer (CT)*

Who is the agent of a cultural transfer (CT)? Who initiates and executes it? Who is responsible? The very wording of our questions would point to an individual anthropomorphic subject, endowed with will, force, reason, autonomy, as well as responsibility. In other words, we enter the realm of a modern theory of action. Yet, such an entity occupying the subject position has already undergone serious critiques, from diverse intellectual camps, especially from poststructuralism.

In the analysis of CTs, it is not easy in every case to pinpoint an individual human subject as the agent. That is not to say human subjects would not or could not participate in CTs, but rather it is difficult to give them full and sole credit for the whole operation. In most instances, their role is somewhat limited to being partial agents intervening in the process without completing it. Their role is thus limited to more restricted interventions, such as having an idea, getting a process underway, being instrumental in one specific phase of the transfer, assuming the function of a facilitator, an intermediary or opponent.

Multiple theoretical considerations plus phenomenal evidence deriving from the empirical observation of cultural practices have made the matter of the CT subject more complex. In order to make our tentative definition functional, we should elaborate on those entities capable of occupying the subject position.

First of all, the subject position can be assumed by collective human agents. The configurations and dimensions of such collective agents might be quite diverse, ranging from an artists' commune to a school of thought or a cinematographic production team. There are also more abstract collectives such as a nation, a social class, and an ethnic group, to name but a few. In a juridical, and even judiciary context, we also have to deal with collective agents identified as legal persons, such as private enterprises and institutions. This last point highlights the fact that questions of copyright or plagiarism as CTs often end up in court. Although this widening of the subject function from an individual to a collective agent impacts our grasp of the CT process, it does not represent a major problem. It might make the analytical identification of the subject more arduous but does not radically impair the logic of action.

A more radical questioning of the subject of action derives from the lessons of psychoanalysis which have the effect of opening and splitting up the internal, psychic unity of the autonomous individual subject. Two important consequences ensue. On the one hand, the subject is broken down into different agents or psychic forces, as identified in the various Freudian topics, so that the entity which supposedly stood as a monolithic and identifiable origin of action is fragmented into a potentially agonistic plurality of entities. On the other hand, the individual subject might lose control over its own action, or at least over its capacity to unify the internal psychic dynamics, that is a capacity necessary for constituting itself as a modern subject.

Another theoretical paradigm which more recently changed the approach to the issue of the subject is Systems Theory.[4] Even without seriously entering the debate on Systems Theory, and its major impact on the configuration of the subject, we can summarize as follows. Systems Theory has introduced the system itself as some kind of a super-subject. Actions formerly attributed to individual agents are now placed under an over-riding agent; i.e., the social

---

[4] One of the best-known representatives of systems theory is the German sociologist Niklas Luhmann, *Soziale Systeme. Grundriss einer allgemeinen Theorie* (Frankfurt/Main: Suhrkamp, 1987), who died in 1998.

system in general, or one of its concrete sub-systems. As a result, actions executed by individual agents are re-categorized as systemic functions, and, to a certain extent, the individual subject gets downgraded to being a mere result of the system's functioning. The individual subject thus loses its initiative and autonomy as agent in the subject function.[5]

Finally, one more but not least transformation of the subject position has to be mentioned. It is the complex problematic of the impact of the new digital technologies combined with the new media on the identification of the agent occupying this position. Our contemporary technoscape and mediascape have indeed invaded the privileged territories of the anthropomorphic subject of action. Everyday technologies and media play an increasingly active role in cultural practices making it more and more difficult to confine them to the role of mere instruments at the disposal of a human agent or else to the role of extensions, or even as prostheses of the human senses.[6] Such an instrumental conception of media and technology would imply that we could do without them while maintaining the privileged position of the subject, although at the expense of losing efficacy in our reach in the world and in society. Yet, the evidence of our contemporary world does not confirm this assumption and actually shows human and machine agents increasingly interwoven. In this case, to be able to analyze certain CTs we would have to install in the subject position a mixed entity of man and machine. In short, the agency of CTs would then be shared between man and machine in proportions determined in each case.

8.1.2   *The Act of Transferring*

As we have already seen, the verb "transfer" is composed of the prefix "trans-" and the verb "feri" (to carry). It means "to carry over, to the other side, beyond". The semantic content of the verb in our definition thus expresses the action proper contained in a CT. Two constitutive aspects of CTs emerge from the semantic structure of this verb: transitivity and vectoriality. Something is being carried from one point to another. Unlike a Brownian motion, this movement is oriented. It has a vector.

There are different perspectives for the observation of such a vectorial movement. This can be illustrated in the German language which, in addition to the verb "übertragen" ("to carry over"), can specify the position of the

---

5   Since CTs are also conceptualized here as a dynamic relation from (sub)system to (sub)system, I am adopting the vocabulary of the systems theory without seriously engaging in its theoretical consequences.
6   As the media theory of Marshall McLuhan, *Understanding Media. Extensions of Man* (London: Routledge and Kegan Paul, 1964), would have it.

observer. "Hinübertragen" indicates the movement away from the observer's position which in our definition is S1, while "herübertragen" indicates the movement towards the observer's position, that is S2. This change of perspective, even when examining the same CT, introduces an important variable into our analysis. Basically, the same CTs can be observed from the giver as well as from the receiver system. If, as it is always the case to a degree, there exists an asymmetry in terms of power between the giver and receiver, this perspective shift makes a significant difference. The same CT may appear as either a case of pillage or theft or else as a case of recuperation and salvaging.[7]

Regardless of the perspective of observation, two minimal conditions must be fulfilled for the CT process to become an object of analysis. First, we require the existence of two different systems; second, a space or border separating these two systems. The process proper and complete of CTs may then be broken down into three operations:

a)   extraction from the giver system
b)   displacement (the act of transferring proper)
c)   insertion into the receiver system

The first operation, extraction, starts with an act of selection. Different kinds of agents can participate in selecting the cultural material to be transferred. Different factors can determine choices, such as a profound subjective desire, the commercial mechanism of supply and demand, the relationship between scarcity and abundance, as well as inequalities in terms of values and prestige. Most of these motivations arise from an asymmetric power dynamic between the two systems. The initial activation for a CT may reside in the giver or in the receiver system and may amount to either exportation or to importation.

However, given the monodirectional asymmetry of this operation, extraction rarely results in an egalitarian exchange which would include something like an equivalent counter-transfer. As would seem to suggest the euphemistic Brazilian term "troca cultural" ("cultural barter").

Depending on the kind of objects involved, "extraction" implies a violent operation towards artifacts or works of art both symbolically and materially. These works are then left in a state of fragmentation, as I have witnessed in the Buddhist cavern paintings in Mogao, China: a clear-cut whole indicated the painting that had been extracted to be transferred to the British Museum in

---

7   These two perspectives clashed for instance recently in Canada in the case of Amerindian "sacred bundles" (sacred items bundled up). The fact that they were recuperated by "white men" and conserved in their museums, was considered by the natives as cases of unlawful appropriation.

London. In this case the giver system perceives this CT as a pillage or as a theft of cultural heritage.[8]

The operation of reinsertion does not necessarily take place in a harmonious way, either. In principle, the receiver system initially tends to perceive the transferred object as a foreign element, with whatever intensity that it might have been attracted in its new cultural environment. A rather long process of systemic reorganization is necessary to accommodate the foreign object which will eventually be inserted positively into the new system and assimilated by it.

This process of recontextualization usually accompanies a strange cultural performance that, to use an oxymoron, might be called 'active forgetting'. In order to reach a certain efficiency in a new system, the object's functioning as well as its meaning in the old system must be forgotten, at least partially. This can be illustrated beautifully by the transfer of the symbol and heraldic element of the white lily passed from the French Bourbon monarchy to the democratic State of Québec and appearing on its official flag (in French called "le fleurdelisé", a contraction of "fleur de lys"). In order to become active as a symbol of modern Québec identity, the fleur de lys' former use as a symbol of the monarchic French colonizer must fall into oblivion.

If this process of recontextualization does not succeed, if the object remains ill-inserted and eventually rejected by the receiver system, we would have to consider it a failed CT. The grafting having been infelicitous, the transferred object will consequently either be ejected from, or else encysted into the system as a foreign body. In the following case study on transhistorical and transcultural transfers of the Baroque, we shall exemplify all three possibilities: assimilation, rejection and encysting.

Last but not least, the analysis of CTs involves the identity of the objects transferred. The breaking down of the process of cultural transfer into the three steps (extraction, displacement, reinsertion) might lead us to believe that an object can be subjected to the process while remaining intact, even unscathed; i.e., be the same cultural object. This would be incorrect, given the systemic logic underpinning the entire process. Not only might the material integrity of an object be seriously in danger and undergo physical changes, but also its identity as a cultural object, even if materially unscathed, will have changed. This is inevitable given the recontextualization and refunctionalization undergone in the new system. The object's new identity and meaning will be determined by its relation to the new cultural environment. This is what Jorge Luis Borges fictionally experimented in his short story "Pierre Menard, autor del Quijote". If Pierre Menard rewrites Cervantes' masterpiece, that is he

---

[8] Today international institutions such as UNESCO are busy trying to restitute such transferred cultural objects to the giver system.

transfers the text to the 20th century and reproduces it "verbally identical" as says Borges, this writing no longer performs the same discursive act as it did in the 17th century. Given the completely different historical and cultural situation into which it is reinserted, Pierre Menard's Don Quixote cannot be the same literary work. According to systemic logic, a cultural object cannot be the same in two different systems.

8.1.3   *The Object of CTs*

What kind of cultural material is being transferred in a CT? The phenomenal diversity of what can occupy the position of the "object" in our definition is almost unlimited. Schematically though, we can break that diversity down into a certain number of categories that need to be distinguished. As we shall see, their difference has an impact on how the process of CT unfolds.

8.1.3.1   The Unique Material Object

The object to be transferred may be unique as a result of either the production process or its identifiable material features. This is the case of an original artwork, for instance a painting or a statue. To be transferred, the piece of art has to be transported as a material object. Given its value, the piece must be handled with care. In the extreme case of an Egyptian obelisk that ends up in Paris, this implies major engineering as well as navigation technologies.

As a unique specimen, often identified in the art system as an "original", this kind of object cannot be located in more than one place. It is here or there, that is, either in S1 or in S2. Its removal from the giver system leaves a mark, either materially as an empty space or, in the subjective perception, as a lack or a loss. In the case of transfers due to wars or civil crimes the giver system might then endeavor to recuperate the object through legal procedures or even through brute force. What makes this category of objects empirically more complex is the concomitant existence of copies and forgeries. Ironically, however, their appearance does not but confirm the uniqueness of the original.

One special object category might be called the "affective originals". Any object, even one with an objective zero value, can become invested positively with personal affect. Even if this object has been serially produced, it then becomes an "original" in our subjective perception. As we know from inheritances, its transfer from one generation to another, and even more between different branches of the same generation might become a very conflictual issue because the authentic "affective original" can only be in one place.

8.1.3.2   The Serial Object

By definition, this category always exists in great numbers, if not "en masse" due to its production technique. At the outset, a multitude of identical objects are produced, be they industrial art works, utilitarian commodities or garments.[9] Hence the opposition of original versus copy no longer applies. This logic does apply already to engravings but also to books after Gutenberg, plus more recently and, a fortiori, also to photographs and films. Such objects usually have an original place or site of production. They are "made in ...". Nonetheless, given their serial nature, they can be present and function at the same time in two or many places and systems. Their transfer, often in terms of export-import, does not bring about their disappearance or loss in the giver system. However, their massive introduction into a receiver system may have major consequences.

In our context of mass culture, the accelerated distribution of such cultural objects, far away from their production sites, manifests a cultural hegemony of the giver system. Today's massive international distribution and consumption of high-tech cultural products, such as films, TV series as well as music, illustrates this situation. Usually cultural analysts and critiques focus on the unloading of North American products (Made in the USA) onto international markets. They scrutinize Hollywood's influence on foreign cultures, but one could just as easily analyze the influence of other centers of production, e.g., Rede Globo (Brazil), Televisa (Mexico) and Bollywood (India).

8.1.3.3 The Symbolic or Semiotic Object

We should not mistake the book – a material object, usually made of paper and ink, sometimes also cardboard and leather – for the text printed inside and for which the book serves as a material support. Given its semiotic nature, the text is more easily transferred than the book. The experience of boxing and moving a personal library will have convinced many readers of this simple fact, especially if we also practice digital transfers of texts or read e-books. Due to its relative independence from the technical support, a text can be transferred with ever greater speed and ease. A giant step has been taken from the medieval copyist to the typographer of the Gutenberg galaxy. Comparatively, though, how to account for the mobility of the electronic text that can be here and there simultaneously and circulate instantly, thanks to the meta-media called Internet? At least this applies to those who enjoy access to the technical hardware devices of diffusion and telecommunication needed to participate in such CTs.

The same applies to images and musical tunes, given that the digitalization of multimedia content treats both the spoken and the written word, as well as other various sounds plus images using the same technological support. It is

---

9   Such as blue jeans which played an important role in the CTs towards countries related to the former Soviet Union.

spectacular how these technological developments have increased our capabilities and the speed of transferential processes within the cultural domain. As these media and technologies function in networks, the circulation of contents takes place through multiple connections. Their mode of functioning actually blurs bilateral relations which makes it difficult to apply analytically our minimal dynamic unit of the CT with its binary vectorial structure. Indeed, this might well represent a limit to the cognitive value of CTs.

8.1.3.4 The Matrix or Generative Object

Instead of transferring a concrete object resulting from a specific process of production, it is also possible to transfer the formula or algorithm used to produce it. In this case, what becomes the object of a CT is the generative matrix; i.e., a virtual configuration containing a powerful productive potential. By adopting the terms of the theory of imitation as an analogical tool, we can affirm that the CT process is no longer located on the level of *natura naturata*, but rather that of *natura naturans*. Obviously if transferred, such an object might have a profound impact on a receiver system.

Applied to literature, this means that a specific text is not really transferred; instead, it is the style manifested by this text; i.e., the literary genre that governed the work's writing, the poetic form employed in a poem. One example would be the *pastiche*. Similarly, in terms of everyday material culture, it is not a specific dish but the recipe for that dish; not someone's garment, but rather the look that inspired the choice of that garment – a look that can be reproduced and recognized elsewhere.

To come back to high technologies, this kind of CT has important economic implications. The inventor of such an object, e.g., a new computer program or a smartphone application, can submit it for licensing dues and earn a lot of money if this program is commercially transferred and adapted to foreign cultures.

8.1.3.5 The Immaterial Object

Finally, immaterial objects also enter the CT process as concepts, values and ideas can be transferred, too.[10] To affirm this is not akin to falling back into the

---

10   The Brazilian critic Roberto Schwarz offers an excellent example of such a CT in his *Misplaced Ideas. Essays on Brazilian Culture* (London: Verso, 1992) that goes back to his article in Portuguese 'As ideias fora do lugar' (in *Ao vencedor as batatas*, Sao Paulo: Livraria Duas Cidades, 1988 [1977], pp. 13–28). Another case in point is the still much disputed transfer of the concept of "human rights", going back to "les droits de l'homme" launched by the French Revolution and transferred from Europe and North America to other cultural systems, usually with political implications.

trap of an old-fashioned idealism. It is important to recognize that whether concept, value or idea, a material support is required to "carry it over". Various media may serve as a support ranging from an image to the human voice and, of course, the printing press. Even electronic media require what we call "hardware" to transfer immaterial contents, however dematerialized and miniaturized they may be.

Although this quick categorization of which objects can enter the CT process might be incomplete, it already provides a good idea of the complexity of CTs. From the first to the fifth category, we observe a progressive dematerialization. However, this does not mean that any object may be transferred without a material support. The basic assumption underlying work with CTs is that nothing can take place in cultural practices without material support and technical devices, not even the transfer of concepts.

8.1.4 Transfers, Intercultural and Intracultural

One more theoretical question must be posed here to determine the reach of the conceptual area that we are exploring. Namely, what kind of different systems are connected by CTs carrying cultural material over from one to another? For nearly three decades, the concept of CTs has enjoyed pride of place in cultural analysis. In fact, the concept was introduced and developed in France by its pioneers Michel Espagne and Michael Werner, and in Germany, by Bernd Kortländer and Hans-Jürgen Lüsebrink, mostly in the context of their research on cultural exchanges between France and Germany.[11] The concept was directly associated with the problematic of intercultural relations, and therefore depended on presuppositions derived from that problematic.

To make these presuppositions explicit, we could argue that in principle a CT takes place between well established, identifiable and recognizable two cultures. In this context, the notion "one culture" has tended to fit into the mold developed over the last few centuries by the European nation state and for its institution. "One culture" was generally understood to be "a national culture", e.g., French, German, or English. Before the concept of CT came into play and in order to render it operative, an internal consistency was implicitly attributed to those national cultures. This consistency contained attributes such as "unity", "identity" as well as "homogeneity". Consequently, the point

---

11   These are a few of their pioneering publications on CTs: Michel Espagne/Michael Werner (eds.), *Transferts. Les relations interculturelles dans l'espace franco-allemand (XVIIIe–XIXe siècles)* (Paris: Éditions Recherche sur les Civilisations, 1988); Michel Espagne, *Les transferts culturels franco-allemands* (Paris: Presses Universitaires de France, 1999); Hans-Jürgen Lüsebrink, 'De l'analyse de la réception littéraire à l'étude des transferts culturels', in *Discours Social/Social Discourse*, 7/3–4 (1995), pp. 39–46.

of departure for CT analysis was the existence of at least two such national cultures. It was also the implied basis on which the concept of cultural transfer could be brought into operation. The process of CT was then seen like some more or less licit cultural trafficking across national borders. Even under such limitations, interest in CTs introduced a certain dynamic into the research on cultural issues. Analysis of such transfers opened a breach in the walls that tended to surround national cultures, often for ideological reasons legitimized by the intrinsic logic of the Nation State. Overall the concept created openings through which a back-and-forth between cultures became conceptually possible and analytically observable. In this sense, this relatively recent orientation in cultural analysis represents progress in our knowledge of cultural life.

Almost a new wrinkle, this positive development in cultural analysis reveals how this opening creates a limitation to the application of CT. How exactly? If we apply it exclusively or at least primarily to intercultural relations; i.e., to cultural mobility between national cultures, we restrict the epistemic potential of the concept explored here. Let us instead go beyond that limitation to consider also those CTs which we might call intracultural. Once we get rid of the more ideological presumption of homogeneous national cultures and observe their empirical reality, we might discover many internal differences. In which case, there is no reason not to apply the CT as an analytical tool within constituted national cultures, too. As a matter of fact, among all kinds of subcultures, or cultural sub-systems, that make up "one national culture". Let us therefore crack open the black box of national cultures and observe their internal dynamics also in terms of CTs. As a first consequence of such a decision, we should obtain confirmation that, indeed, the unity and homogeneity of national cultures are ideological and imaginary constructs.[12] Observing the internal transcultural trafficking of a culture thus allows us to shed a critical light onto those constructs and make visible the mobile internal heterogeneity of (national) cultures. This might lead us to ask radical questions about the consistency of those constructs by bringing to the fore the permanent flux of transfers – unstable, contingent, fragile – that they have as their mission to hide. This kind of microanalysis, in terms of CTs, will amount to a critique of any monolithic view on single cultures.

Beyond de-mystifying, work on the multiplicity of transfers that take place on all levels and in all domains of cultural life will actually reveal the pervasive cultural dynamics. It will bring into focus the permanent processes of

---

12 Cf. Benedict Anderson, *Imagined Communities. Reflections on the Origin and the Spread of Nationalisms* (New York: Verso Books, 1983).

establishing and shifting cultural borderlines, the criss-crossings between the same and the Other, the very paradox that what is peculiar to a culture is often based on forgetting the foreign nature of elements already transferred into that very same culture which has been able to assimilate them. Once we open this wide-ranging zone of intraculturality to cultural analysis, we discover CTs between the most diverse cultural sub-systems. Far from exhaustive, here is a short list of some sites of observation for anyone interested in intracultural transfers. These transfers can take place at the borders or in the contact zones between:

- Cultural strata that correspond, *grosso modo*, to the social stratification: elite culture, popular culture, mass culture, high brow and low brow.
- Different discourses: here the work on CTs catches up with the problematic of interdiscursivity
- Different texts and artifacts: here the work on CTs partially overlaps with that on intertextuality
- Different arts and art forms: here the work on CTs grafts onto the long tradition of interartiality, that is on the comparison and exchanges between different arts
- Different media: these transfers fall into the framework of intermediality, with its specific problematics such as adaptation and remediation.
- Different historical situations: here the work on CTs can contribute to articulate historical projections or resuscitations that are being approached from various angles using terminology like revivals or resurgences, but also anachronisms and non-contemporaneities.

We should keep in mind that all these specific relations may be manifested and activated in the mode of transferential processes within the life of one national culture. Moreover, they can help us to get a better analytical grip on transfers that cross the interstices between two different national cultures. Far from being exclusive or competitive, intracultural and intercultural transfers are very often combined in very complex ways so that in each case our analysis must consider their concrete imbrications.

8.2 Transnational and Transhistorical Mobilities of the Baroque

In the following case study, let us try to apply some of the parameters developed herein for the concept of CTs. More particularly, our analysis will focus on the results of CTs, in other words, on the reinsertion of cultural material into a receiver system. The specific case analysis may be subsumed under the heading "transnational and transhistorical mobilities of the Baroque" and deals with CTs both on an intercultural and a historical axis.

The Baroque as a "cultural material" will be treated within its polymorphous manifestations, in other words, as a style of art, an aesthetic paradigm, and in a much broader sense, as a concrete life style, even an ethos, or more abstractly as a concept, an ideology. In a more restricted application, Baroque refers to specific works of art and other cultural productions.

We contrast here aspects of two different CTs of the Baroque. In terms of results, one is positive; the other, negative. As mentioned, a CT has a positive result if the transferred material is integrated into the receiver system and functions as its own element due to an important forgetting of its initial rooting and meaning in the giver system. As we shall see, this can even lead to a posture of "counter-conquest" when the initially imposed foreign paradigm becomes an identity marker of the receiver system and is aggressively turned against the giver system.

In this sense, the transfer of the Baroque to Latin America was a positive one. The initial giver system was the Iberian Peninsula of the 16th to 18th centuries, with Spain and Portugal as cultural and political centers. The historical context was one of colonization, followed by one of de-colonization.

8.2.1 *Successful Transfer*
This CT must be considered a process of long duration unfolding in two different phases:

8.2.1.1   16th, 17th and 18th Centuries
This was a period of conquest and colonization, which means that this CT took place in a hostile context. The Iberian Baroque was transported over the Atlantic Ocean first by the conquistadors and later by the colonizers. This CT was part of an attempt to impose European Baroque culture on the colonized. The process itself may be broken down into a sequence of different phases. First, the conquerors brought along material objects: single works of sacred art, mostly original statues and paintings "made in Spain" or "made in Portugal". In the next phase, those material objects were usually copies of such works. In the subsequent phase, material as well as immaterial cultural technologies were transferred. On the material side there was writing gear, printing tools, oil pigments, etc. and on the immaterial side, specific know-how and general "cultural literacy" or the support of artists, architects and administrators. The following phase brought about transmission of that know-how and local reproduction of the transferred culture with the help of an indigenous labor force. Finally, the reproduction of foreign cultural elements swerved sufficiently away from the

foreign model to become more and more the colonized's own cultural identity marker. Of course, this went along with an incipient process of decolonization.

During the first phases of this process, still within a colonial context, the Latin American Baroque was called "Barroco de Indias". In fact, in her 1994 book on *Relecturas del barroco de Indias*, Mabel Moraña uses the Gramscian terminology "hegemonic" versus "subaltern" to show how subaltern reproductions of the hegemonic metropolitan model, little by little, introduced local differences which developed into the nucleus of a new cultural identity claim and even into the embryonic emergence of future national identities. In the CT of the Baroque, Moraña observes the early stages of the colony's emancipation from the metropolitan power. In terms of the object of transfer, Moraña refers mostly to discursive practices.

In a different, more Marxian approach, Bolívar Echeverría develops the concept of a Baroque ethos that would have grown on Latin American soil.[13] This ethos blends a strategy of survival and a posture of political resistance. It grew into a new life style which, in Echeverría's broader outlook, could reveal a way out of the capitalist system. He is adamant in giving the indigenous people, in other words the victims of colonization, primary agency in this development. In concrete terms for the natives, the Baroque ethos consisted simultaneously of adopting cultural practices imposed by the colonizer and resisting the colonizer's power by activating their own ancestral way of life. On the other hand, for the American descendants of the European colonizers (the *criollos*), survival was only possible by adopting indigenous values and life styles to a certain extent. The result was a *mestizo* culture whose emblematic figure is the Mexican Virgen de Guadalupe, a combination adopting the Catholic Marian cult carried over from Europe and loading it with indigenous cultural contents.

In her book *América barroca* (1992) the Brazilian historian Janice Theodoro offers yet another narrative to describe and explain the transfer of the Baroque from Europe to Latin America. Her central concept is that of cultural memory, attributed to the agents of the process, both from the giver and the receiver systems. More particularly, Theodoro observes the fragmentation of cultural memory on both sides, hence a need for cooperation which ends up in a culture of miscegenation. The European conqueror and colonizer – mostly men – brings to the new continent a European cultural memory but lacks material support for this memory. Initially, on the new continent, there were no Baroque churches or other Baroque artifacts whatsoever. Hence the danger of losing

---

13   See among other publications his *Modernidad, mestizaje cultural*, ethos *barroco* (Mexico City: Universidad Nacional Autónoma de México, El Equilibrista, 1994), and *La modernidad de lo barroco* (Mexico City: Era, 1998).

this native cultural memory that falls into a precarious state of fragmentation. Therefore, the colonizer needs to reproduce such artifacts. Realizing them requires know how, e.g., architectural plans for churches or imported techniques and technical devices, but also an indigenous work force. Whereas the indigenous agent also has a fragmented memory because he has to construct or create an artifact that does not correspond to his own cultural memory. As a result, this agent supplements his work with elements from his own native culture. That is how, again, a *mestizo* culture emerges and is increasingly claimed as Latin America's own culture over time. Theodoro concludes her narrative with the moment of national identity constructions in Latin America that would correspond to the retotalization of the culture memory.

Despite the difference of their approach, these three narrative accounts of the process of CT agree on its results. The transferred cultural material is increasingly integrated into the Latin American receiver system, to a degree that it can be claimed as part of its cultural identity at the end of the process.

8.2.1.2   20th Century

In Latin America, the movements for national political independence took root at the beginning of the 19th century. They consisted largely in a grafting of the European concept and organization of the Nation State onto the American continent. Most came along with a modern liberal ideology that, true to its European model, was hostile towards the Baroque as a culture related to the "ancien régime" and to pre-modern thought. However, according to some cultural historians, the Baroque continued being reclaimed as a stratum of native popular culture that could support, and even legitimize the emergence of national cultures.

Moreover, it was not until the 20th century that the Baroque was reactivated for identity constructions. Note that this was in Latin America for a Latin American identity, as opposed to either Europe or North Amercia. Again, this mostly was work on the concept, with constant reference to artists, to material culture and to life style. All in all, the CT of the Baroque had gone full circle: the receiver system is claiming as its own that which, centuries before, was transferred to it as a foreign element.

In what is called the "*americanismo*" discourse, more precisely in its mid-20th century version, we can observe an *aposteriori* identity construction that uses the cultural paradigm of the Baroque as a general identity marker. Schematically, this project follows two different strategies. First, there is an essentialist version insisting on an ontological foundation of culture. It does not hesitate to invoke cultural determinism by nature or climate as an argument. This version is concomitant with a typological approach to cultural phenomena that invokes types of style and form and works with cyclical time up to and including the figure of the eternal return. In the European dealings with the Baroque, Eugenio D'Ors (*Lo barroco*, 1944) can be seen as its main representative, if not its emblematic figure. The other version is strategic and inspired by the basic assumption that culture is man-made, therefore, it changes over time and depends on human power relations. This version is concomitant with a historical approach that identifies the Baroque with a chronotope, or a cultural period within a given territory. One of the main representatives of this approach is José Antonio Maravall (*La cultura del barroco*, 1975). We turn here to two different texts, each using one of those strategies through its general outlook. Both these texts are well known within the Latin American essay tradition.

The first text is Alejo Carpentier's "Lo barroco y lo real maravilloso", given as a lecture in 1975 in Caracas, and published later in his book *Razón de Ser*.[14] Carpentier represents the essentialist approach. The second is José Lezama Lima's "La curiosidad barroca", given as a lecture in 1957 in La Havana, and published the same year in his book *La expresión Americana*.[15] He represents the strategic approach, although interspersed with essentialist elements. We shall offer here a selective reading of both texts, foregrounding some of their key features as part of a CT.

It comes as no surprise that Carpentier claims to take his inspiration from D'Ors' typological approach to the Baroque:

> Eugenio D'Ors (...) nos dice en un ensayo famoso que en realidad lo que hay que ver en el Barroco es una suerte de pulsión creadora, que vuelve cíclicamente a través de la historia en las manifestaciones del arte (...) hay un eterno retorno del barroquismo a través de los tiempos en las manifestaciones del arte.
> CARPENTIER 1976, p. 53

> (D'Ors (...) tells us in a famous essay that what the baroque displays is, in fact, a kind of creative impulse that recurs cyclically throughout history in artistic forms (...) there is an eternal return of the baroque in art through the ages.)
> CARPENTIER 1995, pp. 90–91

---

14 References are made to *Razón de Ser (Conferencias)* (Caracas: Universidad de Venezuela, Ediciones del Rectorado, 1976), pp. 51–73. See also the English translation: http://english.duke.edu/uploads/media_items/baroque-and-the-marvelous-real.original.pdf.

15 References are made to *La expresión americana* (México DF: Fondo de Cultura Económica, 1993). In the English translation: 'Baroque Curiosity', in Lois Parkinson Zamora/Monika Kaup (eds.), *Baroque New Worlds. Representation, Transculturation, Counterconquest* (Durham, London: Duke University Press, 2010).

He then lends D'Ors' theory even more authority by affirming the ahistorical nature of the Baroque as a human constant: "El barroquismo tiene que verse, de acuerdo con Eugenio D'Ors – y me parece que su teoria en esto es irrefutable –, como una constante humana" (Carpentier, 1976, p. 53) ("According to Eugenio d'Ors – and it seems to me that his theory is irrefutable in this respect – the baroque must be seen as a human constant". (p. 91)). And, if this were not clear enough, Carpentier explicitly rejects a historical approach that would locate the origin of the Baroque in 17th century Europe, thus recognizing its emergence and flourishment in Latin America as the result of a CT process:

> ... lo barroco visto como una constante humana y que de ningun modo puede circunscribirse a un movimiento arquitectónico, estético o pictórico nacido en el siglo XVII.
> CARPENTIER 1976, p. 56

> (The baroque as a human constant that absolutely cannot be limited to an architectural, aesthetic, and pictorial movement originating in the seventeenth century.)
> CARPENTIER 1995, p. 94

This means that, while using a concept elaborated in European cultural history, Carpentier severs the Baroque from its European roots. For the Cuban author, therefore, the Latin American Baroque has not grown out of a CT but is to be seen as a cultural paradigm native to Latin America.

In order to give this native Baroque an axiological appreciation, he goes further, rejecting negative evaluations that the Baroque has received in Europe, thus preparing the stage for an evaluation that gives the Latin American Baroque superiority over its European counterpart:

> Ese barroquismo, lejos de significar decadencia, ha marcado a veces la culminación, la máxima expresión, el momento de mayor riqueza, de una civilización determinada.
> CARPENTIER 1976, p. 53

> (This baroque, far from signifying decadence, has at times represented the culmination, the maximum expression and the richest moment of a given civilization.)
> CARPENTIER 1995, p. 91

Then there comes the decisive moment in his text when he not only establishes a historical co-extensivity of "America" and "Baroque" but also claims some sort of co-substantiality of both:

> América, continente de simbiosis, de mutaciones, de vibraciones, de mestizajes fué barroca desde siempre.
> CARPENTIER 1976, p. 61

> (America, a continent of symbiosis, mutations, vibrations, mestizaje, has always been baroque.)
> CARPENTIER 1995, p. 98

And furthermore,

> Y por qué es América latina la tierra de elección del barroco? Porque toda simbiosis, todo mestizaje, engendra un barroquismo.
> CARPENTIER 1976, p. 64

> (And why is Latin America the chosen territory of the baroque? Because all symbiosis, all mestizaje, engenders the baroque.)
> CARPENTIER 1995, p. 100

Here we are no longer in a discursive mode of argumentation but rather in a mode of thetic affirmation. This is the moment of deepest essentialism where "America" and "Baroque" are brought to coincide in a unique cultural identity claim. This claim is then argumentatively supported by an implicit theory of cultural determinism:

> Nuestro mundo es barroco por la arquitetura – eso no hay ni que demonstrarlo – por el enrevesamiento y la complejidad de su naturaleza y su vegetación, por la policromía de cuanto nos circunda, por la pulsión telúrica de los fenómenos a que estamos todavía sometidos.
> CARPENTIER 1976, p. 69

> (Our world is baroque because of its architecture – this goes without saying – the unruly complexities of its nature and its vegetation, the many colors that surround us, the telluric pulse of the phenomena that we still feel.)
> CARPENTIER 1995, p. 105

Latin American culture is thus determined by its natural surroundings; i.e., nature, vegetation, colors, the telluric pulse – probably an allusion to volcanic activity. The argument becomes nearly redundant or circular. In short, under such Baroque natural conditions only a Baroque culture can emerge.

Carpentier goes even one step further to claim that given these Baroque natural conditions, to be authentic, the Latin American artist must create Baroque works:

> Tengo que lograr con mis palabras un barroquismo paralelo al barroquismo del paisaje del trópico templado. Y nos encontramos con que eso conduce logicamente a un barroquismo que se produce espontáneamente en nuestra literatura.
> CARPENTIER 1976, p. 71

> (I have to create with my words a Baroque style that parallels the Baroque of the temperate, tropical landscape. And we find that this leads logically to a Baroque that arises spontaneously in our literature.)
> CARPENTIER 1995, p. 106

More than this ethical injunction to be Baroque, the Latin American artist has to obey a spontaneous impulse: he can not *not* be Baroque.

There are minor problems to be highlighted in the logic of this text. For instance, the use of the continental name America to designate just the sub-continent Latin (or Ibero- or South) America. Of course, the same abusive appropriation is practiced in North American discourses. Also, the tropical climate and vegetation – its exuberance, proliferation and abundance can be found in many descriptions of Baroque aesthetics – as representative for the whole sub-continent. This area includes many other kinds of natural environments such as the Argentinian Pampa, the Brazilian *sertão*, and, of course, the Andes. Problematic is also the implicit assumption that all *mestizaje* produces Baroque culture.

Yet the major problem of this text lies in its essentialism. With the various discursive operations shown above, the Baroque is fabricated as a native cultural paradigm grown on American soil. Due to this treatment, it can become the key element in an American cultural identity construction. This whole operation is based on one fundamental assumption: the Baroque was not brought to America, it was always already there even well before emerging in Europe. As such, it necessarily expresses a baroqueness of the natural conditions of America.[16] This denial of the cultural transfer of the Baroque to Latin America is the utmost proof that the CT of the Baroque has successfully undergone its

---

16   In the introduction to his book *Essays on the Literary Baroque in Spain and Spanish America* (Woodbridge: Tamesis, 2008), John Beverly summarizes this essentialist construction: 'Baroque has come to be thought of as a sort of episteme or "deep structure" of Latin America as such' (p. 14) and criticizes it.

transferal to Latin America. The transfer was so successful that the receiver system not only forgot its origin but actively denies it. One can understand that this disavowal is necessary for ideological reasons of identity construction, but in our view it does not correspond to historical facts. Also with its univocal truth claims, this text it is not an essay but rather a thesis text. It might be added here that, in his fiction, Carpentier has treated the Baroque in a much more complex way, for instance in his novel *Concierto barroco*.

Lezama Lima's text is more complex. As we shall see it contains essentialist elements, but they are subordinated to an historic approach. For Lezama Lima it is clear that the Baroque came to Latin America with the Iberian conquistadors and colonialists. He creates the anthropomorphic figure "ese Americano señor barroco" ("this American Baroque gentleman") who appears on the American continent after the first phase of colonization:

> Ese Americano señor barroco (...) aparece cuando ya se han alejado del tumulto de la conquista y la parcelación del paisaje del colonizador.
> LEZAMA LIMA 2010, pp. 81–82

> (This American Baroque gentleman (...) appears when the tumult of the Conquest and the distribution of land to the colonizers are a thing of the past.)
> ZAMORA/KAUP 2010, p. 10

Historically speaking, Lezama Lima clearly sets a *terminus post quem* for the appearance and existence of the Baroque on the American continent. He even explains its being there as the result of a historical transfer:

> Después del Renacimiento la historia de España pasó a la América, y el barroco americano se alza con la primacía por encima de los trabajos arquitectónicos de José de Churriguera y Narciso Tomé.
> LEZAMA LIMA 2010, p. 100

> (After the Renaissance, Spain's history traveled to America, and the American Baroque surpasses the architectural works of José de Churriguera and Naciso Tomé.)
> ZAMORA/KAUP 2010, p. 230

Here the historical narrative is combined with the superiority claim already found in Carpentier; i.e., the development of the American Baroque surpasses its European model. So much for Lezama Lima's identity claim. Nonetheless, he continues founding this claim on a redefiniton of the Baroque for Latin America:

> De las modalidades que pudiéramos señalar en un barroco europeo, acumulación sin tensión, y asimetría sin plutonismo, derivadas de una manera de acercarse al barroco sin olvidar el gótico y de aquella definición tajante de Worringer: el barroco es un gótico degenerado. Nuestra apreciación del barroco americano estará destinada a precisar: Primero, hay una tensión en el barroco; segundo, un plutonismo, fuego originario que rompe los fragmentos y los unifica; tercero, no es un estilo degenerescente, sino plenario.
> LEZAMA LIMA 2010, p. 79–80

> (The different modalities of the European Baroque that we might mention – accumulation without tension, asymmetry without plutonism – derived from conceiving the Baroque as an extension of the Gothic, as in Worringer's cutting definition: 'The Baroque is nothing but a degenerate Gothic'. Our appreciation of the American Baroque will have to be more precise. First, there is tension in the Baroque; second, there is plutonism, an originary fire that breakes the fragments and unifies them; third, our Baroque is not a decadent style, but a culmination.)
> ZAMORA/KAUP 2010, p. 213

We have already seen how, by mere allusion, Carpentier turns a negative attribute (decadent) of the European Baroque into a positive characteristic. Here Lezama Lima is much more explicit and systematic. He replaces one by one the terms European scholars have proposed to define the Baroque by positive terms that define the Latin American Baroque. The same terms which, by the way, become the writer's own through the enunciatory possession mark in the first person: "our Baroque" as opposed to "the European Baroque". Lezama Lima introduces the epithets "tension", "plutonism" and "culmination". This is his manner of setting his own Baroque apart from its European model and counterpart while claiming an axiomatic superiority.

The most enigmatic of those terms is "plutonism". It is derived from Pluto, the Greek god of the underworld. The Christian underworld being the hell, Pluto also represents the flames of the hell, that is a source of caloric energy. We are close here to Carpentier's "pulso telúrico" ("telluric pulse"). Indeed, all the more so because one of the 18th century's two narrative theories on the formation of the planet Earth was named "plutonist" because its main agent was believed to be fire. The other theory was called "neptunist" because it explained the shape of the Earth's surface through the action of water.

What exactly does "plutonismo" have to do with the Baroque? With this defining element, a maximum of energy is attributed to the Latin American version of the Baroque. Again, this element gives it a superiority over any other culture, because it is said to be "el horno transmutativo de la asimilación" (Lezama Lima 2010, p. 90–91) ("the transformative furnace of assimilation", (Zamora/Kaup 2010, p. 222)). Whatever foreign cultural fragment comes close to this kind of furnace or volcano will thus be melted and assimilated into a new cultural identity.[17] Whatever Baroque fragments find their way onto the American continent will similarly be assimilated into the American Baroque. There is an implication that those fragments come from Europe's metropolis where, according to a Spenglerian logic, an old culture is declining; whereas, a younger culture, bestowed with a superior energy, is emerging in Latin America. This represents an extremely active and even violent version of the reinsertion phase that we have identified in the CT process, exclusively seen from the perspective of a strong receiver system.

Plutonism stands out as the most essentialist element and moment in Lezama Lima's text. It effectuates as if by decree a self-attribution of a surplus of energy to one's own culture. And, as with Carpentier's telluric pulse, it locates this energy in Latin America's natural potential. However, what complicates the naturalist essentialism seen in Carpentier is the expression "horno transmutativo" for the furnace is a man-made instrument of assimilation and refers to human technology and action, not to nature.

With such CT dynamics that depict the receiver system as stronger than the giver system, it is quite logical to affirm the superiority of the Latin American Baroque:

> Juana Inés de la Cruz, alcanza su plenitud y la plenitud del idioma poético en sus días. Es la primera vez que en el idioma, una figura Americana ocupa un lugar de primacía.
>
> LEZAMA LIMA 2010, p. 95

> (Sor Juan Inés de la Cruz achieves her fullest expression in a poem that becomes the culminating expression of the period. For the first time in the Spanish language, an American occupies the highest rank.)
>
> ZAMORA/KAUP 2010, p. 225

---

17 In passing we notice here that, as a metaphor for cultural processes configurable as CTs, plutonism, the transformative furnace has exactly the same radical semantic structure as the North American "melting pot". In other words, through caloric energy it has the capacity to transform what comes from abroad, and is perceived as foreign, into one's own identity.

Sor Juana Inés de la Cruz, for Lezama Lima, is part of a trio of emblematic figures. The other two are Kondori, the Peruvian architect, and the Brazilian sculptor João de Lisboa, called Aleijadinho. These three cultural heroes complete Lezama Lima's miscegenated spectrum of the American Baroque: the criollo (Sor Juana), the African-Hispanic (Aleijadinho) and the Inca-Hispanic (Kondori).

What is new in Lezama Lima's text is the conflictual relationship towards European culture as the giver system:

> Repitiendo la frase de Weisbach, adaptándola a lo americano, podemos decir que entre nosotros el barroco fue un arte de la contraconquista.
> LEZAMA LIMA 2010, p. 80

> (Repeating Weisbach's phrase and adapting it to America, we can say that for us the Baroque was an art of counterconquest.)
> ZAMORA/KAUP 2010, p. 213

This figure of the "counterconquest" has had, and still has, a very positive reception in Latin America. It transforms a European scholar's phrase describing the Baroque as the art of the counter-reformation into military terms, thus reversing the colonial relationship between the periphery and the metropolis. Also the very term makes the power relation between two cultures explicit in a military metaphor which already announces the process of decolonization. What stronger identity construction could there be? Not only does the receiver system swallow and assimilate[18] what has been transferred to it, but it also fights back![19]

These two texts belong to the "*americanismo*" discourse and contribute to the construction of a (Latin) American cultural identity. There are two different logics at work in both texts, although in different proportions. One logic follows the *mestizo* paradigm. It is in principle the result of a mixture of different elements or ingredients, originally a biological one. However, here the paradigm refers metaphorically to cultural processes, one of which is the CT. Semantically speaking *mestizaje* produces heterogeneity; i.e., a mixture in

---

18 These two verbs are part of the semantic program of another Latin American metaphor for cultural processes, the "antropofagia" coined by the Brazilian modernists of the 1920s. Antropofagia is not less radical – claiming to erase the identity of the transferred culture – than "plutonism" or "melting pot", but its imaginary is physiological.

19 We could affirm that another Cuban author, Severo Sarduy, did exactly that by developing a new concept of the Baroque and the Neobaroque that became very influential in Europe. Sarduy may therefore be considered as a figure of Baroque counter-transfer.

which the initial ingredients are still recognizable. Yet both texts contain elements of another logic, that is a logic of fusion, of total assimilation of the Other, resulting in a new homogeneity. This second logic tends to override the first one. Notably in Carpentier's text where, while arguing with and within a European concept, the CT is all but denied and replaced by a deep ontology affirming that America *is* Baroque, the Baroque *is* American. In fact, the *mestizo* paradigm is subordinated to this deep ontology. Lezama Lima still argues with historical data, viewing culture as both man made and an instrument of human power relations; whereas, Carpentier sees culture as an essence determined by natural conditions.

8.2.2   *Unsuccessful Transfer*
Still working with the "cultural material" Baroque, we now consider a case where the CT did not succeed. When the transferred material encounters negative forces of resistance in the receiver system, the result may be a partial or total rejection. This can be illustrated with the intra-European transfer of the Baroque from its centers of emergence, specifically the giver systems Spain and Italy with France as the receiver system.

In this case, we can distinguish three different modalities of resistance to the Baroque: progressive suppression, repression and encysting.

8.2.2.1   Progressive Suppression
The process of progressive suppression of the transferred element by the receiver system can be best documented with the case of Bernini in Paris.[20] In 1665, the French monarch Louis XIV invited the Italian architect and sculptor Gian Lorenzo Bernini (1598–1680) to Paris with the mandate to design the expansion of his royal palace, the Louvre. The king was aware of the development of a new artistic style in Italy, one that had already spread beyond the Italian borders and was rapidly garnering international approval. This style, manifested in various arts, was the Baroque, although it was no called so yet.[21] Bernini had just accomplished a major and prestigious work, the Piazza San Pietro in Rome, so the French king wanted to lend his own palace the prestige of both this new style and one of its most illustrious representatives.

---

20   For this case, we rely on Cecil Gould's historical account in his book *Bernini in France. An Episode in Seventeenth-Century History* (London: Weidenfels and Nicolson, 1981).
21   "Baroque" is indeed an exo-genetic concept, it was elaborated after the period to which it refers. See my essay 'The Concept of Baroque', in *Revista Canadiense de Estudios Hispánicos*, 33/1 (Fall 2008), pp. 11–38.

As a guest of the French King, Bernini spent about half a year in Paris (April to October 1665). Already in 1664, before his trip to France, he started drafting projects for the French royal palace. Today, we can document a succession of four projects in which the progressive suppression of the Baroque becomes visible.

The first project was drafted and sent to Paris in 1664. At first glance, it looks very Baroque, with its round and concave ground lines and protruding wings. The superior section resembled a king's crown.

The second project, also drafted in Rome, was sent to Paris in 1664, in response to commentaries already received from Paris on the first project. The design still looks very Baroque with the characteristic round and concave ground lines, but the round "hat" on the top has disappeared.

Drafted in Paris in 1665, the third project appears much less Baroque with its straight lines. The protruding wings are still there but now at right angles. This rendition was probably adapted to the rest of the building after Bernini had finally seen it on the spot.

Before Bernini left for Rome, the ground stone of "his" Louvre was laid in his presence on October 17, 1665. The fourth project was drafted in 1666, after Bernini's return to Rome. The draft itself is lost but was redrawn by the Swedish architect Tessin (accordingly called the Stockholm drawing) based on a model constructed by Rossi that shows the Southern half of the East Façade.

In 1667, the Bernini project was abandoned altogether, under the following circumstances:

> As early as April 1667, and therefore a month before France invaded Flanders, a committee [created by Colbert] consisting of Le Vau, Le Brun and Charles Perron's brother, Claude, had met for the purpose of producing an alternative to Bernini's plan. Colbert had understandably delayed for three months breaking the news to Bernini.
> GOULD 1981, p. 118

The succession of the four projects is visually quite spectacular. We can indeed observe the successive disappearance of the Baroque style. Step by step, the architectural aesthetics of the Baroque, transferred from Italy, is pushed back in favor of a style later called French classical. In the end, resistance to the transfer was stronger than the initial royal motivation. It can be said that this CT was unsuccessful, even that it failed.

It must be added, though, that this negative result, even if it is aesthetically apparent can not be attributed exclusively to aesthetic reasons. Instead, the result emerged from a complex process involving many factors. One factor was

Bernini's personal attitude. He made many negative comments about French culture in general. Another factor was the jealousy of his French rivals. Yet another factor may be traced to intrigues at the French court against the empowerment of the famous foreign artist. Finally, those French architects who had a say, considered the practical and security aspects more than the aesthetics of the façade. All those reasons taken together help explain what occurred but it remains that the French receiver system rejected the CT of the Baroque from Italy.

8.2.2.2 Repression of the "Foreign" Element

In spite of this documented negative reception, the Baroque reached France and found its way into French art works. This was also the case in French literature during the 17th century. In this case another kind of resistance manifested itself. It was not the French authors of the 17th century, but rather French literary scholarship which acted as a negative filter for this CT up until the 20th century. Over a long period, 17th century literature was more or less officially classified as classical. The presence of Baroque elements in it were at most marginal. They were there to be discovered, the CT had taken place, but it became the object of a systemic repression. In short, the elements were not supposed to be recognized, in the double sense of the word, both cognitively and axiologically. In this instance, "repression" perfectly retains its psychoanalytical connotation as a translation of Freud's notion of *Verdrängung*.

This was the case until 1953, when Jean Rousset (1910–2002), a Swiss literary critic and historian working at the University of Geneva, "uncovered" the French literary Baroque.[22] Seemingly it took this external eye to discover the repressed cultural material of Baroque nature which had wormed its way into French literature.

Rousset does not transform altogether the 17th century of literary production in France into a Baroque century. His judgement is much more precise and balanced, but he clearly identifies the Baroque elements present. Moreover, he sees them as the result of a CT from Italy and Spain that met resistance in France:

> La France reçoit, ou refuse, plutôt qu'elle ne donne ; que l'opposition française au Baroque n'est pas aussi générale qu'on pourrait le croire, et que

---

22 See Jean Rousset's *La littérature de l'âge baroque en France* (Paris: José Corti, 1953), followed by *Anthologie de la poésie baroque française* (Paris: Armand Colin, 1961). In his 1998 book *Dernier regard sur le baroque* (Paris: José Corti) he revisits what he calls his own *hypothèse baroque* on 17th century French literature.

> cette opposition, quand elle existe, est en partie, mais en partie seulement, une réaction nationale d'opposition à l'étranger ; que cet étranger est d'abord italien et en second lieu espagnol.
>
> ROUSSET 1953, p. 238

More than 40 years after his initial thesis of *La littérature de l'âge baroque en France*, in his *Dernier regard sur le baroque*, Rousset comes up with an even more differentiated judgment. He insists on the coexistence of the baroque with the classic: 'le baroque et le classique vivent et prospèrent non pas successivement mais simultanément goûtés à la cour et à la ville' (Rousset 1998, p. 28). Yet for Jean Rousset, the historical context remains the same; i.e., the context of a CT from Italy to France, which encountered resistance from the receiver system: 's'affrontent les séductions de l'Italie et les résistances gallicanes' (Rousset 1998, p. 29).

8.2.2.3 Encysting of the "Foreign" Element

Yet another modality of refusing the object of a CT consists of ostentatiously making it appear foreign. Again, this modality manifests a refusal to integrate – and even less to assimilate –the transferred element. It operates as the opposite of a repression that would make it unrecognizable and instead represents an exhibition of the object's otherness. In a written text, for instance, this modality may adopt the discursive procedure of a quotation, thus pointing the finger at the otherness of the transferred element while containing the danger of being "infected" by it.

A good example of this negative dealing with CTs can be found in Marc Fumaroli's introduction to the new edition of Victor L. Tapié's *Baroque et classicisme* (1980). Here is how Fumaroli refers to the Baroque in his text:

> Le point de vue d'un historien aussi attaché à sa discipline que Victor L. Tapié n'aurait su s'accommoder de ce qu'il y avait, dans le *Barockbegriff*, d'hostilité plus ou moins inconsciente contre l'Histoire et en tout cas d'utopie plus ou moins savante. L'Histoire n'était qu'un terrain d'envol pour l'angélisme baroquisant: c'était le sol que l'auteur de *Baroque et Classicisme* était bien décidé à ne pas point quitter. Si le *Barockbegriff* avait un sens, à ses yeux, c'était au prix d'être solidement arrimé à des dates et des lieux.
>
> TAPIÉ 1980, p. 26

By quoting the concept of the Baroque in German, Fumaroli keeps it at a distance from French culture in general, and more particularly from his own text. More precisely in this case, the "foreignness" of the Baroque in France does not refer to some giver system as the homeland of the Baroque (Italy or Spain). Instead, it refers to the homeland of the a-posteriori and exogenous elaboration of the concept of the Baroque in Germanic countries during the 19th and 20th centuries with Burckhardt and Wölfflin in Switzerland, and Gurlitt, Worringer, Weisbach, Hausenstein and Benjamin, among others, in Germany.

Fumaroli insists on marking the Germanic otherness of the concept by using a German word (*Barockbegriff*). He does this nine times in his introduction so that in one and the same discursive gesture, the Baroque is both singled out and rejected as an element foreign to the French language itself. Resorting to a physiological metaphor, we could say that the alien matter is encysted in one's own body.

Quite contrary to what happened in Latin America, the French reception of the transferred Baroque material was not a positive one. Over a long period beginning in the 17th century, the French receiver system used various strategies to keep at a distance and even to reject what was perceived as a foreign element. So, be it by suppression, repression or encysting, the Baroque was not integrated, and even less assimilated. This applies to an architectural project, to a literary style as well as to the very concept of Baroque. Forty years after his "discovery" of the French literary baroque, even Jean Rousset had second thoughts about his use of the term "Baroque". We may thus conclude that the transfer of the Baroque from Spain and Italy to France was unsuccessful.

8.3   Conclusion

Our case study on transcultural combined with transhistorical transfers of the Baroque is focused on the results of CTs. It shows that the transfer of basically the same cultural material can have, under different historical circumstances and in different contexts, very different results. The example of Latin America is an eloquent one. There the Baroque, initially imposed as a foreign cultural paradigm in a colonial context, was progressively integrated and even assimilated in the process of decolonization and political independence, entering into Latin American systems and sub-systems and becoming a strong marker of identity. This was not the case with the intra-European transfer from Spain and Italy which encountered strong resistance in France for a long time.

This case study has illustrated the use of the CT as an analytical tool. As seen in the first part of this essay, the CT is a heuristic instrument that allows us to analyze transcultural mobility. To make it operational, however, certain conditions apply. First, we must reduce the complexity of transcultural mobility by designing a restricted window of observation. The heuristic tool is thus obtained through a "contingent closure" of the infinite object field called "cultural mobility". In order to make concrete empirical analysis possible, it is necessary to extract a dynamic unit configured by binary vectorial relations from multiple vectors and multilateral relations.

Concrete cases of CT may thus be subjected to investigation as processes. The analysis works with a certain number of invariants, such as agents, objects, processes, and power relations, and has to take into account variations deriving from concrete, empirically given situations.

A systemic logic applies to such transfers. What might appear as the "same" object – formally, materially, aesthetically – cannot be the same object within two different systems in terms of functions and meanings. Therefore, it is important to give serious consideration to the processes of de- and recontextualization through which the material to be transferred is being cut off from its initial context. This operation may be thematised in terms of an active forgetting which makes the same material available for the reinsertion into a new cultural context where it can adopt a new functionality.

Note that there is no mechanical application of any kind of research program. As we have seen in our case studies, each analysis requires a precise redefinition of the invariables as well as a careful investigation of the variations arising from different social, political, aesthetic, and mediatic contexts. These considerations can explain the extremely different results in the transfer of the Baroque from the Iberian Peninsula to Latin America on the one hand, and from Italy and Spain to France on the other.

Bibliography

Anderson, Benedict, *Imagined Communities. Reflections on the Origin and the Spread of Nationalisms* (New York: Verso Books, 1983).

Beverly, John, *Essays on the Literary Baroque in Spain and Spanish America* (Woodbridge: Tamesis, 2008).

Bhabha, Homi, *The Location of Culture* (New York: Routledge, 1994).

Carpentier, Alejo, 'Lo barroco y lo real maravilloso', in *Razón de Ser (Conferencias)* (Caracas: Universidad de Venezuela, Ediciones del Rectorado, 1976), pp. 51–73. English translation: The Baroque and the Marvelous Real (1975), in *Baroque New Worlds. Representation, Transculturation, Counterconquest*, ed. by Lois Parkinson Zamora, Wendy B. Faris. (New York: Duke University Press, 1995), pp. 89–108.

D'Ors, Eugenio, *Lo barroco* (Madrid: Aguilar, 1944).

Echeverría, Bolívar, *La modernidad de lo barroco* (Mexico City: Era, 1998).

Echeverría, Bolívar, *Modernidad, mestizaje cultural, ethos barroco* (Mexico City: Universidad Nacional Autónoma de México, El Equilibrista, 1994).

Espagne, Michel, *Les transferts culturels franco-allemands* (Paris: Presses Universitaires de France, 1999).

Espagne, Michel/Werner, Michael (eds.), *Transferts. Les relations interculturelles dans l'espace franco-allemand (XVIIIe–XIXe siècles)* (Paris: Éditions Recherche sur les Civilisations, 1988).

Gin, Pascal/Goyer, Nicolas/Moser, Walter (eds.), *Transfert. Exploration d'un champ conceptuel* (Ottawa: Ottawa University Press, 2013).

Gould, Cecil, *Bernini in France. An Episode in Seventeenth-Century History* (London: Weidenfeld and Nicolson, 1981).

Kortländer, Bernd, 'Begrenzung – Entgrenzung. Kultur- und Wissenstransfer in Europa', in *Nationale Grenzen und internationaler Austausch. Studien zum Kultur- und Wissenstransfer in Europa*, ed. by Lothar Jordan/Bernd Kortländer (Tübingen, Niemeyer, 1995), pp. 1–19.

Lezama Lima, José, 'La curiosidad barroca', in *La expresión americana* (México DF: Fondo de Cultura Económica, 1993), pp. 79–106. English translation: 'Baroque Curiosity', in *Baroque New Worlds. Representation, Transculturation, Counterconquest*, ed. by Lois Parkinson Zamora/Monika Kaup (Durham and London: Duke University Press, 2010), pp. 210–240.

Luhmann, Niklas, *Soziale Systeme. Grundriss einer allgemeinen Theorie* (Frankfurt/Main: Suhrkamp, 1987).

Lüsebrink, Hans-Jürgen, 'De l'analyse de la réception littéraire à l'étude des transferts culturels', in *Discours Social/Social Discourse*, 7/3–4 (1995), pp. 39–46.

Maravall, José Antonio, *La cultura del barroco* (Barcelona: Editorial Ariel, 1975).

McLuhan, Marshall, *Understanding Media. Extensions of Man* (London: Routledge and Kegan Paul, 1964).

Moraña, Mabel, *Relecturas del barroco de Indias* (Hanover NH: Ediciones del Norte, 1994).

Moser, Walter, 'The Concept of Baroque', in *Revista Canadiense de Estudios Hispánicos*, 33/1 (Fall 2008), pp. 11–38.

Rousset, Jean, *Dernier regard sur le baroque* (Paris: José Corti, 1998).

Rousset, Jean, *Anthologie de la poésie baroque française* (Paris: Armand Colin, 1961).

Rousset, Jean, *La littérature de l'âge baroque en France. Circé et le Paon* (Paris: José Corti, 1953).

Schwarz, Roberto, *Misplaced Ideas. Essays on Brazilian Culture* (London: Verso, 1992).

Tapié, Victor L., *Baroque et classicisme* (Paris: Livre de Poche, 1980 [1957]).

Theodoro, Janice, *América barroca. Tema e variações* (São Paulo: Editora da Universidade de São Paulo/Editora Nova Fronteira, 1992).

Zamora, Lois Parkinson/Kaup, Monika (eds.), *Baroque New Worlds. Representation, Transculturation, Counterconquest* (Durham, London: Duke University Press, 2010).

CHAPTER 9

From *Transferts culturels* to *Transferências culturais*: Interdisciplinary and Methodical Dynamics and Translations of the Concept in the Brazilian Context

Wiebke Röben de Alencar Xavier

Abstract

This contribution will focus on an interdisciplinary, panoramic, and analytical view on translation, reception and application of the concept and theory of cultural transfers, in the Brazilian context translated as *Transferências culturais*. Brazilian research based on this concept is relatively new and we found work mostly in the areas of Brazilian Comparative Literature, History, Historiography, Translation Studies, History of the Book and Press, and recently in the area of History of Education. The concept is often intertwined with other international and/or national concepts and theories. After a slow beginning and some resistances against the *Transferts culturels* as an imported concept, we have perceived, over the last few years, more and more considerations and resemantizations of the concept in various disciplines and in the context of some transatlantic interdisciplinary research projects. Some of the newest tendencies in Comparative Literature are focusing on a transnational perspective on Brazilian Literary History, Historiography and Culture.

9.1 Introduction[1]

Since the mid-1980s, processes of cultural transfer as an interdisciplinary object of research have had their own history and bibliography, especially in the German-French context, but also in the wider European and non-European context. This implies transnational projects, case studies on mediators, but also discussions on the possibilities and limits of *transferts culturels* as a methodological concept and theory in context or in competition with other

---

1 This study was financed in part by the Coordenação de Aperfeiçoamento de Pessoal de Nível Superior – Brasil (CAPES) – Finance Code 001.

approaches. In an interview in 2018 with the historian and transfer researcher Alexandre Fontaine of the *Institut für Bildungswissenschaften* (Institute for Educational Science) at the University of Vienna, Michel Espagne not only confirmed the potential of the concept in different cultural contexts than the French-German context, but also underlined the necessity of new appropriations, or rather resemantizations. Through his experiences with the reception of the concept in Russian and Chinese, he has seen how difficult it is to translate the concept, but at the same time he considered its semantic modifications in the process of transfer to be completely legitimate.[2]

This contribution provides an insight into how *Transferts culturels* has been and is imported, discussed and resemantized as a methodological concept in Brazil through different receptions in the academic context of events and projects as well as through the translation of methodological key texts. The focus of interest is on the reception, critiques, and interdisciplinary applications that the concept has experienced in the transatlantic and inter-American research context of the history of the Brazilian press, Comparative Literature, and intellectual history. It will also show which paths it took initially in Latin American and Brazilian German Studies and to what extent it now also plays a role in Translation Studies and the History of Education. In any case, the interdisciplinary transfer and the different applications of the concept in and between different cultural areas are reflected in many ways in the Brazilian Humanities. The concept of *Transferts culturels*, translated as *Transferências culturais*, shows convergences as well as (inter-)disciplinary and conceptual divergences and is combined with various other approaches, depending on the object of research and the mediator.

This applies also to the Brazilian context of the importation of the concept on cultural transfer and its application. Espagne is convinced that it is, above all, the context of the reception that defines what can be imported. And when the foreign reference is integrated into a debate inherent to the context of reception, this reference becomes autonomous in relation to its source and is determined only by the protagonists of the ongoing debate.[3] For the import of the transfer concept and the material research program, especially in the field of literary history, applies an understanding of internationalization "[...] das nicht an die Abstraktionsebene von Theorien und Verfahren gebunden ist,

---

2 Michel Espagne/Alexandre Fontaine, 'Viajando com o conceito de Transferências culturais. Entrevista com Michel Espagne', transl. by Felipe Ziotti Narita, in *Cadernos CIMEAC*, 8/2 (2018), pp. 6–17 (p. 14).
3 Cf. Michel Espagne, *Les transferts culturels franco-allemands* (Paris: Presses Universitaires de France, 1999), p. 23.

diese aber auch zu ihrem Gegenstand machen kann. ([...] that is not bound to the level of abstraction of theories and proceedings but can also make them their subject)".[4]

9.1.1 Transferts culturels *and* Transferências culturais *in Academic Contexts and International Formation*

The interview of Alexandre Fontaine with Michel Espagne from 2018 mentioned at the outset of this article is the most recent product of the discussion on the cultural transfer approach in the Brazilian context of reception. It was translated by Felipe Ziotti Narita, an interdisciplinary and internationally networked Brazilian historian and professor of the *Faculdade de Ciências Sociais e Humanas* of the *Universidade Estadual de São Paulo* (UNESP), and was published at the beginning of 2019 under the title "Viajando com o conceito de Transferências Culturais" in the *Cadernos CIMEAC* of the Universidade Federal do Triângulo Mineiro (UFTM). Narita is currently the chief-editor of this periodical, which was founded by the *Centro de Investigação de Metodologias Alternativas 'Conexão'* in the context of the postgraduation of the Educational Sciences of the UFTM.[5]

But the first reception of the methodological concept of *Transferts culturels* takes place in Brazil long before this translated interview and the translation of methodological key texts on Culturel Transfer. On the one hand, the Universities of Paris, the *École des Hautes Études des Sciences Sociales* (EHESS) and the *Fondation Maison des Sciences de l'Homme* have played an important mediating role in this reception process as educational and research institutions for young Brazilian historians since the 1980s. On the other hand, international research networks, events and projects in the fields of transnational Press History, Historiography, Inter-American Transculturalization Research and International German Studies since the 1990s have contributed in very different ways to the interdisciplinary Brazilian import of the concept.

---

4 Chryssoula Kambas, 'Theorie-Transfers und Internationalisierung der Literaturgeschichte', in *Wie international ist die Literaturwissenschaft?*, ed. by Lutz Danneberg/Friedrich Vollhardt (Stuttgart, Weimar: Metzler, 1996), pp. 287–300 (p. 294). All translations in this contribution are made by its author, Wiebke Röben de Alencar Xavier.

5 In 2017 the translator Felipe Ziotti Narita published the book: *A Educação da Sociedade imperial. Moral, religião e formação social na modernidade oitocentista* (Curitiba: Editora Prismas). He also has a research line on "Transferências culturais e modernidade: circulação de saberes no espaço atlântico (XIX–XX)". In its context, Narita examines the networks of diffusion, reception and reelaboration of knowledge in the light of the material transformations of capitalist modernity, understood as social infrastructures in cities and as spheres of circulation in journals, typographies, books, conferences and other forms of mediation.

9.1.1.1 *Transferts culturels* and *Histoire croisée*
Between 1999 and 2004 numerous research projects, colloquia, and publications on cultural transfer and circulation of almanacs in Europe and the Americas in the field of French-Brazilian Press History already existed. The main participants were Jean-Yves Mollier (Université de Versailles Saint-Quentin-en-Yvelines), Marlyse Meyer (Universidade Federal de Campinas (UNICAMP)), Eliana Dutra (Universidade Federal de Minas Gerais (UFMG)) and Hans-Jürgen Lüsebrink (Saarland University).[6]

In Brazilian German Studies, the reception begins at the XI. Congress of Latin American Germanists (ALEG), organized by the Brazilian Germanist Willi Bolle of the Universidade de São Paulo (USP) in 2003 with the title 'Blickwechsel' (Changes of perspectives). This congress went down in history as the "travelling congress": it began in São Paulo, then went on to Paraty, the birthplace of Julia Mann, the mother of Thomas Mann, and ended in Petrópolis, the seat of the Brazilian imperial family in the mountains of Rio de Janeiro, where Stefan Zweig also spent his last days and then took his own life in 1942 out of desperation and resignation in the face of the events in Europe.

Also in 2003, a first theoretical-methodological key text from the interdisciplinary French field of Historical Sciences was translated into Portuguese, where the concept of cultural transfer plays an important role, but in which the concept of *Histoire croisée* is the focus of interest. This is Michael Werner's and Bénédicte Zimmermann's article "Penser l'histoire croisée: entre empirie et réflexivité" published in the *Annales. Histoire, Sciences sociales* and translated by the Brazilian historian Jaime de Almeida in the periodical *Textos de História* (2003), which recently became available also online.[7] At the almost simultaneous ALEG Congress 'Blickwechsel' in September of 2003, it was also Michael Werner as representative of EHESS in Paris, who gave a plenary lecture on the situation of German Studies in France between literary, cultural and social sciences.

---

6 See first publications of the transnational context of Brazilian Press History in Marlyse Meyer (ed.), *Do Almanak aos Almanaques* (São Paulo: Ateliê Editorial, 2001); Hans-Jürgen Lüsebrink/York-Gothart Mix/Jean-Yves Mollier/Patricia Sorel (eds.), *Les lectures du peuple en Europe et dans les Amériques du XVIIe au XXe siècle* (Brussels: Complexe, 2003); Eliana de Freitas Dutra/Jean-Yves Mollier (eds.), *O lugar dos impressos na construção da vida política* (Belo Horizonte: Anna Blume, 2006).

7 Michael Werner/Bénédicte Zimmermann, 'Penser l'histoire croisée. Entre empirie et réflexivité', in *Annales. Histoire, Sciences sociales*, 1 (2003), pp. 7–36; Michael Werner/Bénédicte Zimmermann, 'Pensar a história cruzada. Entre empiria e reflexividade', transl. by Jaime de Almeida, in *Textos de História*, 1–2 (2003), pp. 89–127.
    https://www.researchgate.net/publication/277096068_Pensar_a_historia_cruzada_entre_empiria_e_reflexividade.

In his contribution, he first problematized, from a French perspective, the term "Germanistik in Frankreich" (German Studies in France), which institutionally did not primarily refer to philology, but to the subject of university teachers in France, who in their research and teaching deal with German literature, language and in the broadest sense cultural studies.[8] In the further course of his lecture, he showed how French German Studies then helped itself out of the crisis in the 1980s. Based on cultural transfer research as well as the transfer and the history of the discipline, Werner emphasizes the opening of new, interdisciplinary research directions in the *Études germaniques* and points out the connection between theory and practice, empiricism and reflexivity. In his remarks, he makes clear both the successful ambitions of the initially German-French C.N.R.S. Research Group around him and Michel Espagne in Paris, but at the same time also refers to the meta-concept *histoire croisée*, which he mediated in São Paulo as a further development of transfer research.

For the predominantly Latin American Germanists and congress guests of European, mostly German Universities, he presents the concept of cultural transfer as an established model that has been theoretically inspired by reception aesthetics, Bourdieu's field theory and neo-hermeneutic approaches. He points out that at the beginning of the 1980s, it was empirically developed by the just mentioned research group led by Germanists in Paris on the basis of the German-French field of relations, but in the meantime it has become an international example far beyond this dimension. He justifies its success above all with the transdisciplinarity of the approach, which has been applied right from the beginning:

> Voraussetzung dafür waren ein anthropologisch fundierter breiter Kulturbegriff, der auch materielle Kultur, Technik und Wissenschaft umfasst, eine sozialgeschichtliche Perspektive, die die sozialen Akteure, die Phänomene von Migration und Akkulturation mit einschließt, schließlich eine konkrete interdisziplinäre Praxis, insofern von Anfang an Historiker, Philosophen, Wissenschaftsgeschichtler, Romanisten, Buchhistoriker, Musik- und Kunstwissenschaftler an dem Projekt beteiligt waren.

> (The prerequisites for this were an anthropologically founded broad concept of culture, which also encompasses material culture, technology

---

8 Michael Werner, 'Zwischen Literatur, Kultur- und Sozialwissenschaft. Zur Situation der Germanistik in Frankreich', in *Blickwechsel. Akten des XI. Lateinamerikanischen Germanistenkongress São Paulo, Paraty, Petrópolis*, ed. by Willi Bolle/Helmut Galle 1 (São Paulo: Monferrer Productions, 2005), pp. 147–158 (p. 147).

and science, a socio-historical perspective that includes the social actors, the phenomena of migration and acculturation, and finally concrete interdisciplinary practice, insofar as historians, philosophers, scientific historians, Romanists, book historians, musicologists and art historians were involved in the project from the outset.)

WERNER 2005, p. 155

However, he notes that, despite all transdisciplinarity, the cultural transfer approach retains a "French" orientation because it adheres to the unity of Social Sciences and Humanities and Cultural Studies by relying preferentially on empirical case studies and often working on the basis of texts and discourses. But at the same time Werner repeatedly stresses that this approach is no longer limited to the French-German context, but is '[...] transversal, übertragbar, übersetzbar, modifizierbar und für andere Terrains adaptierbar ([...] transversal, transferable, translatable, modifiable and adaptable to other terrains)'.[9]

In the end, he presents in even more detail his then most recent research, the meta-concept *histoire croisée*. He defines it as a methodological basis for a history of entanglement, crossings, reflections and intertwinements, with which would be established connections to postcolonial studies and to migration and network research. According to Werner, *histoire croisée* investigates not only research objects that are intertwined or interwoven with each other, but at the same time the concept interweaves itself by, among other things, trying to reflect on its own "Blickwechsel" (changes of perspectives) and to include these reflections in the analysis, in order to achieve a higher degree of reflexivity.[10]

The German specialist public had known the approach for a long time, but the Brazilian and Latin American public reacted very cautiously and critically to Werner's remarks, because there was not yet an interdisciplinary and broad reception of the cultural transfer approach. The lack of resonance at this time was also evident in the article on Swiss-French cultural transfer in the section concerning theories and methods of interpretation, in which the author of this chapter presented the methodological concept on the example of the Swiss Enlightenment author Salomon Gessner (1730–1788) and his works in French translation in the context of Diderot's and D'Alembert's *Encyclopédie* in connection with imagological questions as new and innovative for a literary history of exchange.[11]

---

9   Werner, 'Zwischen Literatur, Kultur- und Sozialwissenschaft', *op. cit.*, p. 156.
10 Cf. Werner, 'Zwischen Literatur, Kultur- und Sozialwissenschaft', *op. cit.*, p. 156.
11 Wiebke Röben de Alencar Xavier, 'Das methodische Konzept Kulturtransfer am Beispiel des Schweizer Aufklärers Salomon Gessner (1730–1788)', in *Blickwechsel*, ed. by Ulrich J. Beil/Claudia S. Dornbusch/Masa Nomura, vol. 3 (São Paulo: Monferrer Productions, 2005), pp. 312–318.

But even before the ALEG in spring 2003, Jaime de Almeida, Professor of History at the Universidade Federal de Brasília (UnB), published his Portuguese translation of Michael Werner and Bénédicte Zimmermann's article on the *Histoire croisée* from the *Annales* in the context of the dossier "Justiça no Antigo Regime" (Justice in the Ancient Regime) in the journal *Textos de História* of the postgraduate program in History at the Federal University of Brasilia (UnB). At first, this happened only recently, this translation, as mentioned at the beginning, also became freely available online, allowing a whole new dimension of reception. But with his translation, which remains very close to the French original, not only was the transfer concept being discussed, but bibliographical references to it have also been translated for the first time, albeit with a critical perspective on the historicity and reflexivity of the concept. The term "transferências" or "estudos das transferências" established itself as a methodological term.

This way, the scientist and Professor also became a cultural agent in his function as a translator. In 1977 and 1978 Almeida completed *Bacharel* and *Maîtrise* in *Histoire* at the Université de Paris VIII Vincennes-Saint-Denis, followed by his teaching degree (1983) and doctorate (1987) in *História Social* at the USP in São Paulo. From 2000–2001 he obtained his postdoctorate at the Université de Paris I Pantheon-Sorbonne. At a later stage, it would be interesting to know whether there were personal contacts between Zimmermann, Werner and Almeida, because the simultaneous publication of the article in the *Annales* and its Portuguese translation as well as Werner's plenary lecture at the ALEG in São Paulo are an indication of consciously mediatory network in theory transfer.

Ten years later, at a German-Brazilian meeting conference in Rio de Janeiro, which was financed by the DAAD and entitled "German Studies in Brazil: Challenges, Paths of Communication, Translations", new paths and perspectives of German Studies in Brazil were discussed and the *Associação Brasileira de Estudos Germanísticos (ABEG)* was founded with the aim of carrying out interdisciplinary research on the very diverse profile of German Studies in the country in the past and present and developing new future perspectives. In the subsequent ABEG Conferences of 2015 in São Paulo, 2017 in Florianópolis and 2019 in Niteroi, there is just always one section in which the concept of cultural transfer has played an important role.[12]

---

12   The 2013 conference is documented in *Germanistik in Brasilien: Herausforderungen, Vermittlungswege, Übersetzungen*, ed. by DAAD (Göttingen: Wallstein, 2014), see for contributions about Cultural Transferts especially Wiebke Röben de Alencar Xavier/ Franziska Schößler, 'Konzepte kultureller Übersetzung. Mit einem Seitenblick auf eine

9.1.1.2 *Transferências culturais* and *Literatura Comparada interamericana*
In the context of the *Literatura Comparada*, the reception of *Transferts culturels* began much earlier in the 1990s within the framework of Brazilian-Canadian research projects and discussions on the possibilities of inter-American comparative literature. Walter Moser, at that time from the Université de Ottawa, and Zilá Bernd, a Brazilian specialist in *Literatura Comparada* at the Universidade Federal do Rio Grande do Sul (UFRGS) in Porto Alegre, Brazil, played a major role in this movement. In this case, however, the path of theoretical-methodological mobility was initially initiated in reverse, namely through the interest of Canadian academics in the

> [...] processos de autonomização cultural, entre eles a antropophagia e a origem da mestiçagem cultural e literária, deslocando clichés acerca da dependência cultural latino-americana em relação aos "modelos" hegemônicos.

> ([...] processes of cultural autonomisation, including anthropophagy and the origin of cultural and literary mestizagem, displacing clichés about Latin American cultural dependence on hegemonic "models").
> BERND 2008, p. 14

Since the early 1990s, events, projects and associated anthologies have been undertaken with a focus on transculturation and inter-American relations, in which cultural transfer processes have played a significant role. The anthology *Confluences littéraires Brésil-Québec: les bases d'une comparaison* (1992), in

---

"Kontextgermanistik", in *Germanistik in Brasilien. Herausforderungen, Vermittlungswege, Übersetzungen*, ed. by DAAD (Göttingen: Wallstein, 2014), pp. 13–28; Wiebke Röben de Alencar Xavier, 'Für eine 'Kontextgermanistik'. DaF, Übersetzung und deutsch-brasilianischer Kulturtransfer im Nordosten Brasiliens', in *Germanistik in Brasilien. Herausforderungen, Vermittlungswege, Übersetzungen*, ed. by DAAD (Göttingen: Wallstein, 2014), pp. 130–132. Under the title 'Traduzir – Transcriar – Transformar' the results of a section of the ABEG from 2015 on cultural transfer and translation are reflected in the Brazilian online journal *Graphos*, 18/2 (2016), ed. by Wiebke Röben de Alencar Xavier and Tito Lívio Cruz Romão. http://www.periodicos.ufpb.br/ojs2/index.php/graphos/issue/view/1859/showToc. The ABEG Conference of 2017 gathers the results of the II Congress of Florianópolis on the ABEG-site http://germanistik-brasil.org/?p=1493 and in September 2019 there is a section in the ABEG- Conference in Niteroi on the topic 'Transferência cultural no campo da Literatura e na Literacia Cient.fica Brasil-Alemanha: um diálogo transcultural' (Cultural transfer in the field of literature and Brazilian-German scientific literacy: a cross-cultural dialogue), coordinated by Thaiane Oliveira (Universidade Federal Fluminense) and Andrée Gerland (Eberhard Karls-Universität Tübingen).

which Zilá Bernd was already involved in the organisation, is particularly worthy of mention. In doing so, it grants Walter Moser a key role for the South-North migration of the concept of cultural anthropophagy, which emerged from the *Manifesto Antropófago* (1928) of the Brazilian modernist Oswald de Andrade. According to Zilá Bernd, Moser has made an essential theorizing contribution to the reflection of questions of identity and its relationship to the national, to migration and cultural transfer, multiculturalism, and cultural mobility on both sides with his groundbreaking contribution 'L'anthropophagie du Sud au Nord'.[13] In Bernd's interpretation,

> [...] nós, brasileiros, podemos reavaliar a abrangência e a atualidade do movimento de 1928, pois ele comporta, segundo o teórico canadense, um ensinamento de base: não há substâncias identitárias preestabelecidas. O fundamento da questão identitária é um processo de interações muito complexo: não é homogêneo, não tem propriedades metafísicas e muito menos determinação biológica [...]. Nesse sentido, o autor considera que o *Manifesto Antropófago* pode fertilizar a reflexão identitária do Norte, embora saliente o caráter potencialmente destrutivo da alteridade contido em sua proposição de base: devorar o outro e apropriar-se de suas contribuições culturais passa necessariamente por sua destruição (aniquilamento). Haveria, pois, no gesto canibal, uma tendência à abolição das diferenças.
>
> ([...] we Brazilians can re-evaluate the scope and actuality of the 1928 movement, because it contains, according to the Canadian theorist, a basic teaching: there are no pre-established identity substances. The foundation of the identity question is a very complex process of interactions: it is not homogeneous, has no metaphysical properties and much less biological determination [...]. In this sense, the author considers that the Anthropophagics Manifest can fertilize the identity reflection of the North, although it highlights the potentially destructive character of the alterity contained in its basic proposition: to devour the other and to appropriate his cultural contributions necessarily goes through its destruction (annihilation). In the cannibal gesture, there would therefore be a tendency towards the abolition of differences.)
>
> BERND 2008, p. 16

---

13   Walter Moser, 'L'anthropophagie du Sud au Nord', in *Confluences littéraires Brésil-Québec. Les bases d'une comparaison*, ed. by Michel Peterson/Zilá Bernd, (Paris: Éditions Balzac, 1992), pp. 113–152.

Zilá Bernd describes here in principle the cultural transfer of Andrade's *Manifesto* and its resemantization in this concept of cultural anthropophagy. Already at the time of its emergence the same manifest destabilized the Brazilian literary institution questioning the Brazilian literary and cultural "caráter nacional" (national character).

A pioneering contribution in the area of *Literatura Comparada* involving cultural transfer processes was also the *Colloque Brésil@Montréal: penser les transferts culturels*, which took place ten years later at the Université de Montréal in 2002. At the same time, Zilá Bernd herself carried out the project *"Transculturalisms/Transferts culturels"* in Canada between 2001 and 2002. Between 2001 and 2004, she carried out the transnational project *"Americanidade e transferências culturais"*,

> [...] o ambicioso projeto de pensar o conceito de americanidade como identidade abrangente, ultrapassando as fronteiras das identidades nacionais, étnicas e de gênero, e procurando refletir sobre autores fundamentais das três Américas para inscrevê-los no âmbito das relações culturais e literárias interamericanas. [...] Trata-se de um projeto de comparatismo literário interamericano que privilegia os processos transculturais ocorridos no continente americano.
>
> ([...] the ambitious project of thinking of the concept of Americanness as a comprehensive identity, going beyond the boundaries of national, ethnic, and gender identities, and seeking to reflect on key authors from the three Americas to inscribe them in the context of inter-American cultural and literary relations. It is a project of inter-American literary comparisons that privileges the transcultural processes that have taken place in the American continent.)
> BERND 2003a, p. 11

In this context, Bernd reflected against the background of the Brazilian-Canadian research discourse above all on the methodical implementation of her project on the basis of "transculturação" (transculturation) and *"transferências culturais"* (Cultural transfers). In her opinion, these are the two concepts that are most adequate to be adopted

> [...] á realidade da condição pós-moderna, na qual há trocas, intercâmbios, perdas e ganhos nas passagens de uma cultura para outra, gerando produtos culturais outros que trazem as marcas indeléveis tanto da cultura de origem quanto da cultura de chegada. O conceito revela-se operacional notadamente quando se trata de refletir sobre as relações

culturais e literárias interamericanas e seu impacto sobre o identitário nas Américas, o que constitui o objetivo maior de nossos esforços de pesquisa no campo dos estudos canadenses e comparados.

([...] to the reality of the postmodern condition, in which there are interchanges, exchanges, losses and gains in the passages from one culture to another, generating other cultural products that bear the indelible marks of both the culture of origin and the culture of arrival. The concept is operational, especially when it comes to reflecting on inter-American cultural and literary relations and their impact on identity in the Americas, which is the main objective of our research efforts in the field of Canadian and Comparative studies.)[14]

BERND 2003b, p. 215

In the introduction to the anthology *Comparative Literature as a Transcultural Discipline*, which emerged from the XXIth Congress of ICLA 2016 in Vienna, the Brazilian Literary Comparatist Eduardo de Faria Coutinho (UFRJ) especially acknowledges Zilá Bernd (Unilasalle) as having given origin to new perspectives in cultural studies and that it is only on the level of a cross- or transcultural perspective that comparatist scholars can envisage the multiple effects of cultural interchanges.[15] In her contribution entitled 'Littératures migrantes: élargissant les frontières des esthétiques transculturelles' she looks back on the last 15 years of her research activities on the *Literatura Comparada interamericana* and mentions as an essential medium for the circulation of methodical and theoretical discussion and results the periodical *Interfaces Brasil-Canadá* (2001–2015), already been quoted here in the context of the concept of cultural anthropophagy. In this periodical, as a principle, no binary schema from North to South but an inter- and transcultural dialogue was established between the participating regions, including Brazil, 'sans passer par le "centre"' ('without passing through the "centre"').[16] Rather, the axis of centrality was replaced by the rapprochement of the South and the North, without establishing hierarchizing perspectives of cultures, and by taking transversal paths, for which

---

14   Zilá Bernd, 'Figuras e mitos da americanidade na ficção brasileira e quebequense', in *Americanidade e transferências culturais, op. cit.*, pp. 214–218 (p. 215).
15   Eduardo de Faria Coutinho, 'Introduction,' in *Comparative Literature as a transcultural discipline*, ed. by Eduardo de Faria Coutinho (São Paulo: Annablume editora, 2018), pp. 10–18 (p. 13).
16   Zilá Bernd, 'Littératures Migrantes. Élargissant les frontières des esthétiques transculturelles', in *Comparative Literature as a transcultural discipline*, pp. 31–40 (p. 34).

research about cultural transfer processes has also played and continues to play an essential role.

9.1.1.3 *Transferências culturais* in Comparative History: History of Brazilian Intellectuals and Print Media

After its initial reception in German Studies, *Literatura Comparada* and History, in 2010, Brazilian historian, Helenice Rodrigues da Silva (1947–2013), presents in her online essay, "*Transferência de Saberes: Modalidades e Possibilidades*", the methodological-theoretical concept of *Transferências culturais* in detail for a larger Brazilian audience for the first time. Based primarily on Michel Espagne's *Les transferts culturels franco-allemands* (1999), she considers various facets that have been added since its development in the 1980s. Her research interest is the development of a Brazilian intellectual history, which goes beyond the national perspective. In this context, she also draws on Werner and Zimmermann's remarks on *Histoire croisée* in order to be able to account for the historicity of Brazilian approaches. She believes that both approaches can be combined.[17]

Like the historian Jaime de Almeida, Helenice Rodrigues da Silva has a history of Brazilian-French education, exile, and research. She graduated in History at the Universidade Federal de Minas Gerais (UFMG) in 1970, but then spent the following 15 years in France during the military dictatorship in Brazil (1964–1985), where, after a specializing at the Université de Franche-Comté in Besançon (1972–1973), she defended her master's degree at the Université de Paris x-Nanterre in 1978 and her Thèse d' État with Jean-Jacques Becker in 1991. The subject was intellectual discourse in the context of the war in Algeria.[18] Between 1984 and 1985, she was a visiting researcher at the *École des Hautes Études en Sciences Sociales* (EHESS) and between 1990 and 1996 she was an associate researcher at the *Laboratoire Communication et Politique - Centre Nacional de Recherche Scientifique* (C.N.R.S.), where she also worked on the history of intellectuals. Only in 1996 she returned to Brazil and became Professor of History at the Universidade Federal do Paraná (UFPR) in Curitiba. Between 2004 and 2005 she completed another postdoctorate at the *Institut d'Histoire du Temps Présent* in Paris. Since that time, her research interest focused on the question of how best to write a form of Brazilian intellectual history that

---

17 Cf. Helenice Rodrigues da Silva, 'Transferência de Saberes. Modalidades e Possibilidades. Transference of knowledge. Modalités and possibilities', in *História. Questões & Debates*, 53 (2010), pp. 203–225 (p. 212).

18 Cf. Diogo da Silva Roiz, 'A trajetória de Helenice Rodrigues da Silva (1947–2013) e a prática da História intelectual no Brasil', in *Cultura Histórica & Patrimônio*, 2/1 (2013), pp. 6–21.

methologically and theoretically should be interdisciplinary, pluralistic, and hybrid, considering the situation of the exile. For this project, in addition to Pierre Bourdieu's field and habitus theory, the methodological concept of *transferts culturels* is introduced, which she presents and discusses in her article as "transferência de sabers",[19] and is essential for the project.

For da Silva, the French concept of cultural transfers is promising for thinking about the transposition of knowledge from one cultural space to another, in which the sociocultural context that gives rise to that knowledge is disregarded in the new space where it is appropriate. Therefore, it is important to study the translations of works and the selection of foreign texts to be studied in a given period, while others are rejected. The concept of cultural transfers, for her, also privileges studies with crossed and connected approaches, comparing different realities and specific moments. With reference to the first publications of Michel Espagne and Michael Werner from the 1980s, she highlights as an object of analysis the processes of selection, mediation, reception, miscegenation, translation, migration, and exchange, among others.[20] And with reference to a note by Hans-Jürgen Lüsebrink and Rolf Reichardt on the history of concepts and cultural transfers (1770–1815) in the periodical *Genèses* (1994), she specifically underscores the role of the theory of intercultural communication:[21]

> Partindo dos discursos de origem, passando pelos veículos de transmissão (mídias e os intermediários culturais) e pelas formas de tradução, de reescrita e de transposição, tenta-se apreender o processo de recepção, desvendado por intermédio das transformações.
>
> (Starting from the discourses of origin, passing through the vehicles of transmission (media and cultural intermediaries) and the forms of translation, rewriting and transposition, one tries to apprehend the process of reception, unveiled through the transformations.)
>
> DA SILVA 2010, p. 209

However, in order to develop the methodical approach for her project, it is not the simple interest of exporting ideas that determines the relevance of the study of cultural transfers, but, in reference to Espagne (1999), she points out, that it is the conjuncture of the receiving context, which, in general, defines, at

---

19   The term itself is translated in the title of her article as "transference of knowledge".
20   Da Silva, 'Transferência de saberes', *op. cit.*, p. 208.
21   Da Silva refers to Hans-Jürgen Lüsebrink/Rolf Reichardt, 'Histoire des concepts et transferts culturels, 1770–1815. Note sur une recherche', in *Genèses*, 14 (1994), pp. 27–41.

a given moment, what can and should be imported.[22] In this sense Silva highlights that it is the 'reception conjuncture that determines what "deserves" to be imported by individuals and groups that transport, from one side to another of a "border", elements of a system to the interior of another system, '[...] é a conjuntura do contexto receptor, que, em general, define, em um determinado momento, o que pode e deve ser importado. ([...] it is the context of the reception context, which in general defines, at a given moment, what can and should be imported)'.[23]

In this focus, with reference to Heinrich Heine as a prototype, Silva explains the significance of intellectuals in exile who, as *"agentes mediadores"* (mediation agents) in history, exercised the function of *"passadores entre culturas"* ("facilitators between cultures").[24] Overall, in the abstract to her article she summarises very well from a globalizing perspective why she considers the cultural transfer approach so important for a Brazilian intellectual history:

> By giving up an epistomological framework of national historiography, the theory of "cultural transferts" paved the way for multilateral studies, involving the processes of inter-relations: interchanges, exports, imports, appropriations, reception of ideas, of models, of values, etc. The broad filed of interdisciplinary research revealed its critical and heuristic value in several areas of the human and social sciences facing the issues inherent to the globalization of knowledge, the interpretation of cultural models and systems of reference.[25]
> DA SILVA 2010, p.

The Brazilian expert in Press History Valéria Guimarães of the *Universidade Estadual de São Paulo* (UNESP) also focuses on the globalization of knowledge. In many international projects and events as well as during her postdoctoral project in 2009 at the *Maison des Sciences de l'Homme* and at the *Université de Versailles-Saint-Quentin-en-Yvelines*, this historian focused on the foreign cultural memory of the Brazilian press and especially on the Brazilian press in French and the dynamics of transatlantic circulation. Indeed, Guimarães is responsible for the Brazilian element of the international research project TRANSFOPRESS, Transnational network for the study of the foreign language

---

22   Cf. da Silva, 'Transferencia de saberes', *op. cit.*, p. 211.
23   Da Silva, 'Transferencia de saberes', *op. cit.*, p. 220. See also Michel Espagne, *Les transferts culturels franco-allemands*, (Paris: Presses Universitaires de France, 1999), pp. 21–23.
24   Cf. da Silva, 'Transferencia de saberes', *op. cit.*, pp. 218–219.
25   Da Silva, 'Transferencia de saberes', *op. cit.*, p. 203.

press, coordinated by Diana Cooper-Richet of the *Université de Versailles-Saint-Quentin-en-Yvelines*.[26]

With an emphasis on the Brazilian-French context, Jean-Yves Mollier and she have already published the first results of their transnational scientific collaboration in 2011 in *Les Transferts Culturels: l'exemple de la presse en France et au Brésil* at L'Harmattan in Paris, also translated into Portuguese in 2012, by the publishing house of the *Universidade Estadual de São Paulo* (UNESP) under the title *Transferências culturais. O exemplo da imprensa na França e no Brasil*. It contains important contributions on identity and alterity in the Brazilian press of the nineteenth and twentieth centuries, on press without borders around the turn of the century, on the Portuguese-language press in Paris in the nineteenth century, on the periodical *Revue des Deux Mondes*, and on transfers and transformations in the case of the press text types *Crônica* (Chronicle) and *Folhetim* (Feuilleton) as well as *Faits Divers* (Divers) between France and Brazil.[27] In the foreword to the Brazilian edition, the Brazilian historian and specialist in Press History, Tania Regina de Luca (UNESP), outlines her view on the application of the concept of *transferências culturais* with special focus on the processes of *"inter-relações"* (inter-relations). In her opinion, this concept opens a field of possibilities by which a traditional interpretation from only one side is replaced by '[...] reciprocidades, múltiplas influências, mestiçagens e modificações ([...] reciprocity, multiple influences, miscegenation and modifications)'.[28] She considers the press particularly suitable for the application of the cultural transfer approach,

> [...] seja pelo seu caráter de empreendimento coletivo, marcante no século XIX e início do XX, período no qual se concentram as análises, seja pelo fato de seus produtos circularem num espaço transnacional, a cargo de um rol diversificado de mediadores, cuja ação concreta é objeto de reflexão em todos os capítulos. Ao lado de novas questões no âmbito específico da História da imprensa e dos impressos, o conjunto que o leitor tem em mãos traz contribuições importantes para pensar a problemática das trocas e das assimetrias, o que extrapola o mundo dos periódicos.
>
> ([...] due to its character as a collective enterprise, marked in the nineteenth century and the beginning of the twentieth century, a period in

---

26   More information about this international network on https://uvsq.academia.edu/TRANSFOPRESSNetwork and about the brazilian group TRANSFOPRESS Brasil http://transfopressbrasil.franca.unesp.br.

27   Cf. Valéria Guimarães (ed.), *Transferências culturais. O exemplo da imprensa na França e no Brasil*, transl. by Kátia A. F. de Camargo (São Paulo: Edusp; Mercado das Letras, 2012).

28   Tania Regina de Luca, 'Prefácio à edição brasileira', in Guimarães, *Transferências culturais*, op. cit., p. 11.

which the analyses are concentrated, and due to the fact that its products circulate in a transnational space, in charge of a diversified list of mediators, whose concrete action is object of reflection in all the chapters. Alongside new issues in the specific field of the History of the press and the printed media, the collection that the reader has in hand brings important contributions to think about the problem of exchanges and asymmetries, which goes beyond the world of the periodicals).

DE LUCA 2012, p. 11

Under the direction of Márcia Abreu (UNICAMP), Jean-Yves Mollier (UVSQ), and Adelaide Machado (Universidade Nova de Lisboa), the international thematic research project *Circulação transatlântica dos impressos - A globalização da cultura no século XIX* took place between 2011 and 2016. Approximately 60 researchers took part in this project and important research results have already been published (Abreu 2016; Granja, Luca, 2018; Poncioni, Levin 2018; Abreu 2017).[29] The aim was to identify the printed works and ideas circulating between England, France, Portugal, and Brazil between 1789 and 1914 and to analyse, from a transnational perspective, the cultural practices associated with the processes of circulation of printed works and ideas.

In the recently published second volume, edited by Tânia Regina de Luca and Lúcia Granja, *Suportes e Mediadores. A circulação transatlântica dos Impressos (1789–1914)*, publishers as well as periodicals are the focus of interest. These have special significance as cultural agents and strategic transport media in the context of dissemination of values, ideas, and faiths in the important moment of formation of national identity. The research carried out in case studies gathered here shows the cultural and political practices prevailing in the Atlantic space in the long nineteenth-century and provides new insights into the complexity and reciprocity of transatlantic circulation based on interdisciplinary and transcultural approaches.

It was evident that the dynamics went far beyond the traditional France-Brazil axis by rediscovering the complex networks, its various supports and actors, established between Brazil, Portugal, France and England, which composed, with reference to Fernand Braudel, a significant part of the cultural life of the "Atlantic world". Methodologically, Granja and Luca, on the basis of the

---

29 *Romances em movimento. A circulação transatlântica dos impressos (1789–1914)*, ed. by Márcia Abreu, vol. 1 (Campinas: Editora Unicamp, 2016); *Suportes e Mediadores. A circulação transatlântica dos impressos (1789–1914)*, ed. by Lúcia Granja/Tania de Luca, vol. 2 (Campinas: Editora Unicamp, 2018); *Deslocamentos e mediações – A circulação transatlântica dos impressos (1789–1914)*, ed. by Claudia Poncioni/Orna Levin, vol. 3 (Campinas: Editora Unicamp, 2018); in English see also *The Transatlantic Circulation of Novels Between Europe and Brazil, 1789–1914*, ed. by Márcia Abreu (Cham: Palgrave MacMillan, 2017).

article 'Transferts culturels et Histoire du livre' (2009) by Michel Espagne, emphasized not only the notion of circulation that assumes centrality, but highlighted that circulation is always accompanied by the

> '[...] problemática das transferências, trocas e mestiçagens, tomadas em diferentes direções e sentidos, o que convida a revisitar o processo de produção, mediação e recepção de objetos culturais. ([...] problematic of transfers, exchanges and miscegenation, taken in different directions and senses, which invites to revisit the process of production, mediation and reception of cultural objects)'. GRANJA/DE LUCA 2018, p. 17

9.1.2 Translation and Asymmetries in the Brazilian Reception of Key Methodological Texts

Michel Espagne is professor at the *École Normale Superieure* (E.N.S.) in Paris and director of research in the *Centre Nacional de la Recherche Scientifique* responsible for the UMR (*Unité Mixte de Recherche*) *8547* "Pays germaniques: Archives Husserl – Transferts culturels", especially for the "LabexTransferS". In addition to being one of the founders of the *Transferts culturels* concept, Espagne is still considered one of its most important representatives. Currently, there is no Portuguese translation of the earliest methodological key texts by Michel Espagne, Michael Werner, or Hans-Jürgen Lüsebrink. Only in the context of cross-cultural research in the area of Press History was carried out the first translation of one of Espagne's articles undertaken by the historian Valéria Guimarães.

Guimarães took advantage of the context of her research on the history of the press and prints and translated *ad hoc* the aforementioned article 'Transferts culturels et Histoire du livre under the title 'Transferências culturais e História do Livro" published in 2012 in the journal *Livro. Revista do Nucleo de Estudos do Livro e da Edição*, the first Brazilian journal for the history of the book and editions.[30] This academic journal, published at the Universidade de São Paulo (USP), is only available in print and has a relatively small circulation, so this methodological text is only accessible to a small audience. Interestingly, this text is not actually considered to be one of Espagne's key works on the concept of transfer, but in Brazil has become significant in the context of recent interest in the field of book and press history.

Translated, it now forms an important theoretical and methodological foundation not only for the already mentioned research projects of Márcia Abreu,

---

30 Michel Espagne, 'Transferts culturels et Histoire du Livre', in *Histoire et Civilisation du Livre. Revue internationale*, 5 (2009), pp. 201–218; Michel Espagne, 'Transferências culturais e História do livro', transl. by Valéria Guimarães, in *Livro. Revista do Núcleo de Estudos do Livro e da Edição*, 2 (2012), pp. 21–34.

Valéria Guimarães, Lúcia Granja, and Tania de Luca, but also an essential basis for a range of academic research work at the Master's and PhD level on topics including Book History, Comparative Literature, and Translation Studies. The cultural transfer approach thus becomes more accessible and consolidates a more frequent discussion in the context of other approaches, which is also reflected in responses to Espagne's translated article.

One can already say that the concrete translation of one of Espagne's methodological texts was not initiated through German Studies, but through the historical disciplines and in the context of new transcultural questions. This also fits in with Espagne's own argumentation in this article, because here he also discusses the cultural transfer approach not as an approach of German Studies in France, but as a concept of the

> [...] recherche en histoire visant à mettre en évidence les imbrications et les métissages entre les espaces nationaux ou plus généralement les espaces culturels, une tentative de comprendre par quels mécanismes les formes identitaires peuvent se nourrir d'importations.
>
> ([...] historical research aimed at highlighting the interrelationships and *métissages* between national spaces or, more generally, cultural spaces, an attempt to understand the mechanisms by which identity forms can be nourished by imports).
> ESPAGNE 2009, p. 201

The translation of his article inspired the Brazilian specialist public, against the backdrop of book history, to undergo a "change of perspective" by examining cultural transfer processes in the context of their own book history, because Espagne focuses on the book as the result of intellectual production and material fabrication, thus making it a predestined object for the application of this approach. Espagne defines what he understands by a "transfert culturel" and highlights both the cultural peculiarity of concepts as a whole and the problematic of traditional perspectives of *"influence"* (influence) and *"rayonnement"* (radiance).[31] He of course looks back on the history of the approach since the 1980s and emphasizes, on the basis of the numerous individual studies that already exist, that the national boundaries of cultural history are only overcome through an almost micrological investigation of the translation process of an object between its source context and a new context of reception. Against this linguistic and sociological background, Espagne notes, for the

---

31   Espagne, 'Transferts culturels et Histoire du livre', *op. cit.*, p. 202.

object book, that a micrological investigation of the translation of the book highlights

> [...] le rôle des diverses instances de médiation (voyageurs, traducteurs, libraires, éditeurs, bibliothécaires, collectionneurs etc.) ainsi que l'incontournable transformation sémantique liée à l'importation. On observera en particulier la transformation qu'une importation culturelle apporte au contexte de réception et inversement l'effet positif de ce contexte de réception sur le sens de l'objet. Il s'agit de combiner une approche sociologique et une approche herméneutique.
>
> ([...] the role of the various mediation instances (travellers, translators, booksellers, publishers, librarians, collectors, etc.) as well as the essential semantic transformation linked to importation. In particular, we will observe the transformation that a cultural import brings to the context of reception and conversely the positive effect of this context of reception on the meaning of the object. It is a question of combining a sociological approach and a hermeneutical approach.)
> ESPAGNE 2009, p. 203

The examples taken from the German-French context are mostly unknown to the Brazilian reading public, but the methodical arguments can be applied to Brazilians' own histories of the book and the press as part of a transcultural literary and cultural history in global context, which is currently also the focus of new research interests in Brazil.

Translations also play an important role in this essay. However, he not only places the function of mediation and the process of translation, as well as its associated semantic transformation through cultural importation, at the centre of his definition for "*Transfert culturel*", but also makes a conceptual distinction between the process of "*traduction*" and "*translation*".

> Une **traduction** n'a pas moins de légitimité ou d'originalité que son modèle. La **translation** des objets culturels n'est pas une déperdition. Cette idée qui, à la suite du philosophe Herder, aurait pu être partagée par les traducteurs parmi les écrivains de la période romantique allemande, est un des présupposés de base de la recherche sur les transferts culturels, qui considère les transformations sémantiques liées à une **translation** non comme une déperdition mais comme une construction nouvelle. La question de savoir si une importation est adéquate ou authentique perd par là même sa pertinence.

(A translation has no less legitimacy or originality than its model. The translation of cultural objects is not a loss. This idea, which, following the philosopher Herder, could have been shared by translators among writers of the German Romantic period, is one of the basic presuppositions of research on cultural transfers, which considers semantic transformations related to translation not as a loss but as a new construction. The question of whether an import is adequate or genuine loses its relevance.)

ESPAGNE 2009, p. 203

At this point, Valéria Guimarães's translation alters the translation of the term at two points. First of all, at the beginning of the above quotation she does not compare "traduction" with the process of "translation", as Espagne does, but instead chooses the term "transposição", through which the process of transfer in Portuguese is interpreted more materially, understood also as translation from one side to the other. And in the second case, in the context of semantic transformation processes, she does not choose "translation" like Espagne, but chooses the term "traduction" this time because it is more oriented towards implicit semantic transformation. The concept of "translação" (translation) is partly occupied by the translation sciences across all languages.[32]

At this point it becomes clear that the translation of this methodical text into Portuguese is of course also a new original against the background of the Brazilian context of reception. This applies not only to the linguistic translation, but also to the content and its reception, because Espagne's detailed explanations from the German-French context of the book history of the eighteenth and nineteenth centuries are at first glance very distant for Brazilian readers. And yet there are always points of contact and parallels with Brazil in terms of content, for example in the context of the production and circulation of works in the German-French context of publishing and book trade history, where Paris, but also, for example, Leipzig, play an important mediating role. A similar role Paris and Leipzig play for Portuguese-language writings in Europe and foreign writings in Brazil during the long nineteenth century.

The Brazilian online journal *Jangada: crítica, literatura, artes* published a second translation of a text by Michel Espagne in 2017, this time focusing on the interdisciplinarity of the cultural transfer method: 'La notion de transfert culturel', published in 2013 in the online *Revue Sciences/Lettres* and translated by Dirceu Magri as 'A noção de transferência cultural'.[33] With a view to

---

32   Cf. Espagne, 'Transferts culturels et Histoire du livre', *op. cit.*, p. 203; Espagne, 'Transferencias culturais', *op. cit.*, p. 23.

33   Michel Espagne, 'La notion de transfert culturel', in *Revue Sciences/Lettres* [Online] 1 (2013), pp. 1–9. http://journals.openedition.org/rsl/219; Michel Espagne, 'A noção de

extending the applicability of the concept to other disciplinary areas and cultural spaces, Espagne describes the development of the concept beyond the French-German context of the history of the Humanities, but in view of the increasing interdisciplinary resonance in other cultural spaces, defines transfer research more generally as part of the "historiographies culturelles transnationales", applicable long ago beyond Europe.[34] The online publication makes Espagne's article accessible to a broad public from the outset in both French and Portuguese.

The Brazilian translator completed his doctorate in *Estudos Linguísticos, Literários e Tradutológicos em Francês* 2014 at the USP and is currently a postdoctoral fellow at the Universidade Federal de Viçosa/Brazil. He also translated Chateaubriand's *Átala* and *René* into Portuguese in 2015. Compared to Valéria Guimarães' translation of Espagne, this newest translation is very easily accessible online and is, therefore, currently receiving a comparatively strong response. The quality of this translation is questionable, containing a number of grammatical and content-related inaccuracies, but can easily be compared due to the online presence of the French source text.[35]

The aforementioned translated interview by Alexandre Fontaine with Michel Espagne, published in the *Cadernos CIMEAC*, is the latest product of the concept transfer and fits in with Espagne's current mediation activities. The historian Alexandre Fontaine, from the University of Vienna, who completed his doctorate in Paris and in Fribourg, Switzerland, is a specialist in Comparative History of Education and Entangled History. He is an associate researcher in the U.M.R. 8547 "Transfert culturel" led by Espagne at the E.N.S. in Paris.

---

transferência cultral', trans. by Dirceu Magri, in *Jangada. Crítica literatura, artes* [online], 9 (2017), pp. 136–147. http://www.revistajangada.ufv.br/index.php/Jangada/issue/view/60/70.

34 Michel Espagne, 'La notion de transfert culturel', *op. cit.*, p. 6.
35 After a brief comparison between the French original and the translation, it can be said that, in addition to spelling mistakes, there are some terminological changes that alter meaning, for example on page 137, where the translator omits Espagne's reference to the German context: '[...] o conhecimento objetivo da área cultural [alemã/allemande] era menos importante do que as alterações a que ela poderia dar origem e, por outro lado, explorar os vetores da transferência ([...] objective knowledge of the [German] cultural area was less important than the changes to which it could give rise and, on the other hand, explore the vectors of the transfer)'. The term "vetores da transferência" at the end of this quotation replaces the term "vecteurs de la translation" in Espagne's French text. (Espagne, Michel, 'La notion de transfert culturel', *op. cit.*; Espagne, Michel, 'A noção de transferência cultural', *op. cit.*)

This interview focuses on key current aspects of the transfer concept and Espagne positions himself with his latest projects. In his answers he emphasizes Heinrich Heine's important role in the development of the concept, the parallelism of mechanisms of circulation and resemantization, the danger of the generalization of the concept, and the importance of philology for the investigation of cultural transfer processes. In this context, Espagne also explains his current research interest in inviting foreign colleagues to write the history of those nations that still dominate global historiography. In this way, he wants to explore the extent to which discourses on global history have, in principle, brought with them a share of imperialism. Espagne also explicitly emphasizes the role of archives in the (re-)construction of the national or foreign memory of national literatures.[36]

Espagne makes it clear that the concept is well-suited to expansion beyond the French-German context and beyond the European context. He sees the future development of the concept integrated into interdisciplinary projects on transnational history and emphasises the need for the concept to be appropriated and re-asserted depending on the cultural context. In relation to the paradox of strengthening and at the same time closing of the societies regarding the foreign cultural memory of a national literature, he says:

> Acho que as transferências culturais de maneira alguma apagam os enrijecimentos nacionais. Ao contrário, andam de mãos dadas. Em toda a história das transferências culturais, há a constatação de uma circulação de objetos ressemantizados que são adaptados à nova cultura e que são uma ponte entre as culturas, com uma circulação que sempre serve para consolidar representações estritamente nacionais. [...] As transferências culturais desejam ser um programa pacifista, mas elas não acabam com a existência de uma espécie de ossificação nacionalista – simplesmente, elas desmantelam essa ossificação. Desse ponto de vista, a Suiça é um bom exemplo, pois se trata de um país que se abriu com ares germânicos, francófonos e italianos, e, ao mesmo tempo, tem consciência de ser um país a parte, com suas regras próprias, temendo ser invadido.
>
> (I don't think cultural transfers in any way erase national hardening. On the contrary, they go hand in hand. Throughout the history of cultural transfers, there is the observation of a circulation of resemantized objects that are adapted to the new culture and that are a bridge between cultures, with a circulation that always serves to consolidate strictly

---

36   Espagne/Fontaine, 'Viajando com o conceito de Transferências culturais', *op. cit.*, pp. 6–17.

national representations. [...] Cultural transfers wish to be a pacifist program, but they do not end with the existence of a kind of nationalist ossification – they simply dismantle that ossification. From this point of view, Switzerland is a good example, because it is a country that has opened up with a Germanic, Francophone and Italian air, and, at the same time, is aware that it is a country apart, with its own rules, fearing being invaded).

ESPAGNE/FONTAINE 2018, p. 15

The final section of this article will describe an example of how the transfer approach has been used in Brazil precisely in the way described above in a concrete interdisciplinary and international research project.

9.1.3 Brazilian Literary History, Historiography and Culture of the Nineteenth Century in a New Global Context

The aim of the international and interdisciplinary research project *Circulação transatlântica dos impressos – A globalização da cultura no século XIX*, which has already been discussed in the context of the concept in research about Press History and which has been conducted under the direction of Abreu, Mollier, and Machado, was to identify the printed works and ideas circulating between England, France, Portugal, and Brazil between 1789 and 1914 and to analyse from a transnational perspective the cultural practices associated with the processes of circulation of printed works and ideas. The historian Roger Chartier comments in the book cover of the first volume *Romances em Movimento* (2016) in a very clear view on how this project breaks with three essential conventional ideas:

> A circulação dos livros e a publicação das obras entre França, Portugal, Inglaterra e Brasil mostram a reciprocidade das trocas e a multiplicidade das interações. Livros em português são editados em Paris, autores brasileiros publicam em Portugal, e autores portugueses, no Brasil. A simultaneidade da publicação e da leitura dos mesmos romances no Brasil e na França destruí a ideia de um atraso cultural do Brasil. As traduções desempenham um papel essencial nesse processo: não somente as traduções dos romances franceses em português, senão também as traduções das obras brasileiras em francês e em alemão. Então, deve-se apagar a ideia de dependência cultural. No Brasil, como na Europa, formou-se um público de leitores que tinha acesso aos romances graças aos folhetins e que lia sem comprar, nos gabinetes de leitura e nas

bibliotecas. Assim, apesar de desigualdades, da duração de viagens, das diferenças das línguas, estabeleceu-se uma autêntica comunidade letrada transnacional.

(The circulation of books and the publication of works between France, Portugal, England and Brazil show the reciprocity of exchanges and the multiplicity of interactions. Books in Portuguese are published in Paris, Brazilian authors publish in Portugal, and Portuguese authors in Brazil. The simultaneous publication and reading of the same novels in Brazil and France destroyed the idea of a cultural backwardness of Brazil. Translations play an essential role in this process: not only the translations of French novels into Portuguese, but also the translations of Brazilian works into French and German. Thus, the idea of cultural dependence must be erased. In Brazil, as in Europe, a public of readers was formed that had access to the novels thanks to the folhetins and that they read without buying, in the reading offices and in the libraries. Thus, despite inequalities, the duration of voyages, the differences in the languages, an authentic transnational literate community was established).
CHARTIER 2016, [book cover]

Like Michel Espagne and Werner, Abreu and Mollier consider the re(visions) of the historical period between 1789 and 1914 particularly important in order to refute traditional views on the opposition of periphery and centre, the idea of the cultural backwardness of Brazil, and on the idea of cultural dependency, or to strongly differentiate them through material studies. They find this period particularly interesting because, at the same time as commercial and cultural articulations intensified, the constitution of independent national states was taking place in part through an affirmation of local peculiarities as the foundation of political sovereignty. These movements were part of a set of exchanges and contrasts with other nationalities. In this context, Abreu refers to the methodology of Cultural Transfers, which plays an essential role in this international thematic project. She specifically cites the "*Avant-propos*" of the collection *Philologiques III* (1994) where the two authors emphasize that the very definition of what is a national literature is practically impossible without the continued recourse to elements of foreign cultures.[37]

---

37   Cf. Márcia Abreu/Jean-Yves Mollier, 'Nota introdutória Circulação transatlântica dos Impressos. A globalização da cultura no século XIX', in *Romances em movimento*, *op. cit.*, pp. 9–13, (p. 10); see also Michel Espagne/Michael Werner, 'Avant-propos', in *Philologiques III. Qu'est-ce qu'une littérature nacionale? Approches pour une théorie*

Additionally, Abreu and Mollier emphasize the idea of circulation, because what matters in the case studies is to observe the two-way movement between Europe and Brazil and not merely the flow of ideas and goods from Europe to Brazil. In other words, it is interesting to think more in terms of connection than of cultural dependence, more in terms of appropriation than influence. Thus, they propose a more differentiated understanding of nineteenth-century culture with an emphasis on its complex transnational relations.[38] Especially in her presentation of the fiction as element of cultural connection, Abreu distances herself from a history of conventional and traditional literature, considering many elements of the Cultural Transfer approach:

> Alargamos o espaço considerado para além da nação, demos importância à leitura e aos leitores (entre os quais se destacam os letrados coetâneos) e prestamos atenção às condições materiais de produção e circulação dos impressos. Além disso, contamos especialmente com fontes primárias (tais como anúncios de publicações à venda; correspondências; pareceres de censura; catálogos de editores; livrarias e gabinetes de leitura; registros de leitura e textos críticos coetâneos), a fim de saber quais eram as preferências dos leitores em certo momento; que relação mantinham os escritores com os livreiros e editores, com os críticos, com o público e com seus colegas; quais eram as obras à disposição, como eram editadas e em que suporte circulavam; quais eram as concepções sobre a produção ficcional no período e como as narrativas eram avaliadas; que lugar ocupavam os romances na vida social e que relação mantinham com o mundo das mercadorias.

> (We widened the considered space beyond the nation, we gave importance to the reading and to the readers (among which the coetaneous literacy stands out) and we paid attention to the material conditions of production and circulation of the printed matter. In addition, we rely especially on primary sources (such as advertisements of publications for sale; correspondences; censorship opinions; publishers' catalogues; bookstores and reading cabinets; peer-reading registers and critical texts), in order to know what the preferences of readers were at a certain point in time; what relationship writers had with booksellers and publishers, with critics, with the public and with their colleagues; what works were

---

interculturelle du champ littéraire, ed. by Michel Espagne/Michael Werner (Paris: Éditions de la Maison des Sciences de l'Homme, 1994), p. 7.
38   Cf. Abreu/Mollier, 'Nota introdutória', *op. cit.*, p. 13.

available, how they were edited and on what medium they circulated; what were the conceptions of fictional production in the period and how narratives were evaluated; what place did novels have in social life and what relationship did they have with the world of commodities.)
ABREU 2016, pp. 16–17

France was a major exporter of fiction, whether in book translations or brochures. But there was also a reciprocity of exchanges and a multiplicity of interactions that are shown in the context of German and French translations of Brazilian novels. They did not travel from Brazil to Europe only in Portuguese. Since the beginning of the nineteenth century, several Brazilian works were translated into French, English, Italian and German, including important textual modifications. The French and German-speaking context was interested in novels by several Brazilian writers, among them the novels *O Guarany* (1857) and *Iracema* (1865), by the romantic author José de Alencar, and the novel *Innocência* (1872) by Alfredo Maria d'Escragnolle, Viscount de Taunay as national productions and best-seller in the long nineteenth century.[39]

In the case of the German context, the novels had several translations. The *Guarany*, for example, circulated in the form of a novel in fascicles in the *Roman-Magazin des Auslandes* in 1872, and was republished and adapted by the emigrant and language teacher, Rudolf Damm, for the *Folhetim* of the *Blumenauer Zeitung* in Blumenau, Santa Catharina, Brazil in 1895. The novel circulated in parallel in an "authorized" translation by Maximilian Emerich, a Prussian military engineer-pontonier and professor at the military school in Rio de Janeiro in 1876. A third translation, by Karl Leydhecker, came out of the *Scherls Taschenbücher* collection in 1911, with a new edition in 1914, a pocket library, offered to a mass public for an affordable price.[40]

In this project, the main methodology used was the concept of cultural transfers, focusing on the circumstances, motivations, translation and editorial strategies, as well as the role of translators and the network of personal, institutional, media and political contacts that enabled the production and

---

39   See Wiebke Röben de Alencar Xavier, 'The Brazilian Novels O Guarany and Innocência Translated into German. National Production and the Bestseller in the long Nineteenth Century', in *The Transatlantic Circulation of Novels, op. cit.*, pp. 145–170; see also Ilana Heineberg, 'French Readings of Brazil. From the Translations of Guarany and Innocencia, to the Exotism of the Novels of Adrien Delpech', in *The Transatlantic Circulation of Novels, op. cit.*, pp. 171–202.

40   Cf. Xavier, 'The Brazilian Novels', *op. cit.*, p. 145.

dissemination of these translations. The objective was to understand the processes of reception and transformation of the Brazilian novel via translation. In the context of these translations, the decisive role of the book's commercialization, the new appreciation of prose through the expansion of the *feuilleton* as a "modern" genre, the great economic and cultural interest of editors and readers in foreign novels, the fascination for the "exotic", the already traditional interest of travelers and scientists in Brazil, with their reports on the fauna, flora and indigenous cultures, but also in Brazil as an attractive country for immigrants, stands out. The decisive role of Brazil's own political and cultural interest in promoting itself as a nation with its own canon of literature, especially with the project of its own national novel, which came to be considered an important element of cultural identity in formation, is also highlighted. At the same time, in the 1860s, the emperor of Brazil, D. Pedro II, financed, the preparation of a history of Brazilian literature, published in Berlin and written in French, by an Austrian scholar: *Le Brésil littéraire. Histoire de la Littérature Brésilienne suivie d'un choix de morceaux tirés des meilleurs auteurs brésiliens* (1863), by Ferdinand Wolf.

Moreover, the inclusion of these two authors of Brazilian Romanticism, Alencar and Taunay, in the list of foreign novels translated for the German-speaking market also allows us to reflect on the complexity of what Michel Espagne calls the "foreign memory" of German-speaking literature and culture at the time. The concept of Cultural Transfers from the article translated by Valéria Guimarães can be placed in this methodological context because it is at this moment, in which Michel Espagne himself had already clearly stated that the observations made in the Franco-German example are very well extended to other national situations. With regard to the transfer of the concept of Cultural Transfer and in connection with considerations on new transcultural dimensions of North-South or South-North relations and dynamics, this example from the Brazilian-German context shows how the studies on the "transculturality of national spaces in Europe" with a focus on instances of translation, cultural transfer, and mediation can be expanded to include various non-European aspects of transculturality.[41] This way, it is possible also to include new transatlantic dimensions of cultural transfers and circulations in the context of German literary history.

---

41 See Christophe Charle/Hans-Jürgen Lüsebrink/York Gothart Mix (eds.), *Transkulturalität nationaler Räume in Europa (18. bis 19. Jahrhundert). Übersetzungen, Kulturtransfer und Vermittlungsinstanzen* (Bonn: V & R University Press, 2017).

9.2 Conclusion

The article has shown the different ways and dynamics through which the concept of Cultural Transfer has come to Brazil since the 1990s and which interests and circumstances have played a role in that. From the outset, historians have played an important role, especially in the history of books and the press, but also as representatives of Comparative Literature and Germanists. Their reception and translation work, the mediation of this approach in the academic environment and the supervision of many master's theses and doctoral theses in recent years, has led to a growing response to the approach in Brazil. One sign of this is that in 2019, the transfer concept and its resemantizations was given significant space at key conferences, that of the ABRALIC (*Associação Brasileira de Literatura Comparada*), to which Ottmar Ette was invited to give a plenary lecture, the ABEG, Congress of *Associação Brasileira de Estudos Germanísticos*, and at the ENTRAD, the *Encontro da Associação Brasileira dos Tradutores*. Here, young scholars presented their projects and research on cultural transfer with Eastern European countries, on German-Brazilian cultural transfer, and on *transferências culturais e circulações* in the context of translation studies.

In the meantime, this approach has developed its own dynamics, despite references to Espagne's texts and is being discussed with other transcultural approaches, such as Ottmar Ette's Transareal studies. It is also discussed with approaches to Vermeer's concept of cultural transfer in Translation studies and receives considerable popularity in the field of *Literatura Comparada*, because it questions the traditional structures of this area in Brazil in a stimulating way. It is now desirable that the questioning and differentiation of North-South disparities and the traditional assumptions about transatlantic relations, the perception and acceptance of the reverse direction of thinking of method transfers, as well as reciprocal dimensions of the research of transatlantic transfers and circulations, find a broader audience, in order to come to a multidimensional and transcultural extension of the transfer approach, in which convergences and above all cultural divergences have their place in methodological discussion and its applications.

Bibliography

Abreu, Márcia, *The Transatlantic Circulation of Novels Between Europe and Brazil, 1789–1914* (Cham: Palgrave MacMillan, 2017).

Abreu, Márcia, *Romances em movimento. A circulação transatlântica dos impressos (1789–1914)*, vol. 1 (Campinas: Editora Unicamp, 2016).

Abreu, Márcia/Mollier, Jean-Yves, 'Nota introdutória Circulação transatlântica dos Impressos – A globalização da cultura no século XIX', in *Romances em movimento. A circulação transatlântica dos impressos (1789–1914)*, ed. by Márcia Abreu, (Campinas: Editora Unicamp, 2016), pp. 9–13.

Abreu, Márcia, 'Apresentação. A Ficção como elemento de conexão cultural', in *Romances em movimento. A circulação transatlântica dos impressos (1789–1914)*, ed. by Márcia Abreu (Campinas: Editora Unicamp, 2016).

Bernd, Zilá, 'Littératures Migrantes. Élargissant les frontières des esthétiques transculturelles', in *Comparative Literature as a Transcultural Discipline*, ed. by Eduardo de Faria Coutinho (São Paulo: Annablume editora, 2018), pp. 31–40.

Bernd, Zilá, 'Mobilidades teóricas interamericanas', in *Interfaces Brasil/Canadá, Rio Grande*, 8 (2008), pp. 13–25.

Bernd, Zilá, 'Apresentação. Americanidade e transferências culturais', in *Americanidade e transferências culturais*, ed. by Zilá Bernd (Porto Alegre: Editora Movimento, 2003), pp. 11–13.

Bernd, Zilá, 'Figuras e mitos da americanidade na ficção brasileira e quebequense', in *Americanidade e transferências culturais*, ed. by Zilá Bernd (Porto Alegre: Editora Movimento, 2003), pp. 214–218.

Charle, Christophe/Lüsebrink, Hans-Jürgen/Mix, York-Gothart (eds.), *Transkulturalität nationaler Räume in Europa (18. bis 19. Jahrhundert). Übersetzungen, Kulturtransfer und Vermittlungsinstanzen* (Bonn: V & R University Press, 2017).

Chartier, Roger, [Book cover], in *Romances em movimento. A circulação transatlântica dos impressos (1789–1914)*, ed. by Márcia Abreu (Campinas: Editora Unicamp, 2016) [book cover].

DAAD (ed.), *Germanistik in Brasilien. Herausforderungen, Vermittlungswege, Übersetzungen* (Göttingen: Wallstein, 2014).

Espagne, Michel, 'A noção de transferência cultural', transl. by Jangada Dirceu Magri, in *crítica, literatura, artes* [online], 9 (2017), pp. 136–147. https://www.revistajangada.ufv.br/index.php/Jangada/issue/view/60/70

Espagne, Michel, 'Transferências culturais e História do livro', transl. by Valéria Guimarães, in *Livro. Revista do Núcleo de Estudos do Livro e da Edição*, 2 (2012), pp. 21–34.

Espagne, Michel, 'La notion de transfert culturel', in *Revue Sciences/Lettres* [online], 1 (2013), pp. 1–9. http://journals.openedition.org/rsl/219.

Espagne, Michel, 'Transferts culturels et Histoire du Livre', in *Histoire et Civilisation du Livre. Revue internationale*, 5 (2009), pp. 201–218.

Espagne, Michel, *Les transferts culturels franco-allemands* (Paris: Presses Universitaires de France, 1999).

Espagne, Michel/Fontaine, Alexandre, 'Viajando com o conceito de Transferências culturais. Entrevista com Michel Espagne', in *Cadernos CIMEAC*, 8/2 (2018), pp. 6–17.

Espagne, Michel/Werner, Michael, 'Avant-propos', in *Philologiques III. Qu'est-ce qu'une littérature nacionale? Approches pour une théorie interculturelle du champ littéraire*, ed. by Michel Espagne/Michael Werner (Paris: Éditions de la Maison des Sciences de l'Homme, 1994).

Faria Coutinho, Eduardo de, 'Introduction', in *Comparative Literature as a transcultural discipline* (São Paulo: Annablume editora, 2018), pp. 10–18.

Freitas Dutra, Eliana de/Mollier, Jean-Yves (eds.), *O lugar dos impressos na construção da vida política* (Belo Horizonte: Annablume, 2006).

Granja, Lúcia/Luca, Tânia de, *Suportes e Mediadores. A circulação transatlântica dos impressos (1789–1914)*, vol. 2 (Campinas: Editora Unicamp, 2018).

Granja, Lúcia/Luca, Tania de, 'Apresentação', in *Suportes e Mediadores. A circulação transatlântica dos impressos (1789–1914)*, ed. by Lucia Granja/Tania de Luca, vol. 2 (Campinas: Editora Unicamp, 2018), pp. 15–32.

Guimarães, Valéria (ed.), *Transferências culturais. O exemplo da imprensa na França e no Brasil*, transl. by Kátia A. F. de Camargo (São Paulo: Edusp; Mercado das Letras, 2012).

Heineberg, Ilana, 'French Readings of Brazil From the Translations of Guarany and Innocencia, to the Exotism of the Novels of Adrien Delpech', in *The Transatlantic Circulation of Novels Between Europe and Brazil, 1789–1914*, ed. by Márcia Abreu (Cham: Palgrave MacMillan, 2017), pp. 171–202.

Kambas, Chryssoula, 'Theorie-Transfers und Internationalisierung der Literaturgeschichte', in *Wie international ist die Literaturwissenschaft?*, ed. by Lutz Danneberg/ Friedrich Vollhardt (Stuttgart, Weimar: Metzler, 1996), pp. 287–300.

Luca, Tania de, 'Prefácio à edição brasileira', in *Transferências culturais. O exemplo da imprensa na França e no Brasil*, ed. by Valéria Guimarães (Sao Paulo: Edusp, Mercado das Letras, 2012), pp. 9–11.

Lüsebrink, Hans-Jürgen/Mix, York-Gothart/Mollier, Jean-Yves/Sorel, Patricia (eds.), *Les lectures du peuple en Europe et dans les Amériques du XVIIe au XXe siècle* (Brussels: Complexe, 2003).

Lüsebrink, Hans-Jürgen/Reichardt, Rolf, 'Histoire des concepts et transferts culturels, 1770–1815. Note sur une recherche', in *Genèses*, 14 (1994), pp. 27–41.

Meyer, Marlyse (ed.), *Do Almanak aos Almanaques* (São Paulo: Ateliê Editorial, 2001).

Moser, Walter, 'L'anthropophagie du Sud au Nord', in *Confluences littéraires Brésil-Québec. Les bases d'une comparaison*, ed. by Michel Peterson/Zilá Bernd (Paris: Éditions Balzac, 1992), pp. 113–152.

Poncioni, Claudia/Levin, Orna, *Deslocamentos e mediações – A circulação transatlântica dos impressos (1789–1914)*, vol. 3 (Campinas: Editora da Unicamp, 2018).

Rodrigues da Silva, Helenice, 'Transferência de Saberes. Modalidades e Possibilidades. Transference of knowledge. Modalities and possibilities', in *História. Questões & Debates*, 53 (2010), pp. 203–225.

Roiz, Diogo da Silva, 'A trajetória de Helenice Rodrigues da Silva (1947–2013) e a prática da História intelectual no Brasil', in *Cultura Histórica & Patrimônio*, 2/1 (2013), pp. 6–21.

Werner, Michael/Zimmermann, Bénédicte, 'Penser l'histoire croisée. Entre empirie et réflexivité', in *Annales. Histoire, Sciences sociales*, 1 (2003), pp. 7–36.

Werner, Michael/Zimmermann, Bénédicte, 'Pensar a história cruzada. Entre empiria e reflexividade', trans. by Jaime de Almeida, in *Textos de História*, 1–2 (2003), pp. 89–127. https://www.researchgate.net/publication/277096068_Pensar_a_historia_cruzada_entre_empiria_e_reflexividad.

Werner, Michael, 'Zwischen Literatur, Kultur- und Sozialwissenschaft. Zur Situation der Germanistik in Frankreich', in *Blickwechsel. Akten des XI. Lateinamerikanischen Germanistenkongress São Paulo, Paraty, Petrópolis*, ed. by Willi Bolle/Helmut Galle, vol. 1 (São Paulo: Monferrer Productions, 2005), pp. 147–158.

Xavier, Wiebke Röben de Alencar, 'The Brazilian Novels O Guarany and Inocência Translated into German. National Production and the Bestseller in the long Nineteenth Century', in *The Transatlantic Circulation of Novels Between Europe and Brazil, 1789–1914*, ed. by Márcia Abreu (Cham: Palgrave MacMillan, 2017), pp. 145–170.

Xavier, Wiebke Röben de Alencar/Romão, Tito Lívio Cruz (eds.), *Traduzir – Transcriar – Transformar, Graphos*, 18/2, (2016). http://www.periodicos.ufpb.br/ojs2/index.php/graphos/issue/view/1859/showToc.

Xavier, Wiebke Röben de Alencar, 'Für eine 'Kontextgermanistik'. DaF, Übersetzung und deutsch-brasilianischer Kulturtransfer im Nordosten Brasiliens', in *Germanistik in Brasilien. Herausforderungen, Vermittlungswege, Übersetzungen*, ed. by DAAD (Göttingen: Wallstein, 2014), pp. 130–132.

Xavier, Wiebke Röben de Alencar, 'Das methodische Konzept Kulturtransfer am Beispiel des Schweizer Aufklärers Salomon Gessner (1730–1788)', in *Blickwechsel. Akten des XI. Lateinamerikanischen Germanistenkongresses*, ed. by Ulrich J. Beil/Claudia S. Dornbusch/Masa Nomura, vol. 3 (Sao Paulo: Monferrer Producoes, 2005), pp. 312–318.

Xavier, Wiebke Röben de Alencar/Schößler, Franziska, 'Konzepte kultureller Übersetzung. Mit einem Seitenblick auf eine "Kontextgermanistik"', in *Germanistik in Brasilien. Herausforderungen, Vermittlungswege, Übersetzungen*, ed. by DAAD (Göttingen: Wallstein, 2014), pp. 13–28.

CHAPTER 10

Relations in a Cultural Triangle: Aspects of Cultural Mediation between Germany, France, and Scandinavia

Karin Hoff, Anna Sandberg and Udo Schöning

Abstract

Studies exploring two-way cultural transfers have provided significant insights and remain necessary. However, such studies can easily be criticised for failing to capture reality, especially if we disregard the fact that studies engaging with reality (or what we call reality) will always be incomplete. Thus, any scientific investigation has to start with the definition of its object, the corresponding aim of the inquiry, and suitable methods. Adopting a different angle or broader perspective on transfers will thus always yield new and different results. Based on these premises and drawing on methodological considerations from previous research on cross-cultural transfer, we planned our investigation of cultural triangular relations between Scandinavia, Germany, and France which was elaborated in three workshops hosted in Göttingen in 2012, in Copenhagen in 2013, and in Paris in 2015.[1] In the following, we will refer to case studies from this project, published in our book series.

---

1 The workshops took place on 12 and 13 June 2012 in Göttingen and on 5 and 6 December 2013 in Copenhagen; the third conference in the series was organised by the Université Paris-Sorbonne on 26 and 27 March 2015 under the title *Réseaux littéraires et artistiques de la première partie du XXe siècle dans le triangle Allemagne-Danemark-France*. Conference proceedings have been published as: Karin Hoff/Udo Schöning/Per Øhrgaard (eds.), *Kulturelle Dreiecksbeziehungen. Aspekte der Kulturvermittlung zwischen Frankreich, Deutschland und Dänemark in der ersten Hälfte des 19. Jahrhunderts* (Würzburg: Königshausen & Neumann, 2013); Karin Hoff/Anna Sandberg/Udo Schöning (eds.), *Literarische Transnationalität. Kulturelle Dreiecksbeziehungen zwischen Skandinavien, Deutschland und Frankreich im 19. Jahrhundert* (Würzburg: Königshausen & Neumann, 2015); Karin Hoff/Udo Schöning/ Frédéric Weinmann (eds.) *Internationale Netzwerke. Literarische und ästhetische Transfers im Dreieck Deutschland, Frankreich und Skandinavien zwischen 1870 und 1945* (Würzburg: Königshausen & Neumann, 2016). The introductions to these volumes give references to literature that has been foundational for this project. The following have been particularly important: Michel Espagne (ed.), *Le prisme du Nord. Pays du Nord, France, Allemagne (1750–1920)* (Tusson: Du Lérot, 2006) especially pp. 5–6, 8. The final impetus for this project came from a conference on French philologist and cultural mediator Claude Fauriel, proceedings have

10.1 Research Topic and Objectives

Considering cross-cultural transfer between Germany, France, and Scandinavia in the nineteenth and twentieth centuries draws together a cultural-historical constellation that has not yet attracted significant attention, despite being an important historical phenomenon. This is due in particular to Germany's central position in this constellation: it is not only geographically situated halfway between Scandinavia and France, but Germany also assumed an increasingly important role in multipolar cross-cultural transfers since the beginning of the nineteenth century and under changing (cultural-) historical conditions. In our project, Scandinavia is regarded as a historical and cultural region consisting of Denmark, Sweden, and Norway with its closely related languages. The idea of a united Scandinavia played a major role in the cultural and political life of the nineteenth century, from the separation of Norway from Denmark in 1814 until the dissolution of the Norwegian-Swedish Union in 1905. At the same time, the Danish-German conglomerate state, with its cultural and linguistic hybridity, ceased to exist. Only after the wars of 1864 and 1871 was Denmark consolidated as a small state and Germany as a unified German Reich. Besides the alternative suggested by pan-Scandinavianism, the nation-building act of creating a perception of Scandinavian unity was common among authors and artists from Denmark, Sweden, and Norway travelling and working in Europe. Accordingly, a European perception of Scandinavia as a single cultural entity can be detected in the period – and still is a factor in the marketing of film and literature from the Nordic countries today. The geopolitical situations and the shifting political alliances between the Nordic countries, as well Germany and France, of course, influenced cultural relations but did not always determine them.

For many Scandinavians, Paris was an obligatory destination for educational and cultural travel in the 19th century; in Germany, Berlin was an important place for Scandinavian artists to travel to as well as settle. However, they also visited cities like Munich, Dresden, and Weimar, and travelled through German landscapes and regions which, like the Harz mountains and the Rhine plain, have become established in cultural history as the ideal landscapes of Romanticism. Writers from the periods of Romanticism to Modernism ranging from Jens Baggesen, Adam Oehlenschläger, Hans Christian Andersen, to Herman Bang, Georg Brandes, Henrik Ibsen, and August Strindberg have not

---

been published as: Geneviève Espagne/Udo Schöning (eds.), *Un historien des langues, des littératures et des cultures. Claude Fauriel (1772–1844) et l'Allemagne* (Paris: Champion, 2013).

only worked in both Scandinavia and Germany, but have also been influenced and inspired by French culture. The names mentioned here also include the first "modern" authors whose texts have been translated from Scandinavian languages into French and German. What is more, some of them published their work in all three languages. Thus, participating in another culture through writing and publishing in a foreign language can be regarded as programmatic.

Although their self-confident participation in several national literatures is of course interesting for us today, in the age of nationalist thinking, this practice appeared as a disadvantage to many authors, because they neither fit into the contemporary literary industry nor found a place in the literary histories first written at the time and built around the idea of the nation state. Several Scandinavian authors were excluded from national monolingual canons and were only re-discovered in the last few years, after having been almost forgotten for a very long period of time. Without doubt, Friederike Brun, Jens Baggesen, and Henrik Steffens (as Scandinavian-German authors) belong to that group of writers who have only attracted one-sided attention or have been ignored altogether.[2]

Since the nineteenth century, new translations and the emerging academic disciplines of literary studies and foreign language philologies have been important sites for cultural mediation between Germany, France, and

---

2 The research project "Grenzgänger" at Kiel University under the direction of Heinrich Detering has resulted in a number of monographs and edited collections which address the conditions and possibilities governing German-Danish cultural exchanges around 1800: Anne-Bitt Gerecke, *Transkulturalität als literarisches Programm. Heinrich Wilhelm von Gerstenbergs Poetik und Poesie* (Göttingen: Vandenhoeck & Ruprecht, 2002); Andreas Blödorn, *Zwischen den Sprachen. Modelle transkultureller Literatur bei Christian Levin Sander und Adam Oehlenschläger* (Göttingen: Vandenhoeck & Ruprecht, 2004); Karin Hoff, *Die Entdeckung der Zwischenräume. Literarische Projekte der Spätaufklärung zwischen Skandinavien und Deutschland* (Göttingen: Wallstein, 2003); Heinrich Detering (ed.), *Grenzgänge. Skandinavisch-deutsche Nachbarschaften* (Göttingen: Wallstein, 1996) and Heinrich Detering/Anne Bitt Gerecke/Johann de Mylius (eds.), *Dänisch-Deutsche Doppelgänger. Transnationale und bikulturelle Literatur zwischen Barock und Moderne* (Göttingen: Wallstein, 2001), and from a Danish perspective: Anna Sandberg, *En grænsegænger mellem oplysning og romantik. Jens Baggesens tyske forfatterskab 1803–1809* (Copenhagen: Museum Tusculanum Press, 2015); Svend Skriver: *Europæerne i 1800-talets danske litteratur. Om Jens Baggesen, P.L. Møller og Georg Brandes* (Copenhagen: University of Copenhagen, 2007) and Per Øhrgaard, 'Die Nachfolge Schillers? Über Oehlenschlägers Corregio und Goethe', in *Das Achtzehnte Jahrhundert, "Deutsch-dänischer Kulturtransfer im 18. Jahrhundert"*, 25/2 (2001), pp. 231–247. And, as another important study: Wolfgang Behschnitt (ed.), *Aneignung – Abgrenzung – Auflösung. Zur Funktion von Literatur in den skandinavischen Identitätsdiskursen* (Würzburg: Ergon Verlag, 2001).

Scandinavia. In France, Claude Fauriel is a case in point. Inspired by German historicism and interested in Scandinavia, he both changed and broadened the French view of literature.[3] Cultivating a very distinct style, he was also the French translator of Baggesen's *Parthenais*, a German-language epic poem which Fauriel had read as a work of eighteenth-century German literature.[4]

More generally, examining how far translations and cultural- and literary-historical scholarship have shaped the image of French literature in Scandinavia and Germany, and German and Scandinavian literature in France, respectively, is an important component in the (re-)construction of the German-French-Scandinavian cultural triangle.[5]

Historically, this exchange was intensified at specific moments. At the beginning of the nineteenth century, the triangle took on a new and distinct shape, and the relations between the participating cultures shifted. Transfer now took place on different terms. In the late-eighteenth and early-nineteenth century, the (re-)discovery of Nordic mythology and medieval literature led to an increasing engagement with the "North" in both Germany and France. Thus, the "Nordic" middle ages were adapted as a treasure trove of new, original literature as opposed to the classicist movements in Europe.[6] At the same time, contemporary Scandinavian literature became popular which gave rise to translations into German and sometimes French. More often than not, Germany mediated these transfers and, in turn, exported its indigenous and new Romantic ideas to the north and west, Scandinavia and Great Britain.

In the same period, scholars began to write the first histories of foreign-language literatures. Based on his journey to Scandinavia, previous German travel writing, and historiographic texts, the French author Jean-Jacques Ampère composed the first history of German and Scandinavian literature in French: *Littérature et voyages. Allemagne et Scandinavie* (1833). Subsequently, French Scandinavian studies evolved in close contact with Germany, both in

---

3 Cf. Espagne/Schöning, *Un historien, op. cit.*
4 Cf. Karin Hoff, 'La Traduction comme médiation culturelle. Claude Fauriel et la *Parthenaïs* de Jens Baggesen', in Espagne/Schöning *Un historien, op. cit.*, pp. 263–279; Udo Schöning, 'Baggesen in Frankreich', in *ejss*, 44 (2014), pp. 254–270.
5 (Re-)construction denotes the historical-hermeneutical approach to facts and their interpretation in the present.
6 Cf. Michel Espagne, 'Herder-Mallet-Arngrímur. Rückläufige Geschichtsschreibung und Kulturtransfer', in Hoff/Schöning/Øhrgaard, *Kulturelle Dreiecksbeziehungen, op. cit.*, (Würzburg: Königshausen & Neumann, 2013), pp. 199–211; Matthias Teichert 'Die Rezeption der mittelalterlichen skandinavischen Literatur in Deutschland', in *Kulturelle Dreiecksbeziehungen, op. cit.*, pp. 241–259; Richard Trachsler, 'Die Rezeption der mittelalterlichen skandinavischen Literatur in Frankreich in der ersten Hälfte des 19. Jahrhunderts', in *Kulturelle Dreiecksbeziehungen, op. cit.*, pp. 261–275.

terms of the topics of their research and the people involved. In the different countries, philologies in general, and foreign-language philologies in particular, have always been engaged in exchange.[7]

Research on the cultural-historical situation just sketched needs to describe and analyse cross-cultural exchanges and relations by considering how participating individuals, groups, institutions, media, and channels, as well as material and immaterial objects interact. These collaborations should be analysed and interpreted both functionally and with respect to their historical context. The emerging patterns can, if necessary, be compared as the trilateral approach allows for the combination of comparative and transfer studies and, thus, acknowledges European entanglements and interconnections.

To this end, we have reviewed empirical studies on the relations between transfers and transformations and, through a comparative approach deployed both methodological perspectives: on the one hand, a typological perspective to explore under what conditions similar phenomena in literature and the arts arise in different social-cultural contexts; on the other hand, a genetic perspective to account for and understand, as far as possible, the sometimes hidden and sometimes visible transfers and their transformations.

Cultural exchanges between France and Germany have already been the subject of an extensive body of scholarship. However, because of their bilateral approach, these studies inevitably entrench the dichotomy of a Western European centre and northern periphery. By contrast, we propose to revise the position and function of the North within the emerging cultural triangle that arises in the nineteenth century.

---

7 Cf. Jean-Marie Maillefer, 'Paul Verrier und der erste Skandinavistik-Lehrstuhl an der Sorbonne', in *Kulturelle Dreiecksbeziehungen, op. cit.*, pp. 213–239; Geneviève Espagne, 'Aufbruch zu einer "Geschichte der Literaturen". Überlegungen des Literarhistorikers Jean-Jacques Ampère (1800–1864) im "deutsch-französischen Beziehungsgeflecht"', in *Kulturelle Dreiecksbeziehungen, op. cit.*, pp. 137–174; Thomas Mohnike, 'Frédéric-Guillaume/Friedrich-Wilhelm Bergmann und die Geburt der Skandinavistik in Frankreich aus dem Geiste der vergleichenden Philologie', in *Kulturelle Dreiecksbeziehungen, op. cit.*, pp. 277–297; Lisbeth Verstraete-Hansen, 'Romanistik in Dänemark. Anfänge, Entwicklung und Ausblick', in *Kulturelle Dreiecksbeziehungen, op. cit.*, pp. 299–320; Udo Schöning, 'Ein Objekt – zwei Projekte? Zu den Vorworten deutscher und französischer Autoren in französischen Literaturgeschichten des 19. Jahrhunderts', in *Literarische Transnationalität, op. cit.*, pp. 243–267; Frédéric Weinmann, 'Die dänische Literatur in den französischen und deutschen Geschichten der Weltliteratur aus der zweiten Hälfte des 19. Jahrhunderts', in *Literarische Transnationalität, op. cit.*, pp. 269–289; Anne-Gaëlle Toutain, 'Hjelmslev et le cercle de Copenhague', in *Internationale Netzwerke, op. cit.*, pp. 219–232.

10.2 Theoretical and Methodological Premises

In the last decades, traditional histories largely based on the model of nineteenth-century teleological and nation-centred historiography have given way to transnational perspectives, engendering comparative and transfer studies. While comparative approaches can bring to light insights on structural history, research on cross-cultural transfer that investigates exchanges between two or more cultures is usually restricted to the historical interpretation of individual examples. In any case, such studies supplement national historiography, which remains essential in itself.[8] However, this entails a problem, evident in the very term "supplement", because it poses the question of the relation between narrowly focused and wide historical perspectives and historiographical representations. In truth, the question concerns the compatibility of a local, regional, or national focus, on the one hand, and transnational panorama, on the other.

In historical studies, the experience of globalisation has fostered the notion of a world-wide network, which consists of subordinate networks that, in turn, are made up of ever smaller networks and lower levels of interactions. In specific contexts, terms like "web" and "network" can be used in a more or less metaphorical sense and invoke different concepts (such as the "World Wide Web") and theories (like graph theory and its influence on different disciplines, such as actor-network-theory in sociology).[9] Using the term "network" as a metaphor allows for empirical research and methodological reflection that theorises the concept, while non-metaphorical uses share the axiom that networks do exist and that the respective object of research can be conceived as a network, or part of one.[10]

---

[8] Cf. Gunilla Budde/Sebastian Corad/Oliver Janz (eds.), *Transnationale Geschichte. Themen, Tendenzen und Theorien* (Göttingen: Vandenhoeck & Ruprecht, 2006); Sebastian Conrad/Andreas Eckert/Ulrike Freitag (eds.), *Globalgeschichte. Theorien, Ansätze, Themen* (Frankfurt/Main: Campus Verlag, 2007); Sebastian Conrad, *Globalgeschichte. Eine Einführung* (München: C.H. Beck, 2013); Ulinka Rublack (ed.), *Die neue Geschichte. Eine Einführung in 16 Kapiteln*, with a foreword by Jürgen Osterhammel (Frankfurt/Main: Fischer Verlag, 2013) (original edition: *A Concise Companion to History*, Oxford, 2011).

[9] Cf. see Bruno Latour, 'On Actor-network Theory. A few Clarifications', in *Soziale Welt*, 47/4 (1996), pp. 369–382; Bruno Latour, *Eine neue Soziologie für eine neue Gesellschaft. Einführung in die Akteur-Netzwerk-Theorie* (Frankfurt/Main: Suhrkamp Verlag, 2007) (original edition: *Reassembling the Social*, Oxford, 2005); Claude Raffestin, 'Réflexions préliminaires I. De l'intérêt du concept de «réseau» dans le champ littéraire', in *Internationale Netzwerke, op. cit.*, pp. 31–36; Sylvain Briens, 'Réflexions préliminaires II. Penser les échanges culturels en termes de réseau', in *Internationale Netzwerke, op. cit.*, pp. 37–43.

[10] Applying the term to an object tends to anthropomorphise it. This evokes the unresolved problem in structural and system theoretical approaches regarding the social formation of the individual and the individual formation of the social.

However, discussing our cultural triangle as a network gives rise to further questions, relating to the evolution and dissolution of networks, their individual, social, and material carriers, and the objects whose transfers create the network. Does the network have a momentum of its own and does it dominate transfers? What about its relations to other networks and the whole? Does it develop nodes on the national, regional, and smaller local level? In how far are these nodes of national and international significance? What does the relationship between transfer and transformation, interaction and interdependence, interpretational sovereignty and competence look like? What about rates of import and export; does the reception of texts follow trends and flows? Finally, moving on from enumerating events and plausible historical facts, research should not just reveal what happened but explain why it happened in a specific way. This opens up further questions concerning structure. Do the processes studied display mechanisms, laws, points of comparison, or possible typologies?

With reference to the genetic perspective, actor-network-theory offers helpful instruments to understand and describe the material, social, and individual dimensions of cross-cultural exchange as well as their interaction. Without doubt, a systematic approach that quantitatively registers contacts and communications in the literary field can be fruitful, for example, to document the frequency and duration of correspondence between scholars or cooperation between publishers, authors, and translators in specific geographical places and periods.[11] However, we have to remember that the circumstances and components of the network cannot always be truthfully recovered. Cross-cultural transmissions are seldom direct and obvious and often hidden or circuitous. Rather than only studying the occasionally obscure path an object might have taken, it is important to analyse the visible result of such an act of transfer.

10.3   Transfer as Transformation

Transfer presupposes an object that is transferred. A cultural object of transfer has imaginary and material dimensions, and its scale can range from a mere idea to a complete *œuvre*. Sometimes its character will be primarily aesthetic, sometimes primarily semantic. The transfer can be a singular event, but it can also be a renewed or parallel transmission, and it can fail, which poses a

---

[11]   Cf. the research project initiated by Joep Leerssen which investigates cultural nationalism in the long nineteenth century. Their platform SPIN (Study Platform on Interlocking Nationalisms) provides digital visualisations of the different webs and networks of the long nineteenth century, www.spinnet.eu.

completely different set of questions. The term is closely enmeshed with the concept of transformation in two respects: in their interplay, transfer changes both the object of transfer and the context of its reception.[12] Hence, we can safely venture the hypothesis that a significant part of the historical dynamics driving cultural evolution can be found in cross-cultural transfers.

Transformations denote medial, formal, or functional modifications that affect an object on its path from the context of its origin to the context of its reception. In an extreme case, this would include the initial perception of the object and its complete integration in the receiving culture. We have to assume that transformations are not random but contingent and that their contingencies can be understood by considering their synchronic and diachronic trajectories.

Transfer studies are guided by the idea that cultural reception is a productive activity, which does not reside in the object but is enacted by the subject or subjects involved in the cultural transfer in a certain context. Reception, however, always entails change, namely of both the object and the recipients and their context. Studies on the (re-)construction of the contexts and consequences of transfers within their cultural-historical contexts have to remember that cross-cultural transfers cannot be adequately described and explained outside their spatial and temporal dimension and respective individual and social conditions.

As already mentioned, research based on a bilateral model simplifies a far more complex situation.[13] However, such research discusses the basic premises of transfer studies and, bearing in mind its limitations, remains useful for analytical purposes. Multilateral studies equally fall short as they can only engage with transfers as a subsection of a larger context. Thus, terms like "web" and "network" are helpful tools as long as they allow for an understanding of the actual conditions of transfers and the description of their spatial structures

---

12   Michel Espagne, 'La notion de transfert culturel', in *Revue Sciences/Lettres* online, 1 (2013), pp. 1–9. http://rsl.revues.org/219. A German translation of the article can be found in: *Internationale Netzwerke, op. cit.*, pp. 45–55.

13   Cf. Udo Schöning, 'Die Internationalität nationaler Literaturen. Bemerkungen zur Problematik und ein Vorschlag', in *Internationalität nationaler Literaturen. Beiträge zum Ersten Symposion des Göttinger Sonderforschungsbereichs 529*, ed. by Udo Schöning in collaboration with Beata Hammerschmid and Frank Seemann (Göttingen: Wallstein Verlag, 2000), pp. 9–43; Udo Schöning: 'Nationallitteraturernes Internationalitet', in *Litteraturhistoriografi (Moderne litteraturteori)*, ed. by Mads Rosendahl Thomsen/Svend Erik Larsen (Aarhus: Aarhus University Press, 2005), pp. 195–213; Udo Schöning, 'La internacionalidad de las literaturas nacionales. Observaciones sobre la problemática y propuestas para su studio', in *Naciones Literarias*, ed. by Dolores Romero López (Barcelona: Anthropos Editorial, 2006), pp. 305–339.

and processes. However, if structures and processes are at stake, as well as the resulting transformations including their semantic and aesthetic implications, a historical-hermeneutical approach is advisable. After all, cross-cultural transfers do not only take place within systems but through individuals acting within spatial, temporal, social, and, of course, systemic frames.

Translations concretise the interconnections of transfer and transformation.[14] Insofar as literary-linguistic interpretation is concerned, transformations become tangible as material, aesthetic, and semantic modification.[15] Other cases are more problematic, and difficulties often begin with the task of defining the contexts between which the transfer takes place. These would shape the interpretative framework to make sense of the resulting object which then has to be defined and analysed depending on these contexts.

While scholarship relying on the concepts of "web" and "network" will neglect or ignore borders, the concept of the "boundary", however problematic, still has to be considered in transfer studies. By contrast with some world-literary and international perspectives, cross-cultural transfer always highlights the differences between the various cultural contexts involved and their specific, not least literary, characteristics. Transfers thus posit boundaries, be they national, geographical, social, cultural, literary, linguistic, or medial. The historical period under scrutiny is shaped by the tendency to subsume these different categories under the umbrella of the nation state, but rather, these categories have to be conceived as overlapping, dovetailing, and intersecting, allowing for permeability and exchange.[16]

---

14 Since the so-called cultural turn in translation studies around 1990 translation is considered not only a linguistic but a cultural activity building on the text's position in two cultures. Thus translation is seen as "re-writing" understood also as editing, anthologizing, abridging etc, see Susan Bassnett/Andre Lefevere, *Translation, History and Culture*, (London, New York: Pinter Publishers, 1990).

15 See *Göttinger Beiträge zur internationalen Übersetzungsforschung*, which present the findings of the collaborative research centre 309 "Die literarische Übersetzung".

16 Cf. Wolfgang Schmale, 'Das Wahrnehmungsmuster 'Grenze' in französischen Blicken auf 'Deutschland', in *Deutschlandbilder – Frankreichbilder. 1700–1850. Rezeption und Abgrenzung zweier Kulturen*, ed. by Thomas Höpel (Leipzig: Leipziger Universitätsverlag, 2001), pp. 173–182; Roberto Simanowski, 'Einleitung. Zum Problem kultureller Grenzziehung', in *Kulturelle Grenzziehungen im Spiegel der Literaturen. Nationalismus, Regionalismus, Fundamentalismus*, ed. by Horst Turk/Brigitte Schultze/Roberto Simanowski (Göttingen: Wallstein Verlag, 1998), pp. 8–60; Michel Espagne, *Les transferts culturels franco-allemands* (Paris: Presses Universitaires de France, 1999), pp. 1–15; Gabriel Layes, *Grundformen des Fremderlebens. Eine Analyse von Handlungsorientierungen in der interkulturellen Interaktion* (Münster, New York, München: Waxmann, 2000) (Internationale Hochschulschriften 345); Bernhard Struck, *Nicht West – nicht Ost*.

10.4 Overview of Results

Our projected (re-)construction of the cross-cultural entanglements between Germany, France, and Scandinavia could not and was never intended to be exhaustive. Rather, we aimed for coordinated yet methodologically different case studies and scholarship of a more exploratory, exemplary, or supplementary character.

The German-French-Scandinavian triangle highlights the close ties that cultural and intellectual actors maintained across national and linguistic borders. Artists, travellers, teachers, and journalists often took on different roles and functions to participate in and instigate exchanges between countries and nations, contributing to the transformation of imported and exported ideas and objects of transfer.[17] Our workshop discussions have revised the established image of Scandinavia as the passive "recipient" of German and French ideas.

Fundamentally, art and especially literature cannot be contained by national borders. Geography cannot explain hierarchies, although it does have practical significance which, however, diminishes with innovations in transport and technology. But as might be expected in our field of research, political, social, and economic conditions are reflected in cultural activities – from the time of the revolutionary wars after the French Revolution and the Napoleonic wars until the wars of 1848, 1864, 1870/71, 1914–1918, and 1939–45.[18]

Frankreich und Polen in der Wahrnehmung deutscher Reisender zwischen 1750 und 1850 (Göttingen: Wallstein Verlag, 2006), pp. 193–200.

17   Cf. Per Øhrgaard, 'Dänen in Paris. P.O. Brøndsteds Reiseeindrücke', in *Kulturelle Dreiecksbeziehungen, op. cit.*, pp. 31–46; Anna Sandberg, 'Frankreich als Imagination und Realität in Kopenhagen um 1800. Malte Conrad Bruun und Jens Baggesen als Mittler im dänisch-deutsch-französischen Kulturtransfer', in *Kulturelle Dreiecksbeziehungen, op. cit.*, pp. 47–76; Udo Schöning, 'Bonstettens Mensch des Nordens und das Problem der nationalen Stereotype', in *Kulturelle Dreiecksbeziehungen, op. cit.*, pp. 77–99; Heinrich Detering, 'Literarischer Dreieckshandel. Hans Christian Andersen zwischen Kopenhagen, Berlin und Paris' in *Kulturelle Dreiecksbeziehungen, op. cit.*, pp. 175–197; Anna Sandberg, 'Herman Bangs Transferfunktion im Dreieck Skandinavien –Frankreich –Deutschland um 1900', in *Literarische Transnationalität, op. cit.*, pp. 147–172.

18   Cf. Raphaëlle Jamet, 'Le jeune Asger Jorn et ses réseaux. L'Allemagne, la France et l'Espagne dans la formation d'un jeune Danois entre les deux guerres', in *Internationale Netzwerke, op. cit.*, pp. 273–286; Francine Maier-Schaeffer, 'Zwischen Dänemark und Paris: Brechts Produktionsverhältnisse im Prisma der imaginären Diderot-Gesellschat (1933–1939)', in *Internationale Netzwerke, op. cit.*, pp. 287–305; Martin Kylhammer, 'Ein kulturhistorischer Fall für die Abteilung Cold Case. Der schwedische Nobelpreisträger Verner von Heidenstam und der deutsche Kulturattaché Paul Grassman', in *Internationale Netzwerke, op. cit.*, pp. 307–327; Laurence Rogations, 'Le Danemark et les Danois dans les journaux et les revues de langue française du XXe siècle. Le spectre de l'Allemagne', in *Internationale Netzwerke, op. cit.*, pp. 113–123.

On the one hand, literary texts continued to travel back and forth across borders and were read and mediated despite political alliances. On the other hand, political events became the subject of heated debates which were by no means free of ideology. Newspapers and magazines provided the main outlets for these controversies. Many writers, such as Herman Bang also worked as foreign correspondents.[19] The works of authors like Henrik Ibsen, Knut Hamsun, August Strindberg, Jens Peter Jacobsen, Herman Bang and Karin Michaëlis were translated into German, and they worked and wrote in Germany and France.[20] In literary history, the eager reception of a specifically Scandinavian "melancholy" and authenticity in Germany figures as a possible solution in the search for alternative models of life and society among Wilhelmine Germans.[21] Rainer Maria Rilke and Thomas Mann, who have been primarily understood as merely being influenced by Scandinavian literature actually engaged in individual and imaginative ways with the North.[22]

The following three brief examples may serve to illustrate the intensive relations and exchanges around 1900: The theatre, the multiple roles of the writer in the example of Herman Bang, and Georg Brandes as cultural mediator.

Theatre (from Vaudeville to Wagner's *Gesamtkunstwerk* and to Ibsen's and Strindberg's modern drama) plays a key role in the history of cross-cultural transfer. Theatre as a form and as an institution fosters an international outlook and remains open to the other arts, which paves the way for new syntheses. Dramatic scripts, the models and sources that have inspired them, stage machinery and acting, director and dramaturg, and stage music and set – all of these aspects are interrelated and soak up external influences, integrating them into new contexts. These transformational processes, which almost inhere in the institution of theatre, often gave rise to new forms and genres that, in turn, were both a reaction to traditional models and part of the development of a European avant-garde. At first, Scandinavian theatres were influenced by new currents from the major European metropolises and tried to follow their

---

19 Cf. Anna Sandberg, 'Herman Bang als Journalist in Paris (1893.)', in *Internationale Netzwerke, op. cit.*, pp. 93–111.

20 Cf. Anna Wegener, *Bibi goes travelling. Producing, rewriting, reading, and continuing Karin Michaelis' Bibi Books 1927–1953. United States, Germany, Denmark, Switzerland, Italy* (Copenhagen: Dissertation, University of Copenhagen, 2015).

21 Cf. Barbara Gentikow, *Skandinavien als präkapitalistische Idylle. Rezeption gesellschaftskritischer Literatur in deutschen Zeitschriften 1870–1914* (Neumünster: Wachholtz, 1978).

22 Cf. Heinrich Detering, 'Brigges Brüder. Rilkes *Malte Laurids Brigge*, die skandinavische Literatur und der fremde Blick', in *Literarische Transnationalität, op. cit.*, pp. 73–196.

examples; but by the turn of the century, Paris and Berlin turned to and received inspiration from Scandinavia.[23]

In newly established theatres in Paris and Berlin, Ibsen and Strindberg were considered pioneers of modern drama. At the same time, *Freie Bühne* and *Kammerspiele* in Berlin were inspired not only by the architecture and design but also by the repertoire of the new Parisian playhouse theatres. The Berlin and Paris theatres staged Ibsen's and Strindberg's plays with success. The cultural transfer functions as a productive exchange between the experimental theatres and individual performances. An example illustrating the international success of Scandinavian drama and theatre is Max Reinhardt's staging of Ibsen's *Ghosts* at the *Kammerspiele* in Berlin 1906. The Norwegian artist and painter Edvard Munch had been creating the programmes and the posters for the Ibsen performances by the French theatre director Lugne-Poë and was then assigned to project the stage designs for *Ghosts*. The successful cooperation with the artist Munch was, thus, carried forward with the expectation of the artist being able to produce a specific Norwegian panorama for the theatre set and evoke a "Nordic" atmosphere. Both of these aspects – the reputation of Munch as well as his Scandinavian creative affinities – would in Reinhardt's opinion guarantee the success of Scandinavian drama in Europe.

The Danish impressionist writer Herman Bang is an exemplary embodiment of the cultural constellation created by the German-French-Scandinavian triangle. From the 1880s, Bang was a journalist and literary reviewer in Copenhagen and introduced his Danish readers to new French literature (authors like Balzac, Maupassant, Daudet, Feuillet, Flaubert, Zola). Bang also used

---

23   Cf. Antje Helbing, 'Französische Anleihen. Die Herausbildung einer dänischen Theaterästhetik bei Knud Lyne Rahbek', in *Kulturelle Dreiecksbeziehungen, op. cit.*, pp. 101–117; Antoine Guémy, 'Kulturtransfer einer Gattung. Das Vaudeville zwischen den französischen, deutschsprachigen und skandinavischen Literaturen', in *Literarische Transnationalität, op. cit.*, pp. 23–43; Sylvain Briens, 'Die Globalisierung des nordischen Theaters am Ende des 19. Jahrhunderts. Der Fonds Prozor der *Bibliothèque Nordique* in Paris aus der Sicht der Akteur-Netzwerk-Soziologie', in *Literarische Transnationalität, op. cit.*, pp. 45–74; Magnus Qvistgaard, 'Henrik Ibsens *Gengangere* und der Kampf um ein neues Theater', in *Literarische Transnationalität, op. cit.*, pp. 73–97; Karin Hoff, 'Interieur und Intimität. Edvard Munchs Beitrag zum Theater der Moderne zwischen Oslo, Paris und Berlin', in *Literarische Transnationalität, op. cit.*, pp. 99–125; Karin Hoff, 'Märchen und Marionetten. Das Märchenspiel der Moderne zwischen August Strindberg, Maurice Maeterlinck, Johannes Schlaf und den Brüdern Grimm', in *Internationale Netzwerke, op. cit.*, pp. 125–143; Antoine Guémy, 'La naissance du cabaret allemand dans le triangle Allemagne-Danemark-France', in *Internationale Netzwerke, op. cit.*, pp. 145–163; Frédéric Weinmann, 'Der alte Taubenschlag am Kreuzweg. Die Bedeutung von Dänemark und Deutschland für Jacques Copeaus *Théâtre du Vieux-Colombier*', in *Internationale Netzwerke, op. cit.*, pp. 165–185.

his position as foreign correspondent for Danish and Norwegian newspapers to culturally position himself in the European context. From 1893–94, he was assisting director at the *Théâtre de l'Œuvre* and was involved in the staging of dramas by Ibsen, Strindberg, and Bjørnsson. Bang's own cultural breakthrough did not happen in Paris but after 1900, when his impressionist prose was translated into German and authors like Thomas Mann, Rilke, Zweig, Hofmannsthal, and Benn acknowledged him as an important initiator of an "impressionist" narrative style. Thus, he had to go through Germany to access the 'space of world literature,' as described by Pascale Casanova.[24]

Herman Bang, Henrik Ibsen, and August Strindberg, who were first influenced by ideas from Berlin and Paris, went on to leave their lasting mark on the continental European metropolises, blazing the trail for the development of a modern aesthetic.[25] On the other hand – especially in times of crisis and war – continental artists and intellectuals like Bertolt Brecht found refuge in Scandinavia and their political and artistic work created in exile affected the cultural climate in their countries of origin. These movements from France and Germany to Scandinavia and back demonstrate the dynamic interrelation between (continental European) centre and (northern European) periphery[26]

Georg Brandes, our third example, embodies a new phase of interaction within this cultural triangle. As a cultural intermediary, he reached in both directions, from the Scandinavian countries to the continental European cultural capitals and back to northern Europe. Spreading the works of Friedrich Nietzsche, he was not only a pioneer in Scandinavia but also in Germany and France.[27] He began by popularising French literature in Germany as well as German literature in Scandinavia and, thus, initiated a turn to modern, naturalist poetry; at the same time, Brandes also drew attention to the burgeoning modern Scandinavian literature in the big European metropolises. His

---

24   Pascale Casanova, *La République mondiale des lettres* (Paris: Le Seuil, 1999), pp. 119–179.
25   Regarding Ibsen see also: Jens Bjerring-Hansen/Torben Jalsbak/Monica Wenusch (eds.), *Die skandinavische Moderne und Europa. Transmission, Exil, Soziologie* (Wien: Praesens Verlag, 2016).
26   This confirms the initial assumption we adopted from Michel Espagne when we started our work on the cultural triangle of France-Germany-Denmark/Scandinavia: "Une des pires erreurs que pourrait commettre l'histoire culturelle de l'espace européen serait d'opposer un centre ou noyau à une périphérie". Cf. Karin Hoff/Udo Schöning, 'Kulturelle Dreiecksbeziehungen – Einleitung', in *Kulturelle Dreiecksbeziehungen, op. cit.*, p. 10; Michel Espagne (ed.), *Le Prisme du Nord* (Tusson: Du Lérot, 2006), p. 5.
27   Cf. Udo Schöning, 'Georg Brandes. Ein Däne als Vermittler französischer Literatur nach Deutschland', in *Internationale Netzwerke, op. cit.*, pp. 57–78; Christian Bank Pedersen, 'L'éthos du *dire-vrai* chez Georg Brandes. Sur *La Guerre mondiale* (1916) et *La Seconde parite de la tragédie* (1919)', in *Internationale Netzwerke, op. cit.*, pp. 203–218.

cosmopolitan and world-literary ambitions, therefore, pointed two ways at once and significantly contributed to trilateral cultural transfers.

Based on the results so far, we can summarise the following: geography and political and socio-cultural traditions underwrite a relatively stable triangle of cultural-historically relevant activities. Larger historical developments determine how the triangle renews itself and how its objects and structures change.

At the turn of the eighteenth and nineteenth centuries, cultural transfers were especially productive, being embedded in general historical processes of modernisation. Around 1800, the end of French cultural hegemony and the (re-)discovery of Nordic mythology marks a first and incisive moment, initiating cross-cultural transfers with the North. New motifs and aesthetics are read not only as the expression of an authentic northern European culture, but they are also adapted in continental European literatures and the slowly emerging philologies. Romantic ideas from Germany spread to other nations and undergird this process.

The period around 1900 sees a second peak in transfers which had lasting consequences. In Paris and Berlin, modern drama and theatre took hold: its scripts were produced by Scandinavian authors, especially Ibsen and Strindberg, whose plays were staged in young avant-garde theatres, first but not only in France and Germany, scandalising their audiences. Their impact reverberated beyond the genre and had a general and lasting influence on cross-cultural exchanges in the cultural triangle.

The nineteenth and first half of the twentieth century are also characterised by political turmoil in Europe. Reactions to the major wars of the second half of the nineteenth century and the First World War are also reflected in various changes in cross-cultural transfers, evident in the example of Scandinavian expressionism.[28]

Finally, we can conclude that, despite contacts and impulses originating from different points in the triangle causing interferences, the (re-)construction of the cultural-historical section comprising Germany, France, and Scandinavia reveals a coherent and clearly outlined structure situated in a larger European, and ultimately global whole.

Translated by Sabina Fazli

---

28 Cf. on this Gunilla Hermansson, *Modernisternas Prosa och Expressionismen. Studier i nordisk modernism 1910–1930* (Göteborg, Stockholm: Makadam, 2015).

Bibliography

Anthologies/Edited Volumes

Behschnitt, Wolfgang (ed.), *Aneignung – Abgrenzung – Auflösung. Zur Funktion von Literatur in den skandinavischen Identitätsdiskursen* (Würzburg: Ergon Verlag, 2001).

Bjerring-Hansen, Jens/Jelsback, Torben/Wenusch, Monica (eds.), *Die skandinavische Moderne und Europa. Transmission, Exil, Soziologie* (Wien: Praesens Verlag, 2016).

Budde, Gunilla/Conrad, Sebastian/Janz, Oliver (eds.), *Transnationale Geschichte. Themen, Tendenzen und Theorien* (Göttingen: Vandenhoeck & Ruprecht, 2006).

Conrad, Sebastian/Eckert, Andreas/Freitag, Ulrike (eds.), *Globalgeschichte. Theorien, Ansätze, Themen* (Frankfurt/Main: Campus Verlag, 2007).

Deting, Heinrich/Gerecke, Anne-Bitt/Mylius, Johann de (ed.), *Dänisch-Deutsche Doppelgänger. Transnationale und bikulturelle Literatur zwischen Barock und Moderne* (Göttingen: Wallstein, 2001).

Detering, Heinrich (ed.), *Grenzgänge. Skandinavisch-deutsche Nachbarschaften* (Göttingen: Wallstein, 1996).

Espagne, Geneviève/Schöning, Udo (eds.), *Un historien des langues, des littératures et des cultures. Claude Fauriel (1772–1844) et l'Allemagne* (Paris: Champion, 2013).

Espagne, Michel (ed.), *Le prisme du Nord. Pays du Nord, France, Allemagne (1750–1920)* (Tusson: Du Lérot, 2006).

Hoff, Karin/Schöning, Udo/Weinmann, Frédéric (eds.), *Internationale Netzwerke. Literarische und ästhetische Transfers im Dreieck Deutschland, Frankreich und Skandinavien zwischen 1870 und 1945* (Würzburg: Königshausen & Neumann, 2016).

Hoff, Karin/Schöning, Udo/Øhrgaard, Per (eds.), *Kulturelle Dreiecksbeziehungen. Aspekte der Kulturvermittlung zwischen Frankreich, Deutschland und Dänemark in der ersten Hälfte des 19. Jahrhunderts* (Würzburg: Königshausen & Neumann, 2013).

Hoff, Karin/Sandberg, Anna/Schöning, Udo (eds.), *Literarische Transnationalität. Kulturelle Dreiecksbeziehungen zwischen Skandinavien, Deutschland und Frankreich im 19. Jahrhundert* (Würzburg: Königshausen & Neumann, 2015).

Rublack, Ulinka (ed.), *Die neue Geschichte. Eine Einführung in 16 Kapiteln*, with a foreword by Jürgen Osterhammel (Frankfurt/Main: Fischer Verlag, 2013; original edition: *A Concise Companion to History*, Oxford, 2011).

Monographs and Articles

Bassnett, Susan/Lefevere, André, *Translation, History and Culture* (London, New York: Pinter Publishers, 1990).

Blödorn, Andreas, *Zwischen den Sprachen. Modelle transkultureller Literatur bei Christian Levin Sander und Adam Oehlenschläger* (Göttingen: Vandenhoeck & Ruprecht, 2004).

Briens, Sylvain, 'Réflexions préliminaires II. Penser les échanges culturels en termes de réseau', in *Internationale Netzwerke. Literarische und ästhetische Transfers im Dreieck Deutschland, Frankreich und Skandinavien zwischen 1870 und 1945*, ed. by Karin Hoff/ Udo Schöning/Frédéric Weinmann (Würzburg: Königshausen & Neumann, 2016), pp. 37–43.

Briens, Sylvain, 'Die Globalisierung des nordischen Theaters am Ende des 19. Jahrhunderts. Der Fonds Prozor der Bibliothèque Nordique in Paris aus der Sicht der Akteur-Netzwerk-Soziologie', in *Literarische Transnationalität. Kulturelle Dreiecksbeziehungen zwischen Skandinavien, Deutschland und Frankreich im 19. Jahrhundert*, ed. by Karin Hoff/Anna Sandberg/Udo Schöning (Würzburg: Königshausen & Neumann 2015), pp. 45–74.

Casanova, Pascale, *La République mondiale des lettres* (Paris: Le Seuil, 1999).

Conrad, Sebastian, *Globalgeschichte. Eine Einführung* (München: C.H. Beck, 2013).

Detering, Heinrich, 'Brigges Bruder. Rilkes *Malte Laurids Brigge*, die skandinavische Literatur und der fremde Blick', in *Literarische Transnationalität. Kulturelle Dreiecksbeziehungen zwischen Skandinavien, Deutschland und Frankreich im 19. Jahrhundert*, ed. by Karin Hoff/Anna Sandberg/Udo Schöning (Würzburg: Königshausen & Neumann, 2015), pp. 73–196.

Detering, Heinrich, 'Literarischer Dreieckshandel. Hans Christian Andersen zwischen Kopenhagen, Berlin und Paris', in *Kulturelle Dreiecksbeziehungen. Aspekte der Kulturvermittlung zwischen Frankreich, Deutschland und Dänemark in der ersten Hälfte des 19. Jahrhunderts*, ed. by Karin Hoff/Udo Schöning/Per Øhrgaard (Würzburg: Königshausen & Neumann, 2013), pp. 175–197.

Espagne, Geneviève, 'Aufbruch zu einer 'Geschichte der Literaturen'. Überlegungen des Literarhistorikers Jean-Jacques Ampère (1800–1864) im deutsch-französischen Beziehungsgeflecht', in *Kulturelle Dreiecksbeziehungen. Aspekte der Kulturvermittlung zwischen Frankreich, Deutschland und Dänemark in der ersten Hälfte des 19. Jahrhunderts*, ed. by Karin Hoff/Udo Schöning/Per Øhrgaard (Würzburg: Königshausen & Neuman, 2013), pp. 137–174.

Espagne, Michel, 'La notion de transfert culturel', in *Revue Sciences/Lettres* [online], 1 (2013), pp. 1–9. https://rsl.revues.org/219. A German translation of the article can be found in *Internationale Netzwerke. Literarische und ästhetische Transfers im Dreieck Deutschland, Frankreich und Skandinavien zwischen 1870 und 1945*, ed. by Karin Hoff/ Udo Schöning/Frédéric Weinmann (Würzburg: Königshausen & Neumann, 2016), pp. 45–55.

Espagne, Michel, 'Herder-Mallet-Arngrímur. Rückläufige Geschichtsschreibung und Kulturtransfer', in *Kulturelle Dreiecksbeziehungen. Aspekte Der Kulturvermittlung zwischen Frankreich, Deutschland Und Dänemark in der ersten Hälfte des 19. Jahrhunderts*, ed. by Karin Hoff/Udo Schöning/Per Øhrgaard (Würzburg: Königshausen & Neumann, 2013), pp. 199–211.

Espagne, Michel, *Les transferts culturels franco-allemands* (Paris: Presses Universitaires de France, 1999).

Gentikow, Barbara, *Skandinavien als präkapitalistische Idylle. Rezeption gesellschaftskritischer Literatur in deutschen Zeitschriften 1870–1914* (Neumünster: Wachholtz Verlag, 1978).

Gerecke, Anne-Bitt, *Transkulturalität als literarisches Programm. Heinrich Wilhelm von Gerstenbergs Poetik und Poesie* (Göttingen: Vandenhoeck & Ruprecht, 2002).

Guémy, Antoine, 'La naissance du cabaret allemand dans le triangle Allemagne-Danemark-France', in *Internationale Netzwerke. Literarische und ästhetische Transfers im Dreieck Deutschland, Frankreich und Skandinavien zwischen 1870 und 1945*, ed. by Karin Hoff/Udo Schöning/Frédéric Weinmann (Würzburg: Königshausen & Neumann, 2016), pp. 145–163.

Guémy, Antoine, 'Kulturtransfer einer Gattung. Das Vaudeville zwischen den französischen, deutschsprachigen und skandinavischen Literaturen', in *Literarische Transnationalität. Kulturelle Dreiecksbeziehungen zwischen Skandinavien, Deutschland und Frankreich im 19. Jahrhundert*, ed. by Karin Hoff/Anna Sandberg/Udo Schöning (Würzburg: Königshausen & Neumann, 2015), pp. 23–43.

Helbing, Antje, 'Französische Anleihen. Die Herausbildung einer dänischen Theaterästhetik bei Knud Lyne Rahbek', in *Kulturelle Dreiecksbeziehungen. Aspekte der Kulturvermittlung zwischen Frankreich, Deutschland und Dänemark in der ersten Hälfte des 19. Jahrhunderts*, ed. by Karin Hoff/Udo Schöning/Per Øhrgaard (Würzburg: Königshausen & Neumann, 2013), pp. 101–117.

Hoff, Karin, 'Märchen und Marionetten. Das Märchenspiel der Moderne zwischen August Strindberg, Maurice Maeterlinck, Johannes Schlaf und den Brüdern Grimm', in *Internationale Netzwerke. Literarische und ästhetische Transfers im Dreieck Deutschland, Frankreich und Skandinavien zwischen 1870 und 1945*, ed. by Karin Hoff/ Udo Schöning/Frédéric Weinmann (Würzburg: Königshausen & Neumann, 2016), pp. 125–143.

Hoff, Karin, 'Interieur und Intimität. Edvard Munchs Beitrag zum Theater der Moderne zwischen Oslo, Paris und Berlin', in *Literarische Transnationalität. Kulturelle Dreiecksbeziehungen zwischen Skandinavien, Deutschland und Frankreich im 19. Jahrhundert*, ed. by Karin Hoff/Anna Sandberg/Udo Schöning (Würzburg: Königshausen & Neumann, 2015), pp. 99–125.

Hoff, Karin, 'La Traduction comme médiation culturelle. Claude Fauriel et la Parthenaïs de Jens Baggesen', in *Un historien des langues, des littératures et des cultures. Claude Fauriel (1772–1844) et l'Allemagne*, ed. by Geneviève Espagne/Udo Schöning (Paris: Champion, 2013), pp. 263–279.

Hoff, Karin, *Die Entdeckung der Zwischenräume. Literarische Projekte der Spätaufklärung zwischen Skandinavien und Deutschland* (Göttingen: Wallstein, 2003).

Jamet, Raphaëlle, 'Le jeune Asger Jorn et ses réseaux. L'Allemagne, la France et l'Espagne dans la formation d'un jeune Danois entre les deux guerres', in *Internationale Netzwerke. Literarische und ästhetische Transfers im Dreieck Deutschland, Frankreich und Skandinavien zwischen 1870 und 1945*, ed. by Karin Hoff/Udo Schöning/Frédéric Weinmann (Würzburg: Königshausen & Neumann, 2016), pp. 273–286.

Kylhammar, Martin, 'Ein kulturhistorischer Fall für die Abteilung *Cold Case*. Der schwedische Nobelpreisträger Verner von Heidenstam und der deutsche Kulturattaché Paul Grassman', in *Internationale Netzwerke. Literarische und ästhetische Transfers im Dreieck Deutschland, Frankreich und Skandinavien zwischen 1870 und 1945*, ed. by Karin Hoff/Udo Schöning/Frédéric Weinmann (Würzburg: Königshausen & Neumann, 2016), pp. 307–327.

Laves, Gabriel, *Grundformen des Fremderlebens. Eine Analyse von Handlungsorientierungen in der interkulturellen Interaktion* (Münster, New York, München: Waxmann, 2000) (Internationale Hochschulschriften 345).

Latour, Bruno, *Eine neue Soziologie für eine neue Gesellschaft. Einführung in die Akteur-Netzwerk-Theorie* (Frankfurt/Main: Suhrkamp Verlag, 2007) (original edition: *Reassembling the Social*, Oxford, 2005).

Latour, Bruno, 'On Actor-network Theory. A few Clarifications', in *Soziale Welt*, 47/4 (1996), pp. 369–382.

Maier-Schaeffer, Francine, 'Zwischen Dänemark und Paris. Brechts Produktionsverhältnisse im Prisma der imaginären Diderot-Gesellschaft (1933–1939)', in *Internationale Netzwerke. Literarische und ästhetische Transfers im Dreieck Deutschland, Frankreich und Skandinavien zwischen 1870 und 1945*, ed. by Karin Hoff/ Udo Schöning/Frédéric Weinmann (Würzburg: Königshausen & Neumann, 2016), pp. 287–305.

Maillefer, Jean-Marie, 'Paul Verrier und der erste Skandinavistik-Lehrstuhl an der Sorbonne', in *Kulturelle Dreiecksbeziehungen. Aspekte der Kulturvermittlung zwischen Frankreich, Deutschland und Dänemark in der ersten Hälfte des 19. Jahrhunderts*, ed. by Karin Hoff/Udo Schöning/Per Øhrgaard (Würzburg: Königshausen & Neuman, 2013), pp. 213–23.

Mohnike, Thomas, 'Frédéric-Guillaume/Friedrich-Wilhelm Bergmann und die Geburt der Skandinavistik in Frankreich aus dem Geiste der vergleichenden Philologie', in *Kulturelle Dreiecksbeziehungen. Aspekte der Kulturvermittlung zwischen Frankreich, Deutschland und Dänemark in der ersten Hälfte des 19. Jahrhunderts*, ed. by Karin Hoff/Udo Schöning/Per Øhrgaard (Würzburg: Königshausen & Neuman, 2013), pp. 277–297.

Øhrgaard, Per, 'Dänen in Paris. P.O. Brøndsteds Reiseeindrücke', in *Kulturelle Dreiecksbeziehungen. Aspekte der Kulturvermittlung zwischen Frankreich, Deutschland und Dänemark in der ersten Hälfte des 19. Jahrhunderts*, ed. by Karin Hoff/Udo Schöning/Per Øhrgaard (Würzburg: Königshausen & Neumann, 2013), pp. 31–46.

Øhrgaard, Per, 'Die Nachfolge Schillers? Über Oehlenschlägers Corregio und Goethe', in *Das Achtzehnte Jahrhundert, "Deutsch-dänischer Kulturtransfer im 18. Jahrhundert"*, 25/2 (2001), pp. 231–247.

Pedersen, Christian Bank, 'L'éthos du *dire-vrai* chez Georg Brandes. Sur *La Guerre mondiale* (1916) et *La Seconde parite de la tragédie* (1919)', in *Internationale Netzwerke. Literarische und ästhetische Transfers im Dreieck Deutschland, Frankreich und Skandinavien zwischen 1870 und 1945*, ed. by Karin Hoff/Udo Schöning/Frédéric Weinmann (Würzburg: Königshausen & Neumann, 2016), pp. 203–218.

Qvistgaard, Magnus, 'Henrik Ibsens *Gengangere* und der Kampf um ein neues Theater', in *Literarische Transnationalität. Kulturelle Dreiecksbeziehungen zwischen Skandinavien, Deutschland und Frankreich im 19. Jahrhundert*, ed. by Karin Hoff/ Anna Sandberg/Udo Schöning (Würzburg: Königshausen & Neumann, 2015), pp. 73–97.

Raffestin, Claude, 'Réflexions préliminaires I. De l'intérêt du concept de «réseau» dans le champ littéraire', in *Internationale Netzwerke. Literarische und ästhetische Transfers im Dreieck Deutschland, Frankreich und Skandinavien zwischen 1870 und 1945*, ed. by Karin Hoff/Udo Schöning/Frédéric Weinmann (Würzburg: Königshausen & Neumann, 2016), pp. 31–36.

Rogations, Laurence, 'Le Danemark et les Danois dans les journaux et les revues de langue française du XXe siècle. Le spectre de l'Allemagne', in *Internationale Netzwerke. Literarische und ästhetische Transfers im Dreieck Deutschland, Frankreich und Skandinavien zwischen 1870 und 1945*, ed. by Karin Hoff/Udo Schöning/Frédéric Weinmann (Würzburg: Königshausen & Neumann, 2016), pp. 113–123.

Sandberg, Anna, 'Herman Bang als Journalist in Paris 1893', in *Internationale Netzwerke. Literarische und ästhetische Transfers im Dreieck Deutschland, Frankreich und Skandinavien zwischen 1870 und 1945*, ed. by Karin Hoff/Udo Schöning/Frédéric Weinmann (Würzburg: Königshausen & Neumann, 2016), pp. 93–111.

Sandberg, Anna, *En grænsegænger mellem oplysning og romantik. Jens Baggesens tyske forfatterskab 1803–1809* (Copenhagen: Museum Tusculanum Press, 2015).

Sandberg, Anna, 'Herman Bangs Transferfunktion im Dreieck Skandinavien – Frankreich – Deutschland um 1900', in *Literarische Transnationalität. Kulturelle Dreiecksbeziehungen zwischen Skandinavien, Deutschland und Frankreich im 19. Jahrhundert*, ed. by Karin Hoff/Anna Sandberg/Udo Schöning (Würzburg: Königshausen & Neumann, 2015), pp. 147–172.

Sandberg, Anna, 'Frankreich als Imagination und Realität in Kopenhagen um 1800. Malte Conrad Bruun und Jens Baggesen als Mittler im dänisch-deutsch-französischen Kulturtransfer', in *Kulturelle Dreiecksbeziehungen. Aspekte der Kulturvermittlung zwischen Frankreich, Deutschland und Dänemark in der ersten Hälfte des 19. Jahrhunderts*, ed. by Karin Hoff/Udo Schöning/Per Øhrgaard (Würzburg: Königshausen & Neumann, 2013), pp. 47–76.

Schmale, Wolfgang, 'Das Wahrnehmungsmuster "Grenze" in französischen Blicken auf "Deutschland"', in *Deutschlandbilder – Frankreichbilder. 1700–1850. Rezeption und Abgrenzung zweier Kulturen*, ed. by Thomas Höpel (Leipzig: Leipziger Universitäts Verlag, 2001), pp. 173–182.

Schöning, Udo, 'Georg Brandes. Ein Däne als Vermittler französischer Literatur nach Deutschland', in *Internationale Netzwerke. Literarische und ästhetische Transfers im Dreieck Deutschland, Frankreich und Skandinavien zwischen 1870 und 1945*, ed. by Karin Hoff/Udo Schöning/Frédéric Weinmann (Würzburg: Königshausen & Neumann, 2016), pp. 57–78.

Schöning, Udo, 'Ein Objekt – zwei Projekte? Zu den Vorworten deutscher und französischer Autoren in französischen Literaturgeschichten des 19. Jahrhunderts', in *Literarische Transnationalität. Kulturelle Dreiecksbeziehungen zwischen Skandinavien, Deutschland und Frankreich im 19. Jahrhundert*, ed. by Karin Hoff/Anna Sandberg/Udo Schöning (Würzburg: Königshausen & Neumann 2015), pp. 243–267.

Schöning, Udo, 'Bonstettens Mensch des Nordens und das Problem der nationalen Stereotype', in *Kulturelle Dreiecksbeziehungen. Aspekte der Kulturvermittlung zwischen Frankreich, Deutschland und Dänemark in der ersten Hälfte des 19. Jahrhunderts*, ed. by Karin Hoff/Udo Schöning/Per Øhrgaard (Würzburg: Königshausen & Neumann, 2013), pp. 77–99.

Schöning, Udo, 'Baggesen in Frankreich', in *European Journal for Scandinavian Studies*, 44 (2014), pp. 254–270.

Schöning, Udo, 'La internacionalidad de las literaturas nacionales. Observaciones sobre la problemática y propuestas para su studio', in *Naciones Literarias*, ed. by Dolores Romero López (Barcelona: Anthropos Editorial 2006), pp. 305–339.

Schöning, Udo, 'Nationallitteraturernes Internationalitet', in *Litteraturhistoriografi*, ed. by Mads Rosendahl Thomsen/Svend Erik Larsen (Aarhus: Aarhus University Press, 2005) (Moderne litteraturteori), pp. 195–213.

Schöning, Udo, 'Die Internationalität nationaler Literaturen. Bemerkungen zur Problematik und ein Vorschlag', in *Internationalität nationaler Literaturen. Beiträge zum Ersten Symposion des Göttinger Sonderforschungsbereichs 529*, ed. by Udo Schöning in collaboration with Beata Hammerschmid and Frank Seemann (Göttingen: Wallstein Verlag, 2000), pp. 9–43.

Simanowski, Roberto, 'Einleitung. Zum Problem kultureller Grenzziehung', in *Kulturelle Grenzziehungen im Spiegel der Literaturen. Nationalismus, Regionalismus, Fundamentalismus*, ed. by Horst Turk/Brigitte Schultze/Roberto Simanowski (Göttingen: Wallstein Verlag, 1998), pp. 8–60.

Skriver, Svend, *Europæerne i 1800-talets danske litteratur. Om Jens Baggesen, P.L. Møller og Georg Brandes* (Copenhagen: University of Copenhagen, 2007).

Struck, Bernhard, *Nicht West – nicht Ost. Frankreich und Polen in der Wahrnehmung deutscher Reisender zwischen 1750 und 1850* (Göttingen: Wallstein Verlag, 2006).

Teichert, Matthias, 'Die Rezeption der mittelalterlichen skandinavischen Literatur in Deutschland', in *Kulturelle Dreiecksbeziehungen. Aspekte der Kulturvermittlung zwischen Frankreich, Deutschland und Dänemark in der ersten Hälfte des 19. Jahrhunderts*, ed. by Karin Hoff/Udo Schöning/Per Øhrgaard (Würzburg: Königshausen & Neuman, 2013), pp. 241–259.

Toutain, Anne-Gaëlle, 'Hjelmslev et le cercle de Copenhague', in *Internationale Netzwerke. Literarische und ästhetische Transfers im Dreieck Deutschland, Frankreich und Skandinavien zwischen 1870 und 1945*, ed. by Karin Hoff/Udo Schöning/Frédéric Weinmann (Würzburg: Königshausen und Neumann, 2016), pp. 219–232.

Trachsler, Richard, 'Die Rezeption der mittelalterlichen skandinavischen Literatur in Frankreich in der ersten Hälfte des 19. Jahrhunderts', in *Kulturelle Dreiecksbeziehungen. Aspekte der Kulturvermittlung zwischen Frankreich, Deutschland und Dänemark in der ersten Hälfte des 19. Jahrhunderts*, ed. by Karin Hoff/Udo Schöning/ Per Øhrgaard (Würzburg: Königshausen & Neuman, 2013), pp. 261–275.

Verstraete-Hansen, Lisbeth, 'Romanistik in Dänemark. Anfänge, Entwicklung und Ausblick', in *Kulturelle Dreiecksbeziehungen. Aspekte der Kulturvermittlung zwischen Frankreich, Deutschland und Dänemark in der ersten Hälfte des 19. Jahrhunderts*, ed. by Karin Hoff/Udo Schöning/Per Øhrgaard (Würzburg: Königshausen & Neumann 2013), pp. 299–320.

Wegener, Anna, *Bibi goes travelling. Producing, rewriting, reading, and continuing Karin Michaelis' Bibi Books 1927–1953. United States, Germany, Denmark, Switzerland Italy* (Copenhagen: Dissertation, University of Copenhagen, 2015).

Weinmann, Frédéric, 'Der alte Taubenschlag am Kreuzweg. Die Bedeutung von Dänemark und Deutschland für Jacques Copeaus Théâtre du Vieux-Colombier', in *Internationale Netzwerke. Literarische und ästhetische Transfers im Dreieck Deutschland, Frankreich und Skandinavien zwischen 1870 und 1945*, ed. by Karin Hoff/ Udo Schöning/Frédéric Weinmann (Würzburg: Königshausen & Neumann, 2016), pp. 165–185.

Weinmann, Frédéric, 'Die dänische Literatur in den französischen und deutschen Geschichten der Weltliteratur aus der zweiten Hälfte des 19. Jahrhunderts', in *Literarische Transnationalität. Kulturelle Dreiecksbeziehungen zwischen Skandinavien, Deutschland und Frankreich im 19. Jahrhundert*, ed. by Karin Hoff/Anna Sandberg/Udo Schöning (Würzburg: Königshausen & Neumann, 2015), pp. 269–289.

Index of Names

Abreu, Márcia   213–214, 220–222, 225–228
Agnetta, Marco   6 n. 16, 17
Allen, Graham   106 n. 5, 121
Almeida, Jaime de   201, 204, 209, 228
Ampère, Jean-Jacques   30, 232, 233 n. 7, 244
Amselle, Jean-Loup   120 n. 11, 121
Andersen, Hans Christian   29, 230, 238 n. 17, 244
Anderson, Benedict   72, 178 n. 12, 196
Andrade, Oswald de   206–207
Anta Diop, Cheikh   27, 42, 111
Antilla, Elina   94 n. 14, 96, 100
Antoine, André   60
Apter, Emily   74, 76, 84
Aragon, Louis   141, 143, 153, 157–160, 163
Archer, William   53 n. 8, 61–63
Armah, Ayi Kwei   111, 119
Ashcroft, Bill   127 n. 11, 131 n. 24, 139
Aubert-Nguyen, Hoai Huong   5 n. 12, 17
Averroes   28

Bachmann-Medick, Doris   6 n. 15, 17
Backer, Harriett   89, 91, 93–95, 98, 101
Baggesen, Jens   ix, 31, 230–232, 238, 245, 247–248
Bakhtin, Mikhail   106
Balzac, Honoré de   240
Bamba, Amadou   119
Bang, Herman   17, 230, 238 n. 17, 239–241, 247
Bassnett, Susan   145 n. 7, 163, 237 n. 14, 247
Bastien-Lepage, Jules   92, 94, 96–97
Baudelaire, Charles   152 n. 19
Becker, Adolf von   14, 90–91, 209
Beerbohm-Tree, Herbert   60
Behschnitt, Wolfgang   231 n. 2, 243
Beller, Manfred   82, 84
Benn, Gottfried   241
Berg, Hubert van den   89 n. 3, 101
Berg, Leo   59, 62
Bergmann, Friedrich-Wilhelm   31–32, 233, 246 (also: Frédéric-Guilluame Bergman)
Bergson, Henri   37

Bernal, Martin   27, 42
Berndtson, Axel   99 n. 22
Bernd, Zilá   205–208, 226–227
Bernini, Gian Lorenzo   191–193, 197
Beverly, John   186 n. 16, 196
Bhabha, Homi K.   7, 168 n. 3, 196
Biely, Andrei   34
Bihl, Liselotte   25 n. 3
Bing, Just   75
Bizub, Edward   152, 163
Blödorn, Andreas   231, 243
Bloom, Harold   68, 84
Bolle, Willi   201, 202 n. 8, 228
Bonnat, Léon   90–92, 95
Borges, Jorge Luis   173–174
Bossuet, Jacques-Bénigne   23
Bouguereau, William   92
Bourdieu, Pierre   65, 69, 84, 92, 98, 101, 145, 202, 210
Brandes, Georg   29, 75, 230–231 n. 2, 239, 241, 247–248
Braun, Friedrich   38–39, 42–43
Brecht, Bertolt   148 n. 15, 238 n. 18, 241, 246
Brecht, George   143
Breton, Jules   94–96, 98–99
Briens, Sylvain   234 n. 9, 240 n. 23, 244
Broomans, Petra   vii, 3–4, 13, 64–65, 68 n. 9, 69, 77, nn. 24–25, 78, 80, 84–85
Broude, Norma   92 n. 11, 101
Bruendel, Steffen   9, 18
Brun, Friederike   231
Burke, Peter   3, 6 n. 15, 18, 64–66, 69, 79, 81, 85
Burnautzki, Sarah   120 n. 11, 121
Burty, Philippe   98 n. 20
Buzzard, Laura   105–106 n. 1, 121

Cahen, Maurice   32
Campos, Haraldo de   154
Cariou, André   101
Carpentier, Alejo   16, 183–185, 187–191, 196
Carter, Angela   152 n. 20, 163
Casanova, Pascale   13–14, 44–55, 60, 62, 65, 73, 76, 85, 145, 163, 241, 244
Catherine II   34

Cazin, Jean-Charles 92
Celestini, Federico 7 n. 18, 9, 18
Céline, Louis-Ferdinand 153
Cervantes, Miguel de 109, 173
Césaire, Aimé 112
Chamfort, Nicolas 128
Chamoiseau, Patrick 108–109, 121
Charles XII 28
Chartier, Roger 220–221, 226
Chateaubriand, François-René de 218
Chen, Yi 74, 85
Christina, Queen of Sweden 28
Clark, Henry C. 129, 139
Claudius, Matthias 35
Clifford, James 126
Cobb, Richard 8 n. 20, 18
Collin, Raphaël 92
Confiant, Raphaël 108, 121
Conrad, Sebastian 234 n. 8, 243–244
Cook, James 8
Cooper-Richet, Diana 4 n. 8, 18, 212
Count of Stolberg-Stolberg, Friedrich Leopold 35
Courbet, Gustave 90
Courtois, Gustave 92
Couture, Thomas 90
Cuvier, Georges 24

Dadié, Bernard 119–121
D'Alembert, Jean-Baptiste le Rond 203
Damas, Léon-Gontran 112
D'Amico, Giuliano 52, 62
Damm, Rudolf 223
Damrosch, David 144, 163
Danielson, Elin 89, 93
Daudet, Alphonse 240
Defoe, Daniel 109
De Gaulle, Charles 116
Delafosse, Maurice 114
Delâge, Denis 5 n. 11, 20
Deleuze, Gilles 5, 71, 85
Detering, Heinrich 231 n. 2, 238 n. 17, 239 n. 22, 243–244
Diderot, Denis 203
Dietze, Antje 4 n. 7, 6–7, 9, 18–19
Diop, Birago 116, 121
Dmitrieva, Ekaterina 33, 42
Dmitrieva, Nina 38 n. 12, 42

Donadey, Anne 122
D'Ors, Eugenio 183–184, 196
Dubois, Margareta 85
Dumas, Alexandre 29, 109
Ďurišin, Dionýz 75–76, 78, 82–83, 85
Dutheil de la Rochère, Martine Hennard 152 n. 23, 163
Dutronc, Jacques 137

Echeverría, Bolívar 181, 196
Egan, Michael 52 n. 6, 61 n. 17, 62
Ehrhard, Auguste 32
Ekman, Kerstin 77
Emerich, Maximilian 223
Engels, Friedrich 113
Epting, Karl 25 n. 3
Erickson, John D 111, 121
Espagne, Geneviève 230 n. 1, 233 n. 7, 243–245
Espagne, Michel vii, 1–3, 5 nn. 12–13, 9, 13, 18, 23, 26 n. 4, 27 n. 5, 28 n. 6, 29 n. 8, 33 n. 10, 39 n. 15, 42–43, 44 n. 1, 62, 66–68, 70, 76–77, 79–81, 85, 142, 146 n. 11, 147 n. 12, 151, 177, 196, 199–200, 202, 209–211 n. 23, 214–220, 221, 224, 226, 229 n. 1, 232 n. 3 n. 6, 236 n. 12, 237 n. 16, 241 n. 26, 243
Ette, Ottmar 124 n. 1, 139, 225
Even-Zohar, Itamar 2, 10, 18, 69, 82, 145

Faria Coutinho, Eduardo de 208, 226–227
Fauriel, Claude 229–230 n. 1, 232, 243, 245
Fendler, Ute 124 n. 1, 139
Fet, Afanassi 34
Feuillet, Raoul-Auger 240
Fichte, Johann Gottlieb 31
Fickert, Jan 6 n. 16, 18
Filion, Louise-Hélène 147, 163
Filliou, Robert 150–151
Flaubert, Gustave 114, 158, 163, 240
Flotow, Luise von 80, 85
Fontaine, Alexandre 199–200, 218, 219 n. 39, 220, 226
Foucault, Michel 5, 118
Frähn, Christian Martin 39
Francart, Johann Balthasar 35
Frazer, James George 24
Freitag, Ulrike 234 n. 8, 243

INDEX OF NAMES

Freitas Dutra, Eliana de   201, 226
Frenzel, Karl   58, 59 n. 14, 62
Frère, Édouard   90
Fricke, Harald   128 n. 12, 139
Frobenius, Leo   112, 114
Fukari, Alexandra   69 n. 12, 87
Fumaroli, Marc   194–195

Gallitzin, Amalie von   35
Garrard, Mary D.   101
Gasimov, Zaur   3, 7, 18
Gasquet, Vasco   129–130 n. 21, 139
Gehrmann, Susanne   138–139
Gellner, Ernest   72
Gentikow, Barbara   239 n. 21, 245
Gentzler, Edwin   69, 146–147, 157 n. 24, 163
Gerecke, Anne-Bitt   231 n. 2, 243, 245
Gérôme, Jean-Léon   92
Gerzymisch-Arbogast, Heidrun   6 n. 16, 18–19
Gessner, Salomon   203
Giehl, Claudia   6 n. 16, 19
Gil, Alberto   6 n. 16, 19
Gjörwell, Carl Chr.   81
Glissant, Édouard   71–72, 85, 126 n. 8, 139
Goethe, Johann Wolfgang von   35–36, 74, 108, 155–156
Gorky, Maxim (also: Gorki)   38
Gorodé, Déwé   15, 124, 127–139
Gould, Cecil   191 n. 20, 192, 197
Gracián, Baltasar   128, 139
Gradus, Jakob   156
Grammaticus, Saxo   10, 146, 158
Granja, Lúcia   213–214, 226–227
Gravier, Maurice   32
Gray, Julie   5 n. 12, 18
Greenblatt, Stephen   84
Greene, Graham   114, 118
Grimm, Jacob and Wilhelm   31
Groot, Georg   35
Grundtvig, N.F.S.   10
Guattari, Félix   71, 85
Gude, Hans Fredrik   91
Guémy, Antoine   240 n. 23, 245
Guignes, Joseph de   24
Guillemette, Lucie   121
Guimarães, Valéria   211, 214–215, 217–218, 224, 226–227
Gunnarsson, Torsten   91 n. 6, 101

Gurvitch, Georges   35
Guthrie, William   24, 43
Gymnich, Marion   125–126, 139

Hale, Thomas   110, 121
Hammershøi, Vilhelm   88 n. 1
Hamsun, Knut   31, 239
Hart, Heinrich und Julius   58
Hartmann, Eduard von   33
Hébert, Louis   121
Heeren, Arnold   43
Hegel, Georg Friedrich Wilhelm   31, 37
Heiberg, Johan Ludvig   31
Heiberg, Peter Andreas   31
Heidmann, Ute   142, 147, 163
Heilbron, Johan   69, 81
Heine, Heinrich   211, 218
Heineberg, Ilana   227
Helbing, Antje   240 n. 23, 245
Helmholtz, Hermann von   33
Helmich, Werner   129–130 n. 20, 139
Herbart, Johann Friedrich   33
Herder, Johann Gottfried   10, 29, 34, 216
Heyne, Christian Gottlob   24
Hippocrates   128
Høffding, Harald   32–33
Hoff, Karin   vii, 11, 17, 229, 231 n. 2, 232 n. 4, 240 n. 23, 241 n. 26, 243, 245
Hofmannsthal, Hugo von   241
Holberg, Ludvig   30
Hölderlin, Friedrich   148 n. 15, 158
Holthuis, Susanne   121
Hongtu, Li   vi, 6 n. 12, 18
Hroch, Miroslav   72–73, 85
Hugo, Victor   29
Humboldt, Alexander von   24, 38
Hume, David   24
Husserl, Edmund   37
Huusko, Tim   97 n. 19

Ibsen, Henrik   10, 14, 32–33, 44–46, 48–61, 230, 239–242

Jacobi, Friedrich Heinrich   35
Jacobsen, Jens Peter   239
Jamet, Raphaëlle   238 n. 18, 246
Janz, Oliver   234 n. 8, 243
Jiresch, Ester   77 n. 25, 85
Johansen, Annette   101

Jolivet, Alfred   32
Jolles, André   130, 139
Jørgensen, Steen Bille   v, vi, viii, 1, 15, 141, 158, 161 n. 30, 163
Jouve, Dominique   129 n. 18, 139
Joyce, James   153
Jullien, François   9 n. 22, 19, 144, 163
Jurt, Joseph   146 n. 9, 147 n. 10, 164
Juvan, Marko   106 n. 2, 121

Kambas, Chryssoula   200 n. 4, 227
Katz, Elihu   4 n. 10, 19
Keilhauer, Annette   3 n. 6, 5 n. 14, 18–19
Kern, Anita   110, 122
Kielland, Kitty   89, 91, 93–95, 98
Kierkegaard, Søren   33
Kirstein, Robert   6 n. 16, 19
Klinger, Friedrich Maximilian   34
Klyuchevsky, Vasily (also: Kliuschewskij, W.)   38, 43
Kojève, Alexandre   35
Konttinen, Riita   89 n. 5, 91 n. 7, 99 nn. 21–22, 101
Kortländer, Bernd   177, 197
Koselleck, Reinhart   13, 27
Kotzebue, August von   34
Kourouma, Amadou   119, 161, 163
Koyré, Alexandre   35
Krejčí, K.   82
Kristeva, Julia   105–106, 118, 122, 147 n. 11
Krøyer, Peder Severin   91, 92 n. 9, 101
Krüdener, Juliane von   35
Kügelgen, Gerhard von   36
Kulessa, Rotraud von   5 n. 15, 19, 146 n. 9, 164
Kylhammar, Martin   246

La Bruyère, Jean de   128
Lacroix, Michel   5 n. 11, 6 n. 17, 19
Lamprecht, Karl   25
Lange, Marit   89 n. 4, 91 n. 8, 94–95 n. 17, 101
Langen, Albert   31
Latour, Bruno   69, 234 n. 9, 246
Laves, Gabriel   246
Lay Brander, Miriam   viii, 15, 124
Leconte de Lisle, Charles   30
Leerssen, Joep   82–84
Lefebvre, Romain   5 n. 12, 18

Lefevere, André   145–146, 163–164
Leguy, Anne-Estelle   viii, 14, 88
Lemke Duque, Carl Antonius   3, 7, 18
Lenngren, Anna Maria   81
LePan, Don   105–106 n. 1, 121
Lessing, Gotthold Ephraim   33
Levin, Orna   213, 227
Lewino, Walter   129, 139
Leydhecker, Karl   223
Lezama Lima, José   183, 187–191, 197
Liebes, Tamar   4 n. 10, 19
Lindau, Paul   58
Linder, Lambert   91
Linnaeus, Carl   24
Lombez, Christine   5 n. 15, 19, 146 n. 9, 164
Lomonossov, Michail Wassiljewitsch (also: Mikhail Vasilyevich Lomonosov)   38
Lotze, Hermann   33
Louis XIV   137, 191
Luca, Tania Regina de   212–214, 226–227
Lugné-Poe, Aurélien-Marie   60, 240
Luhmann, Niklas   69, 170 n. 4, 197
Lundahl, Amélie   89, 93, 96–97, 99
Lüsebrink, Hans-Jürgen   viii, 1, 2 n. 3, 5 n. 13, 8 n. 20, 11 n. 26, 12, 15, 18–20, 23 n. 1, 43, 105, 107 n. 7, 119 n. 10, 120 n. 11, 122, 124 n. 1, 126, 139–140, 142, 164, 177, 197, 201, 210, 214, 224 n. 54, 226–227

Machado, Adelaide   213, 220
Magri, Dirceu   217
Maier-Schaeffer, Francine   238 n. 18, 246
Maillefer, Jean-Marie   233 n. 7, 246
Mallet, Paul Henri   29–30
Mandelstam, Ossip Emiljewitsch (also: Osip Emilyevich Mandelstam)   34
Mann, Julia   201
Mann, Thomas   201, 239, 241
Maran, René   109, 125, 140
Maravall, José Antonio   183, 197
Marjanen, Jani   72, 86
Markina, Liudmila A.   35, 43
Marmier, Xavier   29–30, 81
Marx, Karl   113
Maupassant, Guy de   240
Mauvillon, Éléazar de   30
Mayer, Christine   76, 86
Mbelolo Ya Mpiku, Joseph   118, 122

INDEX OF NAMES

McLuhan, Marshall   171 n. 6, 197
Mein, Georg   19
Menard, Pierre   173–174
Mestcherski, Vladimir (also: Meshchersky or Mestchérsky)   35
Meyer, Marlyse   201, 227
Meyer Ross, Christian   91
Meylaerts, Reine   81, 86
Michaëlis, Karin   239
Middell, Matthias   2, 4 n. 7, 7, 9, 18–19, 23 n. 1, 42–43, 76, 86
Mitterbauer, Helga   7 n. 18, 9, 18
Mix, York-Gothart   201 n. 6, 224 n. 41, 226–227
Moe, Vera   57 n. 12, 62
Mohammed, Askia   115
Mohnike, Thomas   233 n. 7, 246
Mokaddem, Hamid   131, 132 n. 25, 134 n. 27, 135 n. 28, 140
Molière   30
Mollier, Jean-Yves   4 n. 8, 18, 201, 212–213, 220–222 n. 50, 226–227
Monénembo, Tierno   107
Moraña, Mabel   181, 197
Moretti, Franco   70, 86
Morgan, Lewis   24
Moser, Walter   ix, 3–4, 7, 16, 168, 197, 205–206, 227
Moura, Jean-Marc   131 n. 24, 140
Munch, Edvard   88 n. 1, 240
Murdoch, H. Adlai   122
Muusses, Martha A.   77–78, 80
Mylius, Johan de   231 n. 2, 243

Nabokov, Vladimir   35, 141, 143, 153–155, 157–158, 160, 162–163
Narita, Felipe Ziotti   200
Neumann, Gerhard   128, 129 n. 15, 130, 140
Neunsinger, Silke   45 n. 1, 62
Niane, Djibril Tamsir   116
Nietzsche, Friedrich   5, 241
Nordenflycht, Hedvig Charlotta   81
Ntoumos, Veronica   129 n. 17, 131 n. 22, 140

Oehlenschläger, Adam Gottlob   30, 230
Ohrgaard, Per   229 n. 1, 231 n. 17, 238 n. 17, 243, 246–247
Olney, James   113–115, 122
Olsson, Hagar   77–78, 83, 86

Orr, Mary   122
Ouellet, Réal   5 n. 11, 20
Ouologuem, Yambo   15, 105, 109–122

Pageard, Robert   109
Pagni, Andrea   5 n. 14, 19
Pannewick, Friederike   126, 140
Parrot, Friedrich-Georg   37
Pasche, Wolfgang   52 n. 6, 62
Paulmann, Johannes   8 n. 20, 19
Pavlovna, Maria   35
Paz, Octavio   109, 122
Pedersen, Christian Bank   241 n. 27, 247
Pedro II of Brazil   224
Pelouse, Léon Germain   93–95
Perkins, David   68, 86
Perloff, Marjorie   148–149, 164
Peterssen, Eilif   91
Poe, Edgar Allen   152 n. 19
Pokou, Aoura   119
Pollock, Griselda   92 n. 11, 101
Poncioni, Claudia   213, 227
Postlewait, Thomas   53 n. 8, 63
Prendergast, Christopher   46 n. 3, 63
Proust, Marcel   152–153
Pushkin, Alexander   154 n. 23
Pym, Anthony   69, 79–81, 86

Quincey, Thomas de   152 n. 19
Qvistgaard, Magnus   ix, 10 n. 25, 13–14, 56 n. 11, 63, 240 n. 23, 247

Radishchev, Aleksander Nikolajevich   38
Raffestin, Claude   234 n. 9, 247
Rama, Ángel   130, 140
Ramsay, Raylene   129 n. 17, 140
Reichardt, Rolf   210, 227
Reinhardt, Max   240
Rem, Tore   61 n. 17, 63
Ricœur, Paul   10 n. 24, 167 n. 1
Riesz, János   118, 122
Rilke, Rainer Maria   148, 239, 241
Rimbaud, Arthur   114
Rinne, Cia   152 n. 18
Robert-Fleury, Tony   92
Rochefoucauld, François de la   15, 128–129, 139
Rodrigues da Silva, Helenice   209–211, 227
Rogations, Laurence   238 n. 18, 247

Roiz, Diogo da Silva   209 n. 18, 228
Roland Holst-Van den Schalk, Henriette   13, 77–78, 83
Rossi, Carlo   192
Roubaud, Jacques   148–149
Rousset, Jean   193–195, 197
Rudolph, Utto   109
Rüsen, Jörn   111–112, 123
Ruskin, John   152

Sadji, Abdoulaye   119–120
Salnikow, Nikolai   6 n. 16, 20
Samoyault, Tiphaine   106–107, 123
Sandberg, Anna   ix, 11, 17, 229 n. 1, 231 n. 2, 238 n. 17, 239 n. 19, 243, 247
Sapiro, Gisèle   69, 80–81, 86, 145, 164
Savojärvi, Ulla   99 n. 21, 101
Schelling, Friedrich Wilhelm Joseph   37
Schiller, Friedrich   36
Schjerfbeck, Helene   89, 91, 93, 96–99
Schlésinger, Élisa   158
Schlözer, August Ludwig von   37
Schmale, Wolfgang   237 n. 16, 248
Schmeling, Manfred   11 n. 26, 20
Schneider, Lothar L.   58 n. 13, 63
Schöning, Udo   ix, 11, 17, 29 n. 8, 229, 232 nn. 3–4, 233 n. 7, 236 n. 13, 238 n. 27 241 nn. 26–27, 243, 248
Schößler, Franziska   204 n. 12, 228
Schüttpelz, Erhard   125 n. 2, 140
Schwarz, Roberto   176 n. 10, 197
Schwarz-Bart, André   114, 118
Scott, Clive   143 n. 2, 146, 161 n. 32, 164
Senghor, Léopold Sédar   111–112
Shade, John   154–155
Shade, Sibyl   156–157
Shakespeare, William   146, 153–154, 156–157, 159
Shepherd-Barr, Kirsten   52 n. 5, 60 n. 16, 63
Shpet, Gustave   37
Silem, Ahmed   4 n. 8, 18
Simanowski, Roberto   237 n. 16, 248
Simeoni, Daniel   168 n. 2
Sinisalo, Soili   101
Sioui, Georges   5 n. 11, 20
Skriver, Svend   231 n. 2, 248
Snell-Hornby, Mary   69, 86
Solte-Gresser, Christiane   11 n. 26, 20

Sorel, Patricia   201 n. 6, 227
Spoerri, Daniel   141, 143, 149–151, 160, 162–163
Staël, Germaine de   78, 81
Staël-Holstein, Alexander von   39
Stark, Susanne   80, 86
Stefanson, Blandine   138 n. 34, 140
Steffens, Henrik   231
Stehlin, Jakob   35
Still, Judith   106, 123
Stockhorst, Stefanie   5 n. 15, 20
Strindberg, August   32, 230, 239–242
Struck, Bernhard   237 n. 16, 248
Supinen, Marja   101
Sylvan, Otto   75
Szyska, Christian   126, 140

Tacitus   30, 128
Tam, Kwok-Kan   52, 53 n. 7, 63
Tao, Xue   73
Tapié, Alain   101
Tapié, Victor L.   194, 197
Tawada, Yōko   152 n. 18
Teichert, Matthias   232 n. 6, 249
Tessin, Nicodemus   192
Theodoro, Janice   181–182, 197
Thome, Gisela   6 n. 16, 19
Thomsen, Mads Rosendahl   46 n. 3, 55, 63
Thúy, Kim   161, 163
Tieck, Ludwig   29
Tolstoy, Leo   57, 59
Topor, Roland   150
Toutain, Anne-Gaëlle   233 n. 7, 249
Trachsler, Richard   232 n. 6, 249
Trautmann-Waller, Céline   43
Trautz, Birgit   6, 20
Triolet, Elsa   153, 157
Turgenev, Iwan Sergejewitsch   35
Turgeon, Laurier   5 n. 11, 20
Tveterås, Harald   55 n. 9, 63

Uvarov, Sergey   37

Van Tieghem, Paul   74–76, 78, 80–83, 86
Van Tieghem, Philippe Édouard Léon   13, 82, 86
Vauvenargues, Luc de Clapiers, marquis de   128
Vega, Garcilaso de la   28

INDEX OF NAMES

Veit-Wild, Flora 138–139
Venuti, Lawrence 69, 81
Verstraete-Hansen, Lisbeth 233 n. 7, 249
Voltaire 28
Vovelle, Michel 4 n. 9, 20

Wagner, Richard 57, 239
Waldrop, Rosmarie 148
Walter, Reinhold von 38 n. 13
Watkins, Mel 112, 123
Wegener, Anna 239 n. 20, 249
Weinmann, Frédéric 229 n. 1, 233 n. 7, 240 n. 23, 243, 249
Weissbrod, Rachel 6 n. 16, 20
Weitbrecht, Johann Jakob 34
Welsch, Wolfgang 7, 72, 86
Wenusch, Monica 241 n. 25, 243
Werner, Michael 1–2, 6–8, 12, 20, 53, 62–63, 66–67, 72, 75, 80, 85, 87, 177, 197, 201–204, 209–210, 214, 221, 227–228
Westermarck, Helena 89, 91, 93–94, 96–97, 99
White, Hayden 65, 81, 87
Whiteman, Kaye 118, 123

Wiik, Maria 89, 98
Williams, Emmett 141, 143, 149–150
Williams, John 71
Wise, Christopher 120 n. 11, 123
Wismann, Heinz 144, 164
Wittgenstein, Ludwig 148–149 n. 15
Wolf, Ferdinand 224
Wolf, Michaela 69, 80, 87
Wölfflin, Heinrich 195
Wolitz, Seith 118, 123
Wood, Michael 123
Worton, Michael 106, 123
Wundt, Wilhelm 25

Xavier, Wiebke Röben de Alencar x, 16, 198, 200 n. 4, 203 n. 11, 204–205 n. 12, 223 n. 39–40, 228
Xia, Liyang 52 n. 6, 63
Xingjian, Gao 73

Zimmermann, Bénédicte 7–8, 20, 53, 62–63, 67, 72, 75, 87, 201, 204, 209, 228
Zola, Émile 57, 59, 160 n. 29, 240
Zweig, Stefan 201, 241

Printed in the United States
by Baker & Taylor Publisher Services